rough University
, fresh innovative book which, above all, maintains a strong thematic
The analysis is deep-seated, well referenced to key sources, and whilst
nicely balanced with practical cases and examples. Taken in the round,
as an important book and a credit to the the Addison-Wesley collection.'

Manchester Business School
of human resource management is in a state of transition. This book helps
e way towards new thinking about the topic. It articulates the main pressures
onal personnel role and presents some very useful ideas about the breakdown
l organizational structures, managing without unions, and handing over HRM
ty to the line. I learned much from reading this book.'

ward, Policy Studies Institute
a stimulating read, combining insights from sound research and innovative think-
the challenges to management in seeking sustainable competitive advantage. The
er on Managing Without Unions contains a well-grounded discussion of the opportu-
available to management in large, non-union firms and of the reasons why an exter-
union presence constrains managerial prerogative. The discussion has important
plications for management, unions, employees, and, more generally, the health of demo-
atic societies that deserve to be more widely appreciated.'

Luis R. Gomez-Mejia, Arizona State University
'This is truly a path breaking, innovative book that captures the revolutionary changes being
experienced by human resources management. The book is likely to have major impact on
the field for years to come. This is a must read by all managers and academics dealing with
human resource issues.'

William P. Anthony, The Florida State University
'This book is unique and captures the sea-change that we are witnessing in human resources
management. Imagine the changes in the field – no full time workforce, no supervisors,
no personnel managers, no traditional structures – these are but some of the major trends
the book addresses in an innovative and highly readable way. I highly recommend the book
to people who want to learn what human resources management will be like in the future,
not in the past. This book captures it all.'

Herbert G. Heneman III, University of Wisconsin-Madison
'I find the book an interesting and useful compendium of innovations in HR. Its international perspectives are particularly helpful in helping us realize and appreciate the full
range of innovative options available to organizations as they seek optimal ways of maximizing workforce effectiveness.'

Paul Willman, London Business School
'This is an unconventional approach which represents sound academic work in a way
that will appeal to a broad audience. It is both international and interdisciplinary and a
valuable addition to the set of existing books for MBA and executive programmes.'

Keith Sisson, University of Warwick
'A very good review of "best practice" thinking and developments in the management of
human resources. A valuable source of ideas for policy makers and practitioners who want
to understand how the more effective management of human resources can contribute to
competitive advantage, and of up-to-date case material for teachers and students.'

Managing Witl.

Managing Without Traditional Methods

International Innovations in Human Resource Management

Patrick C. Flood
University of Limerick

Martin J. Gannon
University of Maryland

Jaap Paauwe
Erasmus University Rotterdam

and Associates

ADDISON-WESLEY PUBLISHING COMPANY

Wokingham, England • Reading, Massachusetts • Menlo Park, California
New York • Don Mills, Ontario • Amsterdam • Bonn • Sydney • Singapore
Tokyo • Madrid • San Juan • Milan • Paris • Mexico City • Seoul • Taipei

Many of the designations used by manufacturers and sellers to distinguish their products are claimed as trademarks. Addison-Wesley has made every attempt to supply trademark information about manufacturers and their products mentioned in this book.

Cover designed by Crayon Design of Henley-on-Thames
and printed by The Riverside Printing Co. (Reading) Ltd
Typeset by Wyvern Typesetting Ltd
Printed and bound at the University Press, Cambridge

First printed 1995

ISBN 0-201-42774-5

British Library Cataloguing-in-Publication Data
A catalogue record for this book is available from the British Library.

Library of Congress Cataloging-in-Publication Data applied for

We dedicate this book with love and affection to the members of our families.

To the memory of my beloved father, Bartholomew Flood; and to my mother, Catherine, my wife, Patricia, and our sons, Christopher and Patrick Ellis

Doris, Marlies, and Reid Gannon

Marthe and Jochem Paauwe

Acknowledgments

The publishers wish to thank the following for permission to reproduce the material listed.

Figure 2.1 Generic Value Chain; adapted with the permission of The Free Press, a Division of Simon & Schuster, Inc, from COMPETETIVE ADVANTAGE: Creating and Sustaining Superior Performance by Michael E. Porter. Copyright © 1985 by Michael E. Porter.

Figure 5.1 Changes in Union Density 1980–88; adapted with the permission of Blackwell Publishers from Reed, T.F. *et al.* (1995), International industrial relations, in Ferris, G.R. (ed) *The Handbook of Human Resource Management*. Oxford: Blackwell.

Figure 10.1 The human resource base theory of the firm; adapted with permission of Samsom Bedrijfsinformatie from Paauwe, J. (1994) *Organiseren, een grensoverschrijdende passie*.

Excerpted material from: Ivancevich, J., Lorenzi, P., Skinner, S., and Crosby, P. (1994), *Management: Quality and competitiveness*. Burr Ridge IL: Richard D. Irwin. Sims, H. and Lorenzi, P. (1992), *The new leadership paradigm: Social learning and cognition*. Newbury Park CA: Sage. Manz, C.C. and Sims, H.P. (1993), *Business without bosses: How self-managing teams are producing high performance companies*. New York: John Wiley. Reprinted by permission of John Wiley & Sons, Inc.

Preface

In 1991 when Patrick Flood and Jaap Paauwe met while on sabbatical at the London School of Economics, Western economies were undergoing fundamental restructuring. Country after country was experiencing the phenomenon of deindustrialization, corporate downsizing, reductions in full-time workforces, privatization and liberalization of labor markets, and the increased use of radical managerial innovations such as self-managing teams, continuous improvement initiatives, the restoration of line management prerogatives, and changing union–management relationships. Frequently, however, an organization would make a major change in one of these areas without considering fully the organization-wide implications in other areas. These two professors began to speculate that such changes – often introduced in a random, sporadic, and top-down fashion – needed to be placed into perspective so that an integrated and wholistic overview of them could help the practicing manager understand when and how to introduce specific changes without doing violence to the organization.

The initial concept for the book was formed when both Flood and Paauwe were invited to present papers at a conference on industrial relations sponsored by the London School of Economics in Cumberland Lodge, Great Windsor Park, London, that was held on 26 November, 1991. The late Professor Keith Thurley, internationally recognized for his work on the changing nature of managerial work and the concept of a distinctly European style of management, organized the conference and asked Flood and Paauwe to present papers. At this conference Jaap presented a paper, 'Personnel management without personnel managers.' This presentation triggered the concept of the book, as Patrick began to think silently about other changes involving the concept of 'managing without.' In a relatively short space of time these two professors came up with a long list of areas in which 'managing without' was featured. These included managing without: traditional planning systems, traditional structures, traditional owners, unions, supervisors, quality boundaries, personnel managers, and a regular, full-time workforce.

While generating this list came quickly, identifying internationally recognized researchers who had written extensively on these topics was a daunting task. In particular, finding an expert on managing without a complete, full-time workforce proved difficult, even though this topic has become increasingly important throughout the world. Ken G. Smith, a professor at the University of Maryland who was a Visiting Fulbright Professor at the University of Limerick in 1991, suggested that Martin Gannon, an expert on part-time and temporary-help employment, be approached to author this chapter; he was subsequently invited by Patrick Flood to join the team as a senior co-author. Gradually the research team coalesced and eventually included professors from the University of Limerick in Ireland and Erasmus University in the Netherlands, and professors from the following American universities: Maryland, Georgetown, Syracuse, Central Arkansas, and Arizona State.

To ensure that this book was both theoretically sound and helpful to the practicing manager, the authors convened a conference focusing on the proposed book. It was held at the University of Maryland in October of 1993, and its participants included 25 vice presidents of human resource management, all of the authors, and 15 internationally prominent academics who were not involved in the writing of the book. All of the chapters in this book were presented as papers, and extensive and critical feedback was received on each of them. The authors of the papers were asked to use the following guidelines in writing the final versions of their chapters, that is, each chapter should be: theoretically sound, practical and useful, strategic in emphasis, internationally based, case-oriented, and at the cutting edge of trends in human resource management.

In developing this book, we identified two major divisions that became Part One and Part Two. No discussion of the role and contribution of strategic human resources to sustained competitive advantage would be complete without considering the value chain, that is, the primary and support activities which add value to the final good or service. Part One addresses this issue, and it highlights the five capabilities of world-class resource management that go beyond the usual distinction between low-cost leadership and differentiation of products and services as a competitive strategy. These five capabilities are the ability to produce products and services 'right the first time,' speedily, on time, cheaply, and flexibly (Slack, 1991[†]). When combined simultaneously, these factors constitute world-class competitive capability. The simultaneous combination of these factors is the essential task facing top management teams in organizations that are going to successfully compete in the global marketplace in the next decade.

[†] Slack, N. (1991). *The Manufacturing Advantage: achieving competitive manufacturing operations*. London: Mercury Books.

Part Two of the book examines whether or not strategic innovations in human resource management do in fact contribute to value enhancement in the value chain within organizations. Such non-traditional methods include, as suggested above, managing without: traditional planning systems, conventional ownership structures, unions, complex hierarchy, specialized personnel departments, quality boundaries, 'boss type' supervisors, and a complete full-time workforce.

As this discussion indicates, there is a close relationship between Parts One and Two of this book. In understanding the organizational impact of innovations in human resource management, it is important to keep both an upper and lower echelon's perspective on the organization. Often the top management team (TMT) makes one strategic innovation or move that it assumes will have a synchronized value-enhancing response at lower levels of the organization. However, frequently the reality is quite different, as Part Two of the book illustrates. In the final chapter we identify lessons that have been learned from reviewing the experiences of companies throughout the world which have experimented with strategic innovations in human resource management. In the final chapter we also present some new and revised perspectives on theory and practice, and describe what the configuration of human resource systems of the future may look like.

Throughout the book we integrate the various issues and chapters through the use of three major theories: agency theory, transaction cost economics, and the resource base theory of the firm. In the final chapter we argue that it is relatively easy for companies to copy one another's products, designs, advertising campaigns, and so forth. However, human resources represent one factor that is scarce and for which there is frequently no effective substitute. For this reason we refine the resource base theory of the firm into a human resource base theory or model of the firm.

We would like to thank the following people and organizations: Dr Noel Whelan, Dean, College of Business at the University of Limerick; Eamonn Walsh, Thomas Turner, and Michelle Cunningham, University of Limerick; William Mayer, Dean, The Maryland Business School, University of Maryland at College Park; Professor Ken G. Smith, Mercy Coogan, and Jo Anne Schram, University of Maryland at College Park; Dr Jan Verhulp, Dean of the Rotterdam School of Economics, Erasmus University; Philip Dewe, Dean and Professor, Massey University, New Zealand; Nigel Nicholson and Paul Willman, the London Business School; Neil Millward, the Policy Studies Institute, London; and John Kelly, London School of Economics. The Fulbright Commission and the University of Limerick supported Patrick Flood's four-month stay at the University of Maryland in 1993, during the writing of this book. Subsequently, the award of a European Human Capital and Mobility Institutional Fellowship to London Business School (LBS) allowed Patrick Flood to complete this book at LBS in 1995.

In addition, we are very appreciative of the conscientious efforts and patience that representatives of our publisher, Addison-Wesley, demonstrated throughout the project. Our thanks to Jane Hogg and Paula Harris, our editors, who were ably assisted by Victoria Cook. Allison Lock, Academic Sales Advisor at Addison-Wesley, also provided valuable advice at early stages of the project. We also wish to thank Martin Tytler, Production Editor at Addison-Wesley. For their help, and that of others at Addison-Wesley, we are grateful.

International collaboration across three different time zones is not an easy task. Our wives and children endured countless telephone calls at peculiar hours with admirable fortitude and good humor. As Patricia Flood pointed out – the three of us should have gone up in an HRM space shuttle!

Finally, we note that the subject of this book is extremely complex, and it is easy to make factual and interpretative errors when discussing the many issues that need to be addressed. We accept complete responsibility for any errors that this book may contain and ask that you bring them to our attention.

Patrick C. Flood, Limerick, Ireland
Martin J. Gannon, College Park, Maryland, USA
Jaap Paauwe, Rotterdam, the Netherlands
May 1995

Contents

Acknowledgments   vi

Preface   vii

Introduction   xiii

PART ONE

The Case for World-Class Capabilities through Human
Resource Management   1

1 Human resource strategies for world-class
   competitive capability   3
   Patrick C. Flood
   Judy D. Olian

2 Managing without traditional strategic planning:
   the evolving role of top management teams   31
   Ken A. Smith

PART TWO

Non-Traditional Methods: Vehicles for Change   71

3 Managing without traditional structures   73
   Stefan Wally
   Stephen J. Carroll, Jr.
   Patrick C. Flood

4 Managing without traditional owners   105
   Theo van Neerven
   Hans Bruining
   Jaap Paauwe

5 Managing without unions: a pyrrhic victory?   147
Patrick C. Flood
Bill Toner

6 Personnel management without personnel
managers   185
Jaap Paauwe

7 Managing without supervision: how self-managing
teams create competitive advantage   235
Peter Lorenzi
Henry P. Sims, Jr.
Charles C. Manz

8 Managing without quality boundaries   257
Julie A. Kromkowski
Eamonn Murphy

9 Managing without a complete, full-time
workforce   279
Stanley A. Nollen
Martin J. Gannon

10 Competitive advantage through strategic
innovations in human resource management   307
Patrick C. Flood
Martin J. Gannon
Jaap Paauwe

About the authors   327
Author Index   331
Subject Index   337

Introduction

It is now generally accepted that we are living in the midst of a major transformation in the manner in which business is organized and conducted. The international business press is replete with accounts of corporate restructuring as organizations delayer, downsize and introduce new methods and innovative approaches to workforce management. Bookstores all over the world are full of slim 'how to do it' volumes on such diverse topics as *five-minute management, empowerment, mentoring*, and *downsizing* to name but a few. The traditional tried and trusted methods of management espoused by classic scholars such as Fayol, Urwick and Brecht are truly under siege if we are to believe what we read in the popular press. Traditional managerial appproaches based on rationality in organizational design, stockholder supremacy, enduring union–management relations, vertical modes of authority and long-term commitments to employees are being challenged by the practices of organizations desperately searching for new methods to gain a competitive advantage in the marketplace.

Yet delayering and lean management methods potentially expose companies to a new generation of organizational pathologies such as corporate anorexia, increased conflict between different types of organizational members, and decreased commitment to organizational objectives. Euphoria and enthusiasm over the latest management fad can quickly change to disappointment and disillusionment when introduced into a hostile and unreceptive organization culture. Hence managers face a difficult task in unraveling the complexities inherent in new approaches. How do managers know which set of methods seems to work? More importantly, there is a need for balanced theoretical understanding of these trends which will temper the enthusiastic search for panaceas with caution.

This book attempts to go behind these trends to search for theoretical understanding of why they are happening and to assess both the opportunities and difficulties involved in the introduction of such techniques. In Part One we begin our analysis by focusing on the capabilities that must underpin competitive strategies designed to create truly world-class organizational forms. We argue that such organizational forms are characterized by the distinctive competence of the organization to simultaneously combine speed, dependability, quality, and cost-effectiveness. These capabilities seem to characterize those organizations that are most forward looking in their competitive strategy approaches.

We also advance the view that the new theoretical paradigm for integrating human capital perspectives with strategic management is to be found in the resource base view of the firm. According to this theory resources must be valuable, rare, inimitable, and non-substitutable if they are to provide a sustained source of competitive advantage to the firm. We also believe that if the management of human resources is to become a serious theoretically-based subject taught in mainstream strategy courses for future general managers, then the subject area needs to integrate the most powerful theoretical ideas to be found in the strategic management literature, including resource base theory of the firm, transaction costs theory and agency theory. All of these theories, which are primarily economic in orientation, have imparted a rigor to the strategic management literature that is often lacking in the human resource management field.

In Part Two we enumerate and analyze a series of innovations in human resource management which we have observed and which seem to have their origin in the need to create more agile and flexible organizational forms. Our innovations have one common characteristic, namely their focus on *managing without* traditional methods. The list includes managing without: centralized strategic planning, traditional structures, traditional owners, unions, personnel managers, supervisors, quality boundaries, and a complete, full-time workforce. These innovative methods can be contrasted with their more familiar and traditional counterparts: top down strategy formulation, hierarchical modes of governance, traditional stockholders, standardized collective bargaining arrangements, routine and perfunctory personnel management systems, authority-based supervisory and managerial systems, inspection-based quality routines, and permanent, pensionable employment relationships. We attempt to understand both the reasons for these innovations and their impact on the organization in terms of agency theory, transaction cost economics, and the resource base view of the firm. To our knowledge there have been very few attempts to understand strategic organizational innovations in human resource management using these three theories. It is our contention that these theories will become more widely adopted as explanations of such innovations. They focus upon the tensions inherent in the attempt to build strong and cohesive internal human resource capabilities in a business environment which by the very nature of its impermanence encourages the development of low-trust relations.

Thus in Chapter 1 the resource base theory (RBT) of the firm is used to explain how and under what conditions human resources constitute a sustainable competitive advantage. In that chapter transaction costs theory is also used to conceptualize human resource management delivery mechanisms using the make or buy analogy, that is, the firm can either make the product or contract out for it. Then we examine the cultural attributes accompanying two major forms of modern organization – the *Virtual Corporation* (VC) and the *Total Quality* (TQ) organization and the residual role of the human resource department in both cases.

In Chapter 2 the role of the top management team (TMT) is examined in the context of the creation of emergent strategy for capabilities-based or competencies-based competition. The TMT is responsible for crafting adaptive strategies to cope with the continuous changes taking place in the marketplace, which need to be reflected in a contingent internal organizational stucture in which the fixed lattices of job positions and well-defined career paths are frequently eliminated in the adaptation process. As such, the TMT is proactive rather than reactive, and its activities are constantly occurring even when no formal meetings are called. Transaction costs or the costs of doing business are reduced, and the asset base of the firm is strengthened because a greater number of organizational members is involved in the planning process on an active and ongoing basis.

Agency theory (AT) and transaction costs theory (TCT) are both highlighted in Chapter 3 as explanations of the rationale for organizational restructurings which are taking place in numerous countries, many of which result in hybrid organizational forms including the much vaunted, if rarely defined, network organization. The impact of these restructurings both on individuals and the human resource support systems is also explored in that chapter.

Agency theory is the dominant explanatory theory used in Chapter 4 to explore the phenomenon of management buyouts (MBOs) and the role of human resource strategy in creating a successful buyout situation. Information asymmetries and associated motivational issues are also examined. It is argued that, on average, agency costs are reduced in MBO organizational forms.

In Chapter 5 we address the topic of managing without unions, particularly in the context of large high wage non-union companies. This chapter demonstrates that union avoidance by such organizations may represent a pyrrhic victory over trade unions, as the Catch-22 of union avoidance implies that such firms, fearful of union organization, are often unwilling to exercise the freedoms which non-unionism might be expected to confer.

The debate on outsourcing the specialist personnel function is explored in Chapter 6 using transaction costs and agency-based relationships. A typology involving a continuum of minor and major changes and a continuum of internality (make the product in-house) to externality (buy the product) is developed to frame the major issues.

Chapter 7 then explores the issue of managing without supervision, that is, using self-managing teams as an alternative. Transaction costs are reduced when teams are employed, as the number of organizational levels decreases and organizational members are empowered to make their own decisions and carry them out. When operating effectively, such teams provide a strong framework for developing the skills and abilities of their members, thus increasing the asset base of the firm.

In Chapter 8 the focus is on eliminating boundaries separating organizational members, organizational levels, departments, and the customers. When such elimination occurs, the resources in the organization can be harnassed effectively. Not only are organizational members empowered, but also customers, as their opinion about the product and its delivery are actively sought in novel ways.

Chapter 9 examines the new employment relationships that organizations are implementing, particularly the core-and-ring strategy whereby a small group of regular, full-time organizational members is surrounded by different types of employment relationships such as subcontracting and the hiring of temporary workers. Under ideal conditions transaction costs are reduced and the firm concentrates on strengthening the skills and abilities of its core members who constitute its key assets. There is, however, some question as to whether such ideal conditions can be approximated in many situations.

In the final chapter of the book the three theoretical strands of agency theory, transaction costs economics, and the resource base view of the firm are brought together in an integrated model that we call the human resource base theory of the firm. It is our contention that organizational members represent the one asset that is most difficult to copy and that firms must mobilize and motivate them effectively if they hope to achieve world-class competitive capability. Thus, while we emphasize three economic-based theories throughout the book, we end our presentation by describing the dynamic relationships between organizational members that must take place if long-term survival is to occur. In this sense the field of human resource management represents a delicate balance between the technological and impersonal dictates of the marketplace and the all-too-human needs that organizational members seek to fulfill. And, while this book describes several approaches that managers can use to accomplish such balance, in the final analysis it is the responsibility of managers to ensure that organizational and personal goals of members are effectively integrated within specific organizational contexts.

The Case for World-Class Capabilities through Human Resource Management

1

Human resource strategies for world-class competitive capability

Organizations today, by necessity, have become more focused on exploiting sources of competitive advantage in the face of rapid environmental, technological and global economic changes. According to Pfeffer (1994:14), 'as other sources of competitive success have become less important, what remains as a crucial, differentiating factor is the organization, its employees, and how they work.' Additionally, he states that

> [T]he current recognition among strategic management researchers [is] that sustained competitive advantage arises more from a firm's internal resource endowments and resource deployments [particularly its human capital] that are imperfectly imitable than from a firm's product market position.
>
> (Pfeffer, 1994:14)

These 'people' issues used to be the sole responsibility of personnel departments. However, recent research such as that by Fernie, Metcalf, and Woodland (1994) in the United Kingdom using data from a nationally representative sample of workplaces suggests that *specialist* personnel functions appear to detract from both economic and industrial relations performance rather than enhance it.

The specialist personnel function, however, is undergoing dramatic change. In many organizations, the human resource (HR) function is being transformed from a centralized advisory staff function to a proactive and distributed deliverer of personnel systems in support of the business strategy. Relative to the earlier personnel departments that were programme focused (for example, training, recruitment, selection or evaluation), the emerging HR function is a more agile, bottom line and service oriented operation. It is a partner in sustaining the firm's competitive posture in its local, national or global markets. This new HR function is not a stand-alone office or department but is integrated into the core business processes of the firm. It is the driver for achieving innovation, speed and quality *through people*, by re-engineering employee processes throughout all operating systems of a business.

3

In addition to changes in the competitive environment that have prompted re-engineering of the HR function, organizations have also distanced themselves from traditional structures of authority and power. In his seminal work over thirty years ago, Douglas McGregor relates an anecdote that exemplifies this point:

> An agent of the textile workers of America likes to tell the story of the occasion when a new manager appeared in the mill where he was working. The manager came into the weave room the day he arrived. He walked directly over to the agent and said, 'I am the new manager here. When I manage a mill, I run it. Do you understand?' The agent nodded, and then waved his hand. The workers, intently watching this encounter, shut down every loom in the room immediately. The agent turned to the manager and said, 'All right, go ahead and run it.'
>
> (McGregor, 1960:23)

Changes that parallel and support those occurring in internal organizational structures have been implemented in the operations of HR departments. HR specialists who controlled the design and implementation of HR systems are increasingly replaced by line managers who are accountable for delivery of their own human resource management and development activities. Line managers and supervisors *own* the human resource function because they are closest to the employees who represent the unique competencies of the firm. The management of these human resources becomes a direct value-added opportunity for the business, rather than an indirect drain on resources.

The new vision of management is one without the familiar hierarchical base of power, as Kanter points out:

> [Managers] must learn to operate without the crutch of hierarchy. Position, title and authority are no longer adequate tools, not in a world where subordinates are encouraged to think for themselves and where managers have to work synergistically with other departments and even other companies. Success depends increasingly on tapping into sources of new ideas, on figuring out whose collaboration is needed to act on those ideas, on working with both to produce results. In short, the new managerial work implies very different ways of obtaining and using power.
>
> (Kanter, 1989a:86)

According to Kanter's vision, the trappings of leadership have been peeled away in favour of leadership through information and ideas. It illustrates the theme of this book – managing without – exemplified in the HR function, as well as in other organizational structures discussed in subsequent chapters. This new vision of the organization represents a proactive stance to attain competitive advantage, and perhaps it is the *only* way to compete on the global platform. This chapter proposes new organizational forms for managing human resources for world-class competitive advantage, forms shaped around flatter and more agile business operations – a theme expanded upon in subsequent chapters. There are three objectives to this chapter, namely to:

(1) describe the features that typify the world-class organization;
(2) describe the role of the management of human resources in achieving these world-class capabilities; and
(3) outline two radically different organizational models for achieving world-class competitive capability, each having very different human resource management implications.

Specifically, we describe human resource management in the 'quality organization' and in the 'virtual organization'. Both approaches represent the capacity to compete effectively in a sustained fashion, but with a radically different organizational architecture and agenda for the management of human resources than those emphasized in the traditional organization.

The central arguments to be advanced are as follows:

(1) Organizations cannot succeed and prosper over the long term unless they achieve excellence along the multiple dimensions of world-class capabilities.
(2) Successful deployment of the human resource assets of the firm provides the organization with the means to achieve unique, valuable, inimitable, rare, and non-substitutable advantages.
(3) World-class competitive capabilities can take radically different organizational forms, depending on the unique strategic choices made and the conditions surrounding the business.

The search for global advantage

The world of business has become a struggle to gain competitive advantage in a much larger and more demanding marketplace. Markets now stretch across international boundaries, trade barriers have crumbled and distribution channels have become more efficient. State intervention in many markets has diminished and organizations now confront an unequaled number of competitors. Consumer preferences have been ratcheted up, with increasingly demanding calls for higher quality products and services, delivered faster, and at a lower price.

Faced with these unparalleled challenges, organizations search desperately for sources of distinctiveness in their product or service deliverables. It is no longer enough to achieve differentiation on a single dimension of distinctiveness, such as speed to market, or low cost pricing. As Stalk and colleagues (1993:19) point out, in the 1980s companies discovered time as a new source of competitive advantage.

In the 1990s they will learn that time is just one piece of a far more reaching transformation in the logic of competition.' Market survivors and winners in the next decades will do so by combining simultaneously a vector of five competitive abilities. These include the ability to produce goods that are 'right the first time,' quickly, on time, cheaply and flexibly (Slack, 1991: Stalk, *et al.*, 1993). Distinctive capacity to simultaneously combine these five factors can be described as *world-class competitive capability*.

Achieving world-class status through HR strategy

Human resources are part of the strategic asset base of the firm. Using the resource base view of the firm (Barney, 1991; Conner, 1991; Wernerfelt, 1984), we argue in this section that:

(1) appropriate deployment of the human resource assets of the firm provides the organization with unique, inimitable, rare, and non-substitutable advantages;
(2) there is supporting evidence that appropriate human resource deployment adds value to the organization in terms of documented dollar returns; and
(3) these returns are realized because the HR processes focus behaviors into areas that are exploitable for strategic advantage to the firm.

Human resources and the resource base view of the firm

One of the most influential perspectives on strategic management in the 1990s has been the resource base view of the firm (Barney, 1991; Conner, 1991; Wernerfelt, 1984). This particular perspective on competitive advantage highlights the links between the internal resources of the firm, its strategy and financial performance. Barney (1991:101) defines resources as 'all assets, capabilities, organizational processes, firm attributes, information, knowledge, and so on controlled by a firm that enable the firm to conceive of and implement strategies that improve its efficiency and effectiveness.' Resources can be physical, organizational or human. Physical capital resources are comprised of the firm's fixed asset base including plant and equipment, technology and its geographic proximity to markets. Organizational capital resources reflect the firm's structure, and its planning, controlling, and coordination systems. Human capital resources are the pool of human capital attracted and selected into the employment relationship with the firm, and sustained over time within this relationship. The human capital pool includes skills and abilities, as well as less tangible resources such as the tacit knowledge, experience, judgment and collective intelligence of the managers and employees in a firm (Wright, *et al.*, 1994). Further, the characteristics of the pool of human capital are a product of deliberate HR input, throughput and output processes of the firm (see Figure 1.1).

Physical, organizational and human resources represent the opportunities available to the firm for the attainment of a sustainable competitive advantage in its market (Oster, 1990; Porter, 1985). Four criteria must be attributable to a resource in order to provide a sustained competitive advantage (Barney, 1991). It must add positive value to the firm, it should be unique or rare among current and potential competitors, only imperfectly imitable, and non-substitutable with other resources available to competitors (Wright, *et al.*, 1994). As demonstrated below, HR practices meet these criteria and have the potential to be powerful contributors to the firm's performance, provided the organization acts consistently to transform the human capital pool into a source of competitive advantage. As Hall (1992:139) points out, 'the distinctive competence which [Jaguar Cars] enjoys is the ability to build a special type of quality car. This ability is founded upon the skill and experience or know-how, of employees.'

As Figure 1.1 indicates, human capital distinctiveness is not simply an isolated function involving the introduction of human resources into the firm, but it also arises from the dynamic interaction of HRM activities with a whole range of organizational processes such as just-in-time manufacturing, concurrent engineering, organizational

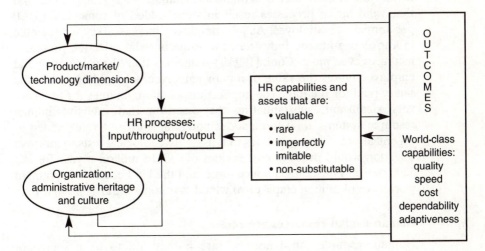

Figure 1.1   Human Resource strategy for competitive advantage: a resource base view.

structures, information technology architecture, and so on (Oliver and Wilkinson, 1992; Snell and Dean, 1992). Do human resources qualify as a source of competitive advantage, according to the parameters articulated in the resource base view of the firm?

Human capital resources are valuable

If the demand and supply of labor is homogenous, that is, employees are perfectly substitutable and all employees are equal in their productive capacity, then of course there is no possibility that human resources add value to the firm (Wright, *et al.*, 1994). However, this is rarely the case as most firms are comprised of distinct bundles of jobs requiring a heterogeneous mix of skills. In addition, organizational attraction strategies result in the availability of applicant pools that differ in their profiles of abilities and dispositions (Heneman and Heneman, 1994; Gratton, 1992). Moreover, over time, internal labor pools become heterogeneous across organizations in both the types and proficiency levels of employee skills, as a result of differentially targeted and effective HRM training and development interventions.

Recent HRM utility models (Boudreau, 1983; Boudreau and Berger, 1985; Cascio and Ramos, 1986) provide a systematic approach for estimating the value of human resource practices to organizations. Schmidt and Hunter (1981) developed a utility model for the valuation of selection programs. They calculated the value to the firm of using valid selection tools to hire an effective budget analyst compared to invalid selection processes that result in selection errors for this job. The value added from a valid hiring process for this one position turned out to be some US$11,000 per annum. Using a similar technique applied to the job of computer programmer, Schmidt, *et al.* (1980) estimated that valid hiring processes result in value added of some US$10,000 per annum per employee. As job complexity increases, say for example in knowledge-intense industries, the value of valid selection processes increases even more. Cook (1993:7) comments that 'the value of a good employee minus the value of a poor employee is roughly equal to the salary paid for the job.' The implications of these findings for firms are very significant, substantiating the assertion that effective human resource systems are a tremendous potential source of value added to organizations. Cook calculates that using psychological tests to improve selection would produce cost savings of US$18 million a year for the 5000 person Philadelphia police force, and the US Federal Government workforce (4 million employees) would save some US$16 billion a year.

Human capital resources are rare

Human resources must also be rare if they are to be a source of sustained competitive advantage. Some might argue that in slack labor markets, when high unemployment levels pervade, firms are in a buyer's market and human resources are anything but rare. Indeed, in situations where work is de-skilled and Taylor-like scientific management principles are practiced, human resources assume a commodity status rather than that of a rare resource. However, when the quality of the input is implicitly factored into the resource, the human capital resource becomes more rare. Wright, *et al.* assert:

> that to the extent that jobs require skills which allow variability in individual contributions (i.e. when job relevant skills are no longer a commodity), these skills should be normally distributed in the population. Thus, under these conditions, high quality human resources are rare.
>
> (Wright, *et al.*, 1993:307)

Examples abound. Consider the New York Telephone Company's recruitment efforts targeted at support employees. 'It tested 57,000 job applicants in 1987 and found that 54,900, or 96.3 percent, lacked basic skills in math, reading and reasoning' (Bradsher, 1990:C3). Motorola reports that 80% of its applicants fail to pass a seventh grade English comprehension or fifth grade math test, and at Bell South, less than 10% of applicants meet all minimum qualification standards (Bank of America, 1990).

Thurow describes the importance of high quality human resources in the following way:

> Consider what are commonly believed to be the seven key industries of the next few decades – microelectronics, biotechnology, the new materials industries, civilian aviation, telecommunications, robots plus machine tools and computers plus software. All are brain power industries. Each could be located anywhere on the face of the globe. Where they will be located depends upon who can organize the brain power to capture them. In the century ahead comparative advantage will be man-made.
>
> (Thurow, 1993:45)

Information technologies that underlie most design and delivery processes in the global markets of today and tomorrow have transformed many industries into knowledge-intensive sectors. As such, the quality of human capital is both critical and in short supply given the knowledge requirements typical of existing and emerging jobs in these sectors (Thurow, 1993). High-quality human capital, that is, human resources that provide unique competitive advantages through design and service innovations or extraordinary quality, is rare.

Human resources are hard to imitate

The human resources available to a firm are hard to imitate for the following reasons. First, human resource capital is formed through an evolutionary process that takes time, and is a product of unique HRM processes. For example, Schneider (1987) has explicated the attraction

– selection – attrition model in which the human capital within organizations reflects an increasingly narrow range of variability in skill and dispositional profiles. This occurs because of a 'cloning' effect – individuals are selected into the organization, promoted and retained because they resemble those making decisions and over time, this leads to a restriction in range in the human variability reflected within the organization.

HR policies and practices are important drivers of the values and behavioral norms that define the organization's culture (see also Chapter 5 on 'Managing without unions' describing the role of HR practices in creating 'strong' organizational cultures). As a consequence of the unique confluence of practices within organizations, the human capital within each organization becomes distinct and difficult to imitate within the short term. This distinctiveness becomes a source of competitive advantage if it is ideally suited to develop and exploit market opportunities.

Secondly, the link between human resources and competitive advantage is imperfectly understood. There is no clean human resource management (HRM) solution that can be reduced to a formula, patented and replicated across organizations. Organizations continuously search for the formula that will work in their unique internal and external circumstances despite the ambiguity between cause (HR processes) and effect (organizational results).

Thirdly, human resources within organizations reflect socially complex structures, predicated on transaction specific patterns that have developed over time, such as the existence of trust and loyalty between parties (or the lack thereof), egalitarian relationships between transactors (or strong hierarchical barriers), or politically motivated (versus discipline-based) decision making, and so on (Hage and Alter, 1993). These patterns are an integral part of the cultural fabric of the corporation that is difficult to imitate, especially across fairly well-established organizations (Kotter and Heskett, 1992; Pettigrew, 1985).

For these reasons, the mix of human capital in firms – characterized by knowledge and skills, behaviors and values – is unique and inimitable in the short term.

Human resources are non-substitutable

A central critique of the non-substitutability of human resources is their potential replacement through alternative hires, technology substitution, or even outsourcing. However, none of these solutions can achieve resource substitution without at least short-term start-up costs, and sometimes permanent damage to the performance potential of the firm (see Chapter 9). Flexible and broad-based intellectual capital is especially critical in the knowledge-intensive industries identified by Thurow (1993). In these industries, human resource substitution becomes even less likely because of the skill and knowledge breadth and flexibility required for performance and the patterns of process coordination that develop among project teams. Moreover, human resources have advantages over non-human (technological) means of task performance. Technologies age and rapidly become obsolete, and are usually fairly narrow in process applications. In contrast, human resources have the potential for skill renewal and avoidance of obsolescence through training and education, and for much broader skill transferability across a wide range of technologies, industries, products, and markets.

HRM creates capabilities that add value

The previous discussion establishes the fact that human capital as a resource possesses the necessary qualities to qualify as a source of competitive advantage, according to the resource base view of the firm (Barney, 1991; Conner, 1991; Wernerfelt, 1984). Beyond the theory, is there evidence demonstrating that HRM practices add value?

HRM effects on the bottom line

Pfeffer (1994) reviews the evidence demonstrating the impact of HRM processes and procedures on firms' financial success and cites numerous illustrations of the point. At the Blue Ridge plant of Levi Strauss, the costs per unit declined by 5.5% during the three quarters following introduction of gain sharing and quality enhancement programs and absenteeism declined by 13% (quoted from Thigpen, 1994:68). The New Universal Motor Manufacturing Company (NUMMI) joint venture between Toyota and GM instituted a radically re-engineered management system including new selection, training, teamwork and production-based pay differentiation in the Freemont, California plant that was previously run by GM alone. Compared to earlier performance levels, the NUMMI venture resulted in a productivity cost and quality advantage of almost 50 percent (MacDuffie and Krafcik, 1986). A seminal multinational study of auto assembly plants in Japan, Germany and the United States (Womack, *et al.*, 1990) found that management and organizational features of the operations explained 36 percent of the inter-plant variability in performance (see also MacDuffie, 1992). Some of the practices underlying these productivity advantages were manpower planning effectiveness (eliminating unnecessary workers), high percentage of workers involved in teams, extensive job rotation, active employee suggestion systems, focused hiring and selection processes, and extensive skill and cross-functional training.

Comparable results have been reported by Oliver, *et. al.* (1994) in a similar study conducted in the United Kingdom. Fernie and Metcalf (1994) in an analysis of over 2000 workplaces in the United Kingdom found that while human resource management (broadly defined to include a range of particular HR practices) does not appear to impact upon the climate of industrial relations, it does impact upon economic performance – defined as productivity relative to other similar workplaces. Relative productivity was found to be higher in workplaces where there is some employee involvement, a pay system contingent upon performance for individuals, single status, and organizational flexibility. Guest and Hoque (1994), in an analysis of the impact of strategic human resource policies and practices in greenfield sites in the United Kingdom, also report positive results. They demonstrate that within their greenfield sample, those firms utilizing the most extensive HR practices report the best HR outcomes (commitment, internal flexibility of staff, and quality of staff), the best employee relations outcomes (industrial disputes, labor turnover, and absenteeism) and the best performance outcomes (in terms of capacity to weather business recessions and quality benchmarked against other UK organizations).

Despite these impressive results, only a minority of employers are re-engineering or sustaining HRM systems as part of their competitive strategy in the marketplace. A US National Commission concluded that:

> The vast majority of U.S. employers aren't moving to 'high performance' work organizations, which requires educated workers, nor investing to train employees. Fully $27 billion of the $30 billion in annual training outlays is spent by ... only 0.5% of all U.S. companies, and fewer than 200 of these employers ... spend more than 2% of their payroll on formal training.
>
> (Karr, 1990:A4)

This lack of generalized movement towards strategic human resource management has also been found by both Millward (1994) and Storey and Sisson (1994) to be true of the British situation.

In addition, many organizations that implemented radically redesigned HRM systems, quality of work life or employee involvement programs have abandoned them. Rankin (1986) concluded that 40 percent of quality of work life or employee involvement programs failed within the first two to three years, and another study concluded that 75 percent of such plans were eliminated after five years (Goodman, 1980). Pettigrew (1985) found that it is often middle managers who are most resistant to the organizational changes needed to make quality initiatives work. In other words, attempts to revolutionize HRM are difficult, can fail and are often short-lived. The central question concerns the critical success factors associated with HRM systems that *do* work.

HRM capabilities that support world-class organizational performance

In the aggregate, as presented above there is evidence that a focus on HRM can enhance the bottom line. What is the process through which HRM adds value? In this section we advance the argument that HRM is a source of competitive advantage to the extent that HRM systems are aligned with critical capabilities.

Appropriately aligned HRM systems are HRM input, throughput, and output processes that focus and stimulate employee behaviors that advance the strategic goals of the business. Another way of expressing this is to say that HRM systems can be either *algorithmic* or *experiential* depending on the nature of the business environment of the organization (Gomez-Mejia, 1992). Algorithmic (rules oriented) HRM systems emphasize behavioral control systems based on standardized operating procedures in the areas of recruitment, selection, rewards, work organization, and employee influence. Experiential HRM systems are more ad hoc and opportunistic in focus, dealing with informal and adaptive performance management feedback and response patterns. HRM systems in slow moving steady state environments can be characterized as routine in nature.

However, if the business environment is in a state of flux where rapid product changes and product innovations are necessary for market success, then an experiential, more ad hoc HRM system may be more appropriate. An HRM system which is opportunistic and adaptive in focus becomes an enabler of market moves, behaviors that are critical success factors in such environments. Of course, this can strain the equity principle so important in eliciting the high levels of employee commitment needed in high performance organizational systems – a further contextual variable which needs to be taken account of in designing experiential HR systems.

Our earlier discussion of the features of world-class organizations identified five critical competitive capabilities or competencies: quality, speed, dependability, cost, and adaptability. Hage and Alter (1993) describe the simultaneous combination of these five characteristics as adaptive efficiency. When suitably aligned, HRM processes create and support adaptive efficiency. However, the simultaneous combination of these capabilities is not a simple linear combination because the confluence of these factors represents a complex and dynamic tension and interdependence. For example, the creation of quality with its emphasis on predictable routines and zero defect products and processes may be at variance with the need to take a product to market quickly and to be highly adaptable, innovative, and flexible. Therefore, the common HRM functions of rewards, work systems, manpower flow, and employee influence (Beer, *et al.* 1984; Truss and Gratton, 1994) may need to combine both algorithmic and experiential features.

Quality capability

Quality capabilities are created by selecting, developing, motivating, and retaining a critical mass of talent that is capable of delivering the highest quality in today's products and processes, but also able to quickly adapt to the delivery needs of *tomorrow's* products and pro-cesses. The development of such a talent pool involves numerous HRM systems, including recruitment and selection, training and development for continuous learning, cross-functional teams and job rotations to develop multi-talented employees, and performance incentives for investment in learning and quality performance (Terpstra and Rozell, 1993). In this regard Schneider and Bowen (1993) have demonstrated in a series of studies in the banking industry that HRM practices inside organizations are significantly correlated with customer perceptions of the quality of services received. Among the HRM practices contributing to customer perceptions of service quality are task design, supervisory feedback and reward practices, career growth and development oppor-tunities, and employee orientation and training practices. Also, best-in-class organizations allocate over 3 percent of their payroll to employee training and development, with some like Corning Glass reporting allocations as high as 7 percent (Olian, *et al.*, 1993). The new Saturn division of GM adopts an 'at risk' pay policy, but the portion of workers' pay that is at risk is tied not to performance, but to invest-ment in training:

> [It] seemed like the ideal solution, not only to emphasize the impor-tance of training, but to help Saturn achieve its quality and produc-tion goals. Doing the right training in the right way at the right time really does leverage [Saturn's] ability to build more cars and increase salary levels . . . Employees received bonuses for the first quarter of 1992 because they exceeded company wide goals for training, produc-tion and quality. In fact, they nearly doubled their training goal of 155,687 hours, logging more than 300,000.
>
> (Geber, 1992:33)

Southwest Airlines, the airline with the highest growth rate and profit margins in the US airline industry today, selects employees by fly-ing customers to its corporate headquarters and involving them in the selection process. As a customer obsessed company, Southwest believes that customers are in the best position to judge candidate qualifications against their own requirements for service (Pfeffer, 1994). Extensive training – representing a credible commitment to customer care – of front-line staff involved in customer interface, was also critical in the successful turnaround of British Airways in the mid-1980s.

Speed capability

Organizational capacity to move fast is a second feature of the world-class competitive organization. HRM practices can affect speed to the extent that they remove buffers to performance (for example, exces-sive bureaucratic requirements), develop responsive HR systems (by pushing the HRM function down to line management, where it happens), and create incentives tied to speed without compromising quality (more *is* better as long as it meets quality requirements). Stalk, *et al.* (1992) attribute Honda's competitive edge in the middle to late 1980s to its ability to reduce cycle time, from design to testing to production. For Honda's new Acura division, this took three years, contrasted with GM's Saturn division, which needed almost double the time to produce less than a third of the car volume. Honda relied on an existing, cross-functionally trained workforce that was sufficiently agile to shift toward a new product line. In contrast, GM had to create a whole new breed of worker. Hence speed facilitated through a capable workforce can provide significant market advantages. The latter point is borne out by a study in the steel industry concerned with the impact of four distinct HRM systems on cycle time (Ichniowski, *et al.*, 1993). The HRM systems varied along a continuum from one anchor emphasizing flexibility and participation (labeled system 1) to narrowly tailored, quantitative production systems (system 4). System 1 work practices push accountability and responsibility down to the line managers and also advocate the empowerment of teams and individual workers. There is a strong emphasis on the development of problem-solving skills, frequent worker management consultation and discussions, gain-sharing compensation, valid selection procedures, and employment security. In contrast, system 4 HRM practices were characterized by infrequent problem-solving strategies or teams, rare worker management discussions or gain-sharing procedures, unsophisticated selection procedures and low employment security, and a strong emphasis on the use of job classifications. The relationship between 'up-time' (frequency of production shifts that met schedule) and a wide range of work practices was documented in the study.

Significant productivity differences emerged for the different HRM systems (Ichniowski, *et al.*, 1993). System 1 had a 98% achievement record on up-time compared to an 88% hit rate under system 4 approaches. Interestingly, simultaneous bundling of a wide range of HRM practices (consultation, empowerment, utilization of tacit knowledge, and so on) was critical to the overall productivity results since specific work practices, in isolation, were found to have little or no effect unless they were part of a larger systemic change.

Dependability capability

World-class organizational systems deliver high-quality products or services *each and every time*. They produce a product consistently and reliably, 'that unfailingly satisfies customers' expectations' (Stalk, *et al.*, 1992). Certainly, the quality movement has emphasized statistical process control systems to provide information on manufacturing variability, in the interest of systematically reducing the variability of a process (Olian and Rynes, 1991). Although machines and technology are frequently the source of some variability, ultimately most performance variability is man-made. This is where HRM systems come into play.

The other driver of dependable production is a performance management system that rewards the 'right' kinds of employee behaviors, with the performance monitoring system sensitive to the level of performance consistency ('what percentage of customers received a follow-up call within the first five days of delivery of the product?'), a reward system that is impacted in a meaningful way by the level of performance reliability (for example, defect rates factored into quantitative measures of performance), and performance improvement systems designed to systematize performance processes and attack sources of unreliability (for example, computerized form letters to provide one of five types of responses to job applicants).

The initial driver of dependable performance is the design process, where the process or product is designed to be right from the start, even if it costs more initially. Vesey (1991) describes the incremental costs of correcting a product or process at later stages of the service or production chain. At each successive phase of the production process (for example, from planning to product design, from product design to process design, from process design to production), the cost of defect correction increases exponentially. To eliminate unreliability at the source, Vesey advocates concurrent engineering processes, relying heavily on multidisciplinary teams comprised of heterogeneously skilled individuals. Here again, selection and training systems play a key part in creating this benchmark capability.

Cost capability

A critical element in achieving incremental cost reductions is the involvement of workers in boosting productivity and eliminating waste through the use of continuous improvement, high involvement teams. Decentralization tends to produce better decisions because individuals with greater tacit knowledge are involved in decision making and can eliminate unnecessarily costly and non-value added tasks at the source.

Evidence on the efficacy of this approach is provided by Levine and Tyson (1991) in a review of some 29 studies on the effects of workplace participation on the costs of production. Of these studies, 14 demonstrated that workplace participation had positive effects on production costs, 2 showed negative effects, and in 13 studies results were inconclusive. The authors concluded that the introduction of team-based participation was more likely to have a significant and durable impact on productivity when front-line employees were involved and when there was substantive and frequent participation in decision making by shop floor employees at the point of production. However, when organizational arrangements such as quality circles occurred in which information sharing was the focus rather than meaningful participation in actual decisions, the benefits were short-lived. While these less involving approaches, such as quality circles, draw on the tacit knowledge and creativity of workers, enthusiasm can often wane because the team lacks implementation authority (see Chapter 7).

Other HRM practices that support a cost capability are gain-sharing plans that reward employees for cost savings. Kaufman (1992) conducted a review of 112 gain-sharing plans in manufacturing, observing the impact on labor hours input into a given product. Workers under IMPROSHARE plans (where bonuses equal half the increase in productivity) reduced defect and downtime rates by 23% in the first year and increased productivity over 15% in three years. Macy and Izumi (1993) conducted a meta-analysis examining the relationship between 44 work practices, and productivity, quality, and costs. Work practices were divided into three main categories: structural work practices (for example, job design, and team work), human resources work practices (training and communications), and technological work practices (computerization, robotics). This meta-analysis of 75 studies contrasting performance before and after introduction of new work practices indicated that the practices were strongly related to increased productivity and reduced costs. In a selected sample of the field studies, introduction of new practices was associated with a 30–40% improvement in performance. The larger the number of new work practices, the greater the increase in productivity and decline in costs. In the NUMMI study cited earlier (MacDuffie and Krafcik, 1986), the new HRM practices in the Freemont California plant resulted in higher quality products with significantly fewer labor hours than was true for any other GM plant, and the plant achieved almost the same levels of performance as the benchmark Toyota plant in Japan.

The evidence demonstrates that HRM practices create cost capabilities by eliminating non-value added processes and by stimulating process innovations. Key HRM processes in this regard are employee involvement strategies, incentive systems through gain sharing, and the development of a workforce capable of process improvements.

Adaptive capability

HRM systems can be rules bound, confining organizational players to the status quo, and benign – neither encouraging nor discouraging innovation – or they can provide the capability and incentives for experimentation and innovation. Adaptive capabilities can be facilitated by the appropriate cross-functional skill building, incentive structures (for example, tying rewards to suggestions and new improvements), and work structures such as teams which facilitate creativity and effective problem solving. The MIT study on auto assembly plants mentioned earlier (Womack, *et al.*, 1990) identified HRM 'buffers' (for example, additional rules or layers of hierarchy) that impede agile adaptability to the needs of the market. In contrast, HRM systems that have created readiness for switches in product and process directions, and incentives for employees to hunger for such changes, position the firm to be the first to adapt in its market. This becomes a source of competitive advantage.

Stalk, *et al.* (1992) demonstrate how adaptive capabilities constitute a competitive advantage in the case of a medical equipment company called Medequip. The company realized that in cases where their sales representatives were allowed to locate on-site with clients, service contracts were renewed at three times the rate of other accounts. They quickly adjusted their administrative and HRM support systems to provide full service to their off-site customer representatives, despite the short-term inconvenience and added resources associated with implementation of this decision. Medequip's adaptive capability was the critical reason behind its successful launch of a new product line and an increase in market share of about 50%.

In summary, we have identified the capabilities of world-class competitive organizations and provided evidence that shows how HRM systems are the enablers of these capabilities. The evidence is over-whelming, even though only a minority of firms approximates this ideal.

Alternative views on managing 'without HRM'

Development of these world-class capabilities into sources of competitive advantage is supported through HRM systems. However, there are alternative organizational forms for enabling these capabilities through HRM. For the purposes of illustration, we describe two alternative HRM forms, each of which is an enabler of the world-class capabilities enumerated earlier. Each reflects an approach to managing without the traditional HRM structure – a theme developed and expanded in Part Two of this book. First, we examine HRM in the *quality organization* and second, we explore HRM in the *virtual organization*. Returning to our model in Figure 1.1 which highlighted the importance of the environmental, organizational, and strategic context for HRM, we see that each form of HRM is both a result of different contextual conditions and a driver of alternative business strategies.

We conceptualize these two alternative forms of HRM using the 'make' or 'buy' analogy, where the quality organization represents the former and the virtual organization the latter. Williamson (1986) describes this decision as one over the establishment of the firm's boundaries, the decision to produce goods or services within the organization or outside the organization using networks of suppliers.

A firm reaching an internal 'make' decision decides to draw on its internal resources using available management, rather than exploiting the market as a resource directing mechanism (Coase, 1937). There are advantages to a firm using internal rather than external market allocation mechanisms. These include the reduction of contracting costs incurred in dealing with buyers and suppliers (Oster, 1990). However, if a firm internalizes transactions and does its buying and selling within the organization, it faces a different set of transaction costs and the management challenge is of motivating the internal workforce.

Alternatively, outsourcing the decision may remove the organization from intimate control over quality and contact with customers, despite the ability to exploit market competition on price and quality to the firm's advantage. Obviously there are tradeoffs, and the question is which set of tradeoffs suits the firm given its market and organizational requirements. Among the factors affecting the firm's decision to make or buy are: the frequency of contact and exchange between the parties to the employment relationship (more frequent leads to a make decision); the market uncertainty over resources (for example, labor supply); availability; greater uncertainty, which leads to a make decision to avoid reliance on the vicissitudes of the market; and the asset specificity (for example, firm-specific training), with greater specificity encouraging a make decision.

The total quality organization and world-class competitive capability

The TQ organization

HR processes within the total quality (TQ) organization can be viewed as the outcome of a decision to support and enable HRM capabilities within the boundaries of the firm. TQ is touted as one of the most important strategic tools to obtain competitive advantage. Reports show that 93% of manufacturing companies and 69% of service firms have implemented some form of quality management (The Conference Board, 1991). Indeed, the majority (64%) of CEOs devote at least one tenth of their time to quality improvement (KMPG Peat Marwick, 1991), and many commit a lot more.

TQ is an entire management philosophy supported through a menu of tools. When successfully implemented, TQ changes the way producers view and interact with each of their customers. Many organizational processes change, including the physical layout of organizations, acquisition of raw materials, product development processes, customer, supplier and distributor relations, and measurement, feedback, and control systems. TQ processes re-focus strategic priorities and change the status and process of management (Olian and Rynes, 1991). Rather than inspecting out defects, the core principles underlying TQ are: customer driven product and process features; building in continuous quality improvement at the source; comprehensive measurement to guide improvement processes; horizontal process and product delivery chains; and employee empowerment to drive improvements.

HRM in the TQ organization

Several HRM processes are critical success factors in the realization of a TQ management system. Emphasis on extensive training and continuous learning systems is required to provide employees with the knowledge and competencies that enable implementation of continuous quality improvements. Advanced career development systems, job rotations, and temporary assignments promote the development of cross-functional skills, and support horizontal (interdepartmental team) processes and problem-solving structures. Organizational reward systems must be designed around relevant quality and reliability measures and extensive 360° feedback systems implemented as the basis for reward processes. Management hierarchies are flattened to motivate and benefit from shop floor involvement in improvement processes. Employee selection systems involve all relevant stakeholders in decision making and are geared toward the skills and behaviors that support TQ. Examples abound of these TQ-based HRM processes (Olian and Rynes, 1991). The Conference Board (1991) notes that companies practicing TQ engage in extensive multi-directional information sharing. Most companies organize employee meetings with top management (79% of manufacturing companies; 73% of service companies), face-to-face short-term teams (92% manufacturing, 97% service), focus groups (46% manufacturing, 71% service), and employee suggestion systems (60% manufacturing, 64% service).

In recognizing the significance of the 'right' kind of raw material, TQ organizations design extensive and systematic procedures to recruit, select, and induct employees at all organization levels (Shook, 1988). For example, Hampton (1988) reports that Mazda and Diamond Star Motors (a Chrysler Mitsubishi company) spend about US$13,000 on each new hire of a production employee. Diamond Star uses a realistic preview video that warns applicants that they must learn several jobs, change shifts, work overtime, make and take constructive criticisms, and submit a constant stream of suggestions in improving efficiency.

The importance of team and teamwork is also reinforced in a number of ways. Self-managing teams become more prevalent as companies advance in their implementation of TQ. KMPG Peat Marwick (1991) found that only 15% of companies in the early phases of TQ implementation used self-managing work teams, compared to 50% in companies with the most developed TQ cultures.

In many companies, teams play a large (or even dominant) role in new employee recruitment and selection. Some TQ firms (such as Honda and WalMart) go as far as evaluating family members as part of the screening process in order to ensure family-wide involvement in the new employer's team. Team interpersonal skills are reinforced through general orientation and training which often lasts several months, even for production workers. Mazda's new hires receive several days of general training, five to seven weeks of technical skills training, and three to four weeks of supervision when first placed on the assembly line.

Similarly General Electric's change to a horizontal organization

> forced major upheavals in [its] training, appraisal and compensation systems. To create greater allegiance to a process, rather than a boss, the company has begun to put in place so-called '360-degree appraisal routines' in which peers and others above and below the employee evaluate the performance of an individual in a process. In some cases, as many as 20 people are now involved in reviewing a single employee. Employees are paid on the basis of the skills they develop rather than merely the individual work they perform.
>
> (*Business Week*, 1993: 20 December, 1979)

Rewards and celebration are used to acknowledge successes and emotionally revive employees to continue in their improvement efforts. Milliken, the Baldridge award winning textile company, has alcoves of excellence, walls of fame and a company news magazine filled with photos and recognition stories (Shonberger, 1990). Xerox conducts a Hollywood style, team celebration event. Over 12,000 employees, customers and employers attend a huge quality fair in one of four US or international locations, all linked via satellite. Pepsi Co. Inc. provides stock options for all of its roughly 100,000 permanent employees to encourage them to celebrate in the success of the corporation (Kanter, 1989b).

Ultimately, HRM in the quality organization is placed – hook, line and sinker – on the shoulders of the line manager. It is the line manager who empowers (or blocks) her workers in taking control of a process improvement. It is the line manager who prompts and encourages employees to seek out new developmental opportunities and to translate what was learned elsewhere into improvements in the work environment. It is the line manager who provides ongoing encouragement (or discouragement) for attempts to experiment with process improvements. It is the line manager who creates an atmosphere that encourages risks and tolerates mistakes, provided the mistakes are based on a reasonable problem-solving strategy. It is the line manager who takes time out to meet with customers and understand their requirements, who provides a role model as a turf protector, or as a team player with other departments. Line managers signal the importance of measurement and feedback based on their posture toward employee and customer feedback on their own behaviors.

The TQ manager's repertoire of HRM practices is a complex set of interrelated behaviors. Pfeffer (1994:244) makes this point well: 'Because of the complementarity among the elements required to manage people effectively for competitive advantage, some observers have noted that such systems are inherently fragile.' He draws on MacDuffie and Krafcik and their discussion of lean manufacturing systems:

> Lean production is . . . fragile with respect to its dependence on human resources. As lean production diffuses . . . it is highly vulnerable to the mass production assumptions and mindsets that have dominated managerial and engineering practice . . . Unless managers keep the skills levels of the work force high, unless they create a culture of reciprocal commitment in which workers will be willing to contribute to process improvement . . . lean production will quickly deteriorate . . . [I]n practice, lean production is not weaker or more prone to break-down . . . [M]aintaining a constant awareness of lean production's 'fragility' is . . . critical to preserving this resilience and flexibility.
>
> (MacDuffie and Krafcik, 1992:212)

There is a wide configuration of sometimes complementary and sometimes tenuously related HRM behaviors that are the means of realizing a TQ philosophy. Leadership at the top is crucial, to signal a jolt to the status quo and to drive out the natural fear of change. However, it is line managers who are the immediate role models of the expected repertoire of behaviors for employees, and if these managers adjust their behaviors in line with TQ prescriptions, they will remove the natural impediments to change and slowly stimulate a re-engineering of organizational cultures.

Hence, the term 'managing without HRM.' In the TQ organization, this means that the HRM function has been permeated throughout the culture, via line managers' role behaviors, and there is no longer a need for HRM to function as a centralized staff function within corporate headquarters. HRM becomes integrated into the core processes of the organization and is used as a tool by the process owners to allocate and stimulate resources (including the human resources) in pursuit of the process goals. Will Potter, President of Preston Trucking and a company repeatedly included in the list of top 100 managed corporations in America, said to one of the authors:

> Human Resource Management is too important to be left to the personnel department. We've eliminated the whole department and put HRM where it should be, in the hands of the managers. On the occasions that we need help or research, we go to consultants. Otherwise, managers want to and should own the management process.

The virtual corporation

The virtual corporation (VC) is a term coined by William H. Davidow and Michael S. Malone (1992). While their particular description of the VC is an all-encompassing mix of management buzz words, empowerment techniques, and inventory control mechanisms, the term has been picked up and used to describe the characteristics of new corporate models that are network based.

The VC

Joint ventures and strategic alliances (see Chapter 3) are but one example of the VC, in essence a temporary and dynamic network of companies that coordinate their activities in order to exploit fast-changing opportunities. Each partner contributes in areas in which it possesses critical advantage, whether in R&D, design, manufacturing, distribution, finance or marketing. The VC or modular company nurtures a few core competency areas in which it enjoys, alone or in partnership, a competitive advantage, and outsources all non-core activities. In theory, the VC can then create a 'best of everything' organization capitalizing on shared costs, skills and access to global markets.

Kingston Technology is one of the world's leading upgraders of personal computers. Located in Southern California, in 1993 sales went from US$140 million to US$250 million, and in 1994 sales were expected to double again. Kingston Technology is a VC, with 220 employees and a tightly knit family of independent companies that function as one in many respects, and are indistinguishable from each other in the eyes of its customers:

> The real secret of [Kingston's] success is its unique brand of corporate organization... Instead of growing as its business grew, adding new capacity or branching into new businesses, Kingston stayed small. It created a rock solid network of corporate partners and farmed work out to them. This isn't mere subcontracting. Kingston and its partners lead complementary corporate lives, sharing capital, know-how and markets. Because each specializes in what it does, Kingston has been able to cut loose from the costs of larger-scale enterprise – and cash in on efficiencies that often elude its rivals.
> ... When Kingston's advertising needs outstripped the capabilities of its design and printing partner, [the CEO] went to the company and said: 'If you grow with us you will have our loyalty.' For Kingston, that meant no shopping around for a better price; on the other hand, it preserved a valued partnership and freed Kingston from having to set up its own department. The arrangement gave the printer confidence to invest in new equipment and even move its operations closer to Kingston. The deals were closed on a handshake, Kingston style.
> (*Newsweek*, 1993:40)

Partnerships in the VC network tend to be fluid, impermanent, informal and opportunistic in basis. The objective of the network of VC partners is to meet and fulfill a specific market opportunity. Once this market opportunity has faded, the network quickly disbands without any cumbersome governance arrangements and consequential costs structures to be dismantled. Byrne and Brant (1993) describe the

VC as a temporary network of independent companies – suppliers, customers, even erstwhile rivals – linked by information technology and sometimes capital structures to share skills, costs, and access to each other's markets, with neither central office nor organization chart, hierarchy or vertical integration.

Apple Computer's strategy of partnering provides a good example of the power of networks (*Business Week*, 1993: 8 February, 98–103). In 1991, lacking the capacity to produce its entire line of Power Notebooks, Apple approached Sony Corporation with a simple request: to manufacture the least expensive version of the Power Notebook. Apple's core competence was its easy to use software, while Sony's core competence lay in its miniaturization manufacturing skills. In 1992, Sony made 100,000 Apple Powerbooks. Later Apple terminated its agreement with Sony. The linkage had served its purpose, namely to bring an entry level product swiftly to market. Through this alliance Apple avoided having to invest in costly and time-consuming R&D and design that – in all likelihood – would have canceled Apple's entry into the portable computer product market.

Technology has a central role to play in the creation of the VC. Roger Nagle, Operations Director at Lehigh University's Iacocca Institute in the United States, envisages a world in which technology could make the creation of virtual enterprises 'as straightforward as connecting components for a home audio and video system by different manufacturers' (Byrne and Brant, 1993:100). Nagle envisages a national information infrastructure linking computers and machine tools across the United States. The creation of this so-called communications super highway would allow far-flung companies to quickly locate suppliers, designers, and manufacturers through an information clearing house. Once connected they would sign 'electronic contracts' to speed link ups without legal headaches. Of course, there are potential dangers with the VC form such as loss of proprietary information or technology through the network, particularly if the network is formed on an opportunistic basis. There are also challenges involved in laterally building trust with outside organizations for managers accustomed to operating within the boundaries of a firm with team members who have many shared experiences and are a product of the same culture.

Byrne and Bryant (1993) offer several guidelines to companies establishing a VC based on lateral alliances. These include: choose the right partnership based on dependability and trust, and bring a particular core competency to the table; play fair – each lateral relationship within the network must present a win–win opportunity for both partnering companies; always put the best and most flexible people into these lateral relationships, for this tells the partner that the alliance is regarded as important; create clearly defined objectives, for both parties need to address 'what is in it for me' and to have a clear idea about what they seek to gain from the partnering company; and create and build a common information technology infrastructure. Key motivating factors for the VC are the elimination of internal overhead and the reduction of transaction costs via the outsourcing of R&D, service or production labor. A byproduct of the decision to outsource core functions is the elimination of the HRM process in the outsourced areas.

The contingency workforce, though not a necessary feature of the VC, is becoming an increasingly prevalent business option for managers, with 44% of CEOs predicting an increase in the use of contingent workers five years from now, and only 9% predicting a decrease (Fortune, 1994). With most CEOs under pressure to squeeze out inefficiencies, many see the contingent workforce as a way of reducing fixed labor costs. This strategy is not without its costs. Temporary employment relationships do not breed employee loyalty to the client company or long-term customer relationships with the changing (temporary) worker. Moreover, company specific or tacit knowledge may take time to acquire, a luxury not available to contingent workers.

Some HRM implications

HRM in the VC

The VC is a form of managing HRM 'without.' It creates organizational capabilities without 'owning' a workforce. The attraction, of course, is cost reduction by exploiting competitive bidding opportunities in the external market, capitalizing on economies of scale that suppliers have achieved, and enjoying the flexibility and cost savings associated with the temporary relationships. Abraham (1990) suggests that there is a cost savings of 15–30% from temporary service workers relative to equivalent full timers, primarily because contractual workers earn fewer or no fringe benefits, and save real estate costs to the extent that they perform the work off company premises. However, such cost savings may be ephemeral (see Chapter 9).

The manager of the core functions preserved within the VC operates much like the line manager within the TQ organization. However, the peripheral functions and players within the VC are ever-changing. There is certainly a reduced need for a centralized or permanent HRM function in smaller, entrepreneurial VCs. The biggest challenge for the HR manager in the VC is to create a palpable organizational culture with core values that are identifiable to both employees and customers. With much of the business of the enterprise in the hands of sometimes unseen, and usually changing hands, this acculturation process is difficult. Moreover, the stress on the core players may be great because of the constant change in their environment and the requirement to permanently adapt to new partners, processes, and potentially higher quality standards. These concerns are somewhat alleviated the more permanent the VC's alliances (as is the case for Kingston Technology), and the greater the confidence that can be placed in the expertise and quality of the VC's partners.

In contrast to the TQ organization in which the entire HRM function shifts to the ownership of the line manager, there is a limited role remaining for HRM specialists in the VC. As suggested earlier, the core competencies of the VC should be managed along the lines of a TQ organization. However, the management of the outsourced or partnered functions may require involvement of the HRM manager. The primary HRM functions within these non-core parts of the VC are manpower planning and competency assessment. Regarding the former role, it falls upon the HRM specialist to create fast and adaptive organizational capabilities through a network of ready and able partners. This requires some foresight into expected manpower requirements. Manpower planning models (Jackson and Schuler, 1990) that delineate expected labor supply and cost functions are relevant here. Additionally, HRM specialists can be important business allies in assessing the quality capabilities of potential and actual VC partners. This is merely an external focus to the usual HRM screening and performance assessment functions. Beyond those two roles, the VC organization has effectively eliminated HRM responsibilities in areas delivered through the VC alliance. Hence, the term 'managing without' in the context of HRM in the VC.

HRM as a core competency

The premise of this book is that human resources are the critical source of competitive advantage to firms. This resource cannot be copied or substituted easily, and the manner in which this resource is combined to create value to the organization is not readily transparent or understandable (Pfeffer, 1994). For these reasons human resources constitute a sustainable source of competitive advantage. HRM practices, if done right, constitute a core competency to businesses because they support and enable world-class competitive capabilities: high quality processes, done fast, consistently, cheaply, and flexibly around changing customer requirements. However, it is our contention that the old way of managing HRM through a centralized staff function no longer works in today's markets of global, rapidly improving, and cut-throat price competition. We offered two alternative forms for the delivery of HRM processes, one in the TQ organization through the line manager as a 'make' process, and one in the VC where activities are associated with the role of core culture builder and 'contract manager' – a 'buy' process. Both forms of HRM – approaches to deploying people that enable more agile service and production processes – better fit the evolving needs of the marketplace than does the more traditional HRM job description. Indeed, we advocate a new form of HRM 'without' the traditional HR function.

References

Abraham, K.G. (1990). Restructuring the employment relationship: the growth of market-mediated work arrangements. In Abraham, K.G. and McKersie, R.B. (eds) *New Developments in the Labor Market*. Cambridge: MIT Press.

Bank of America (1990). Human resource planning, *Perspectives*, 11, 40.

Barney J. (1991). Firm resources and sustained competitive advantage, *Journal of Management*, 17, 99–120.

Beer, M., Spector, B., Lawrence, P.R., Quinn Mills, D., and Walton, R.E. (1984). *Managing Human Assets*. New York: Macmillan.

Boudreau, J.W. (1983). Economic considerations in estimating the utility of human resource productivity improvement programs, *Personnel Psychology*, 36, 551–7.

Boudreau, J.W. and Berger, C.J. (1985). Decision-theoretic utility analysis applied to external employee movement, *Journal of Applied Psychology*, 70, 581–612.

Bradsher, K. (1990). US lag in phone trade seen, *New York Times*, 17 August, C3.

Business Week (1993). The Virtual Corporation, 8 February, 98–103.

Business Week (1993). The horizontal corporation, 20 December, 76–81.

Byrne, J.A. and Brant, R. (1993). The virtual corporation, *Newsweek*, 8 February, 98–103.

Cascio, W.F. and Ramos, R. (1986). Development and application of a new method for assessing job performance in behavioral/economic terms, *Journal of Applied Psychology*, 71, 20–8.

Coase, R.H. (1937). The nature of the firm, *Economica*, 54, 386–405.

The Conference Board (1991). Employee buy-in to total quality. *The Conference Board Report 974*. NY. New York.

Conner, K.R. (1991). A historical comparison of resource base theory and five schools of thought within industrial organizational economics: do we have a new theory of the firm? *Journal of Management*, 17, 121–54.

Cook, M. (1993). *Personnel Selection and Productivity*. Chichester: John Wiley.

Davidow, W.H. and Malone, M.S. (1992). *The Virtual Corporation*. New York: HarperCollins.

Fernie, S., Metcalf, D., and Woodland, S. (1994). What has human resource management achieved in the workplace? *Employment Policy Institute Economic Report*, 8.

Fortune (1994). *The Contingency Work Force*, 24 January, 30–6.

Geber, B. (1992). Saturn's grand experiment, *Training*, 29, (6), 27–35.

Gomez-Mejia, L.R. (1992). Structure and process of diversification, compensation strategy, and firm performance, *Strategic Management Journal*, 14, 381–97.

Goodman, P.S. (1980). Realities of improving the quality of work life, *Labor Law Journal*, 31, 487–94.

Gratton, L.C. (1992). Selecting leaders: practice and trends. In Syrett, M. and Hogg, C. (eds) *Frontiers of Leadership: An Essential Reader*. Basil Blackwell: Oxford.

Guest, D and Hoque, K. (1994). The good, the bad and the ugly: employment relations in new non-union workplaces, *Human Resource Management Journal*, 5, (1), 1–14.

Hage, J. and Alter, C. (1993). *Organizations Working Together*. Newbury Park, CA: Sage.

Hall, R. (1992). The strategic analysis of intangible resources. *Strategic Management Journal*, 13, 139.

Hampton, W.J. (1988). How does Japan Inc. pick its American workers? *Business Week*, 3 October, 84–8.

Heneman, H., and Heneman, R. (1994). *Staffing Organizations*. Homewood, Il: Austen Press.

Ichniowski, C., Shaw, K., and Prennuski, G. (1993). The effects of human resource management practices on productivity. Mimeograph, Columbia University.

Jackson, S.E. and Schuler, R.S. (1990). Human resource planning – challenges for industrial/organizational psychologists, *American Psychologist*, 45, (2), 223–39.

Kanter, R.M. (1989a). The new managerial work, *Harvard Business Review*, November–December, 86–98.

Kanter, R.M. (1989b). *When Giants Learn to Dance*. New York: Touchstone.

Karr, A.R. (1990). Work skills panel urges major changes in school education, job organization, *The Wall Street Journal*, 19 June, A4.

Kaufman, R. (1992). The effects of IMPROSHARE on productivity, *Industrial and Labor Relations Review*, 45, 311–22.

KMPG Peat Marwick (1991). *Quality Improvement Initiatives through the Management of Human Resources*. Short Hills, NJ: KMPG Peat Marwick.

Kotter, J. and Heskett, J. (1992). *Corporate Culture and Performance*. New York: The Free Press.

Lado, A.A. and Wilson, M.C. (1994). Human resource systems and sustained competitive advantage: A competency-based perspective, *Academy of Management Review*, 19, (4), 700.

Levine, D. and Tyson, L.D. (1991). Participation, productivity and the firm's environment. In A. Blinder (ed.) *Paying for Productivity*, Washington, DC: Brookings Institution.

MacDuffie, J.P. (1992). Human resource bundles and manufacturing performance. Mimeograph. Wharton School, University of Pennsylvania.

MacDuffie, J.P. and Krafcik, J.F. (1986). Integrating technology and human resources for high-performance manufacturing: evidence from the international auto industry. In Kochan, T.A. and Useem, M. (eds) (1992) *Transforming Organizations*. New York: Oxford University Press.

Macy, B. and Izumi, H. (1993). Organizational change design and work innovation: a meta-analysis of North American field studies, 1961–1991. In Woodman, R. and Pasmore, W. (eds) *Research in Organizational Change and Development, Vol. 7.* Greenwich, CT: JAI Press.

McGregor, D. (1960). *The Human Side of Enterprise.* New York: McGraw-Hill.

Millward, N.(1994). *The New Industrial Relations?* Policy Studies Institute: London.

Newsweek (1993). *Here's a 'virtual' model for America's industrial giants,* 23 August, 40.

Olian, J.D., Durham, C., Kristof, A., and Pierce, R. (1993). Training and development in world-class companies. University of Maryland (in review).

Olian, J.D. and Rynes, S.L. (1991). Making total quality work: aligning organizational processes, performance measures, and stakeholders, *Human Resource Management*, 13, (3), 303–33.

Oliver, N., Delbridge, R., Jones, D., and Lowe, R. (1994). World-Class Manufacturing: further evidence from the lean production debate, *British Journal of Management*, 5, Special Issue, S53–S65.

Oliver, N. and Wilkinson, B. (1992). *The Japanisation of British industry: new developments in the 1990s,* 2nd ed. Blackwell: Oxford.

Oster, S. (1990). *Modern Competitive Analysis,* London: Oxford University Press.

Pettigrew, A.M. (1985). *The Awakening Giant: Continuity and Change in Imperial Chemical Industries.* Oxford: Blackwell.

Pfeffer, J. (1994). *Competitive Advantage through People.* Boston, MA: Harvard Business School Press.

Porter, M.E. (1985). *Competitive Advantage.* New York: The Free Press.

Rankin, T. (1986). Integrating QWL and collective bargaining, *Work-Life Review*, 5, 14–18.

Schmidt, F.L., Gast-Rosenberg, I. and Hunter, J.E. (1980). Validity generalization results for computer programmers, *Journal of Applied Psychology*, 65, 643–61.

Schmidt, F.L. and Hunter, J. (1981). Employment testing: old theories and new research findings, *American Psychologist*, 10, 1128–37.

Schneider, B. (1987). The people make the place, *Personnel Psychology*, 40, 437–53.

Schneider, B. and Bowen, D.E. (1993). The service organization: human resource management is crucial. *Organizational Dynamics*, 21, 39–52.

Shonberger, R.J. (1990). *Building a Chain of Customers.* New York: The Free Press.

Shook, R.L. (1988). *Honda: An American Success Story.* New York: Prentice-Hall.

Slack, N. (1991). *The Manufacturing Advantage: Achieving Competitive Manufacturing and Operations.* London: Mercury Books.

Snell, S.A. and Dean, J.W. (1992). Integrated manufacturing and human resource management: a human capital perspective, *Academy of Management Journal*, 35, 467–504.

Stalk, G. Jr, Evans, P., and Shulman L.E. (1993). Competing on capabilities: the new rules of corporate strategy. In Howard, R. (ed.) *The Learning Imperative: Managing People for Continuous Innovation.* Cambridge, MA: Harvard Business School Press.

Storey, J. and Sisson, K. (1994). *Managing Human Resources and Industrial Relations*. London: Open University Press.

Terpstra, D.E. and Rozell, E.J. (1993). The relationship of staffing practices to organizational level measures of performance, *Personnel Psychology*, 46, 27–48.

Thigpen, P. (1991) Presentation at Stanford Graduate School of Business, Feb 26.

Thigpen, P. quoted in Pfeffer (1994).

Thurow, L.C (1993). *Head to Head: The Coming Economic Battle among Japan, Europe and America*. New York: Morrow.

Truss, C. and Gratton, L. (1994). Strategic human resource management: a conceptual approach, *International Journal of Human Resource Management*, 5,(3), 663–86.

Vesey, J.T. (1991). The new competitors: they think in terms of 'speed-to-market'. *Academy of Management Executive*, 5, (2), 23–33.

Wernerfelt, B. (1984). A resource base view of the firm, *Strategic Management Journal*, 5, 171–80.

Williamson, O.E. (1986). *Markets and Hierarchies: Analysis and Antitrust Implications*. New York: Free Press.

Womack, J.P., Jones, D.T., and Roos, R. (1990). *The Machine that Changed the World*. New York: Macmillan.

Wright, P.M., McMahan, G.C., and McWilliams, A. (1994). Human resources and sustained competitive advantage: a resource base perspective, *The International Journal of Human Resource Management*, 5, (2), 301–27.

2

Managing without traditional strategic planning: the evolving role of top management teams

In examining and highlighting the role of strategic planning in the modern firm, one might argue that 'Strategic Planning is dead.' Indeed, Henry Mintzberg's recent book, *The Rise and Fall of Strategic Planning* (1994), makes such a case. According to Mintzberg, strategic planning has failed because it is not the same as strategic thinking. Rather than resulting in world-class strategies and capabilities, traditional approaches to comprehensive strategic planning have often been responsible for stifling speed, creativity, and flexibility. Importantly, Mintzberg's point is not that *strategy* is dysfunctional. Rather, the process by which strategy is made is at issue.

James Brian Quinn also called into question the utility of traditional planning approaches to strategy formulation (Quinn, 1980). Quinn noted (1) the tendency for the planning activity to become bureaucratized, rigid, and costly, (2) the often questionable – if not actively destructive – outcomes of the planning activity, and (3) that major strategic decisions were often made outside the formal planning process. Thus, he proposed a process of *logical incrementalism* through which strategy emerges through interactive learning and innovation.

The work of Mintzberg and Quinn is important in that it demonstrates that there are ways to create strategy other than by formal planning. Strategies can emerge as well as being planned (Mintzberg and Waters, 1985). In fact, argues Mintzberg, strategy can be 'deliberately emergent' (Mintzberg, 1987). That is, it is possible to develop strategies by combining deliberation and control with flexibility and organizational learning.

Much of the recent literature on organizational flexibility, learning and competitiveness has focused on teams and team structures (Appelgate, *et al.* 1988; Galbraith, 1977; Manz and Sims, 1987; Snow, *et al.*, 1992). Within this research stream, top management teams (TMTs) have become the subject of a great deal of study (Bantel and Jackson, 1989; Dainty and Kakabadse, 1992; Eisenhardt and Schoonhoven, 1990;

Finkelstein and Hambrick, 1990; Kakabadse, 1993; Keck, 1991; Michel and Hambrick, 1992; Murray, 1989; Myers, *et al.*, 1992; O'Reilly and Flatt, 1989; Wiersema and Bantel, 1992). Hambrick contends that top management teams are the 'key to strategic success' (Hambrick, 1987). We agree: whether deliberately planned or purely emergent, the making of strategy is a primary responsibility of top management. Thus, TMTs are strategic human resources and they play a critical role in crafting HRM strategies for their firms – both of which are important to the development of world-class capabilities.

Objectives

In this chapter we highlight the critical role of TMTs within the conversation on innovations in strategic human resource management. Our specific objectives are to demonstrate the following:

(1) TMTs are strategic human resources in their own right, capable of providing the firm with a sustainable competitive advantage. They should be recognized and managed as strategic human resources.
(2) TMTs can manage the human resources of the firm to allow the bottom-up emergence of strategy. Establishing such a process can lead to the development of world-class strategies and capabilities.

This chapter is divided into three main sections. In the first section, we expand on the discussion of resource base theory introduced in Chapter 1 to provide additional definition of concepts used in this and subsequent chapters. In the second section, we build the case that TMTs are strategic human resources capable of endowing the firm with sustainable competitive advantage. In the third section, we demonstrate how TMTs can manage the firm's human resources to develop world-class strategies and capabilities through a deliberately emergent process based on valuing human resources.

Throughout this chapter we provide examples from AES Corporation, a young, rapidly growing, independent power company (Case study, AES: The Company). We believe that AES is very advanced in its understanding of the role its top management team plays, both as a strategic human resource and in strategically managing the broader human resources within the company to build an organization in which world-class capabilities are developed through a deliberately emergent approach to strategy making.

Case study   AES: The Company

The AES Corporation, formerly Applied Energy Services, develops, owns, and operates electric power plants and sells electricity to utility companies. All of its current plants are cogeneration facilities – a power generation technology in which two or more useful forms of energy, such as electricity and steam, are created from a single primary fuel source, such as coal or natural gas.

AES was co-founded as a privately held corporation in 1981 by Roger W. Sant (Chairman) and Dennis W. Bakke (Chief Executive Officer). Previously, Sant was Assistant Administrator of the Federal Energy Administration (FEA) for Energy Conservation and the Environment from 1974 to 1976, and then Director of the Energy Productivity Center, an energy research organization affiliated with the Mellon Institute at Carnegie-Mellon University, from 1977 to 1981. Dennis Bakke served with Roger Sant as Deputy Assistant Administrator of the FEA and as Deputy Director of the Energy Productivity Center.

AES was formed in response to certain legislative and business environment changes in the regulated utility industry. In response to the energy crisis of the 1970s, Congress passed the Public Utilities Regulatory Policies Act (PURPA). As a result, a significant market for electric power produced by independent power generators developed in the United States. AES was one of the original entrants to this market and today is one of the largest independent power producers.

AES's stated mission is to help meet the need for electricity by offering a supply of clean, safe, and reliable power. The company has pursued this objective by creating a portfolio of independent power plants, all of which use cogeneration technologies. Since 1983, AES has developed, constructed, and is now operating a total of seven plants, and is actively pursuing additional projects in the United States, Europe, and elsewhere overseas.

Pursuing a strategy of 'operating excellence,' AES has established high standards of operation and has been a leader in environmental matters associated with independent power production. All of the solid-fuel projects it owns and operates employ the very best 'clean coal' technologies available, such as scrubbers or circulating fluidized-bed boilers. AES facilities' emissions are consistently well below those allowable under environmental permits, thereby exceeding the standards mandated for such plants under the Clean Air Act. AES has also offset carbon dioxide (CO_2) emissions by funding projects such as the planting of trees in Guatemala and the preservation of forest land in Paraguay. AES has established a better than average safety record for the electricity generating industry. Further, AES plants averaged 92% 'availability' during 1990, 88% during 1991, and 93% during 1992, an above-average measure of plant reliability.

By December, 1990, AES had grown to a company generating US$190 million in revenues on approximately US$1.12 billion in total assets. The company employed approximately 430 people in its plants and at its home office in Arlington, Virginia. In July of 1991, the company went public by selling approximately 10% of the company in an initial public offering. In the same year the company generated US$333 million in revenues on US$1.44 billion in assets. By the end of 1992 the company's market value reached US$1.4 billion. In 1993, AES was ranked 56 on *Fortune's* list of America's 100 fastest-growing companies, the company's third year on this distinguished list. Clearly, the market evaluates AES as a substantial success.

(*Source*: Smith and Sims, 1993)

Company resources and competitive advantage

In this section we overview several concepts central to strategic management and the resource base theory of the firm. This review provides the framework and context for the subsequent discussion of top management teams and how they can create competitive advantage through strategic human resource management.

According to Michael Porter, two central questions underlie a company's choice of competitive strategy: (1) the attractiveness of the industry for long-term profitability and (2) the determinants of the firm's relative competitive position within the industry (Porter, 1980). The first of these questions addresses the environment in which the firm operates. The environment is seen as the source of opportunities for the company to exploit and threats that the firm must avoid. The second question focuses attention on factors internal to the firm. These may be categorized as strengths if they provide the company with the ability to seize opportunities or avoid threats, or as weaknesses if they prevent the company from taking advantage of opportunities or make it vulnerable to external threats (Wheelen and Hunger, 1992). Thus, a popular framework for strategic management suggests that firms compete most effectively by using their internal strengths to exploit external opportunities while simultaneously neutralizing external threats and avoiding internal weaknesses (Barney, 1991).

While much of the strategy literature has focused on the impact of a firm's environment on its ability to attain high levels of performance (Caves and Porter, 1977; Porter, 1980), the resource base theory of the firm focuses on the idiosyncratic characteristics of competing firms and how these characteristics contribute to competitive advantage. Two underlying assumptions are key to the resource base view: (1) firms in an industry are different with respect to the resources they control (such as access to raw materials, product patents, unique production or distribution capabilities, low-cost labor force, and so on) and (2) these resources are not perfectly mobile across firms, with the result that differences between firms can be long lasting. Thus, the focus of attention is on the differences between firms, particularly in terms of the resources at their disposal.

Not all resources controlled by a firm – physical, human, or organizational – may prove strategically relevant. Some resources or attributes may prevent the firm from conceiving of and implementing valuable strategies; for example, a chief executive who is past his prime or set in his ways and who refuses to change although change has become necessary (Hambrick and Fukutomi, 1991). Others may lead a firm to conceive of and implement strategies that reduce its effectiveness and efficiency, as was the case with Midway Airline's ill-fated attempt to expand its successful Chicago-based operations by opening a hub in Philadelphia (Fotos, 1991). Still others may have no impact on a firm's strategy making processes. Such was the criticism leveled at Xerox due to its inability to convert technology generated in the Palo Alto Research Center into marketable products during the 1970s and 1980s (Smith, 1988).

Further, the importance of specific resources may change over time. For example, an investment in a particular technology may provide a competitive advantage until that technology is made obsolete by a newer technology (Pascarella, 1983). This explains why the large capital expenditures by US steel companies failed to keep them competitive with the Japanese firms adopting new technologies.

Importantly, top management plays a central role in relation to firm resources. In general, senior managers are responsible for acquiring and allocating the resources needed by the firm to conduct its business (Bower, 1986). But the role top management plays varies by type of resource. Top managers are responsible for *assembling and allocating* physical capital resources. Top managers both *are* and must *manage* the firm's human capital resources. And finally, top managers give much of their time to *building* the firm's organizational capital resources. In all instances, the objective is effectively using resources to build competitive advantage.

Competitive advantage

According to Porter, 'Competitive advantage grows fundamentally out of the value a firm is able to create for its buyers that exceeds the firm's cost of creating it' (Porter, 1985:3). In other words, a company is profitable if the value it creates is greater than the cost of performing the business functions necessary to create that value. To gain a competitive advantage, a company must either perform value-creation functions at a lower cost than its rivals or perform them in a way that leads to differentiation and a premium price. To do either, it must have a strength or distinctive competence relative to its competitors in one or more of its value-creation functions. Such strengths are the bases for attaining the world-class capabilities identified in Chapter 1. If it has significant weaknesses in any of these functions, it will be at a competitive disadvantage.

Porter demonstrates how value creation is a basis for competitive advantage through the concept of the value chain (Figure 2.1). The value chain consists of primary activities – having to do with the physical creation of a product, its marketing and delivery to buyers and its support and after-sales service – and support activities that provide the inputs that allow the primary activities to take place – including materials management, research and development, human resource management, information systems, and company infrastructure. If a company can gain a distinctive competence in a primary or a support value-creation function, its profit margin will increase. On the other hand, when those functions are weak, the company's value creation will suffer from higher costs or result in an output that is valued less by customers. In either case, its profit margin will be squeezed (see Figure 2.1).

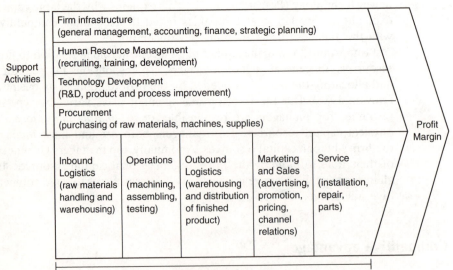

Figure 2.1 Generic Value Chain.
Source: Porter, 1985.

Resource base theory builds upon the concept of the value chain by focusing attention on the various resources that can provide a firm with distinctive competence or relative strength versus its competition in one or more of the value creating functions. From our perspective, a firm enjoys a *competitive advantage* when either of two conditions exist: (1) when it is implementing a unique value creating strategy, one not being implemented by any of its current or potential competitors (Barney, 1991), or (2) when the firm is more effective at implementing value creating strategies than competitors pursuing the same or similar strategies (Porter, 1985). Thus, competitive advantage may result from the utilization of resources that are unique to the firm, or from the more effective use of resources common among competitors (Wilkins, 1989).

Not all resources have the potential for generating competitive advantage – not to mention sustainable competitive advantage. However, this does not mean that common or readily duplicated resources can be ignored. Rather, some resources must be possessed or strategies implemented just to 'play the game.' We think of such resources in terms of providing *competitive parity*. As an example, when Citibank introduced the automated teller machine in the early 1970s, the new technology provided that bank with a significant competitive advantage. Customers moved their accounts to Citibank for the convenience of banking 24-hours a day. However, this competitive advantage enjoyed by Citibank did not prove sustainable. Other banks and financial institutions quicky duplicated the 24-hour banking technology and today 24-hour banking is common. As a result, banks must now provide automated tellers as a basic service if they hope to compete at all.

Some resources possessed by a firm may actually result in *competitive disadvantage*. In these instances, certain resources create weaknesses rather than strengths and rather than serving as a foundation for building competitive advantage, they create barriers to the creation of competitive advantage. For example, capital investment in integrated manufacturing provided Caterpillar Tractor with a competitive advantage throughout the growth years of the 1960s and 1970s. But when Komatsu entered the market with more flexible and efficient manufacturing technology, Caterpillar's high investment in fixed assets created a barrier to the flexibility required during the maturing stages of the industry. In a similar fashion, AES wonders about its portfolio of long-term contracts to provide utilities with electricity at a fixed cost. Today, these are significant strategic resources. But AES wonders about conditions that might change these contracts into barriers to performance, such as major changes in technology or an unanticipated rise in the price of coal.

Profitability: the measure of competitive advantage

Strategy has been defined as the 'continuing search for rent', where rent is defined as a return in excess of a resource owner's opportunity costs (Bowman, 1974). In simpler terms, companies seek to carry out their activities in such a way that their revenues are greater than their costs; that is, they are profitable (Kay, 1990, 1993).

Economic theory suggests that under conditions of pure competition, profitability should be equal for all firms in an industry. However, little examination is required to observe that some firms in an industry enjoy profitability higher than the industry average, and that these abnormal returns persist even when supply and demand within the industry are in equilibrium. Resource base theory argues that two conditions explain this phenomenon. First, not all firms are equally efficient in their use of resources – some have developed a competitive advantage – which explains why certain firms enjoy higher profits than others. Second, the most efficient firms cannot easily increase their output to the point of running less efficient firms out of business because of the presence of isolating mechanisms that restrict the mobility of resources. This explains the continued existence of the less efficient firms (Peteraf, 1993). Of interest, then, are the various ways firms can achieve above-average rates of return, and how firm resources contribute to this achievement.

Ricardian profits are those that result from the exploitation of superior resources that are in short supply. In essence, such profits derive from the effective use of scarce resources – resources that competitors do not have or cannot use as efficiently (Castanias and Helfat, 1991). American Airline's ability to generate profits from Sabre, its computerized reservation system, is an example of a Ricardian profit from a physical capital resource. The unique and rare abilities of CEOs Roy Vagelos (Merck) and Bill Gates (Microsoft) have contributed to the above-average success of their respective companies and demonstrate Ricardian profits from human capital resources. The profitability AES has achieved from its ability to sense and quickly respond to changes in the energy industry (Case study, AES: Informed Opportunism) represents Ricardian profits from organizational capital resources. One question for top managers, then, is how to identify scarce resources and parlay them into Ricardian profits.

Entrepreneurial profits are the result of risk-taking and entrepreneurial insight in an uncertain or complex environment. Above-average profitability often derives to the firm that is able to move most quickly to take advantage of new environmental opportunities. Much of AES's current success is the result of the fact that it recognized early the opportunities for independent power production created by the Public Utilities Regulatory Policies Act. However, these entrepreneurial or *Schumpeterian* profits 'are inherently self-destructive due to diffusion of knowledge' (Mahoney and Pandian, 1992). Thus, the utility

Case study   **AES: Informed Opportunism**

AES has invested a great deal in its ability to sense changes in its industry and respond to them rapidly. As a result, its strategic planning group is less of a planning unit than a data-intensive thinktank. Roger Naill, Vice President and head of the strategic planning unit, explains:

> We think about, should we be in the coal business or the gas business? Should we be building coal plants or gas plants? What is the Clean Air Act going to do to our business? What kind of technology should we be involved in? You know, things like that, that are really sort of fun to think through, and they really change. Bob Waterman [a member of AES's board of directors] called us 'informed opportunists.' The opportunist part is that we take advantage of opportunities. Bob said, 'This market is really changing and these guys,' meaning AES, 'are good at taking advantage of the opportunities even before they erupt.' We're real good at anticipating these markets, jumping in, and figuring out how to do deals. And he said to do that, you need to be informed. You've got to know how the market's changing. And he saw our [strategic planning] group as playing a large role in the informed part. We really keep Roger Sant and the management here current on what's going on in our market environment. So that we can make good business decisions and take advantage of opportunities as they arise. So we really are sort of a policy R&D unit for the company. And I think it's been real productive for the company.

At AES, the planning function is not relegated to the strategic planning group. Rather, the group is charged with providing the information necessary for planning. Naill elaborates:

> I think my role in the strategic planning process is to provide information. It's not to provide a plan. I'm not supposed to write a plan every year and figure out everything, the answer to all the issues and solutions. My role is to provide information to the planners, which turn out to be as broad based a group as we can get in the company. It's all managers, certainly ... We're actually trying to involve everybody. And we provide them information, and then everybody's supposed to brainstorm off of that information.

AES's ability to sense change in its environment and to capitalize on that change, embodied in its planning unit and its open planning process, is a rare and valuable organizational resource. Although the specific actions AES takes in response to change may result in entrepreneurial profits, its fine-grained understanding of its environment contributes to the generation of Ricardian profits.

companies have learned to create their own independent subsidiaries to produce power and now the utilities are AES's largest competitors as well as its largest customers. As entrepreneurial profits derive from speed and timing, a question for top management is: What firm resources facilitate entrepreneurial action?

A third type of profitability takes the form of *quasi profits*, which is the difference between the value of an asset in its first best use and its next best use (Castanias and Helfat, 1991). Whereas Ricardian profits suggest that profit might be derived from a valuable resource regardless of who possesses it, the notion underlying quasi profits is that certain resources gain value as they become specialized to a particular use or firm. For example, the knowledge that a manager develops regarding how to get things done within a particular company represents a firm-specific resource. That knowledge may help the firm become more efficient and more profitable. But the resource is not transferable in that the knowledge is context specific. At AES, the engineering and managerial knowedge that project development team members bring to the company are valuable but generic skills that could be used in many contexts. But the specialized knowledge the team members develop, both about the independent energy business and about AES in particular, increases their value within the company. Further, given the context-specific capability these teams have developed to form, expand, contract, and disband as needed, these 'virtual teams' have become a socially complex, difficult to imitate, human resource (Case study, AES's Project Development Teams). Relative to quasi profits, then, the question for top management is how to derive maximum value by using firm resources in their first best use.

Case study **AES's Project Development Teams**

Once a local or regional utility has agreed to purchase electricity from AES and a power contract has been signed, a *project development team* comes into existence for the length of time necessary to bring the new plant on-line. A project development team has multiple responsibilities including finding a suitable site for the plant, handling public relations with the local residents, obtaining necessary permits or 'permitting,' financing plant construction, and getting the plant operational.

A project development team has a very fluid composition over its life. The team tasked with the Warrior Run project in western Maryland currently has nine members. Only one of these employees was on the team when it first began. Individuals have joined and left the team, and also changed roles within the team, depending on the project demands at any given time. Three team members were added in the past year alone to address specific project needs. One team member compared the project development team to an American football team. During the game, the team puts in different players depending on field position. Similarly, a project development team utilizes different team members based on the stage of the project.

Of course, the development of a new project is an extremely complex and lengthy process, and not all explorations lead to a final launching. Whatever the final outcome, all team members know that their participation is 'temporary' and that they will eventually move on to other teams.

AES's project development teams are an example of a socially complex resource that is the source of quasi profits. The success of the team depends as much on the members' ability to work together in a fluid way as it does on the expertise of the individual team members. This ability is enhanced by AES's corporate culture, which gives priority to the continued development of its high calibre personnel. Thus, even if other companies were to attempt to imitate this strategic resource, there is a significant learning curve to be overcome and no guarantee that the same approach would work in another context.

(*Source*: Kristof, *et al.*, 1993)

A fourth source of profitability takes the form of *monopoly profits*. Monopoly profits result from a deliberate restriction of output rather than an inherent scarcity of a resource (Peteraf, 1993). While some sources of monopoly profits may be illegal – such as collusive arrangements that prevent the entry of new competitors to an industry – others may be the direct result of government sanction, such as the protection provided by import tariffs or the licenses required of certain professions. Still others may result from the presence of mobility barriers such as economies of scale (Caves and Porter, 1977). In all cases, monopoly profits derive from restricting output to levels at or below market demand under conditions that prevent competitors from stepping in to meet the excess demand. Again, top management must be concerned with when and how monopoly profits can be sought.

The power of resource base theory rests in its ability to explain long-lived differences in firm profitability that cannot be attributed to differences in industry conditions (Peteraf, 1993). Firms can use resources to build world-class capabilities in the form of distinctive competencies and parlay these into competitive advantages that result in above-average profitability. The task of identifying these opportunities and organizing to capitalize on them *is the strategic management task of the top management team*. With this framework in mind, we now turn our attention to the TMT and its role as a strategic human resource.

Top management teams as strategic human resources

A major premise of this book is that human resources are strategic and that the effective management of human resources can provide a firm with competitive advantage. More and more, the task of strategic human resource management is being considered a part of the TMT's general responsibility of developing strategies to compete in today's complex and ever-changing environment. But it is important that the TMT itself be considered a strategic human resource. In this section we review the task, structure, and processes of the TMT and examine their implications for creating competitive advantage.

Much of the recent research on top management teams has been based on Hambrick and Mason's 'upper echelons' theory (Hambrick and Mason, 1984). This perspective, inspired largely by the behavioral decision models of the Carnegie School (Cyert and March, 1963; March and Simon, 1958), argues that top management teams have a significant impact on organizational outcomes through their influence on strategic decisions. The theory holds that senior managers make decisions based on their perceptions of the situation – perceptions that are influenced by their cognitive frameworks and personal values. Importantly, the theory recognizes that a manager's cognitive framework and personal values are shaped by previous training and experience. Thus, it is argued, one can make inferences about the strategic choices a team may make by studying observable demographic characteristics of the team, such as age, education, functional background, industry experience, and the like.

The upper echelons perspective is important because it explicitly recognizes that the management of organizations is a shared activity and provides a methodology for studying the influence of top management teams. Since the theory's articulation, researchers have linked top management team characteristics to strategy, organizational innovation, and performance (Bantel and Jackson, 1989; Finkelstein and Hambrick, 1989; Hambrick and D'Aveni, 1992; Keck, 1991; Michel and Hambrick, 1992; Murray, 1989; Smith, K.A. *et al.*, 1993; Smith, K.G. *et al.*, 1994). These studies have demonstrated the validity of the top management team as an important unit of analysis, and additional work is now being done to elaborate how and why these effects occur.

The underlying assumption throughout this literature has been that high-quality top management teams will, on average, outperform low-quality top management teams. Thus, the questions confronting practitioners and academics interested in developing high-quality top management include: What should top management teams look like? What skills and experiences should be represented within the team? What behaviors and processes make the team most effective? How can a superior management team be developed? In short, 'What types of managers, in what combinations, have the best chances of identifying, picking, and implementing successful strategies' (Hambrick, 1987:88; Kakabadse, *et al.*, 1993)?

The task of the TMT

Most textbooks on strategic management recognize the special role played by top management in establishing direction for an organization. The following is typical:

> Strategic decision makers are the people in a corporation who are directly involved in the strategic management process. They are the strategic managers who (with some assistance from staff) scan the internal and external environments, formulate and implement objectives, strategies, and policies, and evaluate and control results. The people with direct responsibility for this process are ... top management. The chief executive officer (CEO), the chief operations officer (COO) or president, the executive vice-president, and the vice-presidents in charge of operating divisions and functional areas typically form the top management group.
>
> (Dess and Miller, 1993:29)

Although the actual composition of the team may differ from company to company, most firms have a group of senior managers who have as their responsibility the making of strategy and the oversight of its implementation.

The formulation of strategy entails defining vision and direction for the firm. This includes developing long-range plans to effectively manage environmental opportunities and threats given the resources (strengths and weaknesses) of the firm. In general, formulation emphasizes analysis and planning; it includes defining the company's mission, specifying achievable objectives, and developing strategies or means of accomplishing the objectives. Decisions regarding mission and objectives include choosing what type of profits are most desirable. For example, *prospectors* – firms that constantly seek new products and new markets – place high priority on the generation of entrepreneurial profits. In contrast, *defenders* – firms that seek to defend strong market positions from would-be competitors – may give priority to monopoly profits (Miles and Snow, 1978).

To be successful in strategy formulation, the TMT must have the ability to fit the firm's resources to the environment. The composition of the team is important in this regard. The background, experience, and values of individual team members – as well as the mix of these characteristics represented by the team – will influence choices of ends and means. For example, research has found that TMTs with younger and more educated members tend to be more innovative in terms of introducing new products and services (Bantel and Jackson, 1989; O'Reilly and Flatt, 1989).

In contrast with formulation, strategy implementation emphasizes action over analysis. Implementation is the process by which strategies are put into action. It requires the creation and execution of action-plans aimed at the accomplishment of long-term objectives. While many implementation tasks are done by lower-level managers, the TMT remains responsible for overseeing and facilitating the process. This entails creating a culture and organizational infrastructure that supports implementation and coordination of activities at the highest level. The ability of the TMT to do this well is likely to result in the generation of quasi profits.

To be successful in strategy implementation, the TMT must have the ability to manage organizational processes. It must be able to translate the company's mission, objectives, and strategies into discrete tasks to be assigned to lower-level managers, and be able to coordinate these activities in an ongoing fashion, including adapting strategies during implementation as changes occur in the environment. Because of the interdependent nature of implementation tasks, the TMT will be central to the coordination process.

Thus, the task of the TMT is extremely complex and has multiple elements (Hambrick, 1993). Given the responsibility to formulate adaptive responses to the environment, the team must continually monitor and interpret external events and trends, and deal with external constituencies. As strategies are formulated, the team must communicate them and monitor their implementation.

Operating at the strategic apex, the TMT confronts an enormity of often ambiguous information. Stimuli are many, often vague, and competing (Hambrick and Mason, 1984; Katz and Kahn, 1978; March and Simon, 1958; Mintzberg, 1979). However, it is this condition that makes the study of TMTs so important. Stimuli are so open to perceptual bias, interpretation, and political manipulation that the specific form and functioning of the TMT will greatly shape what happens to the stimuli, and in turn, to the organization (Hambrick, 1993). Therefore, since TMTs are strategic human resources *in and of themselves*, a critical strategic objective becomes the creation of a superior TMT.

In a general sense, TMT effectiveness comes from a 'fit' between the team and its function. In other words, the team should fit with industry conditions, with the firm's chosen strategy, and with organizational resources (Gupta, 1986; Hambrick and Mason, 1984). Because firms, their contexts and resources are idiosyncratic, there is no such thing as a universally ideal management team (Hambrick, 1987:94). This does not mean that superior TMTs are unattainable. Rather, in the same way that the industry context helps define what firm resources are strategic and have potential for generating competitive advantage, the industry and firm contexts together help define the characteristics of a superior TMT.

Conceptually, teams can be thought of in terms of their composition (who is on the team and what are their characteristics) as well as their processes and behaviors (what the team does). The study of group dynamics encompasses both. We look first at team composition although composition and process are understood to be interdependent: composition influences process and vice versa.

TMT composition and competitive advantage

Research into the nature of effective management has focused on the traits, skills, functions, roles, and behaviors associated with leaders and top managers. Within the context of the TMT, the focus is on variations in group behavior and performance that are consequences of the particular combination of individuals in the group rather than the effects produced by the specific characteristics of individual group members. Thus, the study of superior TMTs must focus on the managerial qualities and skills available to the team as a function of the composition of the team.

Unfortunately, managerial qualities and skills in general, 'are intangible, have no clear blueprint, and are difficult to codify' (Castanias and Helfat, 1991:161). For the sake of discussion, we have divided managerial characteristics into two categories: personality-based qualities – such as values, aptitudes, cognitive style, and demeanor – and experience-based skills. It is not our purpose here to provide an exhaustive review of research findings relating TMT characteristics to strategy and performance. Rather, we focus on some pertinent examples that demonstrate how the TMT is a strategic human resource.

One important managerial quality is a manager's personal values. Such values often derive from upbringing, previous training, and experience. The combination of values represented within the TMT are critical in that they assign 'value' to certain behaviors and organizational outcomes, thereby directly influencing choices of objectives and strategies. According to Hambrick, values affect an executive's contributions to the TMT in three ways.

> First, values cause executives to prefer certain behaviors and outcomes over others. Second, they affect the way in which the person searches and filters data used in decision making. Third, values affect the person's receptivity to any incentives and norms the general manager may try to establish.
>
> (Hambrick, 1987:94)

Where the values of top managers are similar, there is likely to be agreement on objectives and strategies. Where they are different, the choice of objectives and strategies is likely to be fraught with conflict. At AES, the values of the TMT have become the foundation for the company's culture and serve as the filter for all strategic decisions (Case study, AES's Core Values).

Case study   AES's Core Values

An important underlying framework for AES is its four core or 'shared' values. These are:

- to act with integrity
- to be fair
- to have fun
- to be socially responsible.

These values emerged over time, mainly from the founders and officers, and have now been articulated to the degree that they are written and were published as a part of the prospectus for the initial stock offering of the company. Although AES takes pride in its strategic flexibility, one element that stays constant is the four values. Dennis Bakke (CEO) says, 'The only thing that we hold tightly as to what has to be done are the four shared values.' As a result, the values permeate AES and serve to unify the company as it pursues its objectives.

Bakke describes *integrity* as 'it fits together as a whole . . . wholeness, completeness.' In practice, this means that the things that AES people say and do in all parts of the company should fit together with truth and consistency. 'The main thing we do is ask, "What did we commit?"' At AES, the senior representative at any meeting can commit the company, knowing that the team will back him or her up.

Fairness is the desire of AES to treat fairly its people, its customers, its suppliers, its stockholders, governments, and the communities in which AES operates. Defining what is fair is often difficult, but the main point is that the company believes it is helpful to question routinely the relative fairness of alternative courses of action. This may mean that AES does not necessarily 'get the most out of' each negotiation or transaction to the detriment of others. Bakke poses the question; 'Would I feel as good on the other side of the table as I feel on this side of the table on the outcome of this meeting or this decision with my employee or supervisor or customer?'

Bakke also says, 'If it isn't fun, we don't want it. We either want to quit or change something that we're doing.' Sant agrees: 'It just isn't worth doing unless you're having a great time.' Thus, *fun* is the third value. AES desires that the people it employs and those with whom the company interacts should have fun in their work. Bakke elaborates: 'By fun we don't mean party fun. We're talking about creating an environment where people can use their gifts and skills productively, to help meet a need in society and thereby enjoy the time spent at AES.'

The fourth value is *social responsibility*. 'We see ourselves as a citizen of the world,' says Bakke. This value presumes that AES has a responsibility to be involved in projects that provide social benefits such as lower costs to customers, a high degree of safety and reliability, increased employment, and a cleaner environment. 'We try to do things that you'd like your neighbor to do.'

These values have had significant impact on AES's choice of objectives and strategies. For example, Bakke says, 'We have specifically said that maximized profits is not our objective.' In fact, in the company's IPO prospectus, the company stated 'earning a fair profit is an important result of providing a quality product to its customers. However, when a perceived conflict has arisen between these values and profits, the company has tried to adhere to its values – even though doing so might result in diminished profits or foregone opportunities. The company seeks to adhere to these values, not as a means to achieve economic success, but because adherence is a worthwhile goal in and of itself'(*Source*: AES Prospectus 22–3).

(Smith and Sims, 1993)

Aptitudes, like values, are deeply ingrained personality traits that are not likely to change in the short term. They include such characteristics as creativity, intellect, tolerance for ambiguity, attitude toward risk, and cognitive style. The combination of aptitudes within the TMT will also influence the strategic management process. Such characteristics as tolerance for ambiguity and attitude toward risk will influence choices of strategic posture – offensive or defensive – and hence the priority placed on different types of profits. Likewise, people differ in how they process information and make decisions. One distinction in cognitive style is between orderly, analytic thinkers and non-linear, intuitive thinkers. As Hambrick points out, 'The mix of the two modes within a team will greatly affect the team's strategic decisions – both their formulation and implementation' (Hambrick, 1987:95). The appropriate mix of the two styles depends on the context in which the team must operate. For example, a greater proportion of intuitive thinkers may result in greater speed in decision making, an important consideration in rapidly changing environments.

A final managerial quality worth mentioning is the intangible aura, style, or demeanor of the TMT. According to Hambrick,

> Such qualities as enthusiasm, warmth, poise, or stateliness (formality) can be of central importance in constituting a management team. These characteristics would be especially relevant when constituencies are skeptical of the firm's prospects and motives.
>
> (Hambrick, 1987:95)

Empirical evidence bears this out. For example, in a study of financially struggling firms, D'Aveni (1990) concluded that the mere composition of a top group – particularly its 'prestige' – affected the speed and likelihood with which creditors would throw an insolvent company into bankruptcy. Similarly, venture capitalists often consider their 'gut reaction' to the managerial team of a new venture in addition to the quality of the business proposal itself (Sapienza, 1992). Thus, the question is: What demeanor helps the team do its job most effectively?

According to Hambrick, managerial skills 'are more concrete and usually more observable than aptitudes' (Hambrick, 1987:95). Castanias and Helfat categorize managerial skills in terms of their applicability to different situations. They identify generic skills, industry-specific skills, and firm-specific skills (Castanias and Helfat, 1991). Generic skills are those that are transferable across industries, businesses, and firms and include communication, negotiation, economic analysis, planning, delegating, and the like. Such skills are valuable, but not rare. By definition, generic skills do not produce quasi-rents because they are easily transferable between uses. However, to the extent that a team has superior ability in one or more generic skills, such as brilliant negotiating ability, this skill may be parlayed into Ricardian profits. Overall, however, generic skills do not normally provide the basis for a sustained competitive advantage.

By contrast, industry-specific skills include skills and knowledge that are specific to a particular industry. As an example, Hambrick notes, 'If ... strict cost control is a dominant environmental requirement, executives whose expertise and positions are efficiency oriented, for example, operations and accounting, will have disproportionate influence within the TMT' (Hambrick, 1981). Other industry-specific skills might include familiarity with certain industry, technical, or functional-area issues, legal or regulatory factors, marketplace trends, and the like. AES has developed a high level of skill in all facets of the independent power industry, from the energy modelling and strategic research conducted by its planning group to the 'operating excellence' developed at the plants. By definition, industry-specific skills are more rare than generic skills. It is easy to see how superior industry-specific skills may lead to the generation of Ricardian profits. However, detailed knowledge of an industry and skill in using that knowledge may also contribute to the creation of entrepreneurial and monopoly profits, the former through recognition and ability to capitalize on new opportunities, the latter through the ability to see, take advantage of, and in some cases create new barriers to competition within the industry.

Finally, firm-specific skills relate to adding value within a particular firm. For example, Castanias and Helfat cite Roy Vagelos' experience in drug development while Merck's senior vice president for research as adding value to Merck's overall strategy once Vagelos became CEO (Castanias and Helfat, 1991). Vagelos understood Merck's specific strengths and understood how to capitalize on them within the context of the pharmaceutical industry. Thus, the presence of firm-specific skills within the TMT can be used to generate Ricardian profits – by honing skills to a level that they become superior and rare; entrepreneurial profits – by understanding the firm's strengths and how to use them to capitalize on new opportunities; and quasi profits – by understanding the firm's resources and how to use them most effectively.

While individual members of the TMT bring sets of skills to the firm, it is the overall combination of these skills within the TMT that is most important. But just bringing a number of skilled players together does not automatically result in a high-quality 'team.' It is the combination of skills and the ability to use them together in a complementary way that is the essence of teamwork. Without complementarity, there is no synergy; without synergy, the team is not a team at all – it is just a collection of individuals. In sports, this is why 'All Star' teams composed of highly skilled players who are not used to playing together are less elegant in execution than championship teams who have reached the pinnacle of their sport by taking rare and valuable skills and combining them through practice and shared experience.

The composition of the TMT may be considered from a variety of angles. On the one hand, the team may be assessed in terms of central tendencies (average scores) on such observable characteristics as age, level of education and area of study, functional background, experience, and the like. Hambrick and Mason argue that such measures provide a basis for making inferences about difficult to assess traits like values and attitudes. For example, to the extent that age is related to a negative attitude toward risk, TMTs composed of older executives are likely to be less inclined to pursue risky strategies than those composed of younger executives (Hambrick and Mason, 1984). TMTs can also be assessed in terms of dispersion on the same characteristics. For instance, it might be inferred that if the ages of executives on the TMT are widely distributed, the team may experience difficulty working together because of different values espoused by members of different generational cohorts (Pfeffer, 1983). The question becomes how to identify and develop a superior mix of individual characteristics.

The reason for studying TMTs rather than CEOs is that the task of strategic management in most organizations is too big for any one person to carry out alone. The assumption is that the team brings skills in addition to those of the CEO. Clearly, the team should be formed to bring together all of the necessary generic, industry- and firm-specific skills. But there are tradeoffs. The group dynamics literature suggests that specialization of function comes with size, implying that a larger TMT will allow each individual member to refine his or her skills, making them – the skills and the individual – more valuable to the firm (Blau, 1970). But the same literature also finds that as the size of a group grows there is less opportunity for multiway interaction, suggesting that it becomes harder to elicit and coordinate the inputs from team members (Shaw, 1981). Similarly, a larger team is likely to have greater breadth of background and experience, increasing the likelihood that any necessary skill or knowledge is present within the team. But greater diversity of background and experience also suggests a greater breadth of values and aspirations, not all of which will be complementary, that may make it more difficult for the team to work together. Clearly, questions regarding the optimal size and composition of the team are difficult and context-sensitive.

Cohen and Levinthal's concept of absorptive capacity sheds some light on these issues. Absorptive capacity is defined as the ability to recognize, assimilate, and utilize valuable outside knowledge, an ability that in resource base terminology clearly is valuable. It is a function of prior related knowledge. That is, some previous related knowledge must exist before the importance of new knowledge can be assimilated or used. Further, absorptive capacity depends on the individuals who stand at the interface of either the firm and the external environment or at the interface between subunits within the firm. While these interfaces are not the exlusive domain of the TMT, this boundary-spanning role is an important part of its function (Cohen and Levinthal, 1990). Cohen and Levinthal's model implies a tradeoff between the efficiency of communication among members of the TMT and the ability of the TMT to assimilate and exploit information originating from the environment. Specifically, heterogeneity or diversity of background among members of the team improves communication between the organization and its environment by expanding the breadth of information the team can recognize and assimilate. On the other hand, similarity of background and experience, which increases with the time the team is together, improves internal communication between members. This tradeoff may explain Katz and Allen's finding in a study of project groups that the level of external communication and communication with other project groups declined with project group tenure (Katz and Allen, 1982). The implication for TMTs is that, assuming a sufficient level of knowledge overlap to ensure effective communication, interactions across individuals who each possess diverse and different knowledge will augment the team's ability to recognize, assimilate, and capitalize on new information beyond what any one individual can achieve. At AES, the skills and shared experiences of the founding team had significant influence – positive and negative – on the new venture (Case study, AES's Top Management Team).

Case study   AES's Top Management Team

AES has worked hard to develop an open and flexible management structure. Nevertheless, there is a clearly identifiable top management team. Roger Naill, Vice President, provided the following in response to the question, 'Who is the TMT here at AES?'

> Roger, Dennis, and Bob. Roger Sant, Dennis Bakke, and Bob Hemphill. It's pretty clear. They run what's called the office of the CEO and they have some sub-responsibilities within that. For example, Roger is the chairman, and does pretty much what he wants at any point in time. Dennis is clearly focused more on plant operations; sort of the inside, getting the cogeneration plants that are coming down the pipeline up and running. He's getting them so that they will operate excellently. He's mister operations excellence. Hemphill is Executive Vice President, taking care of some internal details. He's also been given the lead for AES Transpower, the international effort, which is now his main thing. But yes, it's clear who's in charge.

One of the strengths of AES's TMT is the shared experience of its members. These shared experiences have contributed to the team's ability to work together and its commitment to a common vision and set of values. Dennis Bakke describes how the relationships of the TMT members predated AES and formed the foundation for the venture:

> I think it starts with the relationship between the two of us when we were in government. We were thrown together. Actually, I helped hire Roger to be my boss in the Federal Government – which can only happen in the Federal Government. I was too young to be the head of Energy Conservation, and yet I was a high-level staff person. I helped hire Roger and he was told that I was his deputy, period – even if he didn't want me as his deputy. From then, we were thrown together, and we developed a tremendous love relationship. It's grown and grown and grown. That was back in 1974. For two years we worked hand in glove in developing strategy for Energy Conservation in the Federal Government. It was brand new. It was a whole new organization. So we had to start from scratch. We had some really exciting people and two of those people became principals here. The top four officers, including Roger and myself, are all from the Federal Energy Administration, Energy Conservation Department. The number three person here is Bob Hemphill. Bob Hemphill is Executive Vice President. He and I, of course, go back even further. He wrote the job description that got me off the Federal Register coming out of the Harvard Business School in 1970. And then we worked together for a couple of years at Health, Education, and Welfare under Elliot Richardson. We went together to OMB [the US Office of Management and the Budget]. Roger and I brought him over to the Federal Energy Administration. He went away for a while to TVA [Tennessee Valley Authority] to get some experience and then came back.

> We finally brought him into AES. So, for 20 years, Bob and I have been friends, and we've probably worked together for about 16 of those years. So that relationship was part of it. So relationships were key.

The members of AES's top management team are cohesive, talk the same language, and understand each other in a way that only results from a great deal of past history together. Further, they are highly trained and experienced in organization, business, and the energy industry. Nevertheless, Bakke confided that when it came time to seek financing for AES's first plant, they ran into quite a bit of difficulty because they had no previous experience in energy production.

> We started the company in 1981. In January we actually formed the corporation ... and we started trying to fundraise; trying to get money for it. We had a business plan. It was incredibly difficult to get people really excited about it. They thought we were consultants. We had a great reputation. We had written a book. We had lots of contacts at Shell Oil, Arco, Sun, Gulf. We had a great reputation in national policy. But not as entrepreneurs. No one took us seriously. Some thought AES was academic. Some thought it was consultants. Some thought it was government policy making. No one thought of us as electricity generators. That was totally ludicrous ... We tried to get $3 million. Five dollars a share, to get $3 million, and it took us nine months. Then we got $1 million that we sold at $2 a share.

AES's founders' knowledge of the energy industry helped them recognize and capitalize on new opportunities. And the company's success largely resulted from the abilities of its high-calibre TMT members and the strength of their long-term relationships and their ability to work together. But AES's experience also demonstrates the problems that can occur when critical skills or experiences are missing from the team and the significance – positive and negative – of a team's reputation.

Other dimensions of team composition that must be considered are the structure of the team, tenure, and succession. Structure relates to such matters as the distribution of power and the nature of relationships among team members. Central to the definition of structure is the extent to which the tasks of team members are interdependent. For example, Michel and Hambrick (1992) suggest that functional heads in a single business company are probably more interdependent than the general managers of strategic business units (SBUs) of a diversified company. Hambrick (1993) suggests that the greater the strategic interdependence of the company's businesses or functional units, the more important a company-wide perspective and the ability and commitment to work together on the part of TMT members. Thus, the nature of the task is an important consideration.

Tenure and succession refer to the length of time individuals have been members of the team and the processes by which members leave and join the team. Research has demonstrated that these are important variables. For example, the organizational tenure of the TMT has been shown to be strongly and consistently associated with strategic persistence or the absence of change (Grimm and Smith, 1991; Wiersema and Bantel, 1992). Fredrickson and Iaquinto (1989) found that increases in TMT tenure give rise to increases in the comprehensiveness of strategic processes – more thorough, analytic, belabored decision making – what they refer to as 'creeping rationality.' Finkelstein and Hambrick (1990) found that the average firm tenure of TMT members was associated with both strategy and performance that conformed to industry averages. All of these findings are consistent with the tradeoff suggested by Cohen and Levinthal (1990) that as teams spend time together, their shared experiences lead to more similar knowledge and values, which – though it may help them communicate with each other – may decrease their ability to innovate.

There is a significant body of evidence to indicate that the composition of the TMT has bearing on the fates of organizations. For example, there has been a consistent finding that young, short-tenure, highly educated TMTs undertake more technological and administrative innovations than the obverse types of groups (Bantel and Jackson, 1989; O'Reilly and Flatt, 1989). Chaganti and Sambharya (1987) showed that the mix of functional backgrounds on the TMT was related to choice of strategy. They classified three tobacco companies according to the Miles and Snow's typology and found the 'prospector' had a greater representation of team members with marketing and R&D backgrounds. Thus, the quality and mix of the skills and knowledge possessed by the members of the TMT are critical.

Unfortunately, although the skills and knowledge represented within TMTs are valuable and can provide for the generation of profits, the general composition of a TMT is relatively easy to imitate and is therefore unlikely to serve as the basis for sustained competitive advantage. While it may not be possible for a competitor to exactly replicate the industry leader's TMT (people are, after all, totally unique), once a particular set of skills is identified as important in a particular industry context, it can often be found or developed. In some cases, this may involve bringing in new team members. In others, it may entail developing new skills within the existing team members – just as AES's TMT had to learn about energy production and the fine points of project financing. Furthermore, 'greatness within a team will not in itself assure strategic success' (Hambrick, 1987:89). Even if a company could hire all of the 'best' talent, there is no guarantee they could work together to produce optimum results, a conclusion obvious from Janis'

(1982) description of the Kennedy administration's handling of the Bay of Pigs. Thus, the discussion must go beyond the composition of the TMT to TMT behaviors and processes, that is, to what the TMT does.

Ancona and Nadler (1989) have identified three processes central to the function of TMTs. These are task management, relationship management, and external boundary management. Task management is the process of organizing to perform the work of the team, which is primarily making and implementing strategy level policy and operating decisions. It involves agenda setting, information sharing, decision making, and implementation support. Importantly, there are many ways through which the components of task management can be carried out. For example, defining the vision for a company and setting the agenda for its accomplishment can be achieved by a charismatic CEO, through a rational planning process, or through an emergent, bottom-up approach. At AES, the strategy-making process (described in the next section) is fundamentally bottom-up, within the context of tightly held core values. The role of AES's TMT has been to develop and manage the process, rather than take full responsibility for setting the company's agenda.

Similarly, strategic decision making can take many forms, including:

(1) *Autocratic decision*: The leader makes a decision without asking for the opinions or suggestions of subordinates, and subordinates have no direct influence.
(2) *Consultation*: The leader asks subordinates for their opinions and suggestions and then makes the decision by himself; the decision is likely to reflect limited subordinate influence.
(3) *Joint decision*: The leader meets with a subordinate or group of subordinates to discuss the decision problem and make a decision together; the leader has no more influence than any other subordinate over the final choice.
(4) *Delegation*: The leader gives subordinates the authority and responsibility for making a decision; limits within which the final choice must fall are usually specified, and the subordinate may or may not be required to obtain the approval of the leader before implementing the decision.

(Yukl, 1981:204)

At AES, priority is given to joint decision making at the strategic level, while decisions regarding plant operations are delegated to plant managers.

Obviously there are many possible routes to effective task management, the best choice among alternatives being dependent on context. What is most important is that the TMT be able to manage its task well. Superior skill in task management processes can result in the generation of Ricardian profits through greater effectiveness than competitors pursuing similar strategies, in the generation of quasi profits through the most efficient use of firm resources, and, to the extent they are chosen as objectives, the generation of entrepreneurial and monopoly profits through the ability to identify and seize opportunities to pursue new strategies or defend current positions.

While task management focuses on the strategic task of the TMT, relationship management involves how the team manages the nature and quality of relationships between team members. The nature of these relationships can be characterized in terms of the degree of openness, cohesion, the level of trust, the quantity and quality of communication, the extent of collaborative behavior, and the like, between team members. Teams that enjoy positive interpersonal relationships and, as a result, work together in positive and supporting ways may be defined as socially or behaviorally integrated (Hambrick, 1993; O'Reilly, *et al.*, 1989; Smith, K.G. *et al.*, 1994). That such integration is important to TMTs was demonstrated by Eisenhardt and Bourgeois (1988) who found in a clinical study of eight minicomputer companies that 'politics' within a TMT – which they defined as observable but often covert actions by which executives enhance their power – consumes valuable managerial time and causes restricted information flows, which in turn lead to diminished organizational performance. Thus, the object of the relationship management process is to create an interpersonal environment that is conducive to maximizing the contribution each team member makes to task management.

Importantly, Stogdill (1959) argues that in any social group that is called together to accomplish a task, there is a tradeoff between task directed and relationship directed behaviors and a balance must be achieved. That is, investing all the team's energy into task accomplishment without giving attention to relationship management will prove counterproductive in the long run since it is the strength of the relationships between members that allow individuals to perform within the team context. Similarly, too much attention given to relationship management can result in a highly integrated group that gets no work done because too much time is given to process and not enough to content. Thus, task management and relationship management should be mutually reinforcing and superior TMTs will do both of these processes well.

The third core process of TMTs identified by Ancona and Nadler (1989) is external boundary management, which relates to how the team deals with factors outside the team and outside the organization. One part of boundary management is defining the boundaries of the organization or the domain of the organization's operations including the populations served, the range of products, and the services rendered. A key dimension of defining boundaries is how flexible they are perceived to be. For example, each time AES enters into a strategic alliance with another organization, it is redefining its boundaries. Another component of boundary management is environmental scanning, which involves looking across boundaries for new knowledge that can be assimilated and used. At AES, the strategic planning unit plays a key role in scanning the external environment through its ongoing research function, while the Operating Committee meetings provide an internal scanning function by providing a mechanism through which plants can learn from other plants' experiences in the pursuit of operating excellence. A final component of the boundary management process is stakeholder management, which involves identifying important actors outside the organization – such as financial markets, the media, key customers, competitors, and governments – and managing relationships with each. At AES, the four core values play an important role in the boundary management process, especially the values of integrity, fairness, and social responsibility.

Before leaving the discussion of TMT processes, it is important to address the issue of managerial incentives. Castanias and Helfat note that,

> 'When top managers have superior skills, whether and to what extent they actively use their skills to generate rents (profits) depends on their incentives to do so. The greater the ability of top managers to collect their earned rents, the greater the incentive to generate these rents'.
>
> (Castanias and Helfat, 1991:163, parentheses added)

However, agency theory points out that overall firm performance may not reflect the superior performance of top management if the managers are able to capture all of the profits from their superior skills in the form of salary, bonuses, stock options, or perquisites. Thus, it is incumbent upon boards of directors to ensure that incentives for top managers are structured to encourage superior management while ensuring that the resulting profits are shared between the managers and the organization as a whole.

Recapitulation

Superior TMTs carry out all of their core processes well, but their dynamics are unique, firm specific, and difficult to imitate. The skills and knowledges necessary to perform well are contingent on industry context, organizational resources, and chosen strategy. For example, one might expect social integration to be more important for prospectors seeking to implement new and innovative strategies than for defenders, with their highly specialized functional structures. Given their complexity and contingent nature, then, do TMTs represent a strategic human resource that can be a source of sustained competitive advantage?

Resource base theory states that for a resource to serve as the basis for a sustained competitive advantage, it must be valuable, rare, inimitable, and have no close substitutes. High-quality TMTs are clearly valuable. Most previous research on TMTs has been directed toward demonstrating that high-quality TMTs will outperform low-quality TMTs.

Are high-quality TMTs rare? Barney and Tyler point out that,

> While the rareness of a firm's high-quality top management team is ultimately an empirical question, it seems reasonable to expect that in some industries, high-quality top management teams are likely to be quite rare, while in other industries, high-quality top management teams are likely to be quite common.
>
> (Barney and Tyler, 1992:37)

Given the heterogeneity and imperfect mobility of human resources, the rareness of high-quality TMTs is probably best considered a matter of degree. Even in industries where there are incentives to invest in high-quality TMTs, not all competing firms will be equally successful in doing so. Thus in all cases it is likely that superior teams will contribute to the highest levels of performance.

Regarding the question of imitability, certain attributes of high-quality top management teams are probably fairly easy to imitate. For example, it would be relatively easy for any firm to assemble a particular mix of functional backgrounds in its top management team. On the other hand, many of the most important attributes of top management teams are very difficult to imitate. Barney and Tyler point out,

> Top management teams are socially complex phenomena. Their successful operation depends upon the development of implicit norms of conduct that emerge over time within a particular organization. The tacit knowledge that makes a team 'work' in one organization may be difficult to describe and difficult to transfer to a different organization ... Morover, even if top management teams could be imitated, there is no necessary reason why one firm's high-quality top management team will necessarily be a high-quality top management team in another firm. The quality of a top management team depends both upon the internal characteristics of the team (for example, the people, their relationship, norms of behavior, patterns of communication) as well as the context within which the team operates.
>
> (Barney and Tyler, 1992:39)

Thus, it appears overall that it is very unlikely that the high-quality top management team of one firm can be directly imitated by other firms.

Virtually no research has been done on the question of whether or not close substitutes for high-quality top management teams exist. Because strategically equivalent substitutes may take the form of similar or dissimilar resources, it seems likely that various dissimilar resources may substitute for certain functions or skills of a high-quality top management team. For instance, a firm may be able to substitute for a competitor's TMT's strong negotiating skill by hiring an accomplished law firm. Or one firm's visionary CEO might be substituted for by another's highly formalized planning process. Further, while a competitor may not be able to directly imitate the industry leader's TMT, it may be able to develop its own high-quality team with the task and process skills necessary to capitalize most effectively on its own unique resource base. But again, substitutability is a matter of degree; while substitutes may exist for specific functions of a high-quality team, it is not likely that any one substitute exists for the total functionality of that team. Thus, even if competitors invest in alternative ways to attain the benefits of a leader's superior TMT, it is unlikely that they will all be successful and a state of resource and performance hetero-geneity will continue.

A firm's unique capabilities in terms of technical know-how and man-agerial ability are important sources of heterogeneity that may result in competitive advantage and the top management team is central to a firm's overall managerial ability. But if several competing firms all have equally high-quality TMTs, then those teams, by themselves, cannot be a source of *sustained* competitive advantage. Further, if prescriptive models of TMT development were ever widely available and easily adoptable, then high-quality TMTs could not be a source of sustained competitive advantage. However, whatever the tendency to invest in high-quality teams, not all competing firms will be equally successful in doing so (because of resource heterogeneity, organizational inertia, barriers to change, and so on) and thus high-quality TMTs will likely be a potential source of competitive advantage for the foreseeable future.

TMTs, human resource management, and emergent strategy

The previous section focused on whether top management teams, as strategic human resources, could in and of themselves be sources of competitive advantage. Importantly, however, a firm may achieve above average performance not only because it has better resources, but also because the firm's distinctive competence involves making better use of the resources it has (Penrose, 1959). Ensuring optimal use of organizational resources is a key task of top management teams (Bower, 1986). In this section, we look at the central role that the top manage-ment team plays in strategically managing the firm's human and orga-nizational capital resources. It is our contention that TMTs can manage human resources to foster the emergence of world-class strategies and capabilities.

In their review of the strategic human resource management liter-ature, Lengnick-Hall and Lengnick-Hall (1988) concluded that tradi-tional approaches to strategic human resource management share three common assumptions. First, that strategic direction has been decided. Second, that strategy implementation deals solely with means to achieve strategic ends and has no explicit role in strategy formulation. And third, that the basic issue – be it employee skills, forecasting, career planning, retention, or training – remains the same; only the answer changes as the strategic conditions change. In contrast, Lengnick-Hall and Lengnick-Hall propose an alternative set of assumptions:

> First ... that the choice of strategy has not been made. Second ... the management of human resources should contribute directly to strategy formulation and to strategy implementation ... Third ... that as strategic conditions vary, the fundamental [human resource] questions that must be addressed also vary because strategic issues reflect strategic contingencies.
>
> (Lengnick-Hall and Lengnick-Hall, 1988:460)

We believe that these alternative assumptions are more in keeping with the concept of emergent strategy. They reveal reciprocal interdependence between a firm's business strategy and its human resource strategy. They not only recognize that organizational goals and the availability/obtainability of human resources are individually important; they imply that the two are interdependent.

It is our purpose in this section to expand the discussion of AES to demonstrate how this interdependence can be managed. We believe that AES has, in fact, integrated its philosophy of human resource management with its approach to making strategy, with the result that highly effective strategies have emerged without the use of formal, top-down strategic planning. The role of the TMT in this context has been to establish and manage this integrated process.

We have identified four major components to AES's emergent strategy process which have resulted from a concerted effort by AES's top management team:

- a team culture
- common values
- investment in human capital
- a flexible strategy process.

Interestingly, these components give AES characteristics of both the total quality organization and the virtual corporation described in Chapter 1. Each component is discussed in turn.

Establishing a team culture

Peters and Waterman described simultaneous loose-tight properties as 'the co-existence of firm central direction and maximum individual autonomy ... Organizations that live by the loose-tight principle are on the one hand rigidly controlled, yet at the same time allow (indeed, insist on) autonomy, entrepreneurship, and innovation from the rank and file' (Peters and Waterman, 1982:318). AES's approach to human resource management is dominated by the company's tightly held core values (recall the case study on AES's Core Values), especially the values of fun and fairness. AES wants the people it employs to have fun in their work – to enjoy using their gifts and abilities productively to help meet a need in society – and to be fairly treated as a full member of the AES team. AES's top management team is of the opinion that if they give employees personal responsibility, hold them accountable, and treat them fairly, they will perform at their peak. Thus, AES's TMT has attempted to build an organizational context that facilitates the company's human resources reaching their potential.

One of the ways that AES has attempted to evoke employee commitment and personal responsibility is the use of teams throughout the organization. AES's plants were originally set up along the lines of traditional industrial organizations, with many hierarchical levels, segmented job responsibilities, and detailed policies and procedures. The plants were running quite well but the TMT became concerned that the way they were running their plants was not consistent with the core values. AES's top management team did not want arbitrary rules, detailed procedures manuals and handbooks, punch clocks, and so on. Rather, said Bakke, 'We wanted a learning organization, where people close to the action were constantly creating and recreating and where these people were making the decisions – strategy, financial, and capital allocations.' The effort to establish teams at the plants became known as 'Operation Honeycomb' (Smith and Sims, 1993).

The basic principle of Operation Honeycomb was to cut the number of supervisory levels to improve communication and get out of people's way. It was important to management to push as much responsibility as possible downward in the organization and then reward responsible action. They were convinced – in keeping with the 'fun' value – that people would like and appreciate the greater personal responsibility. In the words of Roger Naill:

> That was tight. We said, we don't care what structure you come up with, but we do want it to reflect this idea that these guys down here [in the plants] are not puppets. They're going to have a lot of responsibility and a lot of say about what they do, in terms of both their day to day operations and also ownership. You know, financial responsibility. We want them to own stock. We wanted them to have an incentive plan so that if the plant ran well they'd get a lot of money.

On the other hand, what the final plant structure looked like was 'loose.' The mandate was simply to create a structure that provided for everyone having ownership and responsibility for running the plant.

Given this mandate, the plants took primary responsibility for implementing the change. Layers were cut, job categories collapsed, and self-managing teams established. The core values were embraced by plant employees to such an extent that today, when hiring new personnel, more consideration is given to an applicant's fit with the shared values than to his or her technical skills. Top management supported the transition by providing incentives such as stock options and a bonus program – plant employees can receive up to 20% of their salary as a bonus if their plant runs right. Today, virtually all operational decisions are made at the plants.

The principles of Operation Honeycomb are reflective of the total quality organization described in Chapter 1, particularly through the establishment of horizontal relationships and employee empowerment to drive innovation and improvement. At AES, the line managers prompt and encourage employees to seek out new developmental opportunities and to translate what was learned elsewhere into improvements in the work environment. It is the line managers who create an atmosphere that encourages risks and tolerates mistakes. And it is the line managers who signal the importance of performance measurement and feedback.

Instilling common values

AES's top management team has played a central role in the emergence of the team-based structure of the corporation, primarily through mandating the 'tight' principles described by Roger Naill. But the team also plays a continuous and highly visible role in instilling the core values throughout the organization. One process by which the TMT does this is by engaging in annual visits to the plants.

Every officer has to go to one of the plants for a week each year. The visit is more than symbolic; it keeps the top managers in touch with the workers. According to Bakke:

> It's a tremendous time to get to know some of the folks. It lets them give us a bad time. They love it, to see us dirty, or whatever – make fools of ourselves. And partly it's a chance for them to tell us what things are right or wrong.

An important aspect of the plant visits is that they are not for the purpose of reviewing performance or conducting briefings. The executives are there to participate in the everyday activities of the plant by actually carrying out the work assigned to a specific, often labor-intensive job. The executive plant visits have two positive results. First, they provide opportunity for executives to listen to and learn from people with direct experience in the trenches. They also send a powerful message to each employee. In keeping with the company's core values, it communicates that each job is important, and that no one is too good to work at any job, no matter how rough or dirty.

The company has also begun a program of reciprocal visits, where groups of employees from each location make periodic visits to the company home office in Arlington. All of these exchanges evoke a strong sense of loyalty, commitment, and sense of ownership throughout the company, including ownership of the values.

Investing in human capital

Beyond developing a team culture and instilling the culture with the core values, AES's senior management has made a lot of investment in developing its high-calibre personnel, especially those involved in project development work (recall the case study on AES's Project Development Teams). These people are perceived to be valuable and rare and AES views them as key to the company's continued growth. How to keep these people at AES and keep them developing is a major concern.

AES's top managers continually look for ways to provide additional opportunities for their project development personnel. These can often tell how they are progressing by some of the standard HR indicators (salary and responsibility) but not by others (titles, size of office, number of direct reports, and so on). AES's team structure does not lend itself to these latter indicators of success. Rather, progression is more typically recognized through the level of project tasks, level of responsibility, or consideration for special assignments. Bob Hemphill explains it this way:

> If we are successful internationally then that creates real opportunities for that kind of growth to go on. We have bid on a 600 megawatt project in Australia. It's a big deal. If we're going to pull that off, somebody will have to move to Australia very shortly after we get selected. And getting selected doesn't mean the deal is done. All that means is we get to sign the power contract. But you've still got to raise the money . . . a zillion things. So anybody who does that, and takes on that responsibility, is taking on a very big challenge in a very far away country. That's a bunch more than doing a project here, even a fairly big project. That's a real opportunity for more responsibility.

At AES, advancement results from and is rewarded by greater responsibility. Although financial compensation increases with responsibility, AES's top managers believe that the increased responsibility is itself the greater reward. Its intent is to provide opportunity for high-calibre personnel to define their own opportunities for growth, feeding back into the firm's goals and objectives. For example, AES's first international venture was the result of an experienced project development team leader looking for something bigger to do.

AES has also sought to make the most efficient use of its available human resources by keeping staff to a minimum. In resource base theory terms, it has tried to avoid bringing in-house those skills that can be easily procured outside; that is, skills that are valuable but not rare. Rather, AES tries to outsource special or unique skills that are not required 100 per cent of the time. It wants to manage the process rather than do every step of the process. For example, it does not want to gather all of the econometric data necessary to model the energy industry. Rather, it wants to make sure that the data gets gathered by somebody who knows how to do it, and gets analyzed by somebody using the right tools. Similarly, AES does not keep a lawyer on staff because it does not need somebody drafting contracts every day. Thus, outsourcing skills has become common as a way to even out the workload. Note that outsourcing human resources is an emerging topic of research in HRM and is the focus of Chapters 6 and 10 of this book (see, for instance, Bruce, 1994).

Overall, AES wants its human resources to be productive and that is one of the things top management gives its attention to. They constantly review who is working on what to assess the allocation of human resources. They are continually asking such questions as: Is this project really short handed at a critical time? Should we borrow somebody temporarily from another project? Should we assign somebody permanently out of this project into that one? Figuring out how to answer these questions gave rise to the 'virtual' structure of the project development teams (recall the case study on AES's Project Development Teams). The imperative is to get the work done while making sure that all AES people are doing meaningful and useful jobs. Thus, in the structure of its project development teams and its use of outsourced specialty skills, AES exhibits characteristics of the virtual corporation.

Managing strategy flexibly
(Excerpted from Smith and Sims, 1993)

As a result of its team culture, common values, and investment in human capital, AES is prized with valuable and rare human resources. But AES's TMT is not content to have its human resources operate exclusively in their area of expertise. Rather, AES has developed a flexible approach to strategy making that draws broadly on its personnel to formulate as well as implement strategy.

The Operating Committee is the core organizational unit through which strategy is developed at AES. The Operating Committee is composed of the TMT (Sant, Bakke, and Hemphill), all other officers, all plant managers, and the leaders of the project development teams. The committee engages in an annual strategic planning process that is fundamentally bottom-up in approach. First, the strategic planning group prepares and distributes a book of planning data to all participants in the process (recall Case study, AES: Informed Opportunism). Then one-day strategic planning meetings are held at each plant every September. At these meetings the plant personnel come together to address the strategic direction of their own plant and the company as a whole over the next five years. These one-day meetings are also attended by a senior member of the strategic planning group and, typically, two other officers – one of the TMT and one of the other vice presidents.

The meeting is led by the plant manager. The agenda is somewhat structured but discussion fairly loose, designed to get people to talk openly about their ideas and their responses to the discussion materials. Rather than serving as planners, the corporate officers serve as resources, share information, and carry the results of the meeting back to the home office. Summaries of each meeting are prepared and distributed throughout the organization.

For the purpose of strategic planning, the corporate home office is treated as a plant. Participants there include the corporate officers and the team leaders of the project development teams. The meeting is structured similarly to the plant meetings, but it provides a forum for addressing the unique needs and concerns relating to project development rather than plant operations.

Later in September, all senior management (officers, plant managers, heads of project development teams), plus a number of additional representatives from across the company (sometimes chosen at random), meet at a retreat center. This three-day session is the primary corporate strategy vehicle. Attendees are provided with a briefing document (about 200 pages) containing the current strategy statement and reviewing the current market situation, competitors, technologies, potential customers, and the like. This briefing document serves as a basis for brainstorming important issues and decisions facing the company.

All of the attendees will have attended one or more of the one-day plant meetings, and all have responsibility for initiating issues raised and reflecting opinions voiced at these earlier sessions. As in the one-day sessions, a summary document is prepared and distributed.

But strategy making does not end with these annual meetings; rather the process is much more fluid than the above description implies. Strategic issues are often dealt with outside the annual planning structure, in a process that is virtually continuous. Issues raised outside the annual planning structure become topics for discussion and action by the Operating Committee.

The Operating Committee meets for two days each month. On the first day, primary attention is given to implementation issues. The manager of each project, from those in the earliest stages of development to plants currently in operation, gives a short presentation, bringing before the group issues that require brainstorming or decisions. He or she usually identifies several alternatives for action, including the alternative the manager thinks is most appropriate. The discussion following the presentation is likely to address whether the proposed alternative is in accordance with AES's values, as well as the technical and financial aspects of the specific situation. The final decision remains the manager's, but he or she has the resources of the Operating Committee to draw upon.

On the second day, attention turns to more general management issues. Committee members can place any item on the agenda and are encouraged to raise issues that pertain to the values of the company. Topics for discussion may relate to strategy formulation or implementation. In support of this process, the planning group will prepare short, focused reports and briefing documents on selected issues that arise throughout the year. Because the Operating Committee addresses both strategy formulation and implementation issues as they arise, the formulation and implementation processes are truly integrated and continuous and overall strategy is emergent rather than planned.

Results

A number of benefits have derived to AES from the value-driven approach to managing human and organizational capital resources developed by the top management team. First, the emphasis on teamwork has enhanced the motivation, initiative, and accountability of employees throughout the company. Second, AES has developed an environment in which high-calibre personnel are continually challenged with more responsibility, the result being that the company's human resources become more and more valuable over time. Third, AES's approach has led to a highly adaptive, flexible organization in which strategy emerges from the interaction of high-quality people within the context of closely held values. Job assignments, roles, and even strategies are not carved in stone and they sometimes change significantly as the situation demands. Together, the approach developed by AES's top management team has led to high productivity and competitiveness. Bottom line figures speak for themselves (recall the case study, AES: The Company). AES's energy generating plants significantly exceed industry performance standards, a high degree of profitability has been maintained, and voluntary turnover is less than 1 percent.

Summary and conclusion

By now it should be obvious that top management teams are an important topic in the discussion of strategic human resource management.
In the preceding sections of this chapter we have argued that TMTs
are strategic human resources in their own right, capable of providing
the firm with a sustainable competitive advantage; and TMTs can
manage the human resources of the firm to allow the bottom-up emergence of world-class strategies and capabilities in the absence of formal
planning. Strategic human resource management, then, must address
the characteristics and roles of high-quality top management teams
(Hambrick, 1987; Kakabadse, *et al.* 1993).

The extent to which TMTs as strategic human resources can be the
source of sustained competitive advantage is an empirical question.
However, a great deal of anecdotal evidence suggests that TMTs are
strategic human resources, and that they in turn assemble and manage
strategic human resources – both of which can result in competitive
advantage. Should effort be made to build a high-quality top management team? Certainly. Even if high-quality TMTs cannot provide a
competitive advantage, if a company does not invest in its TMT the
lack of a high-quality TMT will result in a competitive disadvantage
when high-quality TMTs become the basis for competitive parity.

The remainder of this book raises issues to be considered by
superior top management teams: namely, those relating to how the
human resources of the firm can be most productively managed. We
believe that managing and liberating human resources is a task of
strategic importance to the firm, and should be a priority of the top
management team. However, innovative human resource management
in and by itself is no guarantee of organizational effectiveness, although
it may well be a stimulus for the reduction of bureaucratic inertia in
many companies.

Downstream from the TMT, the impact of organizational innovations may have unanticipated, even dysfunctional consequences. Thus,
implementing innovations in strategic human resource management
must be carefully monitored. The remainder of the book critically
examines how and in what manner innovations in the management of
human resources may contribute to the resource base of the firm and,
through the creation of world-class capabilities, sustained competitive
advantage.

References

Ancona, D.G. and Nadler, D.A. (1989). Top hats and executive tales: designing the senior team, *Sloan Management Review*, 31, 19–28.

Applegate, L.M., Cash, J.I., Jr., and Mills, D.Q. (1988). Information technology and tomorrow's manager, *Harvard Business Review*, 66, 128–36.

Bantel, K.A. and Jackson, S.E. (1989). Top management and innovations in banking: Does the composition of the top team make a difference? *Strategic Management Journal*, 10, 107–24.

Barney, J. (1991). Firm resources and sustained competitive advantage, *Journal of Management*, 17, 99–120.

Barney, J.B. and Tyler, B. (1992). Top management team attributes and sustained competitive advantage. In Gomez-Mejia, L.R. and Lawless, M.W. (eds) *Advances in Global High-Technology Management*, 2, 33–47. Greenwich, CT: JAI Press.

Blau, P.M. (1970). *Inequality and Heterogeneity*. New York: The Free Press.

Bower, J.L. (1986). *Managing the Resource Allocation Process*. Boston, MA: Harvard Business School.

Bowman, E.H. (1974). Epistemology, corporate strategy, and academe, *Sloan Management Review*, 47.

Bruce, R. (1994). Human resources at the cutting edge, *Accountancy*, 113, 44.

Castanias, R.P. and Helfat, C.E. (1991). Managerial resources and rents, *Journal of Management*, 17, 155–71.

Caves, R.E. and Porter, M.E. (1977). From entry barriers to mobility barriers: conjectural decisions and contrived deterrence to new competition, *Quarterly Journal of Economics*, 91, 241–62.

Chaganti, R. and Sambharya, R. (1987). Strategic orientation and characteristics of upper management, *Strategic Management Journal*, 8, 393–402.

Cohen, W.M. and Levinthal, D.A. (1990). Absorptive capacity: a new perspective on learning and innovation, *Administrative Science Quarterly*, 35, 128–52.

Cyert, R.M. and March, J.G. (1963). *A Behavioral Theory of the Firm*. Englewood Cliffs, NJ: Prentice-Hall.

Dainty, P. and Kakabadse, A. (1992). Brittle, blocked, blended and blind: top team characteristics that lead to business success or failure, *Journal of Managerial Psychology*, 7, 4–17.

D'Aveni, R.A. (1990). Top managerial prestige and organizational bankruptcy, *Organization Science*, 1, 121–42.

Dess, G.G. and Miller, A. (1993). *Strategic Management*. New York: McGraw-Hill.

Eisenhardt, K.M. and Bourgeois, L.J., III. (1988). Politics of strategic decision making in high-velocity environments: toward a midrange theory, *Academy of Management Journal*, 31, 737–70.

Eisenhardt, K.M. and Schoonhoven, C.B. (1990). Organizational growth: linking founding team, strategy, environment, and growth among US semiconductor ventures, *Administrative Science Quarterly*, 35, 504–29.

Finkelstein, S. and Hambrick, D.C. (1989). Chief executive compensation: a study of the intersection of markets and political processes, *Strategic Management Journal*, 10, 121–34.

Finkelstein, S. and Hambrick, D.C. (1990). Top management team tenure and organizational outcomes: the moderating role of managerial discretion. *Administrative Science Quarterly*, 35, 484–503.

Fotos, C.P. (1991). Ailing Midway joins ranks of bankrupt US carriers, *Aviation Week and Space Technology*, 134 (13), 31–2.

Fredrickson, J.W. and Iaquinto, A. (1989). Inertia and creeping rationality in strategic decision processes, *Academy of Management Journal*, 32, 516–42.

Galbraith, J. (1977). *Organization Design*. Reading, MA: Addison-Wesley.

Grimm, C.M. and Smith, K.G. (1991). Management and organizational change: a note on the railroad industry, *Strategic Management Journal*, 12, 557–62.

Gupta, A. (1986). Matching managers to strategies: point and counterpoint, *Human Resource Management*, 25, 215–34.

Hambrick, D.C. (1981). Environment, strategy, and power within top-management teams, *Administrative Science Quarterly*, 26, 252–75.

Hambrick, D.C. (1987). The top management team: key to strategic success. *California Management Review*, 9, 193–206.

Hambrick, D.C. (1994). Top management groups: a conceptual integration and reconsideration of the 'team' label. In Staw, B.M. and Cummings, L.L. (eds). *Research in Organizational Behavior*, 16, 171–213. Greenwich, CT: JAI Press.

Hambrick, D.C. and D'Aveni, R.A. (1992). Top team deterioration as part of the downward spiral of large corporate bankruptcies, *Management Science*, 38, 1445–66.

Hambrick, D.C. and Fukutomi, G. (1991). The seasons of the CEO's tenure, *Academy of Management Review*, 16, 719–42.

Hambrick, D.C. and Mason, P.A. (1984). Upper echelons: the organization as a reflection of its top managers, *Academy of Management Review*, 9, 193–206.

Janis, I.L. (1982). *Groupthink*, 2nd edn. Boston, MA: Houghton Mifflin.

Kakabadse, A. (1993). The success levers for Europe: the Cranfield Executive Competences Survey, *Journal of Management Development*, 8, 12–17.

Kakabadse, A.P., Alderson, S., Randlesome, C., and Myers, A. (1993). Austrian boardroom success: a European comparative analysis of top management, *Journal of Managerial Psychology*, 8, 3–32.

Katz, D. and Kahn, R.L. (1978). *The Social Psychology of Organizations*, 2nd edn. New York: John Wiley.

Katz, R. and Allen, T.J. (1982). Investigating the not invented here (NIH) syndrome: a look at the performance, tenure, and communication patterns of 50 R&D project groups, *R&D Management*, 12, 7–12.

Kay, J. (1990). What makes a company a chart topper? *Accountancy*, 106, 98–101.

Kay, J. (1993). Value-added winners, *International Management*, 48, 44–5.

Keck, S.L. (1991). Top executive team structure: does it matter anyway? Paper presented at the Academy of Management, Miami, Florida, August 1991.

Kristof, A.L., Brown, K.G., Sims, H.P., Jr., and Smith, K.A. (1993). Building the virtual team: an example from AES Corporation. Working Paper. University of Maryland at College Park.

Lengnick-Hall, C.A. and Lengnick-Hall, M.L. (1988). Strategic human resource management: a review of the literature and a proposed typology, *Academy of Management Review*, 13, 454–70.

Mahoney, J.T. and Pandian, J.R. (1992). The resource base view within the conversation of strategic management, *Strategic Management Journal*, 13, 364.

Manz, C. and Sims, H.P., Jr. (1987). Leading workers to lead themselves: the external leadership of self-managing work teams, *Administrative Science Quarterly*, 32, 106–29.

March, J.G. and Simon, H.A. (1958). *Organizations*. New York: John Wiley.

Michel, J.G. and Hambrick, D.C. (1992). Diversification posture and top - management team characteristics, *Academy of Management Journal*, 35, 9–37.

Miles, R. and Snow, C. (1978). *Organizational Strategy, Structure, and Process*. New York: McGraw-Hill.

Mintzberg, H. (1979). *The Structuring of Organizations*. Englewood Cliffs, NJ: Prentice-Hall.

Mintzberg, H. (1987). Crafting strategy, *Harvard Business Review*, July–August, 66–75.

Mintzberg, H. (1994). *The Rise and Fall of Strategic Planning: Reconceiving Roles for Planning, Plans, Planners*. New York: The Free Press.

Mintzberg, H. and Waters, J. A. (1985). Of strategies, deliberate and emergent. *Strategic Management Journal*, 6, 257–72.

Murray, A.I. (1989). Top management group heterogeneity and firm performance, *Strategic Management Journal*, 10, 125–41.

Myers, A., Bryce, M., and Kakabadse, A. (1992). Business success and 1992: the need for effective top teams, *Management Decision*, 30, 17–26.

O'Reilly, C.A., III, Caldwell, D., and Barnett, W. (1989). Work group demography, social integration, and turnover, *Administrative Science Quarterly*, 34, 21–37.

O'Reilly, C.A., III and Flatt, S. (1989). Executive team demography, organizational innovation, and firm performance. Paper presented at the Academy of Management, Washington, DC, August 1989.

Pascarella, P. (1983). Are you investing in the wrong technology? *Industry Week*, 25 July, 38.

Penrose, E.T. (1959). *The Theory of Economic Change*. Cambridge, MA: Belknap Press.

Peteraf, M.A. (1993). The cornerstones of competitive advantage: a resource base view, *Strategic Management Journal*, 14, 179–91.

Peters, T.J. and Waterman, R.H., Jr. (1982). *In Search of Excellence: Lessons from America's Best-Run Companies*. New York: Harper & Row.

Pfeffer, J. (1983). Organizational demography. In Staw, B.M. and Cummings, L.L. (eds) *Research in Organizational Behavior*, 5, 299–357. Greenwich, CT: JAI Press.

Porter, M.E. (1980). *Competitive Strategy: Techniques for Analyzing Industries and Competitors*. New York: The Free Press.

Porter, M.E. (1985). *Competitive Advantage: Creating and Sustaining Superior Performance*. New York: The Free Press.

Quinn, J. B. (1980). *Strategies for Change: Logical Incrementalism*. Homewood, IL: Richard D. Irwin.

Sapienza, H.J. (1992). When do venture capitalists add value? *Journal of Business Venturing*, 7, 9–27.

Shaw, M.E. (1981). *Group dynamics: The Psychology of Small Group Behavior*, 2nd edn. New York: McGraw-Hill.

Smith, D.K. (1988). *Fumbling the Future: How Xerox Invented, then Ignored, the First Personal Computer*. New York: W. Morrow.

Smith, K.A. and Sims, H.P., Jr. (1993). The strategy team: teams at the top. In Manz, C.C. and Sims, H.P., Jr. (eds), *Business Without Bosses: The Emergence of SuperTeams in the World of Work*. New York: John Wiley, pp. 171–95.

Smith, K.A., Smith, K.G., Sims, H.P., Jr., Olian, J.D., and Scully, J. (1993). Top management team characteristics and technological innovation in high-tech companies: exploring the mediating role of group process. Paper presented at the Academy of Management, Atlanta, Georgia, August 1993.

Smith, K.G., Smith, K.A., Olian, J.D., Sims, H.P., Jr., O'Bannon, D.P., and Scully, J.A. (1994). Top management team demography and process: the role of social integration and communication, *Administrative Science Quarterly*, 39, 412–38.

Snow, C.C., Miles, R.E., and Coleman, H.J., Jr. (1992). Managing 21st Century network organizations, *Organizational Dynamics*, 20, 4–20.

Stogdill, R.M. (1959). *Individual Behavior and Group Achievement*. New York: Oxford University Press.

Wheelen, T.L. and Hunger, JD. (1992). *Strategic Management and Business Policy*, 4th edn. Reading, MA: Addison-Wesley.

Wiersema, M. and Bantel, K. A. (1992). Top management team demography and corporate strategic change, *Academy of Management Journal*, 35, 91–121.

Wilkins, A. (1989). *Developing Corporate Character*. San Francisco: Jossey-Bass.

Yukl, G.A. (1981). *Leadership in Organizations*. Englewood Cliffs, NJ: Prentice-Hall.

PART
TWO

Non-Traditional Methods: Vehicles for Change

3

Managing without traditional structures

In the earlier chapters we saw that firms are faced with new realities in globalized competition. Successful competitors must emphasize more than fine-tuning their marketing strategies. As Chapter 1 underscored, to sustain competitive advantage, companies must emphasize the development of the firm capabilities of world-class resource management, namely to simultaneously deliver not only speedily, on time, and flexibly, but also correctly – the first time – and yet as cost-effectively as possible. Meeting these global standards presents the strategists of any company with a daunting challenge, and Chapter 2 has offered insights into the role that top management can play in shaping the capabilities and strategies firms must pursue in this new era of globalized competition.

Despite a boom in the world's financial markets, such trends as downsizing, rationalizing, and restructuring characterized the 1980s. In many industries, the globalization of competition forced world standards of productivity and quality upon firms, some of whom complacently believed that they commanded a competitive edge. At times, strong foreign competition did not jar managers into action. Instead, new, higher standards of performance came from ownership groups that were relatively passive in earlier, more prosperous times. These ownership groups imposing change on organizations included organizations and individuals acquiring existing firms. In addition, established owners, often investment funds, placed their representatives on boards of directors to make changes in existing top management or to at least pressure them into significantly improving organizational performance.

In the aggregate, periods of recession during the 1970s, 1980s, and now in the early 1990s have compelled managers to weigh carefully commitments to people and assets, and to seek the maximum value from those commitments that they do make. In many cases, advances in information systems and other technologies have fostered employee redundancies. In the face of unprecedented competition, corporations have cut costs and downsized often by carrying out various types of restructuring; sometimes they have repeated this process several times. Many managements have turned to outsourcing and developed networks of satellite or cooperating firms to cut operation and research & development costs and to increase overall efficiency and effectiveness (see Chapters 6 and 9).

This chapter's objectives are to examine how firms have adapted to these changing competitive realities and to review theories of organizing work and structuring organizations that offer insights into the catalysts and nature of these changes. We begin with a case description of the Powertech Company. Through the past several years, Powertech has experienced changes that are fairly representative of those that many companies have undertaken. Key issues involving the changing nature of organizational structure that the case presents are then highlighted. Theories of organizational structuring are proffered to offer insights into the nature of company adaptation and to assist organizational designers in structuring their firms effectively. We begin with an overview of traditional theories of organizing work and structuring organizations. We include in this overview an examination of information processing, resource dependency, and institutional theories of organizational structuring. We explain the economically-based theories of agency and transactions cost theories, and how they may help in an understanding of restructuring. Throughout, a variety of case examples is used to illustrate the ways in which firms are structuring to adapt to the new requirements for both survival and success. We begin with the Powertech company.

Case study **Powertech: Development of the Company**

The early years ... from founding to 1978

Powertech is a 300-employee company located in the industrial heartland of the United States. It had revenues of about US$9 million in 1990. It was founded in 1964 by an engineer, Sam Bedingfield, who worked for Apex, a Fortune 500 company. The company was started after Apex refused Bedingfield's recommendation that the company go into a certain line of capital equipment (large motors, transformers, heating units, power supplies, etc.) that the engineer thought had promise. The capital to form the company came from a variety of sources: the personal savings of Bedingfield; investments by some other Apex engineers he persuaded to come with him in the new enterprise; some venture capital from a few wealthy individuals; and bank loans. Most of the company was owned by the engineers, with Bedingfield holding the largest share. The company prospered and grew slowly over the years. Over this time period, it had purchased and then divested itself of some smaller companies, often to obtain new products or technologies. The company's structure consisted of a functional mode of departmentalization with the major departments of engineering, manufacturing, and marketing headed by vice presidents. The vice president of manufacturing was designated as treasurer; manufacturing contained the subunits of purchasing and human resources; and an accounting department reported to the controller. The president/ founder wielded a great deal of power and influence. He had a rather charismatic personality not unlike that of other entrepreneurs, and the entire workforce seemed to admire him greatly. They were quite willing to do whatever he wanted. Since all of the top managers were required to buy company stock, they also had an ownership interest in the company. Managers (all of whom had engineering degrees) and engineers seemed quite willing to work long hours and to exert high degrees of effort on the job. The culture or climate of the organization was very open and informal. There was much joking behavior and relationships among all levels were very warm. Since the core group in the company was engineers, the values of the engineering profession for truth, openness, full disclosure, informal relationships, and power based on expertise were the characteristics of the organization's culture. The capital equipment products of the company were either entirely customized to meet customer requirements for size, performance, shape, and environmental standards or were standardized products that were modified to fit each customer's particular needs. Most of the business of the company involved responding to requests for bids, and the engineering workforce was heavily involved in marketing all the technical products. The engineering department was generally sub-divided into various product groups.

The Taylor-Jones years, 1978–87

In 1978 the company's prosperity was noticed, and it was bought by a US conglomerate, Taylor-Jones, with all of those managers who owned stock selling their ownership interest. Most of the managers stayed on at the company which was managed in a decentralized manner by the new owners, since company performance was high. Managers referred to the new system as that of a benevolent stewardship, and the new parent company was characterized by some managers as rather paternalistic in its style. A few of the older and less competent managers were dismissed and a new manufacturing manager and a new human resources manager for a newly established human resources management unit reporting to the president were hired. The engineering unit consisted of four product groups plus an engineering services unit which provided drafting and other services to the company. With the change in ownership, however, came a different mode of organizing imposed by the parent company. There was more formal planning and less use of a strictly opportunistic or reactive mode to business. Profit goals were established by the parent, but these were not at all unrealistic according to Powertech's managers. Policies were established and put into place. New computer technologies were introduced, including a materials requirements planning system. A main-frame computer was purchased which was used not only for accounting and inventory control but for engineering design as well.

The shifting ownership years, 1987–90

In 1987 the parent, Taylor-Jones company, was purchased by its managers in a highly leveraged buyout. This created a need for a very high cash flow to meet the financial obligations of the company, and much higher profit and short-term performance objectives were imposed on Powertech by the Taylor-Jones managers. The long-time president of Powertech left and was replaced by another individual. Taylor-Jones was then bought by an English conglomerate; Taylor-Jones managers profited very handsomely from this arrangement and retired. The English company was owned by a rather authoritarian business tycoon who immediately fired many individuals and cut costs drastically. A new management system which Powertech managers referred to as a 'reign of terror' was instituted. The Powertech managers hated their new owners. Fortunately for Powertech, however, the new English conglomerate sold off several parts of the Taylor-Jones company, including Powertech. Powertech was now owned by a Boston-based conglomerate, National Energy, which specialized in technical companies. National Energy had been formed from capital provided by a wealthy European family. It was, however, managed by several US MBA graduates of a prestigious busi-ness school. The intention of National Energy was to make Powertech part of another company it owned which made similar products to Powertech in order to increase market share and achieve some economies of scale. After investigation, however, the managers of National Energy felt that Powertech was better managed than its own subsidiary, and they decided to make this subsidiary part of Powertech. The managers felt that Powertech had better planning systems and a more systematic management style than National Energy's own subsidiary, Molar Company. After a few years Powertech elim-inated Molar company, retaining several of its most profitable product lines along with the Molar company names for them. Managers at Powertech brought production of these products to their own location, although they had to build a small additional plant to house some of them.

The National Energy changes, 1990–92

In the 1990s, the president of National Energy gradually made a number of changes in the structure and systems of Powertech. These involved such things as creating a new department of engineering development which would work full-time on developing new products related to the core competence of Powertech. National Energy felt that the operating managers at Powertech did not have the time to work on new products, although they did retain the responsibility for making smaller improvements in present products which would take advantage of new technical processes, new component products, new materials, and cost reduction methods. A new department of software engineering was established in the company, because the controls for all the product lines used more sophisticated computer technologies. All managers and engineers now had their own computers and in general the computer systems of the company were upgraded to reflect the new technological possibilities. A new computer-based materials requirements planning system was introduced. This led to very significant changes in the accounting and purchasing systems used in the company.

The new computers and computer-aided design programs now used by the engineers greatly increased the productivity of the technical workforce. These systems also influenced the manner in which the engineers related to each other in doing their jobs. Bids could be made more quickly since design configurations could be developed much faster than before. Components and parts could be more easily tracked and ordered, reducing inventory levels and making it possible to utilize outside suppliers more effectively. The new computerized inventory control system significantly increased formalization of the manufacturing process, and the systems for handling data established requirements for planning and for data analysis and collection. A new director of quality control was hired and reported to the Powertech president (the old quality control function was under manufacturing). This shift led to newer ideas on what was the most appropriate way to manage this function. The old vice president of marketing was replaced by a highly competent outsider and was moved to a vice president of sales position created to accommodate him. A new director of materials was hired to report to the manufacturing vice president. National Energy imposed new and more stringent profit goals on Powertech and also introduced more precise accounting methods for measuring performance. For example, precise measures of customer delivery, value of monthly shipments and ratios of engineering costs to the sales of various products were now used.

Many older managers and professionals at Powertech were very upset at these changes. They thought that many of the new procedures were inappropriate for their business and distorted behaviors in undesirable ways. For example, the development of new products and the improvement in existing products were felt by many to have declined significantly in Powertech in recent years. Morale was lower and employee turnover was much higher than formerly. However, many managers and professionals were unwilling to criticize the changes for fear of losing their present jobs and not being able to find new ones. Some managers claimed that a 'climate of fear' now existed and that the older, informal, open, and relaxed system had perished to the detriment of the company and the satisfaction of the engineers. Nevertheless, the company did make a profit throughout the recession in the early 1990s.

A new CEO at National Energy, 1992–

In late 1992, a new CEO of National Energy was hired from an aerospace company primarily manufacturing military products and he made several trips to Powertech. Despite the company's profitability, he was highly critical of the way the company operated. He said that the company had to adopt the total quality management (TQM) approach immediately, and he hired a consultant to institute a TQM program in the company and to train all company employees in TQM concepts. He also indicated that a new concurrent engineering approach would be used in the company to speed up the development of new products. This would involve having all functional areas participate up-front in the new product planning process. In addition, he established permanent project groups including those for quality, productivity, and turnaround time for orders, and all managers were assigned to at least one project team and sometimes two. These project teams typically met one full day a week. Managers and professionals spent the other four days back in their functional departments. Thus a matrix organizational structure had been created – each individual employee reported to two bosses – his/her functional boss and his/her project team boss. The relative power and status of these two bosses had not been established by the end of 1993.

Lower-level manufacturing employees also were assigned to these task forces. In addition, many quality circles were created in Powertech. The new National Energy president also decided that the closed office system should be abolished in favor of an open office system where everybody would have access to each other at any time during the day. To that end a brand new plant to replace the old installation has been designed that eliminates private offices and assigns open areas to various product teams that are to be created by Powertech. The long-term plan for the organization as envisioned by the new National Energy CEO is to create a product organization in which all specialties will be assigned to various product groups.

The perception of the present employees toward all of these structural changes and their effects on performance are difficult to determine. Some engineers appear to be quite critical of these changes perhaps because their central role in the company is threatened by them (see Chapter 7). The key discipline now appears to be moving from engineering to accounting – the field of the present CEO of the parent company. Some of the engineers also believe that, in a technical company which makes sophisticated products, an in-depth, profound degree of knowledge is needed which ordinary workers and individuals from such specialties as purchasing, accounting, and marketing do not possess. They feel that their compulsory attendance at so many multidisciplinary meetings is a waste of time because they spend so much time educating those who lack technical knowledge of the company's sophisticated products. In addition, the many meetings significantly decrease the amount of time that is available for accomplishing operating responsibilities such as responding to requests for bids, servicing of field technical problems, and working on incremental product improvements. Since they do not respect higher management any longer, do not own any shares in their company, and do not have any faith in the effectiveness of the many new management procedures adopted, they are no longer willing to work the extra hours in the evenings and on the weekends as they had done a number of years ago. Some of the engineers also feel threatened by the open office concept, believing that they must have privacy and free time to create improvements. Some also feel that the new performance goals do not sufficiently consider the many management tradeoffs that must be made among such factors as costs, quality criteria, customer needs, changing technical requirements (due to environmental regulations, etc.) and other factors. Also, some company managers now fear that they may lose their jobs, because of the many discharges and layoffs that have occurred in the recent past. They believe that there is now an error avoidance culture, instead of the risk-taking climate that was the case in the earlier days of the company's history. Further, such recent episodes as working employees long hours on an overtime basis at the end of the fiscal year to enhance year-end productivity performance and then laying them off at the start of the new fiscal year has significantly worried the human resources management staff. These specialists are concerned about the threat of unionization and turnover among the skilled workers who all are graduates of technical institutes or hold associate degrees from community colleges. Many of the company's managers, its professional engineering staff, and its workforce seem to be quite cynical about the new management programs or 'fads' such as empowerment and TQM, which they believe are unlikely to last for very long. Consequently, they do not feel that the considerable investments in time and effort necessary to make them work well are worthwhile.

Six months after the end of the fiscal year in 1994, the firm's marketing manager realized that the company's bookings for new projects were down 20%. When he asked the engineering vice president why this was so, he was told that maybe the cause was that the engineering managers were just too busy with new activities and responsibilities to make as many inquiries and even bid proposals as they had in the past.

The Powertech case highlights a number of important issues characterizing recent changes in organizational structuring. In Powertech, as in many organizations, a greater reliance on formalization has emerged. Rules, policies, and procedures have become standardized. As trust has declined, communication has tended to follow strictly hierarchical levels. Quantitative, short-term, objective measures are used whenever possible. Specialization has increased, with staff groups emerging and various employee empowerment techniques instituted to harness each and every employee's value-added contribution.

At the same time, at Powertech, as in many other companies, a culture that relied upon trust, loyalty, and camaraderie has been de-emphasized. Instead, teamwork as characterized by physical structures that minimize privacy, and reporting relationships that are sometimes ambiguous have come to the fore. As the financial and control functions seemingly displace the dominance of the technical experts, Powertech's seasoned employees, the solid citizens who embody a battered corporate culture, have been confronted with the need to change. Some have been able to change, while others have not. The survivors seem to be fewer in number with every change in corporate control. No wonder, then, that some employees have come to be more cautious in their behaviors and to feel greater stress in their jobs. As in many organizations, preserving morale at Powertech has become a managerial challenge. Table 3.1 summarizes the issues in structural change that are highlighted by Powertech's recent changes and that characterize the changes in many organizations during the past decade.

Why are these changes occurring in so many of the world's organizations? The answer appears to lie in changes in the nature of competition, advances in technology, and reconfiguration of social institutions in many parts of the world. Competition has been changed by unabated globalization of the world's industries and services. New markets have emerged; others have been redefined; and an increasing number of competitors have appeared from non-traditional locations. The European Common Market agreements, the North America Free Trade Pact, and the ASEAN bloc trading arrangements have all reframed competition at a supranational level – in some cases the trading bloc may come to supplant the nation-state as the most important political and economic unit in world trade. Political change in Eastern Europe also has brought about a collection of new re-emergent free markets that offer access to both untapped consumers and factor markets to all of the world's export-oriented industrial and service firms.

Technological innovations, ranging from the facsimile machine to flexible, computer-assisted manufacturing, have permitted the development of an information-processing or computational infrastructure that minimizes the influence of geographic distance and locational advantage. Within firms, unprecedented information-processing capabilities have allowed organizational designers to transcend the limitations that coordination requirements and cognitive information-processing limitations once imposed. Computerized information systems permit diffuse access to information that workers at all levels can utilize to enhance

Table 3.1 Chronology of organizational changes at Powertech Company

The early years ... from founding to 1978
Key company characteristics:
- closely held ownership
- functional structure
- strong company culture based on values of engineering profession
- reactive market orientation

The Taylor-Jones years, 1978–87
Key changes in company characteristics:
- corporate ownership/'benevolent stewardship'
- more formalized planning, more proactive market orientation
- introduction of electronic data-processing systems

The shifting ownership years, 1987–90
Key changes in company characteristics:
- Taylor-Jones leveraged buyout/ Powertech CEO changes
- English conglomerate purchases Taylor-Jones and divests Powertech
- National Energy Co. acquires Powertech
- Powertech absorbs Molar Company

The National Energy changes, 1990–92
Key changes in company characteristics:
- new product development staff department created
- more formalized and precise controls based on more sophisticated information-processing systems
- erosion of engineering culture

A new CEO at National Energy, 1992–
Key changes in company characteristics:
- new total quality management (TQM) program imposed upon Powertech
- temporary matrix management structure designed to facilitate move towards permanent product divisions
- physical layout changed to open office system
- increasing dominance of accounting profession
- a culture of error avoidance emerges

their job performance and to upgrade their current knowledge skills. These new information processes to some degree mean that the hierarchical reporting relationships embodied in traditional bureaucratic organizations are no longer necessary for efficient information processing and control. Instead, structures encoded into computerized information systems offer firms a sufficient level of control to allow them to first downsize and eventually to empower their employees to act creatively without regard to hierarchical constraints. Such encoded structures also offer firms much greater coordination within and outside the organization without the concomitant coordination costs.

Several of the world's mixed economies, or social democracies, have embraced the zeal for privatization that characterized the Thatcher era in the United Kingdom. Many of these changes are of great magnitude and involve the transformation of communication infrastructures and other fundamental goods and services. New citizen-shareholders have appeared, as the opportunity to own shares in formerly nationalized utilities and other infra-structural industries has become available in

Mexico, the United Kingdom, and Australia; several national governments have decided that a laissez-faire approach will enhance the competitive aspects of their national industries. As part of this market ethos, these government organizations have seen the elimination of thousands of employees and restructuring in a variety of other ways, such as installing new pay-for-performance schemes, as a means to enhance the value of their share offerings. Deregulation of private firms in certain industries, as illustrated by airline and financial services deregulation initiated in the Carter administration in the United States, has also significantly impacted organizational structures and processes, and this deregulation movement has spread to various countries around the world.

Economic, technological, and socio-political changes have redefined the basic nature of many industries. With globalization, not only have consumer and factor markets reached new levels of aggregation and availability, but technological innovations also have redefined minimum efficient scales. New customers and new competitors have required many firms to acknowledge and pursue new global performance standards. As a result, they have sought to divest themselves of assets scaled to older obsolete economies of scale. Companies must not only right-size their enterprises for the present, but must embrace the reality that adaptation has to become an ongoing, dynamic process. The more traditional machine-like bureaucracies that produce reliably, but inflexibly, are unsuited to firms whose environments are volatile and unpredictable. As more and more firms find themselves operating in environments of greater uncertainty, they seek flexible and synergistic new exchange relationships that free them from constraints of commitment to various types of fixed assets (including some human resources).

General Motors offers an example of a great manufacturing company that has restructured in the faces of these forces for change (see the case study, Restructuring at General Motors).

Case study **Restructuring at General Motors**

General Motors has undertaken a very well-publicized restructuring of one of the world's largest companies. Stockholder pressures created by poor competitive results helped instigate these changes in this company. With a worldwide payroll of 710,800 (361,000 in North America), the company has reduced its North American workforce by 74,000 since 1991. In just the last two years, GM headquarters staff has been reduced from 13,000 to 1300 people. They are now forging new alliances with suppliers that greatly add to the performance requirements of such suppliers. Through the use of decentralized decision making, simultaneous management, synchronous organizations, continual improvement, benchmarking, and worker empowerment, all the management catchwords of contemporary global management, the leaders of General Motors have embarked on a transformation that will be ongoing for some time to come. Its decline from 45% of the US automobile market to 35% at the present was a major impetus to such planned changes. General Motors, not Ford or Chrysler, has been the US producer to cede market share to Japanese auto producers. GM's management has had to address the future of the company relative to its US competitors.

GM's new CEO, John F. Smith, has rediscovered GM's traditional distinctive resource, or source of competitive advantage, namely economies of scale in engineering, production, and marketing in a new way. He significantly reduced the US rental car fleet sales that kept plants at capacity but significantly undermined profit margins. In addition to a number of plant closings, he has with the help of the star Spanish cost-cutting auto executive, Jose Ignacio Lopez, saved General Motors some US$4 billion in annual costs. The number of auto platforms from which differentiated models can be built has been reduced from 12 to 5. Nevertheless, a new product launch center and knowledge center to train employees combined with new engineering techniques will allow strong model differentiation and more rapid product development with these new models. He has created a strategy board to identify strategic issues and create and maintain the corporation's vision. In these ways, General Motors has redefined the economies of scale that have been its enduring legacy, but now once again they can be a source of impressive profitability. Still the adjustment remains imperfect. Some stakeholders still seek the overarching benevolence of a bigger General Motors, while unions, for example, pressure General Motors to hire anew now that United States auto demand has restarted an upward trend.

(*Source*: Adapted from Taylor, 1994:54–74)

When corporations of this stature make changes, fundamental relationships with suppliers also are altered. These smaller organizations frequently must restructure themselves, perhaps very substantially, to remain partners with the important customers.

Although performance shortfalls may have pressured General Motors to make changes, even highly successful organizations have had to anticipate change in recent years. Massive restructurings have taken place in both private and public sectors in many nations. According to Apple Computer's former CEO John Sculley, who himself preferred to see his company in another's hands: 'The continuing "reorganization of work itself" is part of a social transformation as massive and wrenching as the industrial revolution' (see Byrne, 1993). Theories of organizational structuring may offer some insights into why these fundamental organizational changes have occurred, and how such organizational structural changes may well continue into the indefinite future.

Understanding structural changes in organization through theories of organizing

Traditional theories of managing

Traditional theories of management held that a single, superior form of management could be identified through rational scientific investigation. For example, Frederick Taylor's scientific management relied on the belief that managers, who possessed greater knowledge, could deconstruct the processes necessary to perform tasks, and could reconstruct them in ways that demanded less skill from workers. Scholars such as Max Weber and Henri Fayol reinforced this belief in managerial legal authority and expert power. Reconstructed task processes would facilitate greater efficiency and require less-skilled workers. The overall result would be more goods at lower prices. This faith in the ability to organize manufacturing work scientifically guided much of industry in the period between the World Wars.[†]

An important aspect of this scientific approach to management was the belief that pay-for-performance schemes could induce employees to harmonize their own and the organization's goals. For example, Chester Barnard, CEO of New Jersey Telephone, wrote on the inducements and incentives managers could rely upon to ensure that organizational members acted cooperatively and in accord with the organization's goals (Barnard, 1938). He addressed the manager's 'zone of indifference' in which the proper inducements could ensure cooperation with an overarching goal. Of course, many of the insights from traditional management theories still guide many organizations. The Lincoln Electric Company and United Parcel Service are smoothly running, efficient, machine-like organizations that still utilize many of these managerial strategies quite successfully (Sonnenfeld and Lazo,

---

† Classic works in management theory include: Weber (1947), Fayol (1949), and Taylor (1911). For a summary of the ideas put forth by Weber, Fayol, and Taylor, see Scott (1992).

1989). Some of the changes at Powertech and at other companies, as summarized in Table 3.1, suggest that depersonalized, economic incentives may be a re-emergent managerial tool used to motivate employees in times when security, belongingness, and status have become impractical incentives. Yet the verities of traditional, scientific-management-based approaches are insufficient to explain the wide-ranging structural changes that are occurring. Factors other than managerial incentive schemes must be behind the restructuring of work.

Traditional theories of structuring

As technological change has significantly impacted organizations through, for instance, previously unimagined information-processing capacity, theories of organizational structure that relate technology to structure have re-emerged. For example, organizational designers have long believed that customizing products with general purpose machinery and highly skilled employees requires a non-bureaucratic structure, in contrast to a firm making standardized products with special purpose machinery and lower skilled employees (Burns and Stalker, 1961; Woodward, 1970). Thus, such theorists have believed that the process technology used would dictate an organization's structure. In the face of ever less-expensive information-processing technology that permits flexible manufacturing with fewer, better-skilled employees, however, the role of process technology in the determination of an organization's structure may have diminished. Instead, many of the craft skills and cultural controls of previous eras have been encoded into improved, computerized machine tools and other information systems. Thus, cheaper computing power has permitted businesses producing customized goods to capture many of the cost savings of mass production; in short, minimal efficient scales of production are steadily declining. Moreover, fewer highly skilled employees are needed to produce these customized goods. Advances in information system technologies may increasingly allow businesses to rely less on employee knowledge and coordination skills. The potential cost savings appear attractive.

This technological imperative in organizational structuring also may be understood in terms of an organization's information processing requirements. For example, Paul Lawrence and Jay Lorsch, two Harvard Business School professors, found that better-performing firms displayed the best consistency between their structural features and the information-processing requirements or contingencies of the environment to which the organization related (Lawrence and Lorsch, 1967). Firms in more complex environments needed to incorporate a requisite variety of organizational integrating mechanisms, such as task forces and permanent teams. In other words, environmental complexity led to organizational complexity. These coordinating mechanisms allowed for the transfer of information across reporting hierarchies. Firms in more stable environments could perform as well with more streamlined structural mechanisms.

These findings helped to explain the historical development of large firms that the Harvard business historian, Alfred Chandler, highlighted in his landmark study of major US firms, such as DuPont and General Electric (Chandler, 1962). As these firms grew, they had to sacrifice the efficiencies of functional formal structures and adopt divisional structures. Organizing along product or geographic lines boosted costs through duplication of functional departments within each of them, but provided firms with the specialization and decentralization necessary to stay closer to their customers and adapt more rapidly to change.

Reinforcing the work of Chandler and Lawrence and Lorsch, Jay Galbraith pointed to environmental uncertainty as the factor that would guide managers in the design of their organizations (Galbraith, 1973, 1977). He suggested that the degree of uncertainty in a firm's environment determined its information-processing requirements and that internal structures and coordinating mechanisms, such as task forces, had to be designed with information-processing capacity capable of meeting environmental requirements. Thus, firms with greater information-processing requirements would more appropriately have more complex and elaborated internal structures than firms that had relatively minimal or straightforward information-processing requirements. In traditional organizations, information processing has generally required high coordination costs. In recent years, information technology has come to serve this coordination function, and it has freed organizational designers to decentralize decision making when desirable without incurring concomitant coordination costs (Bradley, *et al.*, 1993). Powertech, for example, was able to replace its dependence on the control mechanism of the strong engineering-profession-based culture through information systems that allowed it to precisely monitor and control the work processes within the company.

Although changes in the ways that firms can internally satisfy their information-processing requirements may be explained by access to new information technologies, these technologies fall short in explaining the blurring of organizational boundaries that has occurred in recent years. Some of the increasing frequency of interorganizational relationships no doubt can be attributed to the need of organizations to secure a reliable supply of key resources from their environments (Pfeffer and Salancik, 1978). One of the primary means by which firms would ensure reliable access to resources would be through the development of enduring interorganizational relationships or partnerships. We should not forget that key resources may include products themselves, their components, technological processes, and such obvious resources as capital and human resources. The interorganizational relationships created for purposes of obtaining key resources can, of course, take a variety of forms ranging from outright acquisitions and mergers, joint ventures and strategic alliances to licensing or long-term non-contractual trading relationships. All of these types of relationships have increased significantly in recent years as shown by the actions of Powertech, the National Health Service (see Case study), and other cases.

Case study   The National Health Service (NHS)

The National Health Service (NHS) in the United Kingdom, a public sector organization under great external pressures to become more efficient and less wasteful of public funds, has restructured itself to become more efficient and to try to optimize the return on its assets (Flood, 1991). Part of these efforts stems from a need to address an increase in expenditures that greatly outpaced the growth in patients and staff: expenditures increased from £8 billion in 1978 to £26 billion in 1987. Simultaneously, the patient workload increased from 6.5 to 8 million in the same time period, while the patient workload of doctors and dentists rose from 42 to 48 thousand.

In 1993, the implementation of a decentralized, streamlined NHS seems possible. Regional health authorities (RHAs) employed 10,000 staff at their largest; by 1993 that number was 3500. Current plans include replacing the existing RHAs with fewer regional directors and clearer and fewer channels of cash distribution within the system. By 1996, the old RHA system should be replaced (National Health Service, 1993; Caines, 1993).

In general, the NHS has displayed characteristics of an inertial bureaucracy that relies upon promotion from within, consensus management, and internal consistency of policies and rules. The need to contain costs and still provide better services to clients has prompted government leaders to actively embrace the massive undertaking of delegating functions from regions to districts and from districts to hospitals. The intent of this dismantling of the bureaucracy and decentralization of authority is to release resources for patient care. These changes will require significant new HRM capabilities at lower levels as compared to previous periods.

This NHS restructuring reflects many of the changes in other private sector organizations: the restructuring involves downsizing, outsourcing, and establishing networks of specialized but cooperative health organizations all joining their efforts on behalf of the treatment needs of individual patients, the NHS's ultimate consumer. To a large extent, this change has to be achieved through HRM policies and procedures. New training and staffing procedures are crucial requirements needed to empower employees to execute this dramatic change.

However, analyses indicate that frequently insufficient attention has been paid to developing a context receptive to change within those organizations affected and to the processual issues involved in managing large-scale change. Andrew Pettigrew, Ewan Ferlie, and Lorna McKee at Warwick University in their research on the National Health Service (Pettigrew, *et al.*, 1992) have shown that successsful change initiatives involved the creation of a supportive organizational culture, adapting change agendas to their organizational locale, simplifying and clarifying goals and priorities, creating cooperative interorganization networks, sensitive balancing of the inherent tensions between administrative and clinical staff, the availability of key people to lead change, and the enactment of change within a coherent and quality oriented framework. The lack of recognition of these critical factors on the part of central government has created some difficult and highly charged confrontations in the change process.

There have even been instances where the government faced with public rebellion over longer rather than shorter waiting times for operations ignored its own admonitions over the need to control public spending and offered incentives to hospital consultants and staff to work extensive overtime and outside of normal working hours in an effort to clear backlogs on waiting lists and to regain public support.

Insight into the mechanisms guiding the structuring of organizations also has come from the institutional or normative environmental structures that serve as guides or constraint to action (Meyers and Rowan, 1977 and DiMaggio and Powell, 1983 are two groundbreaking papers in neo-institutional theory). Organizational theorists in this tradition have emphasized that managers enact or socially construct their business environments and foster the reproduction of legitimating beliefs that guide their actions. They emphasize that firms are subject to normative, coercive, and mimetic pressures in their environments, and that these pressures cause organizations to structure themselves in ways that afford them legitimacy among the larger set of organizations that control their access to resources. This view of an organization's structure as dependent on the institutional arrangements of its environment helps to explain why organizations in one country might exhibit equivalent structures and practices while recognizing why the modal structures and processes differ from one nation to another. These theorists use the term, isomorphism, to refer to the one-to-one correspondence between the external environment and the organization. In coercive isomorphism governments may require certain types of structures and practices, and large private or public sector organizations may mandate certain structures and practices for their many subsidiary firms. Normative isomorphism can result from the common business school training of managers which, in turn, is reinforced by consistency among text-books and other learning materials. Mimetic isomorphism can stem from the mere public communication of leading company structures and processes in books, articles, cases, or other sources. All of these sources can create a certain type of legitimacy which comes from having struc-tures that display isomorphism with, or conformity to, the normative structures of firms' environments. Of course, such institutional pressures are especially likely to be significant within particular industries as com-pared to the effects of such institutional pressures on organizations across industries or sectors.

In sum, theorists in these various theoretical traditions emphasize that the variability in the structures of organizations can be attributed to the different technologies or environments in which different orga-nizations have found themselves or which they have constructed for themselves. Yet as the world's industries continue to compete on an ever more global scale and political institutions take on ever more extra-national character, the technologies and environments of an ever-increasing number of firms are converging. Increasingly, organizations around the world now share similar information-processing capabili-ties, transportation infrastructures, competitive pressures, and similar political governance precepts that seem to be creating strikingly similar policies, structures, and practices. Still, organizational structures are designed to facilitate the transformation of inputs into outputs and to provide structuring to the employment relationships. The theories addressed until now leave unanswered many of the issues having to do with the nature of changes in employment relationships that are clearly observable around the world, even in such traditional work settings as the Fujitsu corporation (see the following case study).

Case study   **Fujitsu**

Fujitsu is one of the leading Japanese firms and one of the most successful companies in the world. In 1992, Fujitsu ranked number one in computer sales, number two in communication devices, and number four in semi-conductors. In 1991, net sales had increased 16.5% over the previous year, and sales had reached more than US$21 billion overall. In 1993, however, facing a serious recession like most Japanese companies, Fujitsu started to initiate many large-scale changes in its structures and systems (Carroll,

1993). It has downsized considerably and has become much more decentralized. Many of these changes were initiated after it reported losses in 1993, perhaps for the first time in the past several decades. Among these changes, the company announced that it will pay managerial bonuses on the basis of individual performance, not just company performance. It will also initiate an extensive system of flexible hours, so that its employees can structure their work days around their personal needs. These changes are in addition to a planned significant decrease in the size of the workforce through early retirements, transfers of employees to subsidiary companies, and also outright layoffs. The company has now decided that perhaps one fifth or more of its present labor force is superfluous. Hiring schedules have also been greatly cut back and more strategic alliances with companies all around the world are planned.

Theories of organizational structuring based in economics

Some theories taken from economics may clarify why and how the nature of employment relationships appears to be changing so rapidly. That individual self-interest aggregates to the invisible hand as first described by Adam Smith has been one of the cornerstones of economic theorizing for centuries. The economist Kenneth Arrow built on this axiom in the development of agency theory. He emphasized that property rights and self-interest guide economic relationships, but also are closely related to issues revolving around principal–agent relationships (Arrow, 1974). In economies in which property rights are primary, agents are rewarded for acting in owners', or principals', interests. Thus, the board of directors and top management team of a firm would act as agents of shareholders, or principals. More broadly, any employment relationship can be conceived of as a principal–agent relationship. An employee would act as the agent of an employer, the principal. Understanding how to maintain goal alignment – that is, a congruence between the interests of the agent and the principal – is the primary concern of agency theorists. Since these theorists believe that human behavior is characterized by a willingness to engage in opportunistic, self-interested behavior – even if to do so may require guile on the part of the agent – they believe that principals must seek to design reward systems and other motivational mechanisms to ensure that agents will not pursue their own interests but, rather, those of the agent.

Ensuring that agents act in principals' interests causes principals to incur agency costs. Examples of agency costs are monitoring costs and information asymmetry costs. Principals must often incur costs to monitor agent behavior because agents, when it is in their self-interest, may not share important information with principals. Thus, as an example, some shareholders believe that legal proscriptions which dictate the fiduciary responsibilities of managers to act in shareholders' interest may be inadequate. Instead, they seek the institution of reward systems that link managerial compensation to firm performance. Agency theorists would suggest that a reward system so designed would discourage managerial perquisites and empire-building, and focus managerial attention on activities that would enhance shareholder value. There has, of course, been a tremendous amount of activity in recent years with respect to the installation of new pay-for-performance reward systems in industry. Some of these have produced such enormous rewards for the CEOs of some US industrial firms that they have generated considerable controversy and calls for government regulation in this area. Further, all over the world goal setting often associated with various types of merit pay schemes has been initiated for the managers in public sector organizations (Wood and Maguire, 1993). These also can be said to have the primary purpose of aligning the interests of organizational managers or administrators to those of owners (overall government or people of a nation). Similarly, the popularity of leveraged managerial buyouts and other forms of employee ownership in the private sector can be understood as discouraging activities that would not promote shareholder value. When employees, or agents, become owners, or principals, their goals by definition are aligned.

The staff and middle-management functions in organizations provide some insights into understanding how agency costs – the costs of monitoring compliance of the agent with the principals' goals – are embodied in the structures of organizations. Many control and other monitoring functions are designed to ensure that employees, or agents, are acting in the interest of employers, that is, principals. Information system advances have helped to shift these controlling functions from human to technological systems of coordination and have resulted in the ability to 'delayer' organizations as levels of supervision and monitoring become encoded into electronic systems.

These issues become even more clear when considering the structure of an organization as a governance mechanism designed to minimize the transaction costs involved in any relationship between an organization and another party, ranging from employment relationships and buyer–supplier relationships to ad hoc consortia. In particular, the economist, Oliver Williamson, building on the work of the Nobel prize-winning economist, R.H. Coase, has conceptualized the hierarchy, or structure, of an organization as a governance mechanism sometimes best suited to the efficient minimization of the transaction costs involved in a relationship (Williamson, 1975; Coase, 1937). Transaction costs include agency costs, but also other costs; they refer to the costs of initiating and enforcing contracts and other costs incurred in maintaining the ongoing economic system. Transaction costs represent a form of friction in the execution of market transactions. According to the reasoning of transaction cost theorists, the market is the primary form of transaction. However, markets sometimes fail. Transaction costs theory holds that markets fail when transactions are characterized by asset specificity, small-numbers bargaining, or unresolved information asymmetries.

Asset specificity refers to the transaction-specific value – perhaps, sunk costs – of an asset, that is, value that cannot be transferred easily to other exchanges. Transaction costs theory would predict that the greater the magnitude of specific assets involved in a transaction, the less likely the transaction will occur through a market, simply because the transaction costs would be too high. Instead, the hierarchy or structure of the organization would be used to organize the transaction. Much of the unwillingness of firms to commit capital and human assets to projects may be a means of avoiding the costs associated with asset specificity; instead they rely on ad hoc contracting or short-term interorganizational alliances. Since new information technology has reduced coordination, or transaction, costs, the hierarchy of the organization has become a less attractive alternative to the market or hybrid relationship.

Another issue that would dictate how a transaction might be organized is the phenomenon of small-numbers bargaining. The smaller the potential number of trading partners – a situation that could be exacerbated by requirements of significant specific assets – the more likely market mechanisms will fail or be ineffective in the face of overwhelming transaction costs. According to transaction costs theorists, markets will also fail when information asymmetries cannot be cost-effectively resolved or guarded against. Given the complexity of modern organizations and the managerial process itself, information asymmetries are the rule rather than the exception.

In summary, transaction cost theorists hold that when markets fail, hierarchies such as industrial firms emerge as a kind of next best form of gaining the benefits from a transaction. When markets cannot be used to complete transactions, hierarchies can serve as a means of minimizing the transaction costs involved. In recent years, however, transaction cost theorizing has begun to acknowledge a third generic form of governance that is neither a pure market transaction nor a hierarchical arrangement. This intermediate form as manifested in various types of long-term contracting, reciprocal trading, regulation, franchising, and network structures has come to be termed a hybrid form of governance. As indicated earlier in our discussion and in some of the case studies – the UK National Health Service and Fujitsu, for example – these network forms of organizational structures have become increasingly common and indeed have been described as perhaps the natural new form of organization in this post-industrial age.

Each of these different governance structures represents a form of adaptation. In markets, changes in prices have long been recognized as mechanisms for communicating information and attaining efficient adaptation. Similarly, internal adjustments in hierarchies should be viewed as adaptation to changing transaction cost economizing requirements. Network organization can be viewed as offering some of the advantages of both the market and hierarchy in the structuring of transactions. Network forms emphasize longer-run cooperation, learning through information exchange, and an ability to exploit yet still retain tacit (organization specific) knowledge and technological innovation.

Three factors characteristic of the new rules of competition guide the emergence of network forms of organization: (1) the value of know-how or intangible expertise, (2) the demand for speed, and (3) the willingness of transacting partners to demonstrate trust rather than opportunism or guile in the transaction (Powell, 1990). Examples of activities in which intangible, proprietary knowledge may determine success or failure include software development, entertainment, publishing, design, and scientific research. The sharing of the benefit of these intangible knowledge resources appears to occur most readily through network structures, rather than through market transactions or hierarchical relations.

However, we should not lose sight of the symbolic nature of managerial actions. Many times, changes in organizations occur to signal shifts in power (Goffman, 1959; Pfeffer, 1992). Much of what occurs in organizations can be conceptualized as theatrical in that it involves the acting out of power relationships (Mangham and Overington, 1987). The imposition of the TQM system at Powertech by the new CEO of National Energy may be just such an action. Managers often seek to create an image or impression of themselves to an audience of those around them. When managers give attention to certain behaviors or people through rewards or acknowledgements, ceremonies, or simply increased attention to an issue, they symbolically offer significance to these issues, if only because of their perceived power in the organizational hierarchy.

Many of the actions of restructuring that occur in the buying and selling of pieces of corporations and the frequent replacement of top managers in the past decade may be understood from this perspective. Sometimes managers may seek to attain personal goals even if these goals are not in harmony with the efficient structuring of the organization. The shifting ownership years at Powertech may offer an illustration of how contests for corporate control may be motivated by and result in the enrichment of elites without the broader economic interests of the full spectrum of stakeholders taken into account (see Case study, Powertech: Internal Structural Changes).

Case study   Powertech: Internal Structural Changes

By 1993, as compared to the past, Powertech has become a much more formalized company in a process extending over 20 years, with communication now following the hierarchy rather than being very informal and open. There are stringent short-term performance goals imposed on the company and many quantitative measurement and control measures installed. This has continued through adoption of the TQM process which has put a stress on internal measurements of various kinds. The company has many more rules and policies and standardized procedures than before. Managers are very goal-oriented, with many performance goals imposed on the company. The structure has evolved from a very loose simple functional structure to a matrix organization which may ultimately result in a product organization. There are many more specialized individuals and departments at the present time that did not exist in the past such as software engineering, development engineering, and so on. Also, certain functions such as quality control and inventory control and human resource management have been moved from the status of subgroups of other groups to independent organizational units with enhanced power and responsibilities. New empowerment techniques for the workforce such as the creation of many quality circles, putting workers on various task forces, and replacing position titles with the term 'associate', have been adopted. Barriers among specialties have been reduced by the use of multidisciplinary teams and by changes in the physical layout of the plant (removing private offices, creating common and team assigned areas, and so on). The very frequent restructurings occurring over a rather brief period seemed to result in very significant increases in felt stress and decreases in the morale of managers and engineering professionals. It is also possible that company performance has been adversely impacted although that is difficult to determine.

The structural changes in the company seem to stem from a variety of sources, including the company's desire to grow through adding new product accounts. Acquisitions were also carried out to obtain new products and processes. The newly adopted computer technologies seemed to have put considerable pressure on the organization to formalize its procedures in order to incorporate and benefit from some computerized planning and scheduling systems such as MRP. The movement from an employee-owned company to one where the owners are a distant parent company which may have significant debt obligations has imposed significant profit and cash flow and accounting measurement requirements which were not present in its past. Many of the new organizational arrangements, especially the most recent changes such as the use of TQM, quality circles, concurrent engineering concepts, employee empowerment, and the open office concept seem to reflect adoption of what some would call the latest management 'fads' currently being taught in MBA programs; there appears to be a good deal of imitation of programs that other companies in the United States are experimenting with. Changes in top management personnel are related to many of the changes occurring in this company, as the new managers bring to the company practices from their old company. Certainly many of the efforts of new CEOs to show short-term results and to introduce new faddish management techniques appear to stem from a desire to make a favorable impression on company owners and other investment groups. Of course, some changes installed at Powertech by new managers reflect their normative beliefs about ideal management systems based on their experiences in other companies. Some changes such as the enhanced status of the HRM function seem to be a response to new employee regulations and to the fact that Powertech has been sued a number of times by some employees for alleged discriminatory practices in promotion and hiring. Some organizational changes appear to be designed to accommodate personnel problems such as taking advantage of a particularly strong manager or trying to compensate for a weak one.

The Powertech case presents a not atypical example of the significant and frequent structural changes that many companies throughout the world have gone through in recent years. These changes have created significant adjustment problems for the workforce. Some of the changes made seem to have improved organizational effectiveness, and some may have diminished it. There appears to be a wide variety of underlying reasons for the changes in structure.

Using theory to account for organizational restructuring

All of the theories discussed so far are of some help in understanding the restructuring that is taking place in organizations all over the world. We can see from the examples cited such as Powertech, General Motors, the National Health Service and Fujitsu that no one set of variables as identified in a particular theory can explain why restructurings occur or predict the form that such restructurings will take. Of course, a particular theory may be helpful in explaining the timing and form of a particular structural change in a particular organization at some point in its history. Thus, at Powertech, structural change A was carried out because of factor Y, but change B was implemented later because of factors X and Z.

That the cases reveal mixed-motive structural changes is not uncommon. A particular change was created to take advantage of a new environmental opportunity (for example, buy a small firm, and so on), improve the ability of the organization to implement a particular strategy (for example, increase quality), mimic the practices of a leading firm because of normative beliefs or to add to legitimacy, and also to contribute to a positive image of the primary change agent (for example, a new CEO). Over time, these changes form a patchwork of organizational structuring.

In the Powertech case the company made many changes in its structure over time to accommodate both various environmental changes and a chosen strategy of organizational growth and product diversification. In addition, other sources or causes of change included the opportunity to:

- develop new product markets;
- take advantage of new technological systems such as computer-aided design and Materials Resource Planning (MRP) procedures;
- increase efficiency so as to achieve the revenues and cash flows to pay off debt or to satisfy new owners;
- help improve the personal image of new top managers;
- satisfy the normative notions of top managers as to what an effective organization should be;
- mimic other exemplary firms.

The organizational acquisitions that Powertech made and some of its many alliances can be explained by its attempts to acquire very important resources that it needed, including technological processes as well as new products and product components. Also, the economics of transaction costs suggests that the top managers realized it was much cheaper to develop a relationship with an outside organization than it would have been to develop something in-house. Interestingly, Powertech often acquired small organizations for a while and then sold off the smaller organization after incorporating whatever knowledge, products, or processes they needed into their internal operations. Also, some of this particular company's organizational history reflected the norms of its original engineers and these probably were developed in the academic institutions or corporate research facilities in which they studied or worked. Further, the mandated isomorphism from various regulations and the personal intrinsic satisfactions arising from managers and professionals performing better were important influences on the organization's frequent restructuring efforts. Of course, some of these influences were more important at a particular time in the company's history than at other times. Perhaps explanatory and predictive theories of organizational restructuring will have to be superimposed on various stages of organizational growth in order to be truly useful.

The Powertech case also illustrates that for many companies, especially smaller ones, restructuring efforts may stem initially from some imperative imposed by other acquiring organizations who have their own agenda or reasons for making the acquisition. Thus, the restructuring of large organizations automatically imposes restructuring of smaller or dependent organizations, making this a rather complex phenomenon indeed.

Restructuring in the future for world-class competition

It may well be that traditional approaches to understanding how firms structured their organizations have become less helpful in understanding adaptation to the unprecedented volatility and unpredictability of environmental change in today's global economy. For example, traditional theorizing held either that firms sought to fit their structures to environmental contingencies or that the environment selected structures that would be most adaptable. Recently, however, the boundaries between organizations and their environments have become increasingly undefined.

As companies struggle to stay ever closer to their customers, more fluid conceptualizations of structuring mechanisms have emerged. Instead of prizing fit between organizational structure and environmental uncertainty – a goal that leaves managers in rapidly changing situations always at least one step behind – organizations have begun to focus on core competencies, knowledge workers, and an optimally efficient or minimally necessary commitment to tangible assets. In post-industrial economies, proprietary knowledge or information, and the educated worker who embodies them, have increasingly become the focus of many leading organizations. In today's world, managing the firm involves the deployment of these knowledge workers within fluid, flexible networks that promote the optimum improved utilization of this human capital and other organizational resources and strengths. The horizontal organization is one term that has been coined to describe firms that elevate the management of processes over all other factors (Byrne, 1993).

In such an organization, vertical hierarchy is minimized in favor of establishing groups based on process, not function. These groups enable the firm to maximize the efficiency and effectiveness of each process and the talents of those multidisciplinary employees assigned to each of the process groups. These process competencies then constitute a competitive advantage for the firm since they can help achieve a high level of efficiency, quality, and customer service, all at the same time.

Although this type of structure does emphasize the technological imperative theories described earlier, it is actually much more than this and
incorporates factors highlighted by the other theories as well. This type
of structure emphasizes the study of the value-added of each employee
and each activity. Taken together with lean production, these aspects
of network structuring echo the classical concepts of Frederick Taylor's
efficiency model of organizations. Still, these newer organizational
forms represent an evolution of thinking from several past eras.

Any useful new theory is likely to combine factors identified in
several older theories in new and meaningful ways. However, some
research has identified common problems associated with all or most
non-traditional methods of structuring organizations, not the least of
which are misfits between structure and environment, excessive meetings, and increased paperwork (see Miles and Snow, 1992). This
research also has identified why specific types of non-traditional
methods of structuring organizations have failed (see Table 3.2).

In the meantime, as businesses confront the new realities of global
competition, a bifurcation appears to be emerging among the post-
industrial nations. This is contributing to some of the more complex
international organizational alliances that seem to be arising at the present time. Witness the incredibly complex interorganizational relationships of companies such as Fujitsu which has many contractual
relationships with a variety of North American, European, and Asian
companies in other countries. Firms in some countries attempt only to
establish themselves or focus on standardized products or services whose
manufacture or delivery are relatively straightforward and require little
proprietary or tacit knowledge. Such firms must establish themselves as
world-class suppliers. To do so they must focus on cost containment, best
.practices, and other manifestations of the total quality management,
zero-defect ethos that has blessed consumers with unprecedented value,
that is, price/performance tradeoffs, but has forced suppliers to seek
every avenue of cost-containment and quality improvement simultaneously. Of course, some of the traditional theories of structuring can apply
to this situation quite well. In such firms, adapting to these changes has
often had significant implications for employees, and those that can be
replaced by computational infrastructure often are; those who remain
work under increased stress and must continue to develop new skills to
retain and develop marketable skills. Managers may create new forms
of loyalty by securing for current employees the opportunities for learning and upgrading of marketable, rather than company-specific, skills.
Insecure employment relationships may be less stressful for employees
if they can simultaneously acquire the skills required to obtain new jobs
in other organizations, if necessary.

Broadly speaking, a second group of businesses has chosen to unleash
itself from commitment to fixed assets. They engage in knowledge-
intensive industries in which possession of proprietary information and

Table 3.2   Reasons for the failure of non-traditional methods of structuring organizations[†]

Consortia
- participating firms assign only weaker employees to consortia
- undercapitalization
- reluctance to share proprietary knowledge

Matrix organizations
- excessive role conflict because some organizational members report to two or more superiors
- power struggles between the functional and programmatic managers

Joint ventures/strategic alliances
- top managers spend over half of their time on establishing joint ventures but only 8% on establishing management systems
- incompatible organizational cultures
- the joint venture must respond to the unique demands of each of its parents, who may well number three or more (Badaracco, 1992)

Mergers/acquisitions
- unrelated lines of business
- excessive borrowing or debt to finance the merger (Economist Publications, 1994)
- incorrect assumptions, for example, key managers of the acquired company will stay and a boom market does not crash

Network structures/organizations
- suppliers may decide to manufacture *and sell* the products themselves
- firms lose the ability to manufacture a specific product or to offer a distinctive service (The Hollow Corporation, 1987; Miles and Snow, 1992)

† A consortium is a group of organizations that join together to pursue a particular project, usually involving research and development projects. A matrix organization is one in which both functional and divisional chains of command are utilized simultaneously. A joint venture is a form of strategic alliance in which two or more organizations legally create a separate, new organization with its own equity base to pursue a particular strategic activity, such as a new product or new distribution network as an ongoing concern. Mergers involve the combination of two or more organizations into a new organization. Acquisitions are the purchase and incorporation of one organization by another. Network structures involve the disaggregation of major functions and subcontracting out of activities to distinct organizations whose activities are loosely brokered by a network hub or headquarters.

skills that cannot easily be imitated or transferred allows for more than the razor-thin profit margins of the globally competitive manufacturer.

Of course, some of these businesses have chosen to focus on cost-containment where possible, but they try to derive value from knowledge, relationships, and other intangibles that cannot easily be duplicated by global competitors. In the face of global competition, for example, the relationship between buyer and supplier often has changed. This change, however, has often meant that the more powerful buyer has taken advantage of the weaker supplier by squeezing the margins of suppliers and forcing them into debilitating cost-cutting to retain the relationship. Still, in some instances, trust between supplier and buyer has emerged, and cooperative relationships that foster win/win transactions have been established as in the Swiss-based Asea Brown Boveri and US Ford Motor Co. relationship (see Case study).

Case study **Buyer–supplier cooperation**

Asea-Brown Boveri (ABB), a Swiss-based conglomerate, and the Ford Motor Co. entered into a 'deferred fixed-price contract' for Ford's Oakville, Canada paint-finishing facility. This involved a three-step process. First, an appropriation price was agreed upon. This appropriation price was 10% less than ABB's initial bid, but still was a price for which ABB would be willing to deliver the turnkey project. A phase of cooperative engineering, however, would follow the step of establishing an appropriation price. Cost savings discerned during this cooperative phase would be shared according to agreed upon contractual procedures. During this cooperative engineering phase, both Ford and ABB brought their distinctive competencies to the project. Ford had experience in operating such plants, while ABB had expertise in state-of-art technology and process design. This cooperative engineering phase also allowed ABB to shore up subcontractor prices below original estimates, ultimately allowing Ford a savings on the appropriation price. Finally, after the three-month cooperative engineering phase, ABB submitted a final fixed-price bid. The cooperative engineering phase had allowed for a period of learning to eliminate information asymmetries. Costs attributed to this contracting problem could thus be eliminated and a final fixed-price bid would reflect this. Either party could still not participate in the project. In the actual case, ABB offered a price approximately 25% below the initial bid. Initial specifications were substantially met, but the planned execution was remarkably different from Ford's original conception of the facility.

Trust is the key ingredient here. Trust resulted from Ford's need for cost savings, ABB's need to succeed in the project as a success that would make or break this portion of the corporation, and the mechanisms of the cooperative engineering period during which trust could be developed.

(*Source*: Adapted from Frey and Schlosser, 1993:65–72)

Human resource management implications of organizational restructurings

The fallout of organizational restructuring on the HRM function is obviously enormous. Perhaps the first and most important consequence of significant downsizing efforts is that the HRM programs become even more critical to an organization's success. The smaller the labor force, the more important it is that all human resources perform well and that the quality of the HRM systems does impact significantly on the quality of the human resources employed. In addition, the quality of human resources has to be much higher to the extent that the organization itself becomes more complex and that the organization decreases its use of formalistic guides such as imposed procedures. For example, research indicates that as an organization becomes less formalized or less bureaucratic, the quality of managers becomes more highly correlated with unit performance (Gillen and Carroll, 1985). Also, decentralization and increased delegation require human resources to be much more competent than in a more centralized organization. Perhaps this is why a number of research studies now indicate that the quality of HRM programs in companies does relate to higher organizational performance (Kravetz, 1990; Martell and Carroll, 1995).

Network organizations involving strategic alliances among various organizations, many of them from various countries around the globe, also have their special HRM problems and issues. This might be especially difficult in relationships between Japanese and US companies since Japanese companies do not prefer formal contractual agreements while US companies do. Also, attempting to integrate personnel from a number of different cultures is enormously difficult and is a task that few HRM divisions are prepared to do well. The ethnocentrism common in the United States and Japan has created a number of problems for firms from these countries in adjusting to partnerships in other nations (Adler, 1991). International HRM in which individuals must be selected, trained, and compensated for overseas positions is still in its infancy.

Many of the restructurings taking place also appear to require a shift from individualistic-oriented employees to more team-oriented or other-centered employees. This is an outcome of a shift to team management systems, network organizational arrangements, concurrent engineering, and TQM systems. Obtaining such individuals requires changes in some of the more traditional and fundamental HRM systems such as selection, training, performance appraisal, and compensation practices. In attempting to identify more cooperative or more team-oriented persons, companies will probably increase their use of approaches such as observing job applicants completing a simulated group task and allowing current team members to select applicants. The cooperative behaviors to be emphasized and thus shaped must be the focus of the organization's performance appraisal and reward systems. Still, organizations must recognize that they may go too far in eliciting such team or group-oriented behaviors. This can result in such problems as social loafing and 'groupthink' problems where individual effort is reduced and/or where creativity is stifled. As we have indicated, Fujitsu obviously believes that there is too much of a group orientation among its employees and it is attempting to encourage more individualistic behaviors. Selecting more group-oriented employees also places new demands on the design and structure of HRM systems. In a recent study, Carroll and colleagues found that variance among people on an individualistic versus a group orientation scale was related significantly to preferences for different types of selection, performance appraisal, and especially compensation systems (Carroll, *et al.*, 1994). If employee acceptability is one criterion used to choose from among alternative HRM practices, this can impact on the form of HRM systems adopted in the near and far future. Some recent reports indicate that the recent extensive restructurings have tended to create considerable stress and fear among employees in organizations involved in such efforts. This may be one reason why there is some evidence that such restructurings may not have succeeded in achieving their objectives of improving organizational financial performance; GM's latest earnings notwithstanding. There is also evidence that recent restructurings have significantly decreased trust in management on the part of lower-level employees (Hay Group, 1990). This mistrust has undoubtedly been influenced by the fact that CEO earnings have been rising significantly in recent years (while real wages of lower levels has been decreasing) under formulas established by stockholder groups using agency theory to force attention to their interests. Perhaps some of these problems could be mitigated by the increasing tendency to mimic Japanese HRM of utilizing two workforces, one relatively permanent and one temporary, which have different expectations for treatment by the organization (see Chapter 9).

In summary, organizations have been restructuring at an unprecedented level in recent years. These restructurings have tended to involve downsizing, greater decentralization, greater delegation, greater product divisionalization, much more extensive use of strategic inter-organizational alliances, a move from individualistic to more teamwork-oriented systems, and many other changes widely popularized in the professional and academic literature. We have identified the environmental, technological, and economic forces influencing such restructurings along with the various formal theories which attempt to highlight the specific factors that are most important in particular situations. Knowing the important causal factors in restructurings can help predict their frequency and the forms they are likely to take in specific companies. Some of the more obvious implications for human resource management practices associated with these restructurings were identified, and subsequent chapters will analyze many more of them in detail.

References

Adler, N. J. (1991). *International Dimensions of Organizational Behavior*, 2nd edn. Boston, MA: PWS-Kent Adler.

Arrow, K. (1974). *The Limits of Organization*. New York: W.W. Norton.

Badaracco, J.L. Jr. (1992). *Knowledge Link: How Firms Compete through Strategic Alliances*. Boston, MA: HBS Press.

Barnard, C.I. (1938). *The Functions of the Executive*. Cambridge, MA: Harvard University Press.

Bradley, S.P., Hausman, J.A., and Richard L. Nolan. (1993). *Globalization Technology and Competition: The Fusion of Computers and Telecommunications in the 1990s*. Boston: Harvard Business School Press.

Burns, T. and Stalker, G.M. (1961). *The Management of Innovation*. London: Tavistock Publications.

Byrne, J. (1993). The horizontal corporation, *Business Week*. 20 December, 76–81.

Caines, P. (1993). The new regions: more please, *The Health Summary*. October.

Carroll, S.J. (1993). *Changing HRM Systems at Fujitsu*. Working Paper. College of Business, University of Maryland.

Carroll, S.J., Ramamoorthy, N. and Erez, M. (1994). Relationship of individualism-collectivism orientations to preferences for alternative HRM practices. In Symposium: Work Motivation Across Cultures: Theory and Research Application. 23rd International Congress of Applied Psychology. Madrid, Spain, July 1994.

Chandler, A.D., Jr. (1962). *Strategy and Structure: Chapters in the History of the American Industrial Enterprise*. Cambridge, MA: MIT Press.

Coase, R.H. (1937). The nature of the firm, *Economica*, 4, (November), 386–405.

DiMaggio, P.J., and Powell, W.W. (1983). The iron cage revisited: institutional isomorphism and collective rationality in organizational fields, *American Sociological Review*, 48, (April), 147–60.

Economist Publications (1994). Making a meal of mergers, *The Economist*, 10 September, 87–8.

Fayol, H. (1949). *General and Industrial Management*, London: Pitman (first published in 1919).

Flood, P. (1991). The National Health Service (NHS) reforms: implications for management practice at hospital level. Paper presented at London School of Economics, Industrial Relations Research Seminar, Cumberland Lodge, Great Windsor Park, England, 26 November.

Frey, Jr. S.C. and Schlosser, M.M. (1993). ABB and Ford: creating value through cooperation, *Sloan Management Review*, Fall, 65–72.

Galbraith, J. (1973). *Designing Complex Organizations*. Boston: Addison-Wesley.

Galbraith, J. (1977). *Organization Design*. Reading, MA: Addison-Wesley.

Gillen, D.J. and Carroll, S. J. (1985). Relationship of managerial ability to unit effectiveness in more organic versus more mechanistic departments. *Journal of Management Studies*, 22, 351–9.

Goffman, E. (1959). *Presentation of Self in Everyday Life*. New York: Anchor.

Hay Group (1990). *The Hay Human Resource Forecast 1991–2000: Trends Shaping Organizations in the Next Decade*. New York: The Hay Group, 1271 Avenue of the Americas.

Hollow Corporation (1987). *Business Week*, 3 March, 57–74.

Kravetz, D.J. (1990). *The Human Resources Revolution*. San Francisco: Jossey-Bass.

Lawrence, P.R. and Lorsch, J. (1967). *Organization and Environment: Managing*

Differentiation and Integration. Boston: Graduate School of Business Administration, Harvard University.

Mangham, I.L. and Overington, M.A. (1987). *Organizations as Theatre: A Social Psychology of Dramatic Appearances*. Chichester: John Wiley.

Martell, K. and Carroll, S.J. (1995). Which executive human resource management practices for the top management team are associated with higher firm performance? *Human Resource Management* (In press).

Meyer, J.W. and Rowan, B. (1977). Institutionalized organizations: formal structure as myth and ceremony, *American Journal of Sociology*, 83 (September), 340–63.

Miles, R.E. and Snow, C.C. (1992). Causes of failure in network organizations, *California Management Review*, Summer, 53–72.

National Health Service (1993). The new look NHS, *The Health Summary*. London: HMSO.

Pettigrew, A., Ferlie, E., and McKee, L. (1992). *Shaping Strategic Change in Large Organizations: The Case of the National Health Service*. London: Sage.

Pfeffer, J. (1992). *Managing with Power*. Boston, MA: Harvard Business School Press.

Pfeffer, J. and Salancik, G.R. (1978). *External Control of Organizations*. New York: Harper & Row.

Powell, W.W. (1990). Neither market nor hierarchy: network forms of organization, *Research in Organizational Behavior*, 12, 295–336.

Scott, W.R. (1992). *Organizations: Rational, Natural, and Open Systems*, 3rd edn. Englewood Cliffs, NJ: Prentice-Hall.

Sonnenfeld, J. and Lazo, M. (1989). United Parcel Service. In Foulkes, F.K. and Livernash, E.R. (eds) *Human Resources Management: Cases and Text*. Englewood Cliffs, NJ: Prentice-Hall, 448–80.

Taylor, Alex III (1994). 'GM's $11 billion turnaround', *Fortune*, 17 October, 54–74.

Taylor, F.W. (1911). *The Principles of Scientific Management*. New York: Harper.

Weber, M. (1947). *The Theory of Social and Economic Organization*, trans. and eds, Henderson, A.H. and Parsons, T. Glencoe, IL: The Free Press (first published in 1924).

Williamson, O.E. (1975). *Markets and Hierarchies: Analysis and Antitrust Implications*. New York: The Free Press

Wood, R.E. and Maguire, M. (1993). *Private Pay for Public Work: Performance Pay Schemes for Public Sector Managers*. Paris: OECD Press.

Woodward, J. (1970). *Industrial Organization: Behavior and Control*. London: Oxford University Press.

4

Managing without traditional owners: Human resource management and management buyout

Introduction

During the past ten years there has been an unmistakable trend towards strategic re-orientation. Fashionable phrases like 'back to the core business' and 'meaner and leaner' have dominated many discussions in board rooms worldwide. As a result the composition of many holding companies has changed dramatically. In this setting companies are disposing of entire divisions or letting branches strike out on their own. The newly defined strategic course is often either a survival strategy or a deliberate choice made to reinforce the strategic capabilities of the company. At the same time, companies are considering initiatives which restructure incentives at the level of the firm and bring the interest of the owners, management, and workers closer together in order to create a situation of mutual benefit. Such a situation of mutual benefit can be reached only if low-trust relations are transformed into high-trust relations. This chapter examines some significant cases of employee ownership gained through a management buyout and assesses its impact upon economic performance, industrial relations and human resource management (HRM).

Researchers using evidence from different contexts demonstrate that, by and large, there is enhanced economic performance in the great majority of buyout companies.[†] It seems quite likely that the better health of the company has something to do with the alterations in internal labor

---

† Researchers using evidence from different contexts are: for the USA, Kaplan (1988, 1989); Kieschnick (1987) and Singh (1990). For the UK, Wright and Coyne (1985); Thompson, *et al.* (1990a, 1990b). For the Netherlands, Bruining (1992) and Bruining and Herst (1993).

markets associated with the buyout. Suggested causes of improved economic performance are the fact that parent-company overhead costs are eliminated, decision making is quicker, and operational readiness is greater because company policy is determined autonomously.

However, little attention has been devoted to possible contributions to performance improvement achieved through initiatives in the areas of personnel management and industrial relations. Meanwhile, other research has shown that the shape of HRM is influenced by the chosen strategic options of the dominant coalition (see Chapter 2). In the theoretical literature with regard to strategic HRM (SHRM) and industrial relations we find abundant reference to the interrelationships between strategic policies and changes and aspects of HRM.[†] However, with regard to management buyouts empirical evidence seems lacking. This raises the question of whether the buyout involves changes in HRM and whether the newly independent companies use aspects of HRM to promote successful *implementation* of the buyout. When a buyout occurs, HRM seems to become more strategic in focus. The shock effect of the buyout seems to create the need for legitimating mechanisms for organizational change.

A possible schism could of course evolve after the buyout if problems develop and employees do not agree with management decisions, for example, a layoff. This could have some serious motivational effects. The buyout impacts upon motivation, commitment, cost consciousness, self-supervision, horizontal monitoring, and vertical monitoring, and the impact, while generally positive, can also have some negative consequences. In the specific situation of a buyout, management should be aware of the need to address this issue.

After the buyout conventional shareholder structures are questioned and the contribution of HRM to the revitalization of organizations through management buyouts becomes of paramount importance. Strong ties with corporate strategy need to be developed with much attention given to both efficient and effective deployment of personnel, intensive involvement of line management, and the utilization of personnel activities, all of which must be welded into a consistent whole. The ultimate goal is to gain competitiveness by doing things right, fast, on time, cheaply, and flexibly (see also Chapter 1). In this context the key HRM goals become the creation of strategic integration, commitment, and flexibility. It seems worthwhile to trace the extent to which these assumptions are reflected in the actual practice of the newly independent buyout companies studied.[‡]

---

† Studies by Huiskamp (1988), Siegel (1989) and Paauwe (1989) indicate that, in the implementation of strategic decisions, companies often incisively review the use of employees, for example, the substitution of indirect labor for direct labor in order to enhance productivity.

‡ Obviously, HRM is not an isolated department which all by itself determines the fate

This chapter has three objectives. First, we want to highlight the unique features of organizations without traditional owners. We will do so by introducing the phenomenon of the management buyout as a shift from traditional corporate structures to a new organizational design which is expected to be a source of competitiveness. Post-buyout economic performance will be discussed both theoretically and empirically in the second section headed 'Management buyouts'.

Second, we will explore how HRM contributes to the successful implementation of management buyouts by concentrating on the question: Which aspects of HRM are used to enhance the success of buyouts? In the section on 'The contribution of HRM to management buyout success' we present the findings of our research project providing some answers to this question. Following on this we discuss in particular the importance of the extent of equity owned by employees after the buyout and the problem of takers and non-takers. In the final section of the chapter we provide our overall conclusions.

First of all, the case of 'Boekhoven-Bosch' is presented. This illustrates how HRM contributes to the management of an organization after a management buyout, themes which will be explored throughout the chapter.

Boekhoven-Bosch

In the early 1980s the multinational, Elsevier, decided to implement a strategic reorientation by emphasizing its core activities. Consequently, the printing company Boekhoven-Bosch, an Elsevier subsidiary, became an independent firm via a management buyout.

The works council was formally asked to advise.[†] Consultations

---

of a buyout. Rather, an integrated company strategy arises in the interaction of HRM with financial strategy, commercial strategy, and so on, and HRM provides the framework for handling problems every day which otherwise could lead to disaster after the buyout. Schendel (1993) emphasizes that the success of corporate restructuring very much depends upon achieving a fit between three dimensions simultaneously: portfolio of businesses, organization of the work itself, and the financial/governance structure of the firm. Clearly, HRM has a critical role to play within each of these dimensions.

† In the Netherlands so-called works councils have been established in order to provide for legal and formal forms of industrial democracy. The first law on works councils dates back to 1950. Nowadays works councils are mandatory in firms with 100 or more employees, and with more limited tasks and rights in firms with 35 to 99 employees. They are elected from and by the firm's employees and meet with management at least six times a year. Apart from providing information on a number of issues, management needs the permission of the works council for a number of HRM related topics like arrangements in the field of personnel training, personnel evaluation, work consultations, bonus or job-evaluation systems, plans for establishing, altering or canceling labor regulations, and arranging pension, profit-sharing, or savings schemes.

The works council is composed of members elected by the employees of the company from among themselves.

with the works council and the labor unions focused on compensation for the loss of fringe benefits. Once an agreement on compensation was reached, the works council reacted positively to the proposed buyout, as did the trade unions.

In 1988 the organization was examined in depth. This led to a number of recommendations emphasizing the need for the organization to shift to a type of management that leads rather than commands and the introduction of a more strategic approach to human resource management.

This HRM policy covered at least three general areas:

(1) *More attention to human management competency (how leaders interact with other personnel).* Personnel were involved in the business more directly as a means of enhancing a market-oriented attitude. Accordingly, responsibilities were decentralized. Decision making occurred at the lowest possible level. To improve internal communication, team meetings were introduced in each section, as were both informal and formal meetings on the shop floor. Performance appraisals were also introduced. Anything that directly or indirectly touches upon the job was open for discussion.

(2) *Attention to quality-directed efforts, training, and consultation.* For all employees the number of training courses was increased and training opportunities became a recurrent item in performance evaluations. Product quality is pre-eminent at Boekhoven-Bosch. In striving for quality, the organization places heavy demands on the quality of the employees; the emphasis is on final personal responsibility in making decisions and carrying them out effectively.

(3) *An altered relationship between the personnel management department and the line management.* After the management buyout the personnel department was transformed from a specialized, regulating, and bureaucratic body to one with an integral task in management support with a more prominent role for the line management in the implementation of the HRM policy of the company.

From a financial and economic point of view the management buyout was successful. There is remarkable agreement about the contribution of HRM to this success among members of the organization. They feel that the HRM activities initiated after the management buyout have a positive effect on the financial results. Commitment and motivation have increased. The feeling is that the HRM policy has been instrumental in this outcome. The organization has become less centralized, not just because of the reduction in the number of echelons but due to altered communication patterns which have strengthened unity in the firm.

The employees needed some time to grow accustomed to the new forms of consultation and the idea of working together in teams. Therefore pressure mounted at the supervisory level; it was they who were supposed to implement the changes, remind employees of their responsibilities, and request participation and voice if these activities were new for these supervisors.

This case study illustrates how personnel management at Boekhoven-Bosch was revamped following the buyout. Many are sure that without the buyout some crucial changes would have met great resistance. After the buyout everybody has become more aware of the company's problems and more sophisticated in dealing with them.

Management buyouts: international evidence

As the Boekhoven-Bosch case illustrates a management buyout is a specific form of managing without traditional owners, with a great emphasis on strategic reorientation.

There are several motives for managers of parent companies and subsidiaries to participate in a buyout. A major survey of Dutch buyouts by the National Investment Bank (NIB) in 1985 identified two important reasons why buyouts took place:

(1) The parent company faced serious financial troubles and sold its subsidiaries in order to repay debts or to save healthy subsidiaries from bankruptcy.
(2) The parent wanted to pull out of certain industries which no longer fitted into its basic core activities.

Other frequently mentioned motives playing a minor role were:

- different opinions on the company's strategy;
- enhancing management and control at the headquarters of the buyout company;
- obtaining better market opportunities for the parent and/or the subsidiary in order to increase returns on investment;
- management has been very keen for a long time to become owners of the firm;
- external investors took initiatives to divest.

The divisional buyout is far more popular than other sources, such as the independent company in receivership and the shareholder repurchase. This seems to be the case in the Netherlands as well as in the UK and elsewhere in Europe (Wright and Coyne, 1985; Bruining, 1992; Bruining and Herst, 1993). Although the incumbent management team normally executes the buyout, it accomplishes this task largely through the financial assistance of financial backers. The second source of buyouts, which is rising in importance, is the family business having succession problems. Characteristic of the divisional buyout is the combination of an organizational splitoff and a change in ownership and control. In this chapter, however, we highlight and present data only on the divisional buyout.

The early buyouts in the Netherlands mainly stemmed from parent companies having to cope with serious financial troubles. Examples of such parent companies include RSV, OGEM, and Van Gelder Papier. The managers of several of their subsidiaries, not wanting to be dragged into liquidation, bought their firms from the parent companies. Thus the management buyout prevented the subsidiary from drowning with the parent.

The management buyouts we have just mentioned are so-called *defensive* buyouts; in general, the top management lost control over the varied and heterogeneous collection of companies or unrelated diversification, which was not a panacea for the worldwide recession during the late 1970s. Managers, employees, trade unions, and governmental agencies considered such management buyouts to be a device of the last resort to save a company.

In the period 1980–3 66% of all buyouts fell in this category. The growth of buyouts in the Netherlands was helped by the government scheme introduced in 1981 underwriting half of the losses incurred on risk-taking (venture capital) shareholdings provided that certain conditions were met. After some years of experience with buyouts, which became successful by altering their way of management as well as their financial and organizational structures, the reasons motivating buyouts began to change. Recently, unlike the period up to the mid-1980s, there has been a reduction in defensive buyouts. Rather, the emphasis in the market has shifted towards more positive reasons for corporate restructuring. This type of buyout we call *offensive*, because the parent company adopts product-market strategies which concentrate all the available resources on the core business activities. This releases unessential units for possible management buyouts. These activities give the parent companies a competitive advantage over other competitors who continue to carry the overhead costs of peripheral lines of business. Managers of subsidiaries not belonging to these core activities saw their chance and bought their firms from the parent companies. The so-called 'back-to-the-basics movement' has therefore resulted in offensive buyouts. In contrast to the defensive buyouts, the offensive ones are part of the strategic policy of the conglomerate and are, in general, better planned and prepared. This policy is still a major source of buyouts. Without having severe problems, several Dutch conglomerates succeeded in a timely divestment of their subsidiaries which no longer fitted their strategic direction.[†]

[†]   In the period 1987–90 the defensive buyouts decreased to 16%, as the offensive ones increased from 28 to 67%. Across the whole period 1980–90 34% of the buyouts were defensive, 55% offensive, and about 11% not classified.

Buyouts from corporate restructuring, defensive as well as offensive ones, were characteristic of the 1980s, but seem to have staying power also in the following decade. The early 1990s showed a majority of buyouts from (foreign) parent companies which faced financial problems or underwent more active strategic redirections in order to reshape their product portfolios. However, it became evident that family succession was more and more frequently mentioned as a source of buyouts and buy-ins.

Further, the Dutch buyout market may be characterized as displaying several of the necessary conditions for buyout development, especially a need to effect ownership transfer, a healthy venture capital industry, and a legal framework which facilitated such transactions. In the Netherlands, in the early 1980s, management buyouts became a means by which companies could deal with recessionary problems, and these buyouts were supported by the third largest venture capital industry in Europe which was able to undertake such buyout transactions because of a favorable taxation and legal framework. Besides, works councils and supervisory boards frequently made it difficult for unwelcome outside bidders to succeed (Bruining and Herst, 1991:213).

A study of the Dutch Venture Capital Association (NVP) shows that during 1986–90 these institutions realized a 68% increase on their investments in management buyouts originating in the early 1980s (selling prices divided by initial investments). Half of their investments in management buyouts account yearly for ROIs of 15% or more, and a quarter of them for ROIs of more than 50%.

Bruining reports similar findings (Bruining, 1992; Bruining and Herst, 1993). According to this study, the financial ratios of medium-sized and large management buyouts show significantly better cash flow, sales, and return on investment during 1980–90 compared to industry averages. Even in the longer run, for example, three to six years after the management buyout took place, the figures related to these ratios remain statistically better than the industry averages. Bruining completed a sample survey in order to compare different financial ratios of 73 companies after the management buyout with the industry averages (36 small and 37 medium-sized management buyouts). For 22 companies the comparison involved a continuous period of two years; for 21 companies a continuous period of three years; and for 30 firms four or more years. Over a range of seven years, starting from the year in which the buyout took place, we were able to compare the economic performances of different groups of management buyouts with the industry averages. The research shows that during 1980–88 the financial ratios of medium-sized Dutch management buyouts related to cash flow, sales, and ROI were *significantly better* than the average financial ratios of the industries involved. Based on these findings, we conclude that explanations for the statistically better financial ratios of medium-sized management buyouts compared to the industry averages are more firm-specific than industry-specific.

In 1994 we saw a trend towards closer cooperation between Venture Capital Companies of different European countries on the continent which anticipate bigger cross-national border deals in the near future. The Nationale Investeringsbank NV of the Netherlands (NIB) is aiming to expand its venture capital activities beyond the Dutch border. Another Dutch Venture Capital Company, Alpinvest, joined forces with an English investment company, Candover Investment, in setting up a fund for investing in European countries. West German, Spanish, and French partners may be found at a later date.

Analyzing the branches of industry where management buyouts occurred after 1977, we identified a shift from the traditional to non-traditional branches of industry (Bruining and de Jong, 1989). Some examples of the traditional sectors are printing, building, machinery, wood industry, food, and textiles. Examples of the non-traditional sectors are management consulting, software houses, service industries, and highly technical equipment. This chapter indicates that new branches of industry assumed the lead in management buyout transactions after 1984.

If we look at international studies about the economic performance of buyouts, then we obtain the following impression (Wright and Robbie, 1991). Across all buyouts in the UK – a study of the initial consequences of buyout for 111 private sector cases up to late 1983 (a period largely characterized by recession) – 82% showed improvements in profitability, trading relationships, cash and credit control systems, and evidence of new product development. The sample showed considerable changes in employment and management structure (Wright and Coyne, 1985). These findings are supported by a second survey of 57 buyouts over the same period undertaken by Hanney (1986). A subsequent survey by CMBOR of 182 UK buyouts completed between mid-1983 and early 1986, a period of industrial recovery, lent support to these earlier studies, but also found certain differences. For the majority of respondents, trading profits and turnover were found to be 'better' or 'substantially better' than before the buyout and in excess of expectations contained in the business plan (Thompson, et al., 1989). Also, both product development and customer bases are enhanced by the separation from the restrictions imposed by a parent, despite widespread efforts to reduce trading dependence (Wright, 1986). The general state of trading relationships between customers and suppliers seems to improve greatly after the buyout. One third of buyouts which arose because of divestment experienced cash-flow problems afterwards, with pre-buyout difficulties caused by central control of cash flow and post-buyout difficulties involving the servicing of highly leveraged financial structures. About a half of divestment buyouts subsequently made managerial adjustments, with changes in the management team, the appointment of new managers, and changes in the number at management level, each occurring in about one tenth of the transactions. A study of the changes in accounting control systems following a buyout shows that the reintegration of ownership and control enables more appropriate systems to be introduced, especially at the strategic level (Jones, 1988). There was also evidence of a perpetuation of standard performance reports, influenced by the requirements of financial backers who wished to ensure that buyouts were effectively controlled in order to meet their finance servicing costs. Similarly managerial decision making was heavily influenced by the need to meet the financial targets demanded by venture capitalists and other investors.

A study of the longer-term performance of buyouts in the UK using operating performance data confirmed the favorable short-term results, but found that after three years profitability declined (Warwick Business School, 1989). However, this study is quite limited as the longer-term results are based on samples well below double figures, and some firms are not buyouts. Moreover, the figures may be biased downwards, as high performing buyouts which have exited are excluded. A study of 366 buyouts which were funded by the market leader 3i showed that rates of return were above those for all 3i investments, and this study was unable to confirm that performance fell in the longer term (Bannock, 1990). Studies of UK buyouts which have exited by flotation on a stock market show that performance as measured by increases in company value exceeds market indices both prior to flotation and afterwards, although post-flotation performance tended to slow down (Thompson, et al., 1989; Wright, et al., 1987).

While all of this evidence concerning performance improvements in buyouts is strongly positive, it has not been clear what factors have contributed most to the changes which occur. However, a recent study of 28 buyouts has shown that the size of the management equity stake is the most important factor in explaining improvements in performance after a buyout (Thompson, et al., 1989).

In the empirical performance literature two different kinds of theoretical arguments are offered for improvements in economic performance after the management buyout: value creation and non-interventionism. The explanation of value creation due to management interventions asserts that management buyouts are made feasible through major changes in asset management after the buyout. The non-interventionism arguments, such as tax benefits, inadequate leverage, and managerial opportunism or the information asymmetry argument, assume no significant post-buyout changes in the operations of the firm. Such arguments draw upon pre-buyout tax saving, substitution of equity by debt, and undervaluation of the company as the primary drivers of post-buyout gain.

However, our research does not support the tax-saving and inadequate leverage argument, because the significantly higher debt levels of management buyout companies compared with those of the industry averages disappear a couple of years after the management buyout, while performance improvement continues (Bruining, 1992; Bruining and Herst, 1993). Neither does the evidence found in our research support the managerial opportunism argument. If managers buy control of the company because they believe that the company is significantly undervalued by external investors, it is only a question of timing to 'cash out' through a sale or a public offering after the management buyout. Why then do we observe cash flow, sales, and return on investment ratios higher than the averages of the industries? Our conclusions as we shall see are consistent with the empirical studies of Kaplan (1988) and Singh (1990).

Our analysis of the performance literature, together with the results of our comparative financial ratio study of management buyouts and non-management buyouts, convinced us that the value after the management buyout is primarily created by actions of the buyout management team. As Chapter 2 has already shown, the top management team (TMT) plays a dominant role in crafting the internal resource capabilities of the firm. Key actions by the TMT in buyout situations include a flattening of the organizational structure, decentralized decision making, the use of teams, introduction of more focused HRM, and so forth.

Agency theory explanations of post-buyout economic performance

There are, of course, theoretical explanations for the favorable outcomes associated with buyouts. For our explanation we use agency theory. First, we give a financial-economic explanation that is based on theoretical findings about the relationship between the newly independent management team and the investors. Then we give an internal-organizational explanation using empirical evidence about the relationships between the management of the parent company and of the (former) subsidiary and between management and employees of the newly independent company.

The nature of contractual obligations and rights between management and investors is effectively specified in formal contracts. However, the obligations and rights of management and employees are much more varied and generally not as well specified in explicit contractual arrangements. Therefore the organizational-operational analysis of the agency costs, generated at every level of the organization, is more difficult than the financial-economic analysis. Nevertheless, we believe that our analysis in both areas provides insight in the changing relationships between all involved parties after the management buyout.

According to agency theory, the buyout represents a situation in which an existing company makes a fresh start, free from the parent company to which it belonged. Some managers characterize the buyout as an earthquake in the life of the company. We must also stress the meaning of it for the manager himself. He becomes an owner, and the division between ownership and management disappears which in theory can be expected to reduce the shareholder–manager agency problem.

Separating from the parent company is asking for an overwhelming amount of work. After the buyout, in general, one or more changes take place, for example in the products, prices, distribution, promotion, and service strategy. New contracts have to be arranged and new policies and business plans have to be made. In several cases new pension schemes or a new bookkeeping system have to be set up, business staff units have to be reorganized, business insurance has to be taken out, and so on.

As a result of the buyout, the relationships between the internal and external participants and between the internal participants also change. Particular examples include the relationships between investors and management of the newly independent company, between management of the parent and management of its former subsidiary, and between management of the company and employees.

Relationships between internal and external participants and between internal participants constitute the hard core of the agency theory. That is why we make use of this economic-organizational theory for our explanation of the improved economic performance after a buyout, for it emphasizes the relationship between a principal and his agent, who is supposed to pursue the principal's objectives. Agency theory involves the specifications of the contractual relationships between external and internal participants and between internal participants and therefore offers new combinations of risks and incentives for management–employee relationships and the investor–management relationships after the buyout. The new owners of the firm will do their utmost to make the transaction successful; they will tend to use new motivational approaches when dealing with employees so as to generate increased effort and commitment; and they will be sensitive to the demands and needs of the investors who made the buyout possible.

Framework for agency theory

In agency theory the unit of analysis is the contractual relationship between the principal and agent. The essence of the relationship is the delegation of decision-making authority and responsibility to the agent by the principal. The agent makes decisions and carries out activities on behalf of the principal, for which he is rewarded by the principal. According to agency theory, the company is structured by contracts between principals and agents at different levels in the company.

As Chapter 3 has highlighted, if the principal delegates decision-making authority and responsibility to the agent, he is not a priori certain that the agent will carry out the activities and will make the decisions maximizing the principal's interests. This phenomenon is called the agency problem. Because the principal cannot monitor all the decisions and other activities of 'his' agent and uncontrollable factors influence the agent's performance, it is difficult for the principal to determine the extent to which the results depend on the capability, effort, and devotion of the agent.

As a consequence of this information asymmetry the agent has the opportunity for shirking behavior; the agent has the opportunity to pursue his own interests, thereby prejudicing the interests of the principal. Examples are excessive consumption of perquisites, such as expensive automobiles, luxurious board rooms, and an excessive number of subordinates. By these means the agent achieves some power and status, but he tends to reduce the value of the company because of increased overhead and other expenses.

According to agency theory the principal and the agent have conflicting interests and one of them possibly manipulates a commonly shared risk. This phenomenon is generally termed 'moral hazard', and it is the difficulty that the principal experiences in distinguishing between genuine risks, which the agent cannot possibly control, and failure of the agent to take the best possible action that could avoid the dangerous event (Kaplan, 1982:448). In general, all kinds of sub-optimal behavior are covered by the term moral hazard. Also, due to differences in the attitudes toward risk of the principal and his agent, the agency problem can increase.

To protect himself against the risk of moral hazard and other opportunistic behavior of the agent, the principal uses control measures to stimulate the agent to take decisions which are in the interest of the principal. Jensen and Meckling (1976:308) distinguish three kinds of control measures:

(1) *Monitoring efforts.* This activity includes measuring the effort of the agent by means of budget reports and review sessions, and it includes giving instructions to the agent, operating rules to follow, and so on.
(2) *A reward system* for the agent which is connected to his performance. This system contains a sharing of risks and incentives between the principal and the agent.
(3) *Bonding* or the supplementary agreements on the part of the agent. This activity refers to constraints that the agent is willing to accept in order to guarantee the principal that his actions do not harm him.

Fama and Jensen (1983:345) argue that the agency problem can be reduced by breaking up the decision-making process into the following elements:

(1) *Initiation*: the generation of proposals for resource utilization;
(2) *Ratification*: the selection of decision initiatives to be implemented;
(3) *Implementation*: the execution of ratified decisions;
(4) *Monitoring*: the measurement of the performance of agents and the implementation of rewards.

Stages 1 and 3 are labeled 'decision management' and are delegated to the agent; stages 2 and 4 belong to the domain of the principal and are labeled 'decision control.' Thus the delegation of decision making to the agent is restricted to 'decision management,' and it is controlled by using a system of checks and balances; hierarchy is used to implement this system and discipline behavior in order to reduce the risk of making suboptimal decisions. This partitioning of the decision-making process creates an organizationally well-defined environment for analyzing the distinguishing incentive, monitoring, and bonding relationships. Such control measures will reduce the divergence of interests between the principal and the agent in specifying the monitoring relations, the incentive relations, and bonding relations. Hence the agency theory claims that control measures shape the contractual relationship in such a way that conflicting interests are more or less reconciled between principal and agent at an acceptable cost for the principal. The theory does not stress, but does not deny either, that good faith is an important reason for fulfilling both sides of the contract. Rather, agency theory's recommendations are practical: designing adequate monitoring, incentives, and bonding measures in such a way that will stimulate the agent to pursue the principal's interests.

Still, these measures imply costs, the so-called agency costs. We can distinguish monitoring costs, contracting costs, and bonding costs. In spite of these measures there will typically if not always be a difference between the decisions which the agent makes and those which the principal would have taken. Therefore the principal investor always has a residual cash-flow loss, because of the fact that he can never monitor all the activities of the agent.

According to Jensen and Meckling, a distinction can also be made between agency costs of equity and agency costs of debt. Following Bouma and Van de Poel there are also agency costs of the relationship between management and employees (Bouma, 1988; Poel, 1986:117). The central question is whether the agency costs will increase or decrease after a buyout, an issue we can now address. First, we focus on the relationship between investors and the new managers responsible for the buyout. Then we analyze the relationship between the internal stakeholders of the management buyout company, such as management and employees, and the relationship between the management of the parent company and the management of the (former) subsidiary.

A financial-economic perspective

A management buyout tends to result in a better relationship between the investors and the firm's management, and hence in reduced agency costs and an improved economic performance. There are various reasons for these favorable developments (Bruijn, *et al.*, 1990).

In the first place, by participating in the equity of the firm to be bought out, management shows that it has confidence in the success of the buyout. In other words, the management team signals its bright expectations about the subsidiary by supplying a part of the equity capital required to buy the firm from the present owner (the parent company). If this team participates in the equity of the firm it is going to manage, the agency costs of equity will decrease since the probability of conflicts between equity investors and management will be reduced. This is because, by becoming a shareholder in its own firm, the managers will be less inclined to pursue their own objectives, such as maximizing their own salaries or excessive consumption of perquisites (for example, an expensive office and a company jet), since such actions will reduce the firm's profits to which they, as investors, are entitled. The interests of management and external shareholders will converge because of management's stake in the equity. Moreover, the input from the other investors to decisions will help to increase efficiency and profits. If management finances 100% of the buyout, this type of agency cost will be reduced to zero, as the agent then becomes his own principal; in this way the classical ownership-and-control issue is solved. However, such a situation seldom occurs. Because of the large amounts of money involved in a buyout, management usually has to persuade other investors to participate in the firm's equity. Then the agency costs of equity still have to be taken into consideration.

If the buyout is financed with large amounts of debt, for example by issuing bonds, conflicts between shareholders and bondholders may arise which tend to result in agency costs of debt, such as monitoring and bonding costs. Conflicts between shareholders and bondholders may arise because, generally speaking, bondholders are more risk-averse than shareholders. Therefore, bondholders will try to prevent shareholders, including the firm's management, from accepting risky investment projects partly financed with debt. This can be accomplished by including restrictive covenants in the debt contracts, thus leading to a situation in which there is less room to maneuver.

Second, if the employees participate in their firm's equity, the same effects may result since the relationship between management and/or employer and employees can also be conceptualized as a relationship between a principal and his agents. Thus the agency costs of equity will decrease, and the agency costs of debt will increase.

There is a third reason for a reduction in agency costs and an improved economic performance. Usually the management team planning a buyout is assisted by buyout specialists, who perform several tasks such as advising on matters as estimating the buyout price, conducting negotiations with the parent company, and determining the correct moment for letting suppliers and clients know that a buyout is going to take place. Buyout specialists also assist in raising the necessary funds for the buyout. Besides, they often take care of the monitoring function, that is, supervising management on behalf of the investors. Buyout specialists tend to be motivated to perform the monitoring function in a correct and efficient way. If this were not the case, the investors may lose their confidence in them and the specialists may even get a bad reputation, thus inhibiting their chances of arranging new buyouts in the future. Because of the specialists' experience with previous buyouts, they are able to monitor management in an efficient, relatively inexpensive manner. Therefore, bringing in buyout specialists probably results in lower agency or monitoring costs and, accordingly, in improved economic performance.

Fourth, strip financing causing financial unification may decrease the probability of conflicts between shareholders and bondholders, and thus the agency costs of debt will tend to decrease. Financial unification occurs when investors place their money into the different types of securities a firm has issued (Copeland and Weston, 1988:662–3). So bondholders become shareholders and vice versa. Hence the interests of shareholders and bondholders will tend to parallel one another.

Bringing in buyout specialists also leads to financial unification. We have already discussed the various roles that these specialists play in their buyout. Such specialists are representatives of all categories of investors, whether they provide the firm with debt or with equity. It would not be wise for buyout specialists to evoke conflicts between these categories, for instance, by tempting management to accept risky investment projects in order to favor the shareholders while harming the bondholders. Harming the bondholders in this way will result in their refusal to supply these specialists with funds to finance future buyouts. That is why it is essential for buyout specialists to look after the shareholders' as well as the bondholders' interests.

Finally, if large amounts of debt are utilized to finance a buyout, management will endeavour to amortize the debt as soon as possible. In this way the agency costs of debt will soon decline, and the firm's economic performance will normally improve in a few years after the buyout. Discussing going-private deals, which represent a special type of buyout, Hite and Owers argue: 'If large amounts of debt are taken on during the buyout and reduced shortly thereafter, then it seems that leverage has no longer-range purpose, but it functions principally as part of the mechanism to take the company private' (Hite and Owers, 1988:427).

Due to a buyout the agency costs of equity would then decrease while the agency costs of debt may increase or decrease. Therefore, from a financial-economic point of view it is not always possible to predict the effect of a buyout on the total agency costs. If a buyout is completely financed with equity, the agency costs will decrease; if the firm's management finances 100% of the buyout price, this type of agency costs will even be reduced to zero. If a buyout is financed with a combination of equity and debt, the effect on total agency costs cannot be predicted; these costs may increase or decrease.

According to Table 4.1 the agency costs of equity would decrease due to a buyout. The agency costs of debt may increase or decrease. Therefore, from a financial-economic point of view it is not always possible to predict the effect of a buyout on the total agency costs. If a buyout is completely financed with equity the agency costs will decrease; if the firm's management finances 100% of the buyout price this type of agency costs will even be reduced to zero. If a buyout is financed with a combination of equity and debt the effect on total agency costs cannot be predicted; these costs may increase or decrease.

Managerial incentives in buyouts: an intra-organizational perspective

From our practical and mostly qualitative findings we consider how agency costs are likely to behave in the relationship between principal and agent after the management buyout (Bruining, 1992; Bruijn, *et al.*, 1990). Our focus in this section is on the entrepreneurial and behavioral aspects of management, that is, incentives. The central question is the same as in the previous section, namely, whether or not these agency costs will increase or decrease. But we approach this question from a different angle and try to find out whether intra-organizational agency-relationships offer a fruitful opportunity to explain the improved economic performance after a management buyout. Our empirical findings are classified into two categories: rewards and decision making.

Table 4.1 Management buyout and agency costs; a financial-economic perspective

Measures	Agency costs of equity	Agency costs of debt
Managers become shareholders	−	+
Employees become shareholders	−	+
Monitoring by buyout specialists	−	−
Financial unification	0	−
Rapid amortization of debt	0	−

+ = increase; − = decrease; 0 = no effect.

Rewards

The performance-related reward structure after the buyout leads to a higher effort on the part of the manager and the employees, resulting in a better performance of the company. Management and employees work harder, longer and are better motivated because of the financial participation in the company's equity and the reward system, which re-unites residual claims and control at the operational level. Managing a newly independent company without traditional owners means that the effort and commitment create a keen alertness for threats and opportunities influencing the continuity of the company. One might expect that the extra outcome of this incentive system outweighs the contracting costs which is one of the major categories of agency costs. Whenever ratchets do occur in the buyout, management is even more strongly motivated to reach the financial targets in order to obtain a larger part of the shares from the venture capitalist or to lower the company's debt.

Motivation resulting from the reward contract depends on the possibilities that people have to influence the results substantially. It might be expected that the more people are able to influence the performance of the company, the more they will be rewarded by systems that relate to this possibility. A performance-related part of the wages can be used by top management to hold on to its key personnel and to attract others, thus decreasing the chances of shirking or other opportunistic behavior which will tend to harm the company. Because of this disciplining mechanism, we expect lower monitoring costs and shirking and other opportunistic behavior are consequently reduced.

In reducing the agency costs the reward system should be connected to the performance of the company and attuned to some distribution of risks and incentives between principal and agent.

Decision making

The improved speed with which management buyout companies make decisions can be explained by the following observations:

(1) *The thorough knowledge of the actual and future chances of the bought out company.* Management must possess technical knowledge, product knowledge, and initiate major and minor changes. So the speed can be partly explained by the clear vision of the management team about the direction the company will go in, without the roadblocks of other priorities established by the former parent company. There is often an information asymmetry problem here in that managers of the company will know more about the prospects of the company than the employees; this affects equity participation by employees.

(2) *The increasing quality of decision making.* Both case studies and empirical analyses indicate that the quality of decision making

improves after a buyout because the members of the management team tend to be judicious and balanced in their decision making. After all, they are now acting as statutory directors of the company.

(3) *The information gathering effort.* The whole information gathering effort becomes focused on determining and carrying out the priorities of the newly independent company itself, instead of those of the parent company. Frequent and lengthy consultation with the parent company is no longer required.

(4) *The delegation process.* After the buyout the agency problem can be reduced by delegating to the agent the following elements of the decision-making process: initiation and implementation. The remaining elements such as ratification and monitoring belong to the domain of the principal.

(5) *The system of 'checks and balances.'* This system, used in the hierarchy and implemented through budget and reporting measures, and budget and negotiation procedures, has direct implications for the managers and the employees. Negative performance cannot be transferred to the parent after the buyout, and the newly independent company has to cope with it on its own.

This restructuring of the internal organization can be seen as a reformulation of agreements about work constellations and assignments between principals (managers) and agents (employees). The agents must respond to the priorities which the new owners have established. Thus the agent is inclined to act and behave in favor of the interest of the principal, thus creating lower monitoring and bonding costs. Moreover, the principals are inclined to compare and monitor each others' expenses, a process which will prevent excessive consumption.

As a result of increased responsiveness in operations, in structure and in strategy formulating and implementation, total agency costs will be reduced in spite of the increase in monitoring costs.

In this section we used the agency theory to discuss post-buyout economic performance from a financial-economic perspective and an internal-organizational perspective, both in a theoretical and empirical sense. In the next section we want to further concentrate on the internal-organizational perspective. We set up an additional research project aimed at exploring the possible contribution from an HRM point of view to the successful implementation of a management buyout. The contribution of HRM to the success of the buyout is analyzed with reference to the following key concepts: strategic integration, flexibility, and commitment. *Strategic integration* refers to the integration of HRM with strategic planning, coherence across policy areas and hierarchies, and the extent to which HRM practices are operationalized in a consistent and equitable way by line managers. *Flexibility* refers to two potential sources: functional and numerical flexibility. Functional or task flexibility is sought so that employees can be redeployed quickly and smoothly. This form of flexibility is related to qualitative measures, and it is long-term oriented and proactive. The emphasis is on achieving an adaptable labor force. Numerical flexibility is sought so that the number of employees can be quickly and easily increased or decreased in line with short-term changes in the level of the demand of labor. This quantative control is largely ad hoc, short-term, and opportunistic. *Commitment* refers to the idea that increased mutuality between management and the workforce can increase economic effectiveness and human development. The notion of mutual commitment creates a situation where employees (including the management team) have a strong desire to remain a member of the organization, have a strong belief in, and acceptance of, the values and goals of the organization, and have a readiness to exert considerable effort on behalf of the organization.

The contribution of HRM to management buyout success – some research results

In this section we outline the potential contribution of HRM to strategy and improved performance as indicated by the findings of our research. We executed a number of case studies to find answers to our leading question: Which aspects of HRM are used to enhance the success of management buyouts? A total of 12 case studies were carried out; five by way of primary analysis and seven through secondary analysis. Primary analysis included interviews not only with company directors, but also with other staff members (personnel manager, works council, trade union official). In addition, we consulted company documentation. Secondary analysis applied the specific research angle to existing case-study material. The results served to complement findings from the new material provided by the primary analysis case studies. A list of the companies studied is provided in Appendices 1 and 2 at the end of the chapter.

Research results

The framework of analysis which we use focuses on four aspects of HRM:†

† A more detailed description of this analytical research framework is provided in de Jong (1991).

(1) *Principles:* the values and norms on which HRM is based.
(2) *Objectives:* the objectives of HRM and the main avenues of achieving them.
(3) *Action domains:* clusters of mutually cohering activities and instruments by which HRM is implemented. These activities include recruitment, selection, rewarding, appraisal, and training and also matters like staying in touch with trade unions and the works council.
(4) *Actors and decision making:* in the decision-making process we distinguish three actor categories:
   (a) government (legislation, specialized governmental institutions);
   (b) employers (top management, board of directors, line management, specialized staff departments, personnel management;
   (c) employees (works council, committee for working conditions, trade union activists, trade union officials).

On the assumption that the prior position of the companies would have an impact on the choice of HRM tools used to enhance the success of the buyout, we focused primarily on defensive and offensive buyouts (see the previous section).[†]

Principles and objectives

Buyouts provide a good opportunity to completely review labor utilization within the firm and to allow HRM policies to be re-examined in terms of both their internal consistency and likely contribution to organizational performance. Labor utilization is typically reviewed in both quantitative (efficiency) and qualitative (effectiveness) terms.

The desire to deploy personnel more *efficiently* seldom led to (forced) dismissal. Instead, recruitment embargoes (also known as vacancy stops) were more frequently used.

Additional attempts were made to reduce the ratio of indirect to direct functions within the company. The main objective was to tie labor utilization and the actual size of the workforce directly to company strategy. A reduction of the labor force was often carried out because post-buyout human resource management was more emphatically than before aimed at the deployment of a small, regular core of employees who, in view of their expertise and experience, were not easily replaced (see Chapter 9 for a full review of such approaches). This regular workforce is typically expanded with temporary help whenever the workload calls for them. The smaller workforce, the halt on vacancies

---

† A total of 12 case studies were carried out. These provided us with information regarding the management buyout and the structuring of HRM in their company. Moreover, data were gathered on indicators such as motivation, loyalty, willingness to work overtime, employee turnover, absence because of illness, and productivity. In addition, we consulted company documentation.

and/or internal relocation served to create a better business-economic starting position. This accords well with Atkinson's ideas about the flexible firm. Workforce strategy is increasingly oriented to the core/ring (periphery) distinction in the buyout companies which we studied.

The wish to deploy personnel more *effectively* prompted most of the companies in our study to take measures designed to make better use of employee capacities. The reasons behind this differ from company to company. During the period that the companies were still part of the larger enterprise employees tended to assume an attitude of wait-and-see, and motivation was sometimes low or communication with the employees inadequate. In every case which we studied management sought to change attitudes after the buyout by taking decisive actions, as the following interview extracts from Proforms – one of the buyout companies studied – indicates:

> *Proforms* states that 'we mean to cultivate Proformers from now on.' HRM in *Proforms* now particularly addresses itself to increasing both motivation and involvement of all employees: 'We must join hands to keep the show rolling.' The general manager speaks of 'turning people into collaborators in company development.' The starting point for this was increasing the level of open communication. Prior to the buyout 'the view was widely held that the general manager should keep his hands off the work floor,' since this was the plant manager's domain. Management-by-walking-around became an essential part of the management task. In addition, people were given greater responsibility. More was demanded from the workers. Accordingly, training opportunities were expanded and employees at all levels were subject to rigorous performance evaluations. By way of indicating the company's commitment to its employees working conditions were improved. According to *Proforms*'s general manager these measures were successful. Increased communication between employees and management has helped motivation and enhanced involvement. Operational flexibility especially has improved. The rapid rise in the value of shares has, management states, contributed to 'a tremendous rise in employee motivation and involvement, while employee turnover is almost nil.' Increased market-orientation and the need to meet client demands has led to frequent overtime. This is accepted as part of the job. In spite of overtime and a three-shift schedule, absenteeism because of illness is very low at *Proforms*. People speak of 'our company, our capital, and our success' – phrases which one was much less likely to hear before the buyout.
>
> (Abridged from de Jong, 1991)

Both defensive and offensive buyout companies sought to do away with the passive attitude of wait-and-see, to enhance employee motivation and commitment, to render employee attitudes more flexible, more customer-oriented, and more quality- and/or cost-conscious. To a large degree this was achieved through measures envisioned in HRM policy, on the assumption that personnel is a critical success factor for the company. Personal responsibilities are also defined more strictly. More attention is paid to the workers' own responsibility for tasks and more emphasis is placed on efficient and effective management.

Domains of activities

In the area of labor conditions, many of the buyouts studied created merit systems in order to involve employees more than before in the financial fortunes of the company. In several of the companies studied employees either obtained or were granted options on shares. In some cases these occurred at the time of the buyout, in other cases over the ensuing years. The reason why this occurred later in some cases was that obstructive tax laws had to be dealt with first. In addition, the majority of the companies introduced the idea of profit sharing as an additional reward measure. The intention behind this measure generally is greater employee involvement with the company. As the following quotes indicate, the actual size of the equity participation has an important impact upon motivation and commitment levels.

> One assumes that 'The good of the workers and the good of the company coincide.' At *GTI* each employee was given 3 shares at the time of the buyout. It is not surprising, therefore, that participation is insufficiently substantial to increase involvement, or, as one manager commented: 'I think that, if I had 5% of shares my attitude to how the company is doing would be different; unfortunately, however, I don't have that 5%. Also, profit-sharing has nothing to do with your personal efforts. Parts of the company do well, and the feeling there often is that 'they [other sections] take advantage from us.' Since net profit is the basis for profit-sharing, we are talking about the result of the *GTI* community as a whole, and this has nothing to do with your individual responsibilities; but these in fact determine your regular monthly salary and performance perks and thus have much more impact on involvement and motivation.'

According to many, therefore, insubstantial employee participation has not led to greater involvement. Employees do not feel that 'they directly influence the net result and hence the size of the profit-sharing payment or the value of shares.' In most enterprises it is recognized that 'after a few years things are old hat' and the influence of individual employees on profit margins is often negligible. Profit-sharing schemes are therefore looked upon as a kind of recompense; employees are likely to see it as a part of the normal wage and soon become used to it. For this reason some firms caution against profit-sharing schemes. If profits decrease in a poor year and thus the payments drop, dissatisfaction is more likely than if no profit-sharing scheme applied. The expectation is that, certainly in the long run, the effect on involvement is limited. To alter working conditions in this way, then, is to reward personnel materially rather than to enhance their participation and involvement. Other measures are more likely to improve utilization of employee capabilities.

> A member of the management team says that '*GTI* has always given policy priority to the idea of involving people in the firm via their pockets, via profit-sharing and gratuity schemes. These are important elements in the total income. Because the gratuity scheme for management is linked to profit as well, this determines a substantial part of the income, the flexible part. This year the motivational factor may turn out differently. Profit, and hence total income has, of course, been on the rise for years, but not so this year (1993). The company is not doing as well due to the declining market; profits are diminishing and for the first time since the buyout forced dismissals will be unavoidable. Lower profit margins affect income negatively, and this may well prove to undermine motivation. If profits fall management is to blame. In that case dissatisfaction is more likely than when no profit-sharing scheme existed. The danger is that the positive effect is outweighed by negative consequences.'

Whenever possible, post-buyout labor conditions were revised to improve the firm's position on the sales front and/or labor market aspects. In particular, wages and emoluments were adjusted to current norms in the industry. On the one hand, relatively low wages in some firms implied the risk that production personnel – difficult to get at the time of the buyout – would transfer to competitors. In this sense wage adjustment was carried out under pressure of scarcity on the labor market. On the other hand, in view of the sales market, future labor costs need to be contained. Restriction of future pay raises by conforming to industry-wide pay levels is a decision taken under pressure of the sales market. The control of future labor costs is an essential component of the effort to increase a company's competitive edge.

> At *GTI* the view is this: '*GTI* is an enterprise which by its very nature has few assets. *GTI*'s success does not depend on holdings or branches, but on the people who carry out projects: people are the company's primary assets. *GTI* is nothing but people. It is all about putting in hours, and you can't stock up on those. Look, if the price of jam drops you shelve the cans in the stock room and wait for prices to go up; but every hour a mechanic is idle we lose more than just that hour, because labor costs go on. That's why we handle capacity very consciously and borrow a part of the capacity outside. We have to keep labor costs under control.'

In the companies we studied, relations with the employees were intensified after the buyout via internal communication. A large number of companies introduced greater levels of work consultation, readjusted existing communication channels, intensified contact between management and employees and/or works council, or provided the works council and the employees with more and better information. In these ways attempts were made to communicate the company policy objectives more effectively and so change employee attitudes. In addition, efforts were made to increase voice mechanisms, in order to monitor employee sentiment throughout the organization. Increased motivation and involvement of employees was pursued by greater post-buyout emphasis on individual responsibility in the execution of tasks. Individual performance evaluations and follow-ups on these were used to create more feeling of responsibility. On the whole, these measures proved successful. We also found that in time, internal communication, both downwards and upwards, went more smoothly. Nevertheless, the employees and the works council needed some time to get used to the new forms of consulting and the idea of thinking in terms of business performance. To make everyone aware of his own responsibilities to the business is a process which often progresses slowly as employees adjust their thinking.

Improved use of employee capacities was evident also in greater attention to courses and training for employees at every hierarchical level. Eleven out of the thirteen companies studied increased their efforts in this domain subsequent to buyout. In some companies, the need for additional training was a result of greater demands placed on the various functions arising out of the need for the firm to be more responsive to customers. In the majority of cases, then, there was a clear link between the nature of the training proposed and the present or possibly future function likely to be executed by the relevant employee. In a number of firms the demands made on employees became more stringent after the buyout, which implied the need for training. This need was caused by expanding responsibilities at the lower levels and/or facilitating voice and more flexible deployment.

At *Martinus Nijhoff International* the present managers were given additional tasks in the strategic sphere. Their pre-buy-out operational tasks tended to go to the second echelon (as a consequence of the desire to locate decision-making power on the lowest possible level within the organization), so that the responsibilities of middle management increased. Often they found the pressure mounting; it was they who were supposed to implement the changes, remind employees of their responsibilities and request participation. For this reason middle management was given management courses after the buy-out. The courses covered topics such as leadership, quality control, logistics, planning, delegation, conducting evaluation or function interviews and administration. Lower-level personnel was often provided with vocational courses attuned to individual needs. The vocational courses were frequently meant for persons who need retraining because changes in the organization give rise to new functions.

(Abridged from de Jong, 1991)

In addition to the measures mentioned to improve internal communication and enhancement of the training effort, the companies studied of course undertook further initiatives in the area of human resource management. What stands out is that, in spite of different situations and approaches, the measures taken show great mutual consistency and in every case aim at improved use of employee capacities.

Boekhoven-Bosch introduced job profiles and informative and appraisal interviews, linked up with a system of career guidance. The intention is that every employee has a yearly appraisal interview. The immediate boss conducts the interview. If they prefer, both the employee and the boss can invite a third party to be present. The aim of the consultation is to harmonize the employee's function with present and future requirements, and to discuss the opportunities and wishes of the company and the employee. Anything that directly or indirectly touches upon the job may come into purview. Discussion takes place on the basis of equality and the employee is expected to be an active participant in the process. These interviews are therefore looked upon as part of career counselling – an aspect of HRM policy largely neglected prior to the buyout. The job profile supplies the terms of reference for these talks. In 1990 an external agency described some hundreds of jobs in terms of their characteristics and responsibilities. These job profiles are used in the employee appraisal talks, to spot bottlenecks in the delineation of responsibilities and to prevent 'passing the buck.' In addition, accurate job profiles are required to be eligible for (re)certification. Efforts are also made to have commercial persons execute technical tasks and vice versa by means of job rotation and management development. After the management buyout, motivation and involvement increased and the employee attitude changed in the direction envisioned by management. In this connection respondents refer to post-buy-out HRM policy. All agree that the HRM policy has contributed to the success of the company after the buy-out, even though it seems impossible to express this contribution arithmetically.
(Abridged from de Jong, 1991)

Dominant actors in the process of decision making

The values underpinning SHRM (strategic HRM) are often predominantly individualistic and unitarist in focus. This provides a marked contrast to the dominant values of traditional personnel management and more specifically industrial relations which historically emphasized both collective and pluralist values. For many the unitarist implications of SHRM could only begin to have an impact following a much more radical shift of ownership and control. In a situation where the antagonistic model of labor–capital relations tends to have a declining influence, the right atmosphere for the introduction of an individualistic and unitarist version of HRM could be created by a buyout. This arises because both industrial relations and personnel management become more and more subjected to corporate strategy. HRM can contribute constructively to that strategy by emphasizing and promoting strategic integration, commitment, and flexibility.

> An illustration of the unitarist implication of HRM is *GTI Holding*, where the works council takes a realistic attitude. 'This is the first time [in the ten years since the buy-out] that forced dismissals must take place. The works council is sensible about this; they realize that sometimes an operating or business unit is below par and they are aware that sometimes elements must be disposed of. The council thinks about these matters seriously. You can't always salvage everything. In such cases the works council opts for adequate redundancy schemes. They know that you can't keep ballast; in the long run a lot more people will lose their job. No sir, the works council is no idealistic proponent of jobs, jobs, more jobs. They are realistic, but if the occasion calls for it they take their responsibility seriously and put their foot down.' Accordingly, the role of the works council is a substantial one, and its most important meetings are those which have the annual budget and strategies on the agenda.

Management ideology was found to be highly influential in the shaping of post-buyout human resource management. Both the personnel department and line management participated in the design and implementation of (extra) human resource management activities. Line management in particular became emphatically more involved as advisers and implementors of human resource management. Due to the expansion of activities and the increasing integration of personnel tasks in the line the personnel function took on greater significance in a number of the companies. In some other buyout companies the personnel function is kept as small as possible, even when an enlarged or entirely new department is needed because of the vacuum left by the departing parent company's personnel department. After the buyout, external expertise was hired more frequently in these latter companies than was practiced under the old regime (see also Chapter 6). An outstanding feature is that in a large number of the companies studied the advisory influence of the works council on human resource management and on company matters became more evident during the stage of negotiations between the parent and the management team. The information flow to the works council improved and there was growing recognition for the broader importance of the topics dealt with in works council meetings. Subsequent to buyout, the management of many companies increasingly accepted the works council as a serious discussion partner.

> At *GTI* employee participation is not initiated by management alone. The idea entertained by the works council to become shareholders paralleled management thinking. Once this became apparent interdependency and employee participation came quite naturally. There was a high degree of 'we-feeling,' the idea of 'we have pushed off now, so we'll travel together.' The works council, aided by external

experts, participated in a year of intensive preparation. To prevent differences in timing very much attention was given to communication and exchange of information. 'You might say that the role of the personnel section and of the works council has been very large, perhaps the major one.'

Our study clearly demonstrates that the dominant actor is the buyout management team, and that the works council is always involved in the decision. Trade union influence comes forward especially when personnel reductions are envisioned and labor agreements have to be negotiated. After the management buyout the role of line management in the structuring of HRM is expanded.

Employee ownership and the problem of takers and non-takers[†]

Here we will discuss the possible division in the workforce between shareholders and non-shareholders in the newly created buyout company. Share-ownership may potentially either harmonize industrial relations as agents (employees) become principals (owners) or constitute a conflict between takers and non-takers. Whether an employee takes shares to protect his job or to make capital gains, in both cases the financial stake may reduce the employee's perception of a difference between the goal of the firm (to make profit) and the individual (to share the profitability of the company). This may in turn engender more 'cooperative' industrial relations. On the other hand, a division in the buyout workforce between shareholders and non-shareholders may generate new conflicts rather than harmonize labor relations (Bradley and Nejad, 1989). A buyout could split employees into 'haves' and 'have-nots' in terms of those who are interested in seeing their investment grow and those who did not invest. The possible split in the workforce could also result in dual rights. Following a conversion to employee ownership, shareholders may have certain privileges not enjoyed by non-shareholders. This has certainly been the experience in several US employee-owned firms; for example, non-members tend to get the less desired jobs and are excluded from the decision-making process (Bradley and Nejad, 1989).

> To prevent a split in the work force it is not known at *GTI* who owns shares. Shares can be traded freely. 'At *GTI* by now we have no idea who the shareholders might be.' If there were an embargo to the effect that shares can be traded internally only it would in theory be possible to end up with a rift between rich and poor within *GTI*. But this did

[†] With their case study of the National Freight Company (NFC), one of the largest employee owned companies in Europe, Bradley and Nejad (1989) provide an important object-lesson in the effect of employee ownership on employee attitudes.

not happen because no restrictions are made to trading the shares. 'You can look up in the paper how much a share is worth and offer yours for sale. So, there is virtually no concentration of interests within *GTI*, and there is no split in the work force between "haves" and "have-nots."'

The *NFC*'s management has carefully avoided creating a two-tier system of employee rights. Share ownership is kept confidential so that nobody knows who owns shares and who does not. Comparing responses of shareholders and non-shareholders at *NFC*, no differences occurred. Apparently management has been reasonably successful in preventing the development of a division in the work force. Nevertheless, one manager at *NFC* reluctantly admitted: 'It's hard to sack a shareholder. Nobody is meant to know who owns shares, but the pay checks include a deduction for the interest-free loan so we know, and they know that we know.'

(Abridged from Bradley and Nejad, 1989)

Furthermore, if the unitarist perception extends to an additional belief that individual efforts can influence company performance and therefore improve personal rewards, employee attitudes and behavior may be affected in the following ways:

(1) self-monitoring may improve;
(2) horizontal monitoring of colleagues in the same work group may improve, reducing supervision costs;
(3) management shareholders may improve vertical monitoring (Bradley and Nejad, 1989).

Given that employees seem to feel that share ownership creates incentives for cooperation and work effort, one might expect to find that individual self-monitoring improves as a result of becoming a shareholder. Also, a successful conversion may intensify horizontal and vertical monitoring, possibly worsening workplace relations if employee shareholders exert pressure on non-shareholders to increase effort levels.

One *NFC* manager summed up a popular view: 'There is no difference at this depot between the effort levels of shareholders and non-shareholders, because the shareholders have pulled up the effort levels of non-shareholders.' Another *NFC* branch manager perceived the situation somewhat differently, with the implications for improved industrial relations: 'It depends who's got the shares. In this depot the right people have got shares. The people and the stewards who have been with the company for a long time are shareholders and they are the leading lights.' One said: 'at *NFC* head office we are working harder, but that is because our work-load has increased and the staff levels have stayed the same.' At the operational level, a similar view was expressed by a branch manager: 'Everyone is working harder, not because of the buyout but because of increased volume.' One clerical worker said: 'There are more managers around now. There's been no change in workers' attitudes but managers are more motivated. Previously the government paid the bills, now they're looking for waste.'

(Abridged from Bradley and Nejad, 1989)

This observation suggests the influence of horizontal monitoring, that is, employee shareholders helped and encouraged other workers to work harder because they felt their stake would be affected by the effort of others. If employees increase their horizontal supervision as a result of becoming shareholders, such a change in work behavior could have an important impact upon the firm. In contrast with an expected decrease of vertical supervision by the management as a result of the increased horizontal supervision by the employees, some managers of companies which we studied did acknowledge increasing their vertical supervision, but they attributed this to the increased demands of being privatized in competitive markets and the increased volume of business. After the buyout the management in the companies studied became more cost conscious, placing increased demands on the employees. Both shareholders and non-shareholders agreed that this was the case, suggesting a broad increase in vertical monitoring.

Overall, however, the effects of individual share ownership are frequently confounded by the effects of increased participation in decision making which may accompany a change in ownership (Goldstein, 1978; Johannesen, 1979; Long, 1978). Earlier studies have suggested that the benefits of increased participation in decision making may be greater than those of becoming individual shareholders. The best outcome, however, would result if the two effects occurred together. Companies that combine employee ownership with employee involvement programs show substantial gains in performance.

In conclusion, it seems that after the buyout perceptions of the incentives of employee share ownership are clearly related to whether an individual owns shares or not. Moreover, this perception exists at all levels in the organization. Shareholders in the companies that we studied also appeared to gain significantly more personal satisfaction from the company's success.

After the buyout both vertical and horizontal monitoring has increased. The findings suggest that to achieve a very large increase in horizontal control, a high proportion of the manual employee work group may have to be shareholders. Moreover, vertical monitoring (by the management) has increased.

Furthermore, although shareholders were more likely than non-shareholders to regard the buyout as a success, that difference in view does not seem to have built up resentment among non-shareholders. Management's avoidance of a structure of differential rights, and the care taken not to raise hopes of greater participation in decision making, appear to have been successful.

The overall findings suggest that employee ownership does have the potential to harmonize industrial relations; it does not appear to create a new division in the workforce between shareholders and non-shareholders or create expectations from employee ownership that could not be met.

Summary and conclusions

In this chapter we have shown that buyouts as organizations without traditional owners have a unique mixture of features which distinguish them from other companies, as discussed in the second section on management buyouts. They represent a shift from traditional corporate structures to employee-owned organization, whereby the division between ownership and management disappears.

Improved performance after the buyout

The phenomenon of the buyout not only occasions a shock effect, but increases the willingness to change as well. Hence it is the right moment for the management of the newly independent company to implement change, including adjustment of labor conditions and personnel arrangements. It is evident that post-buyout economic performance tends to improve and that HRM contributes to this improvement.

Management buyout and taking advantage of momentum

The event of a buyout provides a cornucopia of opportunities for management to be critical, to 'dot the i's', and to institute corrective actions where needed. A crucial advantage is the momentum for change that a buyout evokes. Under normal circumstances management tends to proceed slowly and is impeded by bureaucratic inertia, employee aversion to change, and the resistance from labor unions and works council. During and immediately after a buyout such forces against changes disappear or are minimal.

Agency costs

The earlier section on management buyouts describes the changed relations after the buyout between investors and management of the buyout company and between internal participants. This description suggests an explanation for the improved economic performance after a buyout. The central question in this second section was whether the agency costs will increase or decrease after a buyout. We approached this question from two angles:

(1) the financial-economic angle; and
(2) the internal-organizational angle.

In this section we concluded that – as a result of increased responsiveness in operations and structure, and in formulating and implementing strategy – total agency costs will be reduced. Our research shows that by making the firm as flexible as possible, post-buyout management is able to reduce risk. Value after the buyout is primarily created by actions of the buyout management team, which tends to succeed in taking several effective measures that increase operational, structural, and strategic flexibility on the one hand and improved economic performance on the other. Management possesses a strong influence over the selection of the most appropriate techniques to make the best use of the available human and capital resources.

Duration of the success

In general, post-buyout performance of companies in the short term improves. While the longer-term picture is unclear, performance does not appear to decline. Whether buyouts themselves remain as a permanent or a transitory form of organization is the subject of considerable debate. While some buyouts have now reverted to traditional ownership and management, the majority have not done so. To this extent buyouts represent a new organizational form. But it has to be recognized that the buyout is also a part of the lifecycle of the firm – a point also emphasized in Chapter 3.

Consistency with HRM measures

Our analysis demonstrates that specific aspects of HRM contribute to the success of the company. The rationale for a buyout, whether defensive or offensive, appears to have no effect on the nature and intensity of the measures taken. But would these measures have been implemented if no buyout were carried out?

The labor factor in a quantitative sense seems directly linked to the buyout: the buyout is the immediate occasion for personnel reduction, freezes on hiring, and/or internal reallocations. It is probable that such changes would have taken place even if no buyout were carried out. Then again, a buyout implies a shock effect whereby willingness to change increases both among the newly independent management and the employees. A buyout acts as a catalyst for the implementation of change.

One might ask, though, whether the study was too one-sidedly based on successful buyouts. Increased emphasis on the labor factor might also be a consequence of improved post-buyout economic performance, which would allow more room to shape HRM. Still, our analysis and case studies (especially the specific sequencing of causes and effects) tend to support the hypothesized connection, that is, that HRM is supportive of the success of an buyout.

Strategic HRM

In particular, SHRM helps to create competitive advantages for companies. A buyout creates conditions whereby managers have a new found freedom of maneuver to institute changes in their approach to HRM. Everybody is committed to making the buyout a success. It becomes clear to everyone 'why changes are necessary,' 'what the goals are,' and 'how they are to be achieved.' The most critical HRM feature in achieving the desired change is commitment, of all parties. Commitment can be created by increased employee involvement and equity ownership, which are the crucial elements in a buyout. Management and employees do not have a choice; they now must begin to share the same goals, which leads to a situation in which changes are easily accepted.

In conclusion

Our analysis indicates that post-buyout personnel management has the following characteristics:

(1) In the pursuit of post-buyout success, employees are considered to be a critical factor for gaining competitive advantage.
(2) Starting from this fact, HRM changes key aspects of traditional personnel management so that they are consistent with the overall company strategy.
(3) Mutual consistency and coherence of the various personnel instruments and activities is more emphasized after the buyout than before it.
(4) After the buyout the improvement of mutual relations is stressed, as are improving the use of employee capacities and expanding their responsibilities.
(5) Line management in particular becomes emphatically more involved as advisers and implementers of HRM. After the buyout their role in the structuring of HRM is expanded.
(6) Management typically accepts the works council and/or union as a serious discussion partner. Thus employee ownership possesses the potential of harmonizing industrial and workplace relations.

HRM in the sense described above contributes to economic performance through the realization of greater strategic integration, flexibility, commitment, employee motivation, and employee quality in tandem with optimal cost efficiency. Further, our findings reveal that HRM in the buyout company has strong ties with company strategy, and that increased attention must be given to efficient and effective deployment of personnel, intensive involvement of line management, and the utilization of personnel activities. While buyouts can and do fail, by and large they are successful, especially when all of the important stakeholders see a close relationship between non-traditional HRM strategies and improved financial performance.

References

Bannock, G. (1990). *The Economic Impact of Management Buy-outs*, London: 3i.

Bouma, J.L. (1988). De markt voor vennootschappelijk bestuur; deel 2: Agentschapsrelaties en tucht door overname, *Maandblad Bedrijfsadministratie en Organisatie*, 92, (1099), 256.

Bradley, Keith and Nejad, Aaron (1989). *Managing Owners: The National Freight Consortium in Perspective*. Cambridge: Cambridge University Press.

Bruijn, R.P., Bruining, J., Herst, A.C.C., and de Jong, A.C. (1990). Corporate restructuring in the Netherlands: management buyout performance and agency theory. Paper presented at the Seventh International Conference of Europeanists, Washington, March. In CMBOR Occasional Paper 22, University of Nottingham, p.29.

Bruining, J. (1992). 'Management buy-out'. (dissertation) Erasmus University; Rotterdam.

Bruining, J. and de Jong, A.C. (1989). *Holland Management Buyouts – January 1985–October 1989*. Centre For Research In Business Economics, Erasmus University, Rotterdam, 6.

Bruining, J. and Herst, A.C.C. (1991). Management buy-outs in the Netherlands. In Blackstone, L. and Wright, M. (eds). *Economist Guide to European Buy-Outs*. London: Economist Publications.

Bruining, J. and Herst, A.C.C. (1993). Management buy-outs, risks and returns: evidence from Holland, Paper Finbeldag 1–11, Erasmus Universiteit, Rotterdam.

Copeland, T.E. and Weston, J.F. (1988). *Financial Theory and Corporate Policy*. Reading, MA: Addison-Wesley.

Fama, E.F. and Jensen, M.C. (1983). Separation of ownership and control, *Journal of Law and Economics*, 26, 327–49.

Goldstein, S.G. (1978). Employee share-ownership and motivation, *Journal of Industrial Relations*, 20, (3), 311–30.

Hanney, J. (1986). Management buy-outs: an offer you can't refuse, *Omega*, 14, (2), 119–34.

Hite, G.L. and Owers, J.E. (1988). The restructuring of corporate America. In Stern, J. and Chew Jr., D.H. *The Revolution in Corporate Finance*. Oxford: Blackwell. 418–27.

Huiskamp, M.J. (1988). Ondernemingsstrategie en arbeidsverhoudingen, *Economisch Statistische Berichten*, 22 June, 595–99.

Jensen, M.C. and Meckling, W.H. (1976). Theory of the firm: managerial behavior, agency costs and ownership structure, *Journal of Economics*, 3, 305–60.

Johannesen, J. (1979). VAG: a need for education, *Industrial Relations*, 18, (3), 364–69.

Jones, C.S. (1988). Accounting and organisational change: an empirical study of management buyouts. Paper presented at the 11th Congress of the European Accounting Association, Nice, April.

Jong, A.C. de (1991). *Effectief sociaal ondernemingsbeleid bij een management buy-out; een exploratief onderzoek*. Rotterdam: Stichting Moret Fonds.

Kaplan, R.S. (1982). *Advanced Management Accounting*. Englewood Cliffs, NJ: Prentice-Hall.

Kaplan, S.N. (1988). 'Sources of Value in Management Buyouts'. (dissertation) Cambridge; Massachusetts: UMI Dissertation Information Service.

Kaplan, S.N. (1989). The effects of management buyouts on operating performance and value, *Journal of Financial Economics*, 24, 217–54.

Kieschnick, R.L. (1987). *Managements Buyouts of Public Corporations: An Empirical Analysis*. (dissertation) University of Texas; Austin: UMI Dissertation Information Service.

Lichtenberg, F.R. and D. Siegel (1989). The effects of leveraged buyouts on productivity and related aspects of firm behavior, National Bureau of Economic Research, Working paper series, no. 3022, Cambridge, Massachusetts.

Long, R.J. (1978). The effects of employee ownership on organizational identification, employee job attitudes and organizational performance: a tentative framework and empirical findings, *Human Relations*, 31, (1), 29–48.

Paauwe, J. (1989). *Sociaal ondernemingsbeleid: tussen dwang en ambities*, Alphen aan den Rijn. Samson Bedrijfsinformatie.

Poel, J.H.R. van de (1986). *Judgement and Control: Individual and Organizational Aspects of Performance Evaluation*. Groningen: Wolters-Noordhoff, 117.

Schendel, D. (1993). Introduction, Corporate restructuring, *Strategic Management Journal*, 14, Summer 1993 Special Issue, 1–3.

Singh, H. (1990). Management buyouts: distinguishing characteristics and operating changes prior to public offering, *Strategic Management Journal*, 11, 111–29.

Thompson, S., Wright, M., and Robbie, K. (1989). Buy-outs, debt and efficiency, *Journal of Applied Corporate Finance*, 2, (1), 76–85.

Thompson, S., Wright, M., and Robbie, K. (1990a). Management buy-outs from the public sector: ownership form and incentives issues, *Fiscal Studies*, II, (3).

Thompson, S., Wright, M., and Robbie, K. (1990b). Management equity ownership, debt and performance: some evidence from UK management buyouts. The Centre for Management Buyout Research; University of Notttingham. Occasional Paper, 1–22.

Warwick Business School (1989). *The Long-term Performance of Management Buy-outs*. University of Warwick; Coventry: Touche Ross.

Wright, M. (1986). The make-buy decision and managing markets: the case of management buy-outs, *Journal of Management Studies*, 23, (4), 434–53.

Wright, M. and Coyne, J. (1985). *Management Buyouts*. London: Croom Helm.

Wright, M., Robbie, K., and Coyne, J. (1987). *Flotations of Management Buyouts*. London: CMBOR/Spicer and Pegler Associates.

Wright, M. and Robbie, K. (1991). UK Performance Studies of MBOs. In Bonnet, M.P.B., Bruining, J., and Herst, A.C.C. (eds). *Handbook for MBOs, Theory and Practice*. Deventer: Kluwer Bedrijfswetenschappen, 111–14.

Appendix 1 Case studies: primary analysis

Case study   Buyout company, **Boekhoven-Bosch**; parent, **Elsevier-NDU**
(1987: 460 employees – printing)

In the early 1980s multinational publishing company Elsevier decided to implement a strategic reorientation. Owing to technical over-capacity in the graphic industry profit margins were dwindling. To cope with the competition of US publishers, cost effectiveness had to improve via greater efficiency and improved performance. Elsevier opted for a concentration on core activities. On 8 October 1986, the printer Boekhoven-Bosch, an Elsevier subsidiary, became an independent firm again via a management buyout. Financing was by two participating companies, together holding 58.4% of the shares; the general manager gained 5% of the shares, as did the Employee Consortium; 41.6% remained with Elsevier. At the time of buyout the workforce comprised some 450 employees which made the company one of the larger ones in the Dutch graphic industry. Boekhoven-Bosch is an offset printer, specializing in printing journals, telephone books, public transport schedules, and tariff books. Telephone books are produced in a joint venture with printer R.R. Donnelly & Sons, Chicago. Boekhoven-Bosch is a full-service company handling typesetting, printing, binding, and distribution. Over the years following the management buyout trading results and net profit improved. The buyout was an offensive one.

Case study   Buyout company, **GTI Holding**; parent, **SHV-concern (NL)**
(1984: 8275 employees – technical services)

GTI Holding is one of the largest Dutch organizations in technical services in utility and industrial building, shipbuilding, and offshore in Northwest Europe. Its service includes design, installation, operation, and maintenance in all technical disciplines such as electrotechnology, telecommunication, heating, airconditioning, and related technologies including measurement and instrumentation technology, security systems, industrial automation, and electronic control systems. GTI's workforce stands at

8275. The company has a network of more than 80 divisions and branches located in the Netherlands, Belgium, Germany, and the UK. SHV is its parent company. Toward the end of the 1960s SHV took over a number of firms active in the area of installation and technological enterprise. The installation firms were united in 1970 in the Groep Technische Installatie (GTI). In 1984 GTI became independent via a management buyout. A year later, GTI Holding entered the Amsterdam Exchange. At the time of the buyout all GTI employees were given three GTI shares; 10% of the shares could be bought privately by the employees. In addition, the PPM (Personnel Consortium) obtained 25% of the shares. At an administration office personnel can obtain PPM shares, which in turn has GTI shares. This third block is a mixed security construction and employee instrument. The buyout had an offensive character.

Case study Buyout company, **Dordtse Kil Holding**; parent, **Compagnie Française de Navigation Rhénane**
(1988: 240 employees – shipbuilding and tooling factory)

The basis for Dordtse Kil Holding was laid in 1917, when the Compagnie Française de Navigation Rhénane (CFNR) established De Biesbosh-Dordrecht. This French shipping company needed a support station for its Rhine fleet. The holding's activities consist of building and repair of river craft, barges and flat-bottoms, construction of passenger bridges for airports, building contracting, and the exploitation of flat-bottoms. Vessels and passenger bridges are delivered both in the Netherlands and abroad. Major export countries are Germany, France, and the UK. Shipbuilders experienced a number of lean years. Toward the end of the 1970s and the early 1980s the slowing economy did not leave shipbuilding untouched. As recently as 1987 employment in Dutch shipbuilding suffered a 30% decline. At the close of 1990 Dordtse Kil Holding employed approximately 250 full-time workers. The French company sought to sell its shares in the context of the privatization policy of the French government. The unstable results of Dordtse Kil Holding, too, were a consideration in the decision to seek a buyer for the shares. The major reasons given for the management buyout were the continuity of the company, guaranteed employment, and forestalling unwanted takeovers. CFNR threatened to withdraw its floating reserves from the company and intended to sell its block of shares soon, leaving the company with unforeseeable consequences. Accordingly, the management buyout was a defensive one. The holding company Verdam took over the shares. At the time of the buyout the participants in this company were the general manager of Dordtse Kil

Holding (75% of shares) and two middle managers (12.5% each). In 1989 the general manager presented 5% of his shares to the employees.

Case study Buyout company, **Martinus Nijhoff International**; parent, **Wolters Kluwer** *(1989: 105 employees – publishing)*

Martinus Nijhoff International is a service organization in the field of distribution of books, journals, and other reference works aimed at domestic and foreign scientific publications. Books and journals are acquired worldwide from publishers. Libraries are a major group of buyers of the company's services. The company head office is in The Hague, with branches in Boston, Sofia, and Taipei. Martinus Nijhoff International is one of the few companies operating in this market. Swets & Zeitlinger in the Netherlands and Faxon and Ebsco in the United States are its competitors.

In February 1991, Martinus Nijhoff International had 150 full-time employees. Although the company's net result was positive it did not meet the stipulated return-on-sales norm of 7%. Parent Wolters Kluwer further felt that the activities did not sufficiently mesh with those of the concern. Wolters Kluwer was willing to sell to the highest bidder. In 1988 Zwets & Zeitlinger attempted a takeover, but towards the end of the year they pulled out because of fierce resistance by works council and trade unions. Works council and trade unions were strongly opposed to the takeover because Zwets & Zeitlinger would not guarantee employment, so that some 80 out of the 105 jobs were threatened. Immediately following termination of these talks, the buyout initiative was taken. The management buyout may be considered an offensive one. After the buyout two members of the management team had 60% of shares, 30% each. The remaining 40% went to ODH Financial Markets, the external consultancy during the talks.

Case study Buyout company, **Triumfus Onion Products**; parent, **Suiker Unie** *(1990: 80/20 employees – onion products)*

Triumfus Onion Products (TOP), located in Gravenpolder (the Netherlands), sells onions of various grades and processes onions into a variety of products. The firm's quality policy is tuned to buyers who demand a constant, high quality. About 80% of the production is for export, mostly to Germany, the United Kingdom, Spain, the United States, Indonesia, Brazil, and Argentina. In February of 1991 TOP employed 19 full-time employees. During the peak period (summer) use is made of temporary workers; depending on the size of the harvest 100–300 school youths are put to work. TOP's history goes back to 1940, when the company was established. In 1986 the Suiker Unie, a sugar beet growers' cooperative looking for diversification, bought TOP. It soon became clear that the Suiker Unie had made a poor acquisition, since the onion processing firm suffered heavy losses. In spite of the introduction of a new quality policy and investment of a few million guilders for new machinery, the situation did not improve and the firm continued to operate at a loss. In October 1990 the Suiker Unie decided to sell TOP or, failing that, to close it down as of 31 December 1990. The management buyout may therefore be seen as a defensive move. After the buyout the company workforce was reduced, so that 60 jobs were lost. Two managers became owners. They each took 50% of the share capital of the newly established company.

Appendix 2 Case studies: secondary analysis

Case study   Buyout company, **Crown van Gelder**;
parent, **Van Gelder Papier**
(1983: 260 employees – paper)

Crown Van Gelder produces wood-free, white paper. The company is
located in Velsen (the Netherlands) and has a division in Fribourg
(Switzerland). The company produces quality industrial specialties for a
specific and mostly narrow market. The products are for the most part
sold to firms in the EU. In 1989 72% of its turnover was export.

Case study   Buyout company, **De Reus**; parent,
RSV
*(1983: 300 employees – electrotechnical industry
(elevators))*

De Reus produces elevators. The company is located in Krimpen aan de
Ijssel (the Netherlands) with branches in Alkmaar (the Netherlands),
Mariakerke (Belgium) and Paris. Elevators are produced to lift both
persons and goods. At present 25% of the turnover is via worldwide
export.

Case study   Buyout company, **Plasthill**; parent,
Solvay (Belgium)
(1984: 50 employees – chemical works)

Plasthill, located in Hillegom (the Netherlands), fabricates polythene foil.
Products are sold in the Netherlands, Belgium, Germany, France, the UK,
and the Nordic countries. From 1970 to 1979 Plasthill was a division of
Philips, which sold this non-core activity to the Belgian chemical concern
Solvay.

Case study   Buyout company, **Van Nelle**; parent, **Nabisco Brands (US)**
(1985: 1700 employees – foods, coffee, and tobacco)

Van Nelle produces proprietary brands in the market of food and stimulants. The company has various brands in the Netherlands, Belgium, Germany, and the United States. In 1977 Van Nelle was fully taken over by the American company Standard Brands (which in 1981 merged into Nabisco Brands).

Case study   Buyout company, **UT-Delfia**; parent, **Unilever**
(1986: 420 employees – compound food industry)

UT-Delfia (UTD) produces mixed feed for cattle, poultry, pigs, and horses. The company has a number of processing plants in the Netherlands and one in Belgium. UTD imports about 90% of its raw materials from North and South America and Asia. The products are sold mostly in the Netherlands.

Case study   Buyout company, **Proforms**; parent, **Burroughs (US)**
(1986: 70 employees – graphics)

Proforms is a printery located in Heerhugowaard (the Netherlands). The company offers a number of specialist products important for (business) data retention, and up to 1986 was part of the US computer firm Burroughs.

Case study   Buyout company, **Atlas Venture**; parent, **NMB**
(1986: 25 employees – banking (venture capital))

Atlas Venture is a venture-capital company in Amsterdam, with branches in Boston and Munich. It holds a number of participation companies whose objective is to enhance the risk-carrying capacity of enterprises and, if need be, to provide them with active guidance. The capital provided often serves to allow an enterprise to cope with temporary difficulties such as financing rapid expansion, financial problems during successions, and management buyouts.

Case study   Buyout company, **National Freight Consortium**; parent, **state/privatization**

The NFC is the largest and most diverse road freight transport, storage, and distribution company in Britain, with interests in the travel business and property management. The National Freight Company (NFC) is one of the biggest buyouts of its kind in Europe. In February, 1982, during the early stages of the British government's privatization program, the former National Freight Corporation was bought by an employee consortium. Since this historic purchase, the NFC's performance has been outstanding.

5

Managing without unions: a pyrrhic victory?

Until recently, 'managing without unions' scarcely rated a mention in the international industrial relations literature. In the 1970s, non-union companies were not considered to be a significant part of the industrial relations scene. In Western Europe, trade unions were still strong, with union density rates averaging about 45%. With the possible exception of the United States, which has experienced secular decline since the Second World War, trade unions internationally looked to be in a healthy position, and even in the United States some sectors of unionism such as government employees experienced growth.

Indeed, it appeared to some commentators only a matter of time before all significant concentrations of employees became unionized. By the late 1980s, however, the position had altered dramatically, as Figure 5.1 illustrates. Trade unions were now experiencing relentless pressure emanating from fluctuations in the business cycle, structural change in host nation economies, and the advent of new and sophisticated approaches to human resource management designed to reduce the felt requirements for union representation among employees. Suddenly, the non-union company, previously ignored, was now worthy of investigation. However, researchers found that non-union companies were much more difficult to study.

Despite this situation some researchers (McLouglin and Gourlay, 1994; Scott, 1994) have managed to penetrate the non-union environment and have given us rich insights into a relatively uninvestigated area. The empirical research reported in this chapter reflect the results of just such an investigation. It focuses on an intriguing dilemma – namely that some large, non-union, and highly profitable companies are unable to fully exploit the many supposed benefits of non-union status.

In this chapter we first explore the issue of managing without unions by presenting two brief case examples which bring into perspective the

Figure 5.1 International changes in union density, 1980–88.
Source: Reed, *et al.*, 1995.

challenges faced by managers in pursuing union avoidance strategies. Next we examine the reasons why employees join and employers avoid unions and reflect upon these reasons in terms of the three main theoretical perspectives used in the book: agency theory, transaction costs, and the resource base theory of the firm.

In the second section we examine the key causal forces which have led to the growth and diffusion of the non-union sector internationally and consider which set of factors determines whether a firm will adopt a union suppression versus a union substitution approach. In the third section we identify the role of employment practices in high wage companies in creating a robust non-union culture and examine the Catch-22 of union avoidance which faces some large non-union companies. Finally, we conclude by considering some of the implications that this Catch-22 has for both unions and employers.

Non-unionism: issues and challenges

Many factors, as we shall see, are associated with the drive towards non-unionism. While ostensibly there seem to be many advantages associated with the non-union approach from the perspective of managers and employers, there are also difficulties, problems, and unresolved issues. To illustrate, we begin with two short cases of 'managing without unions' drawn from the United States and the United Kingdom which dramatize some of the potential problems associated with such approaches.

Case study   **Even in the United States, non-unionism is not as easy as it looks.**

In 1993 Polaroid, Du Pont, and Electromation appeared before the US National Labor Relations Board (NLRB) charged with violating the National Labor Relations Act of 1935 which was designed at least in part to prevent the establishment of 'company unions.' In December 1992 the NLRB ruled that Electromation, a manufacturer in Indiana had acted illegally in establishing 'action committees' of employees designed to focus on workplace issues. Similarly, Du Pont has had to disband its safety committees and Polaroid's 30-member board of employees has been ruled illegal.

The origins of these issues lie in the 1920s when hundreds of US companies such as Goodyear set up work councils or company-based unions. These were ostensibly designed to promote teamwork but from the perspective of organized labor were union-busting devices constructed so as to convince employees that they had no need for a union. In 1935 Senator Robert F. Wagner championed the passage of the National Labor Relations Act, which as part of the 'New Deal' program explicitly encouraged collective bargaining, establishing the rights of employees to join unions, setting standards for union elections, and specifying certain unfair labor practices of employers.

Potentially, the establishment of company works councils and even team-based quality improvement initiatives are suspect as they could be construed to violate the rights of employees to join unions.

Case study   Evidence from the British Workplace Industrial Relations Surveys indicates the unacceptable face of non-unionism

Recent evidence from the British Workplace Industrial Relations (WIRS) surveys suggests that employees in the non-union private sector are at a considerable disadvantage when compared with their unionized private sector counterparts. Non-union employees in Britain receive, on average, much less information from management, are provided with fewer information/communication channels, and work in organizations with fewer health and safety representatives than their unionized counterparts.

Further analyses indicate that non-union private sector workplaces (when compared with their unionized counterparts) experience higher accident and injury rates, as well as more dismissals of a non-redundancy nature, and they provide fewer grievance and disciplinary procedures to their employees. In addition, non-union workplaces experience more compulsory redundancies and higher levels of labor turnover, but virtually no strikes. Absenteeism levels within non-union firms were viewed by survey respondents to be as good as their unionized counterparts.

While the climate of employee relations was seen by managers to be good in non-union workplaces, issues of 'morale' were viewed as problematic, perhaps because of the labor turnover problem cited earlier. Pay comparisons reveal an interesting picture – the non-union companies in the private sector record greater pay dispersion and a higher incidence of low pay. Pay is more often determined by market forces and performance than in the unionized private sector. Non-union workplaces also record higher usage levels of contingent workers and fewer personnel specialists than their unionized counterparts.

(*Source*: Adapted from Millward, *et al.*, 1992:363–5)

Dilemmas and potential answers

These two cases raise several interesting issues. In the British case we see that employees in non-union workplaces are disadvantaged relative to their unionized counterparts on a host of communication and 'voice issues.' Paradoxically, the US case reveals that – due to the unique institutional and legal arrangements prevailing in North America – even when management attempts to introduce 'voice mechanisms' such as consultation committees, they may be in violation of the Wagner Act which was designed to prevent companies from 'interfering with, restraining, and coercing employees.'

The picture painted by the British WIRS data suggests that there is a real danger that unorganized workers can expect more informal but much less favorable institutional arrangements for 'voice' and due process than workers employed in unionized private sector workplaces. One can see that non-unionism confers (in the British, private sector context) considerable 'freedom to maneuver' upon employers in terms of their employee relations strategies and in terms of organizing more flexible working arrangements. However, from the perspective of these employees, greater flexibility in working arrangements does not translate into higher wages or more favorable working conditions.

This is good news for British trade unions faced with a continuing debate about their relevance to a modern 'enterprise led' economy. Interestingly, the WIRS data also raises some policy questions for would-be labor law legislators (Millward, 1994). If unions do not organize in currently unorganized private sector workplaces, what governance arrangements need to be legislated for in order to prevent the potential exploitation of non-union employees? This debate is currently prominent in the United States.

Defenders of non-union approaches, of course, can argue that the WIRS data on non-union companies is size related, deriving from the fact that non-union workplaces are typically smaller, and many of them are independent in the sense that they do not belong to part of a larger enterprise. Based on this evidence, the highly visible and proactive human resource strategies deployed by companies such as Marks and Spencer, IBM, and others must, at least in the British context, be regarded as 'atypical' (Blyton and Turnbull, 1994). This is not a trivial point as much of the laudatory literature on non-unionism has, until recently, had a narrow empirical base from which to extrapolate. It is also an important caveat to bear in mind when reading the section of this chapter describing the Catch-22 of union avoidance which derives solely from an analysis of the experience of *large* high wage non-union organizations operating in the Irish Republic.

Why do employees join unions and employers avoid them? Some international evidence

The reasons why employees join unions are diverse. Some employees experience dissatisfactions with their work environment and see unions as a mechanism for negotiating improvements. Other employees experience peer pressure to join the union or are forced to join, particularly in situations where a pre-entry closed shop exists. Brett (1980) suggests that there are two main reasons why employees join unions.

(1) The employees' initial interest in unionization is triggered by dissatisfaction with working conditions but the individual employee feels powerless to change these conditions.
(2) Employees may attempt to organize a union if they believe in the concept of collective action and they believe that unions will yield positive rather than negative outcomes for them.

Business cycle effects on union joining

George Bain and his colleagues have used econometric models to analyze union growth and decline in several countries (Bain and Elsheikh, 1976; Bain and Price, 1983). Their research suggests that inflation, pay increases, unemployment, changes in the labor market, and the attitude of government strongly influence membership growth and decline. When inflation rates are high, unions enjoy a 'credit effect' to the extent that they can secure pay increases for their members in the place of perceived erosion of living standards (the 'threat' effect) caused by inflation. These authors found that inflation and pay rises increased union membership but that unemployment had a dampening effect on the rate of unionization.

Governments which are sympathetic to unions (for example, the Labour Governments in the United Kingdom in the 1970s) aid the level of unionization. This is due in part to the high employment concentration in the public sector: when governments encourage union recognition, large sectors of relatively 'captive' employees are exposed to typically successful, union recruitment drives. However, as Klandermans (1986) points out, refinements of these models (Visser, 1985) show that in several Western European countries increased unemployment did not lead to a hemorrhaging of union members, and in some countries even led to a gain. In certain countries such as Denmark, unions occupy a central position in the social security system even to the point where unemployment benefits are administered through trade union organized labor exchanges. The net result is that, in such countries, many unemployed former union members continue to retain their union membership. However, unions in other countries such as Ireland have found that the creation of a special low-cost category of membership for unemployed members, in itself, does not provide a major retention device for unemployed members. Additionally, in the United States where many large corporations administer job insurance, pensions, scholarships, and so on, unions have seen these services to employees taken outside their domain of influence, further exacerbating their rate of decline.

Contextual influences on union joining

Klandermans (1986) divides studies of union joining into two categories:

(1) collective joining via union certification in the United States;
(2) individual joining via voluntary membership.

The research on individual voting behavior in certification elections (Brett, 1980; Lawler, 1986) demonstrates that job dissatisfaction and the belief that unions are instrumental in improving these terms and conditions of employment provide the best explanation of individual voting behavior in union elections.

Interestingly, however, Klandermans notes that background variables such as age, seniority, education, gender, race, and the nature of work carried out added little explanatory value to the analyses that have been completed (Klandermans, 1986). However, there is a variety of methodological problems with some of these studies which suggests that these latter findings are not completely robust.

Research on individual decisions to join a union is relevant where employees have a choice about joining a union or where pre-entry closed shop conditions do not apply. Dutch research (Van de Vall, 1970; Klandermans, 1984a, 1984b, 1984c) has shown that the individual decision to join unions hinges around three motive categories:

(1) *Reward motives*. People join unions where they perceive that the expected benefits of union membership (protection against arbitrary dismissal, job control, financial and moral support during strikes, and so forth) outweigh the perceived costs of membership (financial dues to the union, potential hostility of employers' reactions, and so on).
(2) *Collective motives*. People join unions because of their perceived role in creating a just and equitable society, and where they believe that collective rather than individual action is likely to be more successful in achieving these goals.
(3) *Social motives*. People join because of the social pressure which they experience both on and off the job. Social pressures can be very strong in situations where high levels of union membership already exist in the relevant workforce.

In these situations, non-membership can be seen as counter-normative behavior eliciting a variety of pressure tactics such as 'being sent to Coventry' (an isolation tactic). A study of Dutch hotel workers cited by Klandermans found that 39% of the variance in union joining behavior was accounted for by these three motives (Klandermans, 1986). The three main theoretical perspectives used in this book – the resource base view of the firm, agency theory, and transaction costs – are supportive of these research findings on union joining behavior. Examined from the perspective of resource base theory, union joining may be viewed as a rational attempt by unions to influence the physical, organizational and human capital resource base of the firm. Provided unions gain suffcient bargaining strength through increased membership, they can influence even the fixed asset base of the firm through such mechanisms as board-level participation. Unions have been particularly successful in this regard in Germany where co-determination has had demonstrable economic benefits. The impact of unions on the firm's organizational capital resources has also been demonstrated: managers and owners are forced to tighten up loose and often ill-defined organizational arrangements. Similarly, the firm's human capital configuration is affected by unions when they negotiate internal labor market arbitrage mechanisms such as seniority rules and rules governing promotion, layoffs, and dismissals. All of these mechanisms buttress individual employees against the vagaries of arbitrary employer action.

Union joining behavior is also consistent with both agency theory and transaction cost perspectives. Unions mediate in the classic principal–agent relationship, but act on behalf of agents, namely employees. Unions, by negotiating egalitarian-based rules governing internal labor markets, attempt to reduce the potential 'moral hazards' inherent in managerial behaviors such as 'favoritism on the job.' They also reduce transaction costs for their members by providing economy of scale benefits in negotiations with employers and the de facto substitution of a hierarchical union governance form in the place of dispersed individual-level negotiations between employees and employers.

Why do employers try to avoid unions?

The main perceived advantage for management in avoiding trade unions has been the ability to pay lower wages than unionized competitors, and the ability to make potentially unpopular decisions without facing an organized challenge from the workforce. Whether unionization actually does affect competitiveness is debatable. In fact, in the 1970s an interesting school of thought developed in the US which suggested that unionization went hand-in-hand with higher productivity. A number of researchers working at Harvard University discovered from a statistical study that industries in states with high rates of unionization seemed to have achieved higher rates of productivity than the same industries in the states with low unionization (Brown and Medoff, 1978; Freeman and Medoff, 1984). Possible explanations of the relationship found in this study lie in the fact that unions, by raising wages, attract better qualified and experienced employees who stay longer with the firm because of the locking-in effect of union negotiated pension schemes and the fact that jobs in the non-union sector do not pay as well as their unionized counterparts, paricularly in the United States. In addition, by reducing wage dispersion in the workplace, unions can potentially affect job satisfaction, athough the relationship between job satisfaction and productivity is empirically tenuous.

Several criticisms have been made of their analysis, with some of the criticisms coming from the same researchers. First, their comparisons of productivity were based on value added, and therefore it is possible that the apparently better performances from the unionized sectors were due to monopoly effects. This would arise where one or more unionized companies had a virtual monopoly in a particular market, and thus higher wages negotiated by unions could be passed on to consumers in the form of higher prices.

Another criticism, which is particularly pertinent in the present context, is that even if unions do not reduce productivity, they do reduce profits, and thus, at least in the longer term, competitive advantage. Research into union effects on profitability has been surprisingly limited and relates primarily to the United States. In one important study, Clark found that unionism decreased the pre-tax rate of return on capital by 4.1 percentage points or by 19% relative to the sample mean (Clark, 1984). In the case of firms with low market share (less than 10%) Clark found that unions reduce profits by 4.7 percentage points or by 40% relative to the sample mean of 11.1%. However, no change was discerned by Clark in the case of firms with more than 35% of market share. In other studies, Ruback and Zimmerman (1984) found that there were substantial falls in equity value associated with union representation, and Connolly and colleagues (1985) found that unions were able to capture rents associated with intangible capital investments in R&D rather than with short-lived advertising expenditures. This later finding would suggest that unions may impact negatively on long-run growth.

Obviously a great deal depends on the character of the union movement in a particular country and on union density. It seems unlikely that the larger Japanese manufacturing companies have lost out significantly through union representation, for all large manufacturing companies in Japan are unionized, albeit by Japanese-style 'company' unions, and these same companies have demonstrated their ability to compete internationally, make large profits, and invest heavily in R&D. To return to the Harvard research of the 1970s, Freeman, Brown, Medoff, and others postulated a number of reasons why unions may enhance productivity, and many of these arguments still have force (Brown and Medoff, 1978; Freeman and Medoff, 1984). Their main argument is that unions lock workers into jobs by gaining better pay and conditions for them. Thus, turnover of experienced workers is reduced, speed and quality can be more easily maintained, and waste is kept to a minimum. Because investment in training is not lost through high turnover, more training is likely to be given in the future. Other points put forward include such arguments as: unions, through a 'shock' effect, smarten up management; better communication channels enable workers to suggest improved ways of doing things; and the better morale of unionized workers improves their performance. Table 5.1 summarizes some further US studies on the mainly negative impact of unions on shareholder value, profitability, and productivity.

Although in recent years the Harvard researchers have revised their views to some extent, their research does suggest that in many situations unions do not inhibit productivity as much as is popularly supposed.

The research findings listed in Table 5.1 suggest that union recognition is more likely to be associated in the US context with a decline in shareholder wealth. These negative results, Kleiner (1990) argues, may also help explain why low-wage firms, which have potentially the most to lose from an organizing drive, are the most likely to engage in union avoidance techniques (Abowd, 1989; Becker, 1987; Becker and Olson, 1986; Ichniowski, 1986; Katz, *et al.*, 1985; Kleiner, 1990; Kleiner, *et al.*, 1980; Neumann, 1980; Richard and Zimmerman, 1984; Thomas and Kleiner, 1989).

There is still, however, a widespread perception among managers in multinational companies that unions have even a wider impact. The following is a list of alleged disadvantages of unions quoted by managers and researchers, namely that unions:

- raise employment costs
- make change more difficult
- encourage trivial grievances
- protect unsatisfactory workers
- impede communication
- promote an adversarial industrial relations climate
- inhibit individual rewards
- provide a platform for trouble makers
- impose restrictions on production
- inhibit flexibility
- impose unnecessarily high manning levels (Toner, 1987).

Again these findings are consistent with the propositions advanced by the resource base theory of the firm, agency theory and transaction costs – when viewed from a managerial perspective. For example, a managerially inspired resource base perspective would argue that

Table 5.1   The mainly negative impact of union activities on organizational performance (as reported in the US research studies indicated)

Union event period	Productivity effect	Profit/share price effect	Time
Election (Ruback and Zimmerman, 1984)	N/A	Union loss reduces shareholder equity by 1.86%; union win reduces shareholder equity by 3.84%	1962–84
'Unexpected' wage settlement (Abowd, 1989)	N/A	Each US$1.00 gained by either side cost other side US$1.00	1975–82
Concession bargain (Becker, 1987)	N/A	Increases shareholder equity by 8%	1982–83
Two-tier Agreement (Thomas and Kleiner, 1989)	N/A	Increases shareholder equity by 1.0% to 4.1%	1983–86
Strikes (Neumann, 1980; Becker and Olson, 1986)	N/A	Reduces shareholder equity by 1.0% to 4.1%	1962–82
Grievance activity (Ichniowski, 1986; Katz, et al., 1985; Kleiner, et al., 1980)	1 standard deviation increase in filings reduces productivity by 1.5% to 6.7% related grievances	Increase from zero to average level of grievances reduces profit by 14.6% (Ichniowski)	1970–80

Source: Kleiner, 1990.

owners, faced with the potential restrictions placed upon managerial prerogative by unions will – where anti-union sentiment is strong and where unions do not enjoy a high degree of social legitimacy – be strongly motivated to pursue the non-union option. The arguments advanced in this regard are that unions reconfigure the resource base of the firm in ways that are detrimental to shareholders and the long-run survival of the firm. They supposedly accomplish this goal by redistributing shareholder wealth to employees, thus negatively impacting the firm's capacity to attract investment; impairing managers' ability to alter the skill base of the firm in response to changing market conditions arising from the restrictions placed upon the right to hire and fire; and by imposing restrictive due process governance arrangements within the firm.

Additionally, unions viewed from an agency theory perspective are seen as an unnecessary and obtrusive filter in the relationship between the principal and agent, imposing even further monitoring costs upon employers and protecting shirking behavior on the part of some recalcitrant employees from employer retribution.

Further motivation to pursue a union avoidance strategy is presented by the increase in transaction costs necessary to negotiate and administer the union contract and create a 'dualist' infrastructure within the firm. This dualism refers to the need to create dual communication channels in unionized environments – one following traditional collective bargaining contours, the other oriented towards direct and individualized communication with employees. However, as we shall see in our discussion of the Catch-22 of union avoidance, a paradox pevails in that transaction costs are not appreciably reduced in large high wage non-union firms where there is a strong external union presence interested in recruiting members in such firms.

A theoretical explanation of the non-union phenomenon and the Catch-22 of union avoidance

Kochan and colleagues have developed a comprehensive and integrated theoretical framework which attempts to explain the emergence of the contemporary non-union phenomenon (Kochan, *et al.*, 1986). Figure 5.2 outlines an adapted version of the Kochan *et al.* model of the emergence of non-union employment relationships. It can be seen from this model that the emergence of non-union companies and the diffusion of the non-union system is integrally linked with a broad range of explanatory factors. These factors include the external environment, managerial values, and business strategies coupled with the impact of the firm's industrial relations/HRM policies and practices. These are seen as contributing forces to union recognition or non-recognition.

The external environmental variables

The external environmental variables outlined by Kochan and colleagues include labor market and workforce demographics, product markets, technological change, and government policies. The argument advanced is that where labor markets are slack, unions are weakened, bestowing greater freedom on the part of managers to choose the non-union option.

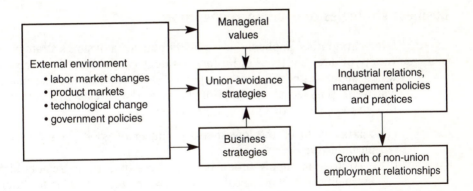

Figure 5.2   The emergence of non-union employment relationships.
Source: Kochan, *et al.*, 1986.

Workforce demographics are also viewed as an important influence, as generally females have a lower propensity to unionize than men, although this is certainly due in part to the limited availability of unions willing to organize in industry sectors where there is a high concentration of female employees (Green, 1990). Product markets also exert an important influence. The product market impacts upon employee relations in a number of different ways. Irrespective of whether the firm is union or non-union, where labor cost containment pressures are particularly high, they will influence the type of employee relations strategies pursued at the level of the firm. For example, if labor costs are a large proportion of total costs and if the organization is pursuing a strategy of low-cost leadership, then it can be expected that very tight, codified labor relations policies and practices will be pursued at the level of the firm with the objective of containing labor costs at the minimum possible level. In the United States, for example, where there is a non-union wage differential of some 15–20%, one can see why firms wishing to contain labor costs opt for the non-union strategy. That is, by going non-union it is frequently cheaper.

Technological change is also relevant, for it can erode jobs which are traditionally the domain of trade unions, for example blue collar, low-skilled and semi-skilled occupations. Government policies in turn can accentuate or ameliorate this drag on union membership growth. This is illustrated in the case of the United States where there has been a resurgence in the right to work laws which, again, remove incentives on the part of individuals to join unions. Even in Ireland where there has traditionally been support for trade unions, it has been noted that since the 1980s, the Industrial Development Authority is not as directive as it used to be in recommending union recognition to incoming foreign direct investors into Ireland (McGovern, 1989).

Business strategies and union recognition

Every firm either implicitly or explicitly pursues a business strategy. A variety of different types of business strategy can be identified, each of which significantly affects the type of employee relations strategies which are pursued at the level of the firm. Porter classified competitive strategies into two major approaches:

(1) a strategy to be the lowest-cost producer of goods or services in an industry;

(2) a strategy to supply products or services that are extremely high in quality or technologically innovative in such a way as to differentiate the product or service from competing firms (Porter, 1980).

The latter strategy, it is argued, allows the firm to sell its products at a price premium. According to researchers such as the Boston Consulting Group, this approach generates significant above-average returns to firms pursuing such a strategy (Buzzel and Gale, 1987). In turn, the business strategy and the extent of competition in the firm's product market have a significant impact upon the type of industrial relations and human resource management policies and practices which are pursued at the level of the firm. It can be expected that aiming to be the lowest-cost producer (low-cost leadership) in a particular industry (and particularly where labor costs are a high percentage of the cost of manufacture) will have a significant impact upon managerial strategies to control costs, including labor costs at the level of the firm.

By contrast, the firm which is pursuing a differentiation strategy may be generating a significant stream of revenue in a growth situation, which will lead to an entirely different set of competitive pressures at the level of the firm. It is generally agreed that firms wish to match their business strategies and human resource management strategies. If the external environment is one of rapid change, turbulence, and reactivity, ideally a coherent approach aimed at matching human resource strategy to the external environment will be developed. Thus, for example, a premium may be placed upon attracting and retaining flexible, innovative, and entrepreneurial employees in a highly reactive market. An *experientally* based human resource strategy (see Chapter 1) developed in such circumstances may seek to exclude trade unions from any role in the organization because of the potential constraints which they place upon employer action. This will, of course, not always be the case, as recent British WIRS data have shown that large unionized companies avoid these potential constraints by extensive experimentation with employee involvement practices (Sisson, 1993). Managerial values therefore must play an important part in the union recognition decision, although how these values interact with human resource practices across varying industry contexts and national cultures is by no means fully understood.

The role of managerial values in shaping union recognition

Kochan and colleagues (1986) argue that the values of the dominant coalition have a tremendous impact upon the decision of an organization to recognize trade unions. These authors point out that managerial values act as a lens through which environmental pressures or opportunities pass in the process of producing and formulating organizational responses. Options that are inconsistent with accepted values are rejected and discounted as being outside the range of all acceptable alternatives, or not even consciously considered. In the case of the United States, deep-seated opposition to unions is a key element in the ideology of US management. Thus, company country of origin could potentially be a very powerful explanatory variable in determining union recognition or non-recognition. If such a scenario were correct, one would expect that foreign investors of US origin would be unlikely to recognize trade unions in offshore locations. Similarly, Japanese companies would be expected (because of the traditional arrangements in their home country) to go for a single union deal – it being the closest approximate to the establishment-based unions in Japan; and British and Scandinavian companies would be expected to recognize trade unions in offshore investment locations (Guest and Hoque, 1994). However, to date, there is little supportive evidence on this point.

Factors determining union suppression and union substitution approaches

Two very different strategies in relation to union avoidance may be adopted. The first of these may be described as the union suppression approach, for example strenuously resisting union organizing drives, including the use of coercive tactics by managers to stay union free. The second is the union substitution approach which focuses on removing the triggers to unionization within the organization. According to Kochan and colleagues (1986), it was mainly the large companies which utilized union substitution strategies in the United States. Large firms with significant financial resources are in a situation where they can employ specialized personnel and employee relations staff which act as replacements for typical union-provided functions such as grievance channels, due process, wage negotiations, and so on within the organization. Firms which are unable to bear the costs of sophisticated approaches, including the development of a significant employee relations staffing ratio, are more likely to opt for the union suppression approach. This is because of the fact that managers in smaller organizations are more likely to hold doctrinaire neo-unitarist values which do not countenance trade unions as being relevant to their particular organizational context. Some evidence of this can be found in the

Irish and UK context which indicates that there is considerable opposition to unions among small, hi-tech, service and clothing companies (McGovern, 1989; Ram, 1994).

There is a range of environmental and organizational conditions which also appear to increase the probability that an employer will choose the direct suppression approach to union avoidance (Kochan and Katz, 1988:191). Among these are the presence of a hostile social and political environment towards unions: employment of low wage or unskilled workers with few labor market alternatives; an abundant supply of alternative workers; lower recruitment and training costs; low profit in a highly competitive industry; smaller firms; the lack of professional personnel staff; and the willingness to litigate union challenges through administrative and judicial procedures. It is extremely difficult, however, to measure how many firms actively oppose unions, though such direct suppression tactics have certainly increased in many countries over the past 10 years.

Strategies to reduce incentives to unionize

The alternative approach focuses on eliminating the triggers to unionization, for example, poor supervision, perceived inequities, low levels of job security, and comparatively low levels of pay.

Strategies used to eliminate triggers to unionization typically include some of the following (Kochan and Katz, 1988):

(1) Pay and conditions, including fringe benefits equal to or greater than those paid to workers employed in comparable industries and firms.

(2) A high rate of investment by organizations in training and career development.

(3) Considerable effort to create secure employment and avoid layoffs as much as possible.

(4) Sophisticated systems of organizational communications and information sharing.

(5) Informal mechanisms for or encouragement of participation in decision making about how the work is to be carried out.

(6) Development of a psychological climate that fosters and rewards organizational loyalty and commitment.

(7) Creation of a rational wage and salary administration, equitable performance appraisal, and promotion systems that reward merit and also recognize seniority.

(8) A non-union grievance procedure usually without binding arbitration.

(9) Location of new production facilities in rural areas or in areas only sparsely unionized.

(10) Use of employee selection devices that weed out workers who might or might not be pro-union.

The purpose of these policies is to obtain workers who are simultaneously satisfied with the economic rewards from work, the intrinsic aspects of their jobs, and their ability to influence decisions having to do with their work. Some of the best examples among mature companies that apply the above soft human resource management approaches to retaining a non-union status include: International Business Machines (IBM), Eastman–Kodak, Digital Equipment Corporation, Motorola, Marks and Spencer, Wang Electronics B.V., and Verbatim. Toner's studies of large non-union companies in Ireland show these companies develop a strong corporate culture built upon their employment practices which acts to reduce the perceived demand for unions amongst their employees (Toner, 1987) (see Figure 5.3).

Toner's study compared employee perceptions of human resource policy and practices among a sample of 248 workers drawn from three large non-union and four large unionized plants. Each of the plants was foreign owned, operated in the electronics industry and with one exception had been set up in either the late 1960s or the 1970s. Variations in attitudes to some 19 personnel policy and practice items were examined between the unionized and non-union employees. Typical item content referred to issues such as management style, grievance handling, satisfaction with supervisors, pay, and fringe benefits. Statistically significant and more favorable attitudes were found among non-union employees on 14 of the 19 items examined. The research reported later in this chapter derives from the detailed follow-up case study and interview work conducted at these seven plants.

Industrial relations, HRM policies and union avoidance

Human resource policies and practices of the above type can be expected to have a significant impact upon whether firms recognize trade unions or not (Beaumont, 1987, 1991; Beaumont and Harris, 1988; Fiorito, *et al.* 1987; Guest, 1987; Milner and Richards, 1991). There are a number of ways in which the HRM policies and practices outlined above could act to reduce the incentives for unionization. If we accept as a starting point that felt inequities and dissatisfactions with the work environment can create a demand among employees for union representation, then we can begin to view HRM policies and practices as perhaps substituting for the functions and activities which trade union services supply. If good pay and conditions are provided within the firm, individual developmental and training needs are catered for; and if extensive communication, briefing, and information services to employees exist, then one of the major functions of trade unions,

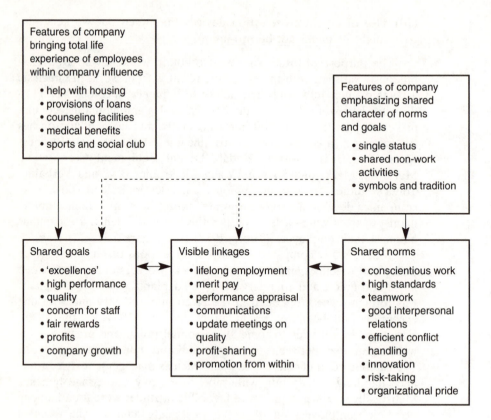

Figure 5.3 Model of a strong non-union culture.
Source: Toner, 1987.

namely the negotiation and improvement of such conditions and services, is eroded. As we have seen earlier, however, within the non-union sector, typically only the large, high wage companies are either in a resource-rich position to provide such services or possess the sentiment to do so (Blyton and Turnbull, 1994).

An explicit human resource strategy often also includes references to creating a culture and climate which creates a sense of 'mutuality' among employees and managers at the plant level. This can have the effect of reducing the demands for unionization. Pay-for-performance systems which recognize individual contribution and merit have also been found to be a common feature in large non-union companies (Toner, 1987). The provision of career development and training opportunities in firms, plus an above-average expenditure on training, would also appear to be a characteristic of large non-union companies. Further, selection methods designed to filter out people who are prone to unionize have been found by researchers to be one of a battery of techniques used by non-union companies (Foulkes, 1980). Briefing and communication techniques may also be expected to be well developed in large non-union companies. Also, the extent to which line managers are dominant within firms exerts a significant influence on the way in which human resource policies and philosophies are developed and promulgated at the top level of the organization.

Kochan and colleagues (1986) argue that during the 1970s human resource professionals lost ground to line managers with the result that the motivation to actually pursue non-union alternatives was felt first by line managers and high-level corporate executives, *not* by industrial relations and human resource management practitioners responsible for interaction and negotiations on union matters. Chapter 6 makes a similar point in relation to the decline of the power and influence of the personnel specialist. Indeed, when viewed historically, many industrial relations professionals in the United States, the United Kingdom and Ireland rose to positions of influence within companies by virtue of the fact that there was a need to develop strong collective bargaining arrangements in order to produce quiescent trade unions at the workplace level.

The Catch-22 element in union avoidance and the 'Americanization of industrial relations'

Unions exist, at least in part, as a means by which workers protect themselves against managerial prerogatives. It follows that a firm which seeks to take advantage of the absence of unions cannot do so through exercising managerial prerogatives in such a way that would induce unionization. For instance, if a firm manages to create a union-free environment, and then decides to take advantage of this by lowering wages, the workers are likely to organize to prevent this. This is particularly true in the case of US multinational corporations (MNCs) locating subsidiaries in European countries with a strong union tradition. A US company may work hard to create a non-union environment, and then, ironically, find that it is unable to take advantage of it because the local unions are eager to recruit members.

It is perhaps important at this point to reiterate the distinction made earlier between two types of non-union companies, or rather two different external contexts within which they are created. The first external context is one in which there is little threat of union organization, which may occur where:

(1) the industry or firm is so marginal that workers and/or unions realize that unionization would put it out of business;
(2) the industry or sector operates in a highly competitive environment and the union organizers realize that there are few 'pickings' for

the workers, and, consequently, for the union. In general, as Barbash (1984) observed, unions target only the profitable industries, though this may be more true in the US than elsewhere;

(3) the legal framework makes union organization difficult, as in the United States, particularly in the 'right to work' states;

(4) social and political factors facilitate unscrupulous employers in suppressing union activity, sometimes violently;

(5) workers are apathetic, badly educated, or poor, and are fearful of engaging in any activity that might endanger their livelihood. This applies mainly in some Third World countries where union density is below 10%. However, it can also apply in pockets in more developed economies.

In these situations management may take advantage of the absence of unions to pay wages at minimum local market rates and to make all the major decisions about the business unilaterally.

The second external context is one in which there is considerable threat of union organization, and this may exist when:

(1) union enmity in the particular area or industry is already high, or where there are legal pressures on employers to recognize unions;

(2) the industry or sector is particularly profitable, or where a firm has established a niche or monopoly position which would make it relatively easy to pass on union-induced wage increases to consumers;

(3) union organizing efforts in the area or sector are comparatively aggressive;

(4) a previously profitable organization or sector is undergoing a process of rationalization.

In these situations a firm may still decide to adopt a non-union policy, in spite of the difficulties involved, to avoid the alleged disadvantages of unions listed earlier in this chapter. These firms cannot, however, take full advantage of the absence of unions, since to do so would itself induce unionization. Foulkes refers to such companies as 'large' non-union companies, and although this description by no means applies to all such companies, it will serve as a useful shorthand for the remainder of the chapter (Foulkes, 1980).

Limited focus of collective agreements

In order to understand what advantages a company can possibly gain from non-union status, it is useful to consider the scope of the standard collectively bargained union–management agreement. In general, in the process of collective bargaining, workers frame their demands in precise rather than in qualitative terms: 'Precise, quantitative demands give a concreteness and urgency to the opposition of groups that vaguely felt, but unfocused, dissatisfactions about the quality of life would never do' (Lockwood, 1958:388). In a collective bargaining context, wages also take on an important symbolic character (Hyman, 1972:123). Kornhauser suggests that: 'a stated goal of higher wages may veil unverbalized strivings for self-respect and dignity or vague hostilities toward the boss, the machine, and the entire industrial system (Kornhauser, *et al.*, 1954:64–5).

Hyman (1972) remarks that the reason why certain strivings are unverbalized and certain motivations unstated may be that these are unsuited to the language and the structure of collective bargaining. A wage claim is readily comprehensible, whereas non-wage issues are far less easy to formulate precisely. Ironically, however, in the process of making precise quantitative demands, unionized workers may have to sacrifice some of the unverbalized strivings and motivations. The formulation of demands in precise terms may mean that other less quantifiable options have to be foregone.

The quantifiable elements of the employment contract which are negotiated by the union approximate in a general way to the lower order needs identified by Alderfer (1972). At any rate it can be stated that unions in general do not concern themselves with higher order needs which are rather abstract and immaterial, and are less subject to quantification, and therefore do not fit comfortably into a collective bargaining context. Unions will, however, bargain about 'motivational' factors insofar as aspects of these are measurable and objective. For instance, with regard to achievement, and growth and advancement possibilities, unions will often insist on seniority as a basis for promotion. With regard to the work itself, and responsibility, the union may look for monetary reward for changes in work practices or increases in responsibility. In regard to recognition, unions have tended to oppose individual positive recognition on the grounds that it weakens collectivism. However, on the whole, unions do not particularly concern themselves with the satisfaction of higher-level needs.

The distinctive element of personnel policies in large non-union companies is that they attempt to exploit the 'motivational' or 'higher order' factors, while not neglecting the demotivational potential of lower order factors. Should they neglect the latter they would demoralize the employees and might well trigger union organization. When they exploit the motivational factors, this is less likely to happen. For instance, a large non-union company may decide to institute a policy of promoting on merit rather than on seniority. In a non-union setting, this is unlikely to cause much dissatisfaction, or trigger unionization, unless it is seen to be implemented in an unfair way. This is because it does not take place in the context of a collective bargaining relationship, but that of an individual relationship in which the contractual element is not stressed.

Figure 5.4 suggests which of the perceived disadvantages of unions

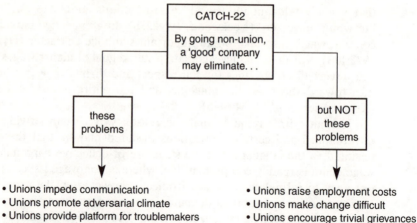

Figure 5.4 The Catch-22 of union avoidance.

a large non-union company might side-step, though if it does so in a crude or impersonal fashion it will adversely affect morale or encourage unionization. This list is derived from observation of behavior in unionized and non-union companies, but it is consistent with the theoretical considerations outlined above (Toner, 1987). The various points highlighted in Figure 5.4 will now be examined in some detail.

Employment costs

In the case of basic pay and conditions, large non-union companies cannot afford to take advantage of union absence to impose less favorable conditions than those a union would achieve. Indeed, on these issues the large non-union companies tend to give rather better conditions than unionized companies. Toner (1987) found that wage rates in large non-union companies were marginally above those in comparable unionized firms (1–4%). Interestingly, in both types of companies, when workers were asked how satisfied they were with basic pay, the outcome was almost exactly the same. However, in the case of fringe benefits, 75% of workers in the non-union companies considered them 'very good' or 'good', as against 37% in the unionized companies. A factor here is not only the desire of non-union employers to have good relations with employees, but also the fear of unionized employers to give fringe benefits for fear that they come to be seen as part of the negotiated package, to be improved on if possible.

Job security

In the case of job security, until recently 'lifelong' employment was a central plank in the personnel policies of the large non-union companies. Quinn Mills, commenting at the time about the unbroken policy of IBM on job security, pointed out that a policy of full employment (or even a general belief that such a policy of lifetime employment exists) is the major prerequisite for building trust with employees (Quinn Mills, 1988). In recent years many of the large non-union companies have been forced by market conditions to reduce their workforces. However, in general their severance packages have been extremely good in situations where union organization was a significant threat.

Thus a non-union policy does not offer the possibility of a 'hire and fire' policy. There is some evidence that, in the absence of a union challenge, non-union companies may find it easier to employ temporary, part-time and contract workers. However, Toner found that the employment of workers on a temporary basis for long periods did cause resentment in the large non-union companies studied, especially if these workers were let go. The hiring of temporary staff can be constrained in unionized companies, particularly where union membership is a condition of employment. Nevertheless, one can easily find examples, both in the public and private sectors, of 'temporary' appointments dragging on for years in unionized organizations.

Dismissal of unsatisfactory workers

A commonly cited problem related to unions is that they make it more difficult to dismiss unsatisfactory employees. In Toner's research two supervisors in a unionized company stated:

> In A. Ltd. you are well aware that they have a union and that they are well represented. People cannot be sacked here. When I was a shop steward here I was representing a man who was to be sacked. I found out that the supervisor had no documentation so the man got back. In the other (non-union) company he would be gone. (Supervisor 1)

> As regards the advantage of being union or non-union, one question that has always come up is that of the unsatisfactory employee. We can't dismiss them. If we have people who are not suitable attitudinally, we can't get rid of them. (Supervisor 2)
>
> (Toner, 1987:366)

But a large non-union company may also be reluctant to dismiss unsatisfactory employees, or to crack down on absenteeism, for fear of encouraging unionization. In Toner's research, a supervisor compared the situation in two companies in which he had worked:

> How do the jobs compare? Y Ltd. was highly unionized. I felt when
> I came here first that we were not doing things because we did not
> have and did not want a union. For instance, absenteeism in Y Ltd.
> was 4–5%; here it went as high as 25% on some shifts. To be honest
> we are spoiled because of the unions.
>
> (Toner, 1987:147)

Resistance to changes

A common complaint made about unions is that they make change
more difficult. A shop steward in one company studied by Toner
described one manager's attitude on this point:

> The production manager here has had classical management attitudes
> towards the union ... He was paranoid at first. He was previously in a
> unionised engineering company where they have a lot of restrictive prac-
> tices. They would not agree to changes in their work without extra pay.
>
> (Toner, 1987:75)

In another company studied by the same author the managing director
and two of the supervisors were asked if the presence of the union
made it more difficult to make changes:

> Does the union make it more difficult? Yes it does, no use saying it
> doesn't. It could influence your decision. If something is traditional it
> is hard to get something different done. (Supervisor)

> It is necessary with a union to list down all the parties who will be
> affected; and to consider what assurances will be given to the union.
> (Managing director)

> The union makes a big difference here indeed. If you have a problem
> the union has to be taken into account and you can't get an answer.
> I'll see the shop steward before I do something or not do it.
> (Supervisor)
>
> (Toner, 1987:365)

However, a lot seems to depend on the nature of the industry. In
the face of rapid technological progress, and intensified international
competition, most unionized workers are realistic about the need for
constant change.

For instance, in Toner's study a number of interviewees emphasized the flexibility within the electronics industry:

> Restrictiveness is not in this industry. There is never-ending change,
> some quite revolutionary change. People are used to this situation
> from day one. No one would get support here for restrictive practices.
> There was a move to a new building recently but nobody looked for
> relocation money. (Shop steward, Company X)
>
> (Toner, 1987:74)

Insofar as unionized workers do tend to make change more complicated, do large non-union companies then have *carte blanche* with regard to making changes? In practice large non-union companies go to considerable trouble communicating proposed changes to employees. A supervisor in one large non-union company stated:

> Communications here have to be good. Things are changing very often. The product line is changing. Orders are often cancelled. We all need to know what is happening. The ordinary employee is naturally listened to.
>
> (Toner, 1987:186)

Employees in both unionized and non-union plants were asked how they would rate the extent to which changes affecting their work were discussed with them beforehand. Perhaps surprisingly, 57% of the non-union employees rated their companies as very good or good in this respect, as against only 26% of the unionized workers. However, in the absence of a union, there is a smaller possibility that management will get into a situation of having to bargain about change.

Dealing with minor grievances

Another common complaint about unions is that to encourage the venting of trivial grievances wastes a lot of management time and may lead to more generalized disputes. Toner quotes a number of supervisors expressing this view:

> When people have a shop steward they tend to run with every little tittle-tattle. That does happen here. If there is someone there to crib to, people will crib. The shop steward is a good shoulder to cry on. (Supervisor 1)

> People take advantage of the union and bring up grievances because it is there. (Supervisor 2)
>
> (Toner, 1987:365)

However, Toner found that the workers in the large non-union companies studied were more satisfied with their grievance procedures than their unionized counterparts, with 76% of the former considering grievance procedures good or very good, compared with 48% of the latter. In the large non-union companies 87% of the employees surveyed considered that their complaints were taken 'very seriously' or 'quite seriously', compared with 62% in the unionized companies. Non-union companies use a variety of mechanisms to bring grievances to the surface and hopefully to solve them. Apart from the key role played by well-trained supervisors, large non-union companies also deploy special personnel staff, sometimes called employee representatives whose job it is to keep their finger on the employee relations pulse.

Non-union companies also use various meetings or fora at which grievances can be raised. Among its informal channels of communication, one large non-union company lists:

- weekly coffee sessions with the chief executive
- functional coffee sessions
- informal one-to-one meetings
- casual social conversations.

The grievance channels in large non-union companies frequently get quite complicated, as the personnel manager in one large non-union company reported:

> As regards grievances, we allow employees to talk to as many people as they want to. [The employee] is asked to talk to the supervisor first, but his destiny is not controlled by that one man. But the problem of going over people's heads is always a grave danger. We have two personnel reps. They are very high-powered people. In the case of grievances the first line is the supervisor, then the personnel rep. We have to convince two groups of people that the role of the reps is not disadvantageous to them, the employees and then the supervisors.
>
> (Toner, 1987:163)

So, in general, the business of dealing with apparently trivial grievances is not one that can be avoided by a large non-union company. On the contrary, as we have seen, these companies seem to go out of their way to encourage employees to articulate their grievances. In a highly unionized environment, the monitoring of grievances is a constant worry for the management of large non-union companies.

The managing director of one unionized company, who had previously been managing director of a large non-union company, summed up this preoccupation:

> The management of a company that is unionized is not constantly conscious of it being union. Whereas when I managed a non-union company I was always aware that it was a non-union company. Non-union companies have a powerful incentive to keep things right to keep the union out. I've been concerned how paranoid about unions the non-union companies are. Non-union companies wonder if they pay too much. Unionization would be a constant threat in this country. Company X ran into problems. The people said, 'We're fond of this company but we had better protect ourselves' so they joined the union. In cases of redundancy the unions offer the best protection. There is evidence that if it were not for the union movement the non-union companies would not pay as well as they do.
>
> (Toner, 1987:385)

Potential for motivational factors in non-union companies

The perceived disadvantages of unions mentioned above are not ones that can be simply side-stepped by large non-union companies. Large non-union companies must pay just as much attention to 'lower order' factors as their unionized counterparts. However, to return to Figure 5.4, in theory at least, large non-union companies may be able to side-step some of the problems listed on the left-hand side of Figure 5.4, and thus bring the 'motivational' factors more into play.

Individual rewards

Two supervisors spoke about the 'leveling' effect of unions:

> The union caters for the lowest common denominator, for instance, in the matter of output levels. A union takes away flexibility regarding incentives apart from promotion. The union is a leveller. The largest group of workers set the parameters. They become a pressure group. The union brings an equalisation of wage rates. The differentials have been narrowed here. (Supervisor 1)

> I think the non-union companies achieve a better result because they reward people better individually. They can increase somebody's rate. I noticed this in factories in England. But with union negotiations everyone is on the same level and it takes away initiative. I hear this mentioned in my shop – 'Why bother to work harder?' (Supervisor 2)
> (Toner, 1987:365)

This leveling of wages and conditions is not merely an accidental by-product, but is of the very essence of classical trade unionism. The argument was that individual bargaining between the employer and worker gave rise to competition between individual workers and tended to result in lowering wages and conditions of employment; wages would be kept down to what could be demanded and secured by the weakest bargainers of the labor group. This concern led to the union principle of uniformity in regard to all conditions of work and pay where competition between workers could take place.

By contrast, a belief in individualism is fundamental to the large non-union companies. This was particularly true of IBM, on which many of the other non-union companies tried to model themselves. A central thrust in IBM's strategy was to develop an entrepreneurial and risk-taking spirit among its employees. This need for individualism at IBM derives from the influence of Tom Watson Jr. and incentives have played a central role in the IBM culture. Of course, in this regard IBM merely reflects deeply held beliefs of US society. Part of the US business ideology, dubbed 'The American Way of Life', is the belief that individualism is a mainspring of the US economic and political system.

Indeed, a study of international differences in work-related values (carried out, incidentally, among IBM employees worldwide), identifies the United States as the most individualistic of 53 countries studied. Hofstede (1984:154) comments:

> The United States is the major exporter of modern organization theories, but its position of extreme individualism in comparison to most other countries makes the relevance of some of its theories in other cultural environments doubtful.

In the absence of a union, with its strongly anti-individualistic culture, a company should be able in implement a policy of individual reward, thereby enhancing motivation. However, non-union companies must ensure that any incentive is seen to be fair. In one company studied by Toner the implementation of a merit pay scheme appeared to be one of the factors that triggered the unionization of the plant. A supervisor stated:

> Top management was autonomous before the union came in and it is not good industrial relations to have a 'take it or leave it' attitude. Personally, I never condone unfair treatment, but you would have cases where two people were working on the same machines side by side and getting two different rates of pay for no apparent reason.
>
> (Toner, 1987:375)

A shop steward gave a similar opinion about the merit pay scheme:

> Before the union came in you might have three people in one area all doing exactly the same work, and each getting different rates of pay. If you were 'well in' you got the A rate. The system did not go down well because it was too dependent on how you got on with certain people.
>
> (Toner, 1987:375)

Improved communications

A second advantage that a large non-union company might derive from the absence of a union is that it may be able to free up lateral communication in the company. In a unionized company communications can become quite bureaucratic, with great emphasis on procedures, and a wariness on the union side about informal communication channels. A shop steward in a foreign-owned (not US) unionized company commented:

> The union is the main channel of communication between management and workers. The company does not want to have it any other way. The company wants a single recognizable entity, which is the union, to deal with. If more informal meetings were mooted, the union would probably oppose them.

It would be more advantageous to the company, rather than to the workers, to be more personable and to adopt the 'American' approach. The union would feel the company was propagandizing the workers and would be uncomfortable with this. At the same time, if the company really wanted to set up channels of this kind, there is probably not much the union could do about it. However, as long as the company is under _____ [nationality] command such a thing will not happen. It would be seen as an abdication of power to listen to opinions from the floor.

(Toner, 1987:172)

An employee 'rep' in one of the large non-union companies considered that there was a great sense of freedom in the company compared with union companies, in the sense that employees could talk to anyone: 'In a union shop barriers go up all over the place' (Toner, 1987:173). He had been training officer in both types of companies and claimed that in a union company a training officer could not be on the floor or talk to people without the shop steward wanting to know why: 'If I spoke to somebody the steward would be up to him in a minute to ask what I wanted (Toner, 1987:173).'

Apart from the charge that unions can create a climate where informal discussion between management and employees is made more difficult, it is also sometimes alleged that the presence of unions complicate communication related to the work process. Two supervisors in a large non-union company made this point strongly:

> The steward is an extra person on the scene. Here, if we want to build up targets we talk to the twenty people involved. In a union company the union will have their attention. You can't sell the idea through the shop steward so quickly. In a union house the shop steward is set up as a barrier to communication. You are not able to do so much. (Supervisor 1)

> When you talk about a union you are talking disruption and loss of production. If you have to go through fifteen people to get something done, the union eats away your authority. (Supervisor 2)

(Toner, 1987:124)

Nevertheless, precisely the opposite point of view was expressed by a number of staff in a unionized light engineering company surveyed:

> A. Ltd. saw the union as more of an ally. Their attitude is, if they are in a union we can talk to them, we have a procedure. You can be better organized in a plant with a union if you have the right people at the helm. Flexibility has improved immensely. The company can move people around. The unions have ok'd it. (Supervisor)

> The union keeps the whole place together. A minority of workers can often lead people and paint a certain picture, but when they are all brought together they see if differently.
> The union may talk to people and influence them. (Supervisor)

> Management in union companies can do things and see if the union reacts. The union will tell us if we are not doing things right. (Managing director)
>
> (Toner, 1987:363)

Brown and Medoff (1978) also suggested that collective bargaining can open up an important channel of communication between workers and management. The matter can best be summed up by saying that the absence of unions gives the non-union companies more options in creating both formal and informal communication channels. Whether these are always more effective channels than would exist in a unionized set-up seems less certain, depending to a great extent on the ingenuity and determination of management.

Avoidance of adversarial climate

In Toner (1987) two senior managers mentioned the potential for unions to create an adversarial climate:

> In companies that start off with a union a polarization develops. You will hear management say things like, 'We'll face them' or 'We'll take them on.' I have never heard that said here. (Personnel manager, non-union company)
>
> Unions will have to say 'We are going to get you more'. . . The unions are in the business of saying, 'Your employer is not dealing with you well enough.' They promote the idea that management have more to give. (Managing director)
>
> (Toner, 1987:136 and 365)

From a non-union company point of view, the main problem with a polarization of this kind is not so much that it increases wage costs, or leads to arguments, but that it inhibits the development of a strong company culture. It can be argued that the starting point for the large non-union company is not that it is non-union, but that they have a shared culture.

This involves sharing a vision that is based on a clearly stated set of values describing both the organization's mission (purpose) and the methods for realizing it. Toner found less identification with management among workers in unionized plants compared with their counterparts in non-union companies. In response to the question, 'To what extent do you think of management and employees in your company as being on the same side?,' 60% of the non-union employees responded 'completely' or 'to a great extent,' whereas 56% of the unionized employees ticked 'to some extent' and 23% 'hardly at all.' Many unions and their representatives in plants would subscribe to the arguments put forward by such writers as Hyman (1972) on sources of conflict in industrial work situations, including:

(1) *Job Security.* The worker's desire to establish a right to his job as a potential source of conflict.
(2) *Power and control.* The exercise of managerial control as a persistent basis for conflict.
(3) *Income distribution.* What is income for the employee is cost for the employer.
(4) *The nature of modern industrial work.* The fact that much work cannot be expected to possess much meaning or creativity.

Hyman acknowledges that there exists an area of common interest between those who control industry and those who work in it; namely, that if the firm goes bankrupt, both suffer losses. Yet, clearly, this degree of solidarity is far less than is required for the kind of culture espoused in IBM.

Unions also possess a strong culture of their own designed to facilitate a solidaristic orientation. This can be most clearly seen in material symbols, such as banners and badges. It can also be observed in language used in union circles, employing such terms as 'brother,' 'scab,' 'blackleg,' 'rank-and-file,' and so on. Many of the tactics employed by union members would be considered unethical, even by their own members, if employed in other areas of life. Examples would include sending a fellow-worker 'to Coventry,' preventing people from working by mass picketing intended to intimidate, excluding non-members of the union from employment, preventing the operation, either by themselves or others, of essential services, or failing to carry out the lawful instruction of their employer. An organization with such a strong and distinctive culture could well be considered to represent 'a different drummer.'

Nevertheless, in practice, unions do not always seem to inhibit the creation of a strong company culture. In Toner a supervisor is quoted as saying:

> With the union the only time you actually get collective action is during the pay bargaining. There are different shades of trade unionism.
>
> (Toner, 1987:121)

In fact this would correspond to the general view of trade unions in Japan, where identification with the company culture is at its strongest. In the West, two different developments have contributed to making the unions less fearsome at the plant level. In the first place, better management and more proactive policies have drawn the unions' teeth in several areas. In the second place, the general decline in union density due to economic factors, as well as the growth of sophisticated human resource management, has forced unions to take part in a kind of 'Dutch auction' whereby unions are motivated to compete in offering terms most favorable to the employer. This development has been noted in Britain, where a northern regional secretary of the Transport and General Workers Union (TGWU), Joe Mills, described the contest for representation rights in the new Nissan plant in Tyne and Wear as being forced to parade before prospective employers like beauty queens. He argues that, instead of seeking to recruit members, unions have offered themselves as recruits to management – reversing the whole principle of trade unionism (Huxley and Tighe, 1985). In short, the absence of a union may allow a company to adopt an outwardly unitary, as against pluralistic, stance towards their employees and to attempt to build a single unified organization culture. However, the difficulties of doing this equally well in a unionized establishment can be exaggerated.

Flexibility, manning levels and restrictive practices

Unions, particularly craft unions, are traditionally associated with a lack of flexibility in work practices. However, as mentioned earlier, much depends on the industry. For instance, a report on the computer industry in Ireland by a US consultancy firm (Burns Christopher, Inc., 1986) stated that though some employers have invited the participation of a union, they found no indication that labor unions have resulted in manning level or work restrictions of any sort. In Toner the personnel manager of a large non-union company commented:

> Since the Irish Productivity Council was founded, unions in Ireland have generally been OK as regards productivity... I have personally experienced union obstruction about promotion, but it was often due to other problems... Flexibility is not much different whether unionized or non-unionized; people are people and you have got to get commitment.
>
> (Toner, 1987:121)

Nevertheless, in the same study, there was a good deal of anecdotal evidence that unions do have some impact in this area, particularly in relation to production levels. But some of the experiences cited date from earlier years, and other comments may have been largely impressionistic:

> In V. Ltd. (electronics company) I had a bad experience with the union. After three weeks with the company, working as an assembler, my numbers were not very good, about 220, when the target was 250. The supervisor pointed this out to me. The operator at the next bench overheard and she made a big fuss and called in the union. I had to go to a meeting with the supervisor and the shop-steward. I was very embarrassed. I thought the supervisor was probably right and she was encouraging me because she saw I was a good worker...
>
> Another example of flexibility here was in the _____ department where we were able to reduce the quality check and increase production by 50 units per hour. You could not do this in a union house

... There are differences between here and a union shop. In a union shop if a girl had a quota of 260 she would stop when she reached it, she would not do 270. (Supervisor, non-union company)

(Toner, 1987:76)

But a few interviewees made the point that where production levels in unionized companies are bargained, measurement is more exact, and this can lead to tighter controls:

It is hard to compare this and the last (union) job. There was a measured day rate, so there was a specific amount to do and the length of breaks was laid down exactly in calculating the rate. Here there is no set rate. (Supervisor, non-union company)

In a unionised situation measurements tend to be exact. We have been attempting to discuss productivity deals here. In fact we have lower manning levels than the norm, dating from our non-union days. In a union situation we would have had to bargain our helpers. This would be seen as a union gain but it would also be a contribution to productivity. (Managing director, union company – formerly non-union)

(Toner, 1987:77)

With regard to demarcation, comments from a number of supervisors in non-union companies suggested that non-union companies were able to take considerable advantage of staff flexibility to an extent that might be seen as minor exploitation in a union house:

If we had a union it could cause difficulties here. I might have an oddball job. I am a toolmaker but we have great flexibility. A guy will do anything here. There is no demarcation. We don't encourage switching but it is possible. There have been occasions when the office girls have got involved in packing in order to get special orders out on time. (Supervisor, non-union company)

(Toner, 1987:78)

Conclusion

In general, it is not certain that non-union status ensures significantly greater flexibility than union status. The nature of the industry may be more significant. Some industries, generally more traditional ones, have a history of demarcation and inflexibility. In these industries non-union status might theoretically bring greater flexibility, but in practice non-union status is not a realistic option because of the high 'unionateness' (Lockwood, 1958) of the industries in question. In the case of modern industries, such as electronics, software, and pharmaceuticals, a culture of flexibility has in any case developed, mainly because these industries have matured in a climate of intense national and international competition.

In this type of industry there seems to be currently little advantage in the area of flexibility to be gained from non-union status. Moreover, if the absence of a union is taken advantage of to gain flexibility, there is likely to be a limit to the tolerance of workers in this respect, especially where practice in unionized establishments is well known.

An important intermediate case can be found in traditional industries where deregulation, privatization, or 'demonopolization' are the order of the day. In this case a new company may initially gain considerable competitive advantage through a non-union policy, not only through paying lower wages and salaries, but also through greater flexibility. A notable example of this has been the airline business, where a host of non-union airlines, such as the ill-fated People's Express, sprang up in the 1970s and 1980s. It is difficult to predict whether the competitive advantage gained in these cases will be long term. The staff of these companies are well aware that management is taking advantage of their non-union status and attendant flexibility. For them, the tradeoff is a job which is still reasonably well paid, a job which would probably disappear if union rates and conditions were imposed.

It should not be forgotten, moreover, that unions have important societal welfare effects which have impinged directly upon the democratic process in pluralist societies – reducing inequalities in income distribution, enhancing pension coverage for blue-collar workers (who otherwise might fall prey to the vicissitudes of the market), and ensuring that potentially dictatorial political regimes do not go unchallenged. The British WIRS evidence also indicates that non-unionism in the private sector by no means always follows the high wage, high involvement approach popularized in those books written about the large non-union type companies. While, as we have seen, some large non-union companies provide extensive and progressive human resource practices designed to win the hearts and minds of employees, they are best viewed as 'atypical' within the non-union sector.

Moreover, it seems that the threat of becoming unionized forces even the most progressive of these large non-union companies to be consciously viligant in monitoring their own management to ensure that human resource policies and practices are implemented in a consistent and equitable fashion. 'Managing without unions' for these large high wage companies is a far cry from the supposed freedoms that union avoidance might be expected to confer. It is an empirical question as to how many of these large non-union companies would continue to invest in their high wage, high commitment strategies in the absence of unions. Non-unionism for the latter category of firms would indeed seem to represent a form of pyrrhic victory.

References

Abowd, J. (1989). The effect of wage bargains on the stock market value of the firm, *American Economic Review*, September, 774–801.

Alderfer, C.P. (1972). *Existence, Relatedness and Growth*. New York: The Free Press.

Bain, G.S. and Elsheikh, F. (1976). *Union Growth and the Business Cycle*. Oxford: Basil Blackwell.

Bain, G.S. and Price, R. (1983). Union growth: dimensions, determinants and density. In Bain, G.S. (ed.), *Industrial Relations in Britain*. Oxford: Basil Blackwell.

Barbash, J. (1984). *The Elements of Industrial Relations*. Madison, WI: University of Wisconsin Press.

Beaumont, P. (1987). *The Decline of Trade Union Organisation*. London: Croom Helm.

Beaumont, P. (1991). Trade Unions and HRM, *Industrial Relations Journal*, 22, (4), 300–9.

Beaumont, P. and Harris, R. (1988). The North-South divide in Britain: the case of trade union recognition, *Oxford Bulletin of Economics and Statistics*, 51, 413–28.

Becker, B.E. (1987). Concession bargaining: the impact on shareholders' equity, *Industrial and Labour Relations Review*, 40, 268–79.

Becker, B.E. and Olson, C.A. (1986). The impact of strikes on shareholders' equity. *Industrial and Labour Relations Review*, 39, April, 415–38.

Blyton, P. and Turnbull, P. (1994). *The dynamics of employee relations*. London: Macmillan.

Brett, J.M. (1980). Why employees join unions, *Organisational Dynamics*, Spring, 53–4.

Brown, C. and Medoff, J. (1978). Trade unions in the production process, *Journal of Political Economy*, 86, (3), 355–78.

Burns Christopher, Inc. (1986). Ireland as a Site for Information Operations. Salem, Massachusetts. Report Commissioned by Industrial Development Authority.

Buzzel, R.B. and Gale, B.T. (1987). *The PIMS Principles, Linking Strategy to Performance*. New York: The Free Press.

Clark, K. (1984) Unionization and firm performance: the impact on profits, growth and productivity. *American Economic Review*, 24, (4), 893–920.

Connolly, R.A., Barry, T., and Hirschey, M. (1985). Union rent seeking, intangible capital, and market value of the firm. Mimeograph. University of North Carolina at Greensboro, January.

Fiorito, J., Lowman, C., and Nelson, F.D. (1987). The impact of human resource policies on union organising, *Industrial Relations*, 26, (2), 113–26.

Foulkes, Fred K. (1980). *Personnel Policies in Large Non-Union Companies*. Englewood Cliffs, NJ: Prentice-Hall.

Freeman, R.B. and Medoff, J.L. (1984). *What do Unions do?* New York. Basic Books.

Green, F. (1990). *Trade union availability and trade union membership in Britain*. Manchester: Manchester School of Economic and Social Studies, 58, 378–94.

Guest, D. (1987). Human Resource Management and Industrial Relations, *Journal of Management Studies*, 24, (5), 503–23.

Guest, D. and Hoque, K. (1994). The Good, the Bad and the Ugly: employment relations in new non-union workplaces. *Human Resource Management Journal*, 5, (1), 1–14.

Guest, D. and Rosenthal, P. (1992). Industrial relations in greenfield sites. Mimeo, Centre for Economic Performance, Industrial Relations Conference, London School of Economics, Centre for Economic Performance, London, March.

Hofstede, G.H. (1984). *Culture's Consequences*. (Abridged edition.) Beverly Hills, CA: Sage.

Huxley, J. and Tighe, C. (1985). New look union at Nissan plant, *The Sunday Times*, 28 April.

Hyman, R. (1972). *Strikes*. Glasgow: Fontana/Collins.

Ichniowski, C. (1986). The effects of grievance activity on productivity, *Industrial and Labour Relations Review*, 40, October, 75–89.

Katz, H.C., Kochan, T.A., and Weber, M. (1985). Assessing the effects of industrial relations systems and efforts to improve the quality of working on organizational effectiveness, *Academy of Management Journal*, 28, September, 209–526.

Klandermans, P.G. (1984a). Mobilisation and participation in trade union action: a value expectancy approach, *Journal of Occupational Psychology*, 57, 107–20.

Klandermans, P.G. (1984b). Mobilisation and participation: social psychology expansions of resource mobilisation theory, *American Sociological Review*, 49, 583–600.

Klandermans, P.G. (1984c). Membership meetings and decision making in trade unions. Paper presented at the EGOS Colloquium on trade unions in Europe: the organizational perspective. 11–13 October, Amersfoort, The Netherlands.

Klandermans, P.G. (1986). Psychology and trade union participation: joining, acting, quitting, *Journal of Occupational Psychology*, 59, 189–204.

Kleiner, M. (1990). The role of industrial relations in industrial performance. In Fossum, J.A. (ed.) *Employee and Labour Relations*, Washington, D.C: Bureau of National Affairs.

Kleiner, M.M., Nickelsburg, G., and Pilarski, A. (1980). Grievances and plant performance: is zero optimal?, Proceedings, Madison, Wisconsin, Industrial Relations Research Association.

Kochan, T. and Katz, H. (1988). *Collective Bargaining and Industrial Relations*. Irwin, Il: Homewood, 191.

Kochan, T.A., Katz, H.C., and McKersie, R.B. (1986). *The Transformation of American Industrial Relations*. New York: Basic Books.

Kornhauser, A., Dubin, R., and Ross, A.M. (eds) (1954). *Industrial Conflict*. New York: McGraw-Hill.

Lawler, J. (1986). Union growth and decline: the impact of employer and union tactics, *Journal of Occupational Psychology*, 59, (3), 217–31.

Lockwood, D. (1958). *The Blackcoated Worker: A Study in Class Conciousness*. London: Allen and Unwin.

McGovern, P. (1989). *Union Recognition and Avoidance in the 1980s in Industrial Relations in Ireland: Contemporary Issues and Developments*. University College, Dublin.

McLouglin, I. and Gourlay, S. (1986). *Enterprise without unions: industrial relations in the non-union firm*. Buckingham: Open University Press.

Milner, S. and Richards, E. (1991). Determinants of union recognition and employee involvement: evidence from the London Docklands. *British Journal of Industrial Relations*, 29, (3), 377–91.

Millward, N. (1994). *The new industrial relations?* London: Policy Studies Institute.

Milward, M., Stevens, M., Smart, D., and Hawes, W.R. (1992). *Workplace Industrial Relations in Transition*. Aldershot: Dartmouth.

Neumann, G. (1980). The predictability of strikes: evidence from the stock market, *Industrial and Labour Relations Review*, July, 525–35.

Porter, M. (1980). *Competitive Strategy*. New York: The Free Press.

Quinn Mills, D. (1988). *The IBM Lesson: The Profitable Art of Full Employment*. New York: Times Books.

Ram, M. (1994). *Managing to survive: working lives in small firms*. Oxford: Blackwell.

Reed, T.F., Beaumont, P.B., and Pugh, M.F. (1995). International industrial relations. In Ferris, G.R., Rosen, S.D., and Barnum, D.T. (eds) *The Handbook of Human Resource Management*. Oxford: Blackwell.

Richard, R. and Zimmerman, M.B. (1984). Unionization and profitability: evidence from the capital market. *Journal of Political Economy*, 92, (6), 1134–57.

Ruback, R. and Zimmerman, M.B. (1984). Unionization and profitability: evidence from the capital market, *Journal of Political Economy*, 92, (6), 1134–57.

Scott, A. (1994). *Willing slaves: British workers under Human Resource Management*. Cambridge: Cambridge University Press.

Sisson, K. (1993). In search of HRM. *British Journal of Industrial Relations*, 31, (2), 201–10.

Thomas, S. and Kleiner, M. (1989). Two-tier collective bargaining arrangements and shareholder equity. Unpublished Manuscript, University of Minnesota.

Toner, W.P. (1987). Union or non-union: contemporary employee relations strategies in the Republic of Ireland. Unpublished PhD, London School of Economics.

Van de Vall, N. (1970). *Labour Organizations*. Cambridge: Cambridge University Press.

Visser, J. (1985). Vakbondsgroei en vakbondsmacht in West Europa, *Tijdschrift voor Arbeidsvraagstukken*, 1,(1), 52–69.

6

Personnel management without personnel managers: varying degrees of outsourcing the personnel function

Introduction

Current developments such as intensified competition, accelerated technological progress, and a shorter product lifecycle create more exacting markets. These market demands affect the areas of cost effectiveness, quality, flexibility, innovativeness, and speed. Often these demands have to be met simultaneously if sustainable competitive advantage is to be achieved. Such demands have fundamental consequences for the structuring of the organization and its management of resources, including its 'human resources.' Given this situation, the unavoidable fact is that organizations must focus on their core activities and core competencies. Activities not falling within these categories must then become possible candidates for outsourcing. In the language of transaction cost economics the pros and cons of 'make' (in house) or 'buy' (outsourcing) decisions must continually be analyzed. Viewed from this perspective the traditionally configured specialist personnel function becomes a potential candidate for outsourcing.

In addition to this shift in emphasis from *make to buy*, we can also identify a related tendency towards greater involvement of line managers. One of the essentials of the strategic human resource management (SHRM) approach – next to its close alignment with business requirements – is its emphasis on shifting responsibilities from staff to line management. Line managers are typically required under a strategic human resource philosophy to 'discover' and recognize the crucial role of human resources in developing the five capabilities of world-class performances, that is, the ability to produce products and services 'right the first time,' speedily, on time, cheaply, and flexibly (see Chapter 1). Line managers must become the implementers of human resource policies if such strategies are to succeed. It stands to reason, then, that this perspective must lead to increasing pressure on the traditional role of the personnel management specialist. Taken to its logical conclusion, this perspective could eventually imply that the HRM approach leads to 'personnel management without personnel managers.' The BSO/Origin case study below is ample evidence that this possibility is not mere fiction. On the contrary, it could well represent the shape of things to come.

This chapter, using research from various countries, illustrates that profound changes in the personnel function are being implemented in many companies. In order to give a clear overview of the various changes in HRM delivery systems – both minor and major – affecting the personnel function we developed a four-cell typology (matrix) of which the two dimensions are as shown in Figure 6.1:

(1) The distinction between *internalizing* (the shift from specialist staff to regular line management) and *externalizing* (the shift from 'make to buy') that is, completing the personnel function activity in-house or contracting with others to do it.
(2) The depth and scope of the intervention: does the implemented change affect the organization as a whole (*major change*) or does it only have an impact upon the domain and mode of operation of the personnel department itself (*minor change*).

In this chapter we first examine the issues involved in managing without personnel managers by presenting a short case, which brings into perspective several of the issues faced by managers pursuing such a strategy.

Next we present an overview of recent organizational trends and developments, all of which emphasize the increasing importance of human resources, in order to identify their possible effects upon the personnel function. In particular we focus on those effects which are related to the shift of responsibilities from specialist staff departments to regular line management. Line managers are increasingly pressed to optimize the rendering of specialist staff services. This process of optimization can often be realized by applying the principles of the marketplace (market forces) and by using the analytical device presented by transaction cost economics in order to decide whether to make or buy specialist personnel activities.

Then we present a systematic overview of the various possibilities of internalizing (shift from specialist staff to line management) and externalizing (shift from make to buy). Finally, we address the issue of whether we really need personnel managers or whether we can do without them. We link this debate to an examination of factors/variables which explain the presence or absence of a personnel management department.

Focus of change / Extent of change	Internalizing (shift from staff to regular line/workers)	Externalizing (outsourcing)
Minor changes		
Major changes		

Figure 6.1   Alternative HRM delivery mechanisms.

Case study   BSO/Origin: The shape of things to come[†]

Leaning back in his chair Eckhart Wintzen, founder and CEO of BSO/Origin, reflected on the beginnings of his company. 'When I started out, I was fortunate in that I was not hindered by any knowledge of proper management techniques. Otherwise I might have ended up doing things the traditional way.'

From humble beginnings in the Netherlands in 1976, BSO/Origin has blossomed into a multinational organization, specializing in the selling of software. The company offers a comprehensive range of products ranging from integrative information systems and operations to consultancy and facility management. Rapid growth has meant that it now employs more than 4000 employees working in more than 80 different business units throughout the world.

A distinguishing feature of BSO is that, under Wintzen's leadership, the company's strategies all add up to a highly innovative approach to management. The single most important of these strategies is that the company structure is based on the distinctive idea of cell division. This means that, as soon as a branch of BSO employs a hundred people, it splits into two separate companies. This is exactly like biological cell-replication and reflects a truly organic organization. This continuous process of cell-splitting supports BSO's geographical extension and its very flat hierarchy enables the effective use of informal and face-to-face communications. Further, the structure is commercially flexible, enabling the autonomous divisions to respond rapidly to local market trends. The principle of cell-division also assures a high degree of employee commitment

---

† The introductory case of BSO/Origin is based upon the following interviews and reports: Wintzen (1991, 1993); PW (1994); BSO/Origin, 1992:79.

and maximum possibilities for self-actualization. As Wintzen points out: 'Our employees love the cell-philosophy approach, because it allows them maximum play for their own initiatives and creativity. By keeping staff size limited to 100 in each cell, people are really able to see the fruits of their own labor.'

Every cell is responsible for realizing its own targets within the framework of the overall corporate strategy. Also, every cell is able to function independently; as Wintzen has stated: 'In nature, things grow without any supervision. An onion, for example, grows because it has a message built into its cells, not because it has a chairman of the board. And if nature can do it, why can't companies?'

Specialist staff departments are absent from the BSO structure. While there are some small specialist departments at the top corporate level, the various cells or business units assume responsibility for their own profitability, marketing, recruitment, selection, appraisal, and workforce planning. Such tasks become the responsibility of the line manager(s) in charge. In this structure there is no need for a specialized personnel department.

At all levels of the organization formal and informal communication is very important. For example, selection interviews are carried out by employees within each unit and these employees also have an important say in the appraisal process. Every month informal meetings are held to discuss developments in information technology, projects assignments, and staffing policies. All employees are responsible for their own training and development, and each employee is allotted approximately 5% of their workable hours for this purpose. Every month, group managers will meet with employees to discuss progress in terms of individual career development. Twice a year each unit organizes a weekend get-together and in this highly informal atmosphere the aim is to develop better communications and interpersonal relationships. Families are not left out. They too attend and take part in the activities. Needless to say, motivation and commitment is high. As a result employee turnover is below 5% per year.

Wintzen himself strongly believes in his philosophy of delegating authority and responsibility as much as possible so that employees will have the best opportunity to use their skills and develop their potential. According to Wintzen,

> Two preconditions are important. First of all the objectives of the company must be well-known to everybody. Everyone must be able to see a clear relationship between his contribution and the objective of the organization... Secondly, it is important that this responsibility is related to visible jobs that can be measured... The possibility of measuring will get lost if, for example, many specialist staff departments are involved in the carrying out of a particular job. Measuring also creates challenge in a job: One can check to what degree the stated target has been reached. Moreover, measuring will allow the possibility of appraisal by others. It creates the opportunity for applause, which is highly motivating.

With this philosophy the emphasis at BSO/Origin is on a totally integrated management. As indicated above, staff departments hardly exist within the business-units. Such a structure develops a whole new organizational culture. This new culture conflicts with the more traditional approach to management in which staff and line functions are clearly separated. BSO and the Wintzen philosophy operate without the need of a specialized personnel function and may well reflect the shape of things to come in traditional organizations seeking innovative change.

An overview of actual developments

The origins of the personnel management department

Not surprisingly, the roots of personnel management are fairly diverse. However, certain developments are somewhat international (see, for discussions, Tyson and Fell (1986) in the UK and Cascio (1992) in the USA) and primarily owe their existence to the process of industrialization.

Case study   Paternalism and the first personnel manager in the Netherlands

In the Netherlands at the turn of the twentieth century the initial impetus toward social organization policy came from entrepreneurs such as Stork and Van Marken. They were prototypes of the paternalistic entrepreneur, men who knew 'their' workers, knew what was 'good' for them, and acted accordingly. Van Marken noted that in his firm the workers became alienated from their job. He attributed this to the enormous growth of the Yeast and Methylated Spirits Works in Delft, and considered the establishment of a workers' association to be an excellent instrument by which to combat this alienation. Van Marken also developed a kind of 'scheme of needs.' He held that employees needed not only job security and steady wages; other needs perbtained as well: recreation, training and 'moral betterment.' To meet such needs, he created a personnel function.

(*Source*: Bakker, *et al.*, 1989:8)

The roots of personnel management can also be traced to the bureaucratization of organizations. The growth of large-scale organizations, spreading applications of bureaucracy and the rise of specialist sections and departments (accounting, production planning, and so forth) all fostered a need for managing personnel.

In many cases the personnel function originated in the accounting department. Traditionally, accounting departments were responsible for a variety of ad hoc activities related to staffing and staff retention: recruitment, selection, salary administration, implementation of legal regulations and conditions stipulated in collective bargaining agreements, canteen stock maintenance, maintenance of wash-up rooms, and so on. Such activities became too bothersome for the accounting departments, and eventually they became the responsibility of newly created personnel departments.

The literature attributes subsequent developments in personnel management to concomitant developments in organization theory, such as the scientific management movement (Taylor), scientific administration (Fayol), human relations (Elton Mayo), and the revised view of human relations as human resources or as individuals capable and willing to assume responsibility (McGregor). Each school of thought stresses a particular image of man's nature, a concurrent emphasis in personnel activities, and a self-image of the role that personnel management should play in organizations.

More recent developments in personnel management (from the mid-1970s onward) generally demonstrate a more business-led approach to personnel issues. The rise of strategic management leads to greater attention being given to the value added concept of human resources, that is, the value that human resources add to the final good or service. This approach tends to encourage workforce planning and human resource utilization in terms of both today's and tomorrow's needs. It is this approach which when pressured by international competition sometimes expands into (strategic) human resource management (SHRM), often linked to a strategy of differentiation and complex organizational structures.

The challenge of increasing complexity

Increasing levels of organizational complexity cannot be solved by using more control and hierarchy. The only effective way for an organization to cope on a long-term basis with such an increasing degree of complexity (which at surface appears to manifest itself as 'chaos', because the underlying patterns are too complex to understand at first sight) is to enlarge the potentials and possibilities for self-regulation. This is achieved through empowerment strategies, encouraging self-monitoring, and by inculcating high levels of organizational commitment.

An enlarged degree of autonomy and flexibility can be effected by a regime involving several measures. A first category of measures taken by many organizations is to reduce the number of managerial levels and thus the commitment to the 'command and control bureaucracy' (Dichter, 1991:147). The aim of this type of intervention is to refocus the organization so that customers are once again the primary emphasis. Examples of these kinds of interventions are the removal of hierarchical levels (Keuning, *et al.*, 1993), the decentralization of entrepreneurship close to specific product market combinations (Aken, *et al.*, 1993), and the emphasizing of integral or unit management (Wissema, 1992).

The above-mentioned structural adjustments are useful, but not sufficient by themselves. Management and employees need to be provided with greater autonomy and responsibility. This can be achieved by a second category of measures and approaches aimed at expanding tasks, developing competencies and increasing responsibilities. More specifically we refer to approaches like empowerment, the development of self-managing teams (Manz and Sims, 1993), and the introduction of socio-technical measures and improvements in order to speed up the quality of working life.

Once we have been able to enhance the self-autonomy of management and employees, we must realize that at the same time mutual dependency has increased (Mastenbroek, 1993). Exchange of information and abundant access to it for everyone is necessary in order to establish coordination, both in a formal and informal way. It goes without saying that the manner in which human resources are treated is crucial in bringing about this self-autonomy of managers and employees.

Both the structural adjustments and the measures aimed at enlarging autonomy lay a solid foundation for a third category of interventions centering on business processes. In this respect we, of course, refer to approaches like business process re-engineering (Hammer, 1990), strategic quality management, and business process improvement (Harrington, 1991). The familiar image of the organization as a layered cake of functions, departments and hierarchic levels will disappear. Instead, we get a new organizational design in which processes of management and business, that lead to output and added value, have a central place. Needless to say, the role of people – individually or working in teams – as supporters and enablers of these processes is crucial.

Finally, as all these changes begin to take effect, the boundaries between the organization and its environment become more and more blurred. This blurring of organizational boundaries is enhanced by such developments as strategic alliances, especially in the field of research and development, outsourcing, and network forms of organizations.

Schematically, these changes and their impact associated upon the way organizations are structured can be presented as shown in Figure 6.2.

In summary, organizational structures are emerging where the emphasis is on greater flexibility. Employees must therefore work within

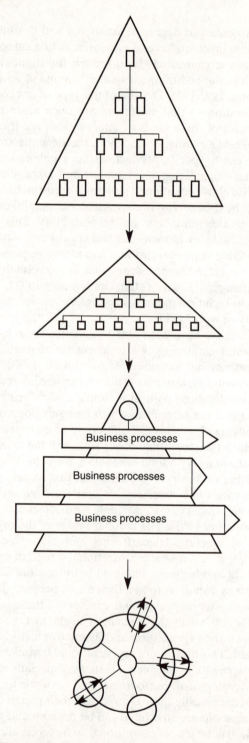

Figure 6.2 From hierarchy to business processes.

a more strategically oriented structure which is closer to the market. They must assume greater decision-making powers and accept more responsibilities in carrying out their tasks. In essence, the whole focus of the organization is towards its core activities and core competencies and the crucial role of workforce management.

Competencies as a source of sustainable competitive advantage

There is still another important reason for the growing significance of human resource management. To ensure that the organization sustains its competitive edge, there must be less of an emphasis on existing products, services, and markets, and more of an emphasis on core competencies (Prahalad and Hamel, 1990) and core capabilities (Bartlett and Ghosal, 1989). It is these core competencies that will guarantee a flow of new products and services for the future.

The competencies and capabilities at issue here are the development and communication of knowledge, adaptability, the combining of distinct technologies and production techniques, and the ability to transcend functional boundaries in order to cooperate. Quinn (1992a, 1992b) refers in this respect to 'knowledge-based service activities,' which are at the heart of an 'intelligent' business, that is, activities that cannot easily be duplicated by competitors. For this reason a real sustainable competitive advantage usually derives from developing depth in skill sets, experience factors, innovative capacities, know-how, market understanding, databases, or information distribution systems. According to Quinn, service activities, of which the performance and quality are highly dependent on the way human resources are being selected, developed, and managed. A study by Hall (1992) supports the growing significance of human resource management. Based on a survey among top managers, Hall establishes that resources like product or company reputation, employee know-how and skills, and company culture are crucial in contributing to the success of the organizations studied.

Personnel management: too important to be left to personnel managers?

The emergence of strategic HRM

Needless to say the aforementioned developments have given a strong impetus to HRM becoming more strategic in focus. They also imply that line managers are inclined to attach more importance to the whole issue of human resource utilization in the process of generating added value. This emphasis is also reflected in the more serious studies on SHRM, whose definitions have one thing in common: *a closer alignment to business* (we refer to, among others: Armstrong, 1992; Guest, 1987, 1989, 1990; Hendry and Pettigrew, 1990; Kluytmans and Paauwe, 1991; Storey, 1989). More specifically the defining characteristics of strategic HRM (SHRM) can be outlined as follows:

(1) The idea that people are essential to the success of an organization. Improved use of their capacities leads to enhancement of company performance.
(2) Complete integration of the HRM strategy into the corporate strategy. On the one hand, the business context is decisive for the deployment of workers. On the other hand, workers' capabilities can put a stamp on what is strategically desirable and possible.
(3) Emphasis on the importance of mutual consistency and coherence of the various personnel instruments and activities in order to achieve flexibility, commitment, quality, and customer-orientation.
(4) HRM as a line responsibility, in which special staff expertise is limited to support, advice, and partial implementation.

Referring to the Harvard model of Beer and colleagues (1984), these defining characteristics imply that it is not enough anymore to develop and implement personnel techniques and activities that are simply able to manage organizational human resource flows (in-, through-, and out). Strategic HRM adds the additional dimension of contributing towards establishing competencies like flexibility, quality ,and customer-orientation and commitment.

No wonder that line management is becoming more involved and is looking for clues in order to optimize the contribution from the personnel function. In combination with trends like *back to the core business* and *leaner and meaner* the shift from specialist staff to line management is evident.

Shift from line to staff

Specialist staff departments emerged only because organizations grew large. It is only large companies that can afford the 'luxury' of assigning certain managerial tasks to a specialist. Over the first 60 years of the twentieth century we saw organizations systematically grow bigger. The profitable efficiency achieved through mass production was sufficiently attractive to strive for maximum expansion. From the late 1970s onward the tide seemed to turn: larger organizations began to decentralize and subsidiaries were privatized or made independent (see Chapter 4). One reason for this change was that at a given point, the efficiency returns gained through growth were nullified by higher costs due to increasingly complex coordination. Furthermore, a large organization tended to have an alienating effect on many employees, thus eroding performance and motivation. Another reason for the trend towards decentralization is that the organization's environment keeps changing rapidly. A large organization could no longer react quickly. Smaller, leaner, and meaner units were created whose ability to respond immediately to changes in the environment owes much to the fact that their managers were charged with integral and total management of the unit. This made such managers responsible for all aspects of management: acquisition, production, sales and, of course, personnel.

It goes without saying that the developments sketched above had an impact on specialist staff departments generally and on personnel departments in particular. As Schuler (1990:51) notes:

> Companies are beginning to recognize the importance of people to the business's success. More human resource issues are really people related business issues in that they influence the essence of the business – profitability, survival, competitiveness, adaptability, and flexibility.

The assignment of integral management to line managers, the tendency towards decentralization, and the creation of smaller units imply that the role and position of personnel/human resource staff functions need to be reconsidered.

Changing roles and expectations for the personnel manager/HR manager

To be sure, this readjustment and recalibration has been going on for some time. Tyson (1987), struck by the increased fragmentation of the personnel function which he describes as its 'Balkanization,' distinguishes three Weberian ideal types or models:

(1) *The clerk of works model.* Personnel management as an administrative support activity with no involvement in business planning. All authority is vested in line managers. The principal activities for these personnel staff will be recruitment, record keeping, and welfare.
(2) *The contract manager model.* An approach concerned with confronting unions with a system, as part of a comprehensive policy network. Acting on behalf of line managers, the personnel department staff are experts in the trade union agreements, in fixing-day-to day issues with the unions, and responding in a reactive way to problems.
(3) *The architect model.* Personnel executives seeking to create and build the organization as a whole. This creative vision of personnel means contributing to the success of the business through explicit

policies which seek to influence the corporate plan, with an integrated system of controls between personnel and line managers. The personnel function is thus represented within the dominant coalition in the organization.

Armstrong (1988:25), however, notes that the contract manager model is dying out due to the diminution of trade union bargaining power (see also Chapter 5). Because line management displays a newly found self-confidence, the majority of personnel staff out of necessity fall back on the 'clerk of works model, performing routine administrative work ... whilst a few elite architects of strategic human resources policy continue to operate at the corporate headquarters level.' Even so, the 'clerk of works' model is no longer a secure shelter in view of the rising tendency toward accountability, the need to be able to illustrate the costs/benefits of a function, and the growing requirement that personnel information systems provide tough, quantifiable data. Given this interest and the expertise of accounting departments in this area, the danger is that they will become important competitors of the personnel staff according to Armstrong (1988:27).

Differentiation in roles will inevitably mean differentiation in dominant value patterns. In this connection Torrington (1988) points to the traditional man in the middle approach, in which personnel management in the past increasingly assumed a third-party role between management and employee, particularly due to the influence of legislation. Under the influence of strategic HRM thinking this traditional role is gradually shifting to a regular management function. Motorola's CEO Robert Galvin notes that in the final decade of the twentieth century human resource professionals are turning into members of the management team. They are expected to manage people-related issues, that is to say human resource activities are addressed from a business perspective (Schuler, 1990:50).

Carroll (1991) also envisages a shift in HRM roles, as a consequence of the more pronounced links to business needs and, thus, a greater requirement to contribute to organizational effectiveness. In additon to the traditional roles of policy formulator and provider of personnel services, Carroll expects certain roles to take on greater importance:

(1) *Delegator.* This role enables line management to serve as primary implementors of HRM systems.
(2) *Technical expert.* This function encompasses a number of highly specific HR-related skills.
(3) *Innovator.* As innovators, HR managers recommend new approaches to solving HRM-related problems, such as productivity.

Does this mean that, with respect to the dominant value pattern, personnel managers will now have to conform to business-economic criteria (bottom line, profits, effectiveness, and so on)? The analysis by Legge (1978) offers two options or strategies for HR professionals:

(1) *Conformist innovator.* The personnel specialist who identifies with the objective of organizational success, emphasizing cost benefit tradeoffs and conforms to the criteria adopted by managerial colleagues, who usually have greater power.
(2) *Deviant innovator.* The personnel specialist who identifies with a set of norms that are distinct from, but not necessarily in conflict with, the norms of organizational success. Power derives from an independent, professional stance when working with managerial clients.

In our evaluation at the end of this chapter we will deal with this issue more extensively.

Apart from this shift in emphasis in the role and relation between line and staff and the values at issue, there is still another conceivable option, namely that personnel activities are carried out by others, either internally or externally. Art Maine, Senior Personnel Manager at Revco, puts its this way:

> The real role of HR is in the areas of human productivity, quality and performance, yet these are being done increasingly by line managers, especially in the highly innovative successful mid-sized companies. The HR staff just do the administrative stuff which could be downloaded someday to the accounting and legal departments.
>
> (Schuler, 1990:49)

In our next section we will deal with this topic extensively both from a theoretical and empirically based perspective.

Alternative/innovative ways of performing the personnel function

Theoretical approaches

Due to the increased importance of the human factor we have already indicated that line management demands the optimization of the contribution of the personnel function. In this respect the following questions are crucial in deciding to carry out particular activities within or outside of the boundaries of the firm:

(1) Is the personnel activity at issue a genuine requirement? Does it in fact add value?
(2) If the answer is yes, should we then do it ourselves or should we outsource the activity (externalization)?

(3) If we should do it ourselves, should we then carry out activities through the specialist staff or by/via regular line management and/ or workers (internalization)?

By internalizing we mean the shift from specialist staff departments to regular line management and/or workers. In its extreme form this shift or downloading of activities – possibly in combination with contracting out – may yield a personnel management without personnel managers, of which the BSO case is a striking demonstration. Externalizing implies a shift from the in-house 'make' option to the so-called 'buy' option (outsourcing). To match this trend an increasing number of agencies are making themselves available. Obviously, the decision to make or buy is subject to a whole range of considerations including effectiveness, quality, efficiency, accessibility, speed of delivery, and associated costs of monitoring. Williamson's transaction costs theory (1985) offers a very useful analytic framework for this kind of decision.

As already outlined in Chapter 3, Williamson's starting point is his argument that the process of splitting work has given rise to specialization and that this in turn leads to a need for coordination between functional specializations. Such coordination can take place in one of two possible ways: either via the external labor markets on the basis of price, or within the organization itself as a result of carefully considered planning of activities. But both ways have costs attached to them. For example, using the market will lead to the cost involved in bringing buyer and seller together and in setting up and policing the transactional contract, whereas using the internal organization will lead to the cost involved in coordination. Through the comparison of the costs involved in completing the transaction, either through the marketplace or through the organization itself, the optimal choice between making or buying can thus be made. In the matrix section that follows (p. 200) we will offer a number of possibilities for outsourcing the personnel function or elements of it. The analytical framework of transaction cost theory will offer a useful guidance in specific circumstances as to whether or not (or parts thereof) should be outsourced the personnel function.

In 1986 Torrington and McKay (1986) pointed to the growing threat of contracting out of regular personnel activities to external agencies. Their survey in the United Kingdom indicated that activities such as training, recruitment and selection, and management development were eligible for contracting out, while activities like employee relations, pay, manpower planning, and appraisal remained the province of the internal personnel department. Relying on the core/periphery model of Atkinson (1984, 1986) (see also Chapter 9), they came to the alarming conclusion that, evidently, external consultants are becoming quite successful in penetrating the core activities of the personnel function.

In a more recent study, however, Adams (1991) indicated that application of the core/periphery model to the personnel function is an oversimplification. If, for example, Atkinson's model of the flexible firm is applied to the personnel function, we still lack a conceptual framework for the trend towards internalizing, that is, 'the move of some organizations towards devolving personnel functions to line managers – who are, in the model's own terms, undisputed members of the "core workforce".'

The distinction between core and peripheral personnel activities does, however, contribute to the insight that personnel can be considered as a bundle of separable functions and so opens the way to fragmentation (Tyson's Balkanization) such that personnel work is more prone to be performed by expert consultants (Torrington, 1989).

As noted above, Adams (199:44) holds that the core/peripheral distinction and its frame of reference of transaction-cost economics (make or buy) might be too gross to aid analysis. In relation to externalizing – and in view of current developments – she proposes a more finely meshed scheme which introduces into companies the discipline of the marketplace without substantially altering the employment contract. Examples include cross-charging between divisions and the rise of paid-for 'internal consultancy.' Accordingly, Adams developed a 'scale of increasing degrees of externalization, understood as the application of market forces to the delivery of personnel activities.' She distinguishes a progression of four alternatives for the corporate personnel department:

(1) specialized in-house units or agencies
(2) internal consultancy
(3) business within a business
(4) external consultancy.

In-house agencies are used in organizations where cross-charging between departments operates. This may be looked upon as a first step toward internal consultancy. It involves the introduction of charging customers for the personnel activity provided by the consultancy, in order to turn the activity into a profit rather than a cost center. One step further and we have the business within a business, in which the organization subcontracts the operation to an individual or group of individuals who set up their own business. Businesses within a business act very similarly to external consultancies, except that they may retain special links with the parent organization (Adams, 1991:45). The framework developed by Adams offers excellent opportunities to chart the available alternatives for structuring the personnel function. These alternatives need not exclude the personnel manager as a kind of broker matching the manager's need for expertise and the host of external resources offering different products (Torrington, 1988:8).

Alternative approaches: an overview of possibilities found in reality

Having outlined the various trends that have an impact upon the way the personnel function is carried out, we now present our findings, which focus on two tendencies, namely internalizing and externalizing. As already mentioned internalization implies the shift from specialist staff towards line management and/or regular workers.

In order to make use of the framework developed by Adams we supplement our definition of externalization (a shift from in-house activities to outsourcing) with the definition put forth by Adams: 'the application of market forces to the delivery of personnel activities.' In addition, we distinguish between minor changes, which can be applied without radically altering the existing organizational structure, systems, and culture; and major changes, which have an impact upon the whole organization and cannot be implemented in an isolated way. This allows us to represent the various possibilities in a two by two matrix, as illustrated in Figure 6.3.

Drawing upon the case study evidence, we provide examples illustrated by the matrix, and in so doing gain an overview of available options to carry out the personnel function, given the context of current trends. Naturally, a firm may apply these tactics and strategies simultaneously, depending on specific contingencies. Scale is another obvious influence on the possibility for applying the various tactics in the matrix. In his transaction economics approach, Williamson (1985) draws attention to the fact that the frequency of the transaction is an important characteristic in weighing the 'make' or 'buy' options. For example, the choice between outsourcing or in-house execution

Focus of change / Extent of change	Internalizing (shift from staff to regular line/workers)	Externalizing (outsourcing)
Minor changes	**A** • integral management • self-managing teams • core and peripheral personnel activities	**B** • outsourcing partially • contract management • specialized in-house units • internal consultancy/profit center
Major changes	**D** • personnel management without personnel managers	**C** • agencies • leased employees • teleworking

Figure 6.3 Alternative HRM delivery mechanisms found in practice.

of outplacement activities depends very much on the number of eligible persons, and this in turn has to do with the size of the organization. Accordingly, when discussing the various tactics and strategies we also take into account their applicability in larger and smaller organizations.

Below we successively discuss the minor changes in the area of internalizing (section A of the matrix); next we treat the externalizing changes, distinguishing between minor adaptations (section B) and major revisions (section C), although in many cases the transition will of course be a gradual one. Section D of the matrix represents the most extreme shift from staff to line, namely personnel management without a personnel manager, and deserves our special attention. It is in this connection that we present our cases, the considerations and motives on which they were based, the advantages and disadvantages of the approach, and the special industrial relations arrangements that may develop in companies without a personnel department. On the basis of empirical data we also comment on the factors/variables that can explain the presence or absence of a personnel management department.

Minor changes in the shift from staff to line

Relative to quadrant A of the matrix (see Figure 6.4) we describe three possibilities – integral management, self-managing teams, and the core-periphery model – each of which implies that components or tasks of the personnel function are transferred to the line management or the regular workforce. Transfer of the activities implies a shift in the package of specialist personnel department tasks, possibly in tandem with retrenchment. Such interventions can take place without the need of radical adjustments in the organizational structure and operating systems.

Integral management

Given integral or total responsibility for a specific business-unit or business-process and accountability for output and results, a manager logically bears responsibility for the budgetary means and the employees entrusted to him. Such responsibility must be predicated on relevant competencies. In connection with competencies in the personnel area, we normally think of recruitment, selection, appraisal, reward, and

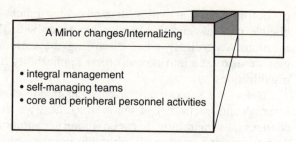

Figure 6.4 Section A: Minor changes/Internalizing.

training. To transfer these tasks implies a great deal of change in the relation between the specialist personnel department and the line manager who is given integral responsibility.

Self-managing teams

In organizations oriented to the social-technical systems approach and working with semi-autonomous groups or so-called self-managing teams (see Chapter 7), there are also opportunities to shift tasks from specialist staff departments to the regular workforce. Manz and Sims (1993) provide a list of team responsibilities which allows us to identify a number of tasks which lighten the load of traditional personnel departments:

- assigning jobs
- training team members
- setting team goals
- assessing internal appraisal
- resolving internal conflicts
- electing internal team leader
- testing for competency
- selecting team members.

This means that self-managing teams (for a more extended treatment, see Chapter 7) imply two effects. First, there is less need to introduce certain personnel tasks separately, because they are inherent to the nature or character of self-managing teams. Second, it becomes possible to delegate tasks or activities to the team provided, of course, that appropriate instruments are developed.

Cascio (1992:423) describes the use of self-managing teams at General Motor's Saturn Plant as follows:

General Motors invested eight years and US$3.5 billion in its medium-tech Saturn Plant at Spring Hill, Tennessee, just south of Nashville.

To build small cars, as good or better than the Japanese, Saturn's 3,000 employees operate in terms of a labor–management agreement which is very nearly unique in the US. The United Auto Workers share in every aspect of the business, from the executive suite down to assembly. Workteams on the line are given an unprecedented scale of responsibilities: next to having direct voice in shop-floor operations the teams interview and hire new members, schedule work and vacation, order materials, and assume budget responsibility.

Core and peripheral personnel activities

In dividing tasks between line and staff we can – in analogy to Atkinson's core/ring model of the flexible firm (see Chapter 9) – distinguish core tasks of the personnel department and more peripheral tasks. An early enumeration of core tasks at the corporate level is given by Purcell (1985) and Sisson and Scullion (1985):

- corporate culture and communications
- policy formulation and monitoring
- human resource planning
- cabinet office service/sounding board
- management development
- outside lobbying/internal advice
- information coordination
- consultancy/mediation
- personnel services for small units.

Schuler (1990) notes a similar development in the identification of strategic HRM core activities and mentions these six:

(1) business person
(2) shaper of change
(3) consultant to organization/partner or line managers
(4) strategy formulator and implementor
(5) talent manager
(6) asset manager and cost controller.

The studies cited by these writers indicate that increasingly there are fewer specialist personnel tasks to perform in such areas as recruitment and selection, training and development, appraisal, rewards, and so on. Naturally, up-to-date data systems must be available for these activities, and the personnel function or an external agency should have such technical expertise, but the subsequent implementation can be left to regular line management. Viewed from an HRM function at the corporate level, regular personnel activities related to the in-, through- and outflow of human resources are becoming an increasingly peripheral task which – if tools and systems are up to date – can very simply be delegated to line management.

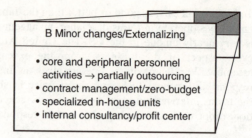

Figure 6.5   Section B: Minor changes/Externalizing.

Minor changes introducing an increasing degree of externalization

The possibilities in our next quadrant (section B, Figure 6.5) illustrate the necessity of our extended definition of externalizing, which not only involves outsourcing (shift from make to buy) but also an increased application of market forces to the in-house delivery of services.

Core and peripheral personnel activities

Carrying further the distinction between core and peripheral personnel management tasks, we can apply it to outsourcing of non-core tasks. This 'make' or 'buy' decision may be facilitated through the use of the conceptual framework of economic organization theories, including agency and transaction cost economics, and attention to matters such as transaction frequency, degree of organization specificity, and the costs of monitoring contracted-out tasks. Adams (1991), charting externalization tendencies, studied the following activities: graduate recruitment, executive search and selection, temporary staff recruitment, training and development, outplacement and redundancy counseling. An earlier study by Torrington and Mackay (1986) also includes management development, computers/data base, and job evaluation. Reviewing these studies, we conclude that this list covers more than just peripheral tasks: some activities, such as management development or training, will certainly be considered core activities in many organizations. The critical point is that certain components can be contracted out for various reasons:

- cost reduction, efficiency
- quality level, expertise/specialist knowledge, effectiveness
- (temporary) shortage of time in the in-house department

- ability to compare with other firms in the same branch (bench-marking)
- need for impartiality and independency.

All of these emphases are apparent in the following case study (de Vries and Paauwe, 1994):

Case study   **UK's Customs and Excise Department subject to market testing**

In the beginning of the eighties the Thatcher administration introduced initiatives to reduce public spending. For that reason an Efficiency Unit was set up in order to stimulate and check reduction plans/schemes of the various departments and offices. In spite of this policy, however, government spending still remained at too high a level, so in 1991 'market testing' was introduced. The various departments and offices of local government have to subject themselves to competition. They have to put out their services to tender, for which the following procedure has been developed. First of all, the service must be described for which both the in-house team and outside competitors are invited to bid. Both parties do their utmost to make an offer with the best price–quality ratio. In-house teams are being helped by consultants to develop their bid and to find methods in order to improve their way of rendering services at the lowest price possible. Of course, these in-house teams are highly motivated in view of the prospect of losing their jobs if they fail to win the bid. Initially traditional support services like cleaning, safe-keeping/guarding, and catering were subject to market testing and privatized.

Recently Customs and Excise has started market testing in areas such as payroll, typing, lots of training activities, and a large part of the employee selection process. Performance appraisal is seen as a possible activity for the near future.

In the beginning the unions did not like market testing, because they were afraid of privatizing and losing their jobs. In November 1993 there was a one-day national strike in order to demonstrate their discontent. Nowadays the unions are more satisfied because they have agreed that Customs and Excise will do all it can in supporting the in-house team in formulating their bid. According to a publication of Her Majesty's Treasury (Competing for quality, November 1991) the advantages of market testing are:

- competition helps ensure value for money
- focusing on performance outputs will produce clearer standards and improved quality of service

- an explicit customer–supplier relationship
- external and in-house bidders will be given the opportunity to be more innovative in their field
- monitoring of contract and service level agreement (contract for the in-house team) will focus on the output, objectives, and targets required in improving the efficiency and effectiveness of services.

(*Source*: de Vries and Paauwe, 1994)

Contract management/zero-budget

Contract management/zero-based budgeting basically means that each department starts each year with a 'zero' budget; it must justify each budgetary request. A 12-month contract is concluded with the various business units or divisions. The personnel department takes care of a number of annually recurring tasks at a negotiated price. When an appeal is made to this department for ad hoc or incidental tasks, an hourly rate applies. The contract is based on an average number of tasks per employee, for example, appraisal, career counseling, complaints, and so on. The remainder of the budget has to be filled in by the personnel department by offering attractive 'services' on the internal market, for instance, strategic work conferences in the context of desired cultural change or a specific training program appropriate to the implementation of formulated strategic company policy.

Case study   **PTT Post**

PTT Post (Mail) is a good example of a recently privatized company that has introduced contract management in order to restructure its personnel services/activities. It employs about 60,000 people in the Netherlands. At the corporate level it still has a corporate personnel department; however, at the business unit level the line managers in charge of the unit and the decentralized personnel staff departments are subject to the principles of contract management. So every budget year it negotiates a number of services and activities.

(*Source*: Uijlen and Paauwe, 1994)

Specialized in-house units

Further, specialized in-house units offer an alternative way of running a particular personnel service, which is subject to market forces, without necessarily involving a great deal of outsourcing. They very often operate in companies that are accustomed to cross-charging between departments.

Case study **Rabofacet**

Rabofacet (500 employees) is a subsidiary of the RABO-Bank company, one of the larger financial institutions in the Netherlands. Rabofacet's main activities are in the field of information- and data processing and telecommunication. Both product/market/technology combinations and specialist staff departments have been organized as business-units. Regular standardized personnel services (such as recruitment and appraisal) have a yearly budget, whereas for more specific services like training and development or OD-activities (organizational development) the business-unit is being charged by the personnel unit on the basis of an agreed upon hourly rate.

(*Source*: Uijlen and Paauwe, 1994)

Internal consultancy/profit center

Compared with the preceding alternative, the option of having an internal consultancy as a separate profit center is more market-driven. According to Adams (1991:45) it involves the introduction of 'charging' customers for the personnel activity provided by the consultancy in order to turn the activity into a profit center rather than a cost center. For example:

Case study **AKZO Coatings**

AKZO Coatings is a subsidiary of one of the leading Dutch multinational chemical companies. AKZO Coatings employs about 2400 people. Organizationally, it is made up of business-units. Its personnel department is considered to be a profit center and is located at corporate level. Every line manager in charge of one of the business-units buys the services of the personnel unit on the basis of a previously negotiated contract. This means that the business-unit manager is confronted with forced shopping. However, for some activities like training and development or a specific consultancy assignment, a manager can turn elsewhere.

(*Source*: Uijlen and Pauuwe, 1994)

Major changes vis-à-vis externalizing

It should be understood that the above alternatives and examples, though arranged in the quadrant of minor changes/externalizing, actually represent a fluid transition to more incisive kinds of externalizing, like full outsourcing of all personnel activities, making an abundant use of leased employees, and teleworking. These are discussed below, and quadrant C (Figure 6.6) gives an overview of the various possibilites under the heading 'Major changes/Externalizing.'

External consultancies/agencies

First, although outsourcing as such has been around for some time and its use keeps expanding, it is frequently partial. Complete outsourcing of all personnel activities is rare. Still, there are recent examples of firms that turn for complete structuring of all specialist personnel activities and handling of benefits to external consultancies or agencies, perhaps after temporary creation of a business within a business which, according to Adams (1991:45):

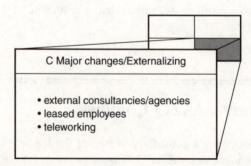

Figure 6.6 Section C: Major changes/Externalizing.

allows the organization to subcontract the operation to an individual or group of individuals who set up their own business. Depending on the size of the operation, these individuals remain self-employed or go on to become direct employers in their own right.

Case study   Workforce Solutions: an IBM spin-off

In 1991, IBM decided to spin off its huge human resources operation (annual benefits costs US$1 billion-plus for its 158,000 domestic employees) into a separate company called Workforce Solution (WFS). Providing all human resources to IBM's 13 business units, WFS is now saving IBM some US$45 million per year in the form of reduced staffing, consolidation of offices and new technology. WFS features tailored speciality areas – ranging from occupational health to career development – and offers customized benefit packages. As of the end of 1992, WFS is handling business for other companies as well.

(*Source*: *Business Week*, 10 May, 1993:58)

Making independent specialist staff departments and subsequently externalizing them is a development taking place especially in large-scale companies. They are the ones that have the expertise and manpower, and are able to award work or orders during the initial period of change. This is not true for smaller firms. Nevertheless, in these firms there are also interesting possibilities for complete outsourcing, for instance, in the form of regional service organizations set up by employer organizations.

Case study   Regional centers for personnel affairs

In Holland the Dutch Federation of Christian employers has established a number of regional Centers for Personnel Affairs. Small companies (on an average less than 100) are regular subscribers to these centers, which entitle them to one or two days of specialists' personnel service per week in order to deal with a variety of personnel issues and activities. Thanks to this kind of tailor-made personnel work they can do without an employed personnel management professional. Recently, the temporary employment agencies have also discovered this new market segment and have set up subsidiaries in order to provide for interim personnel management assistance on a commercial basis.

This sort of alternative is very attractive, certainly for smaller companies whose scale is insufficient to cover indirect costs or overhead related to a fully-fledged personnel department.

Leased employees

In addition, implementation of core-ring strategies may involve changes in the package of tasks completed by the personnel function (see Chapter 9). To make use of a flexible workforce (for example, short-term contract workers, agency temporaries, and on-call workers) does not necessarily mean a reduction of the organization's activities. After all, temporary staff involve a lot of administration and introductory training, and the personnel costs associated with such flexible workers may be equal to or more than those associated with the permanent staff. An exception to this is the recent phenomenon of leased employees. Employee leasing is an arrangement whereby a company transfers to, and subsequently leases its employees from, a leasing organization. While the company retains the right to hire, fire, lay off, promote, or reprimand the labor force, the leasing organization handles personnel administration including payroll, payroll taxes, employee benefits programs, and sometimes even direct supervision. In this way the employees of small firms can share in health, life insurance, pension plan, and compensation schemes otherwise unavailable to them. Attorneys say that to preclude possible liabilities client companies should be sure to choose financially solid leasing organizations. Currently there are some 1500 leasing firms operating in the US (cf. *Marketdate Enterprises*, April 1991:15–16).

Employee leasing seems suitable for smaller firms who themselves are unable (due to the small size of their operations) to professionally structure their handling of personnel services and benefits.

Teleworking

New organization concepts such as network forms of organization or the so-called dispersed organization, in combination with the flexibility provided by electronic mail and telefax, expand opportunities for teleworking or telecommuting. Rapid development and use of technology has provided the infrastructure for expanding the employment of teleworkers. Various arrangements are in use:

(1) *The lone telehunters.*   Freelancers and/or subcontractors, operating in a very independent way, are not very likely to form a group or to socialize with the company. The relation with the company is only based on results (contract management).
(2) *The lone teleworkers.*   They appreciate a strong link with the company and are mainly motivated by the possibility of establishing the right balance between work and non-work. The relationship with the company is based on trust.
(3) *Tele-outposts.*   Processing factories located close to the people in search of work. For example, in the Netherlands some companies have arranged for their information-processing needs through a tele-outpost in India, where well-qualified labor is both abundantly present and relatively cheap.

The above-mentioned forms of teleworking or telecommuting can significantly contribute to the externalization of personnel activities and a reduction of in-house personnel tasks. They do, however, presuppose an entirely different approach to leadership, motivation, and performance monitoring. Moreover, not every individual can cope with the pressure of working alone or without direct supervision of superiors or colleagues. For this reason Cascio (1992:427) is skeptical, even though in the US the infrastructure is well established and relatively inexpensive to use. 'Mix and match' programs that allow workers and managers to prearrange a schedule of days spent at home and in the office are the most common and most popular telecommuting arrangements, according to Cascio. In those cases, however, it is more likely that special personnel arrangements will increase in relation to the available facilities.

Major changes towards internalizing

In the area of major changes/internalizing there is only one possibility left: personnel management without personnel managers.

As stressed in the previous section on personnel management, the

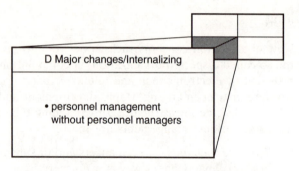

Figure 6.7   Section D: Major changes/Internalizing.

HRM approach, with its emphasis on strategic integration and intensive involvement of line management, could ultimately lead to a situation of personnel management without personnel managers. That this is no mere speculation was demonstrated by the BSO/Origin case at the beginning of this chapter. To obtain more insight into the shift of personnel responsibilities from staff to line we (Hulleman and Paauwe, 1992) studied a limited number of companies who, although employing more than 350 persons, do not have a separate specialist staff department to implement the personnel function. The number of companies was limited, not only because of the scope and nature of our study, but also because these are exceptions. Still, in combination with research cited previously, these exceptions help us to answer the question: Do we really need personnel managers, and what factors/variables can explain the presence or (partial) absence of a personnel management department?

More specifically the following questions are addressed:

(1) Why do some fairly large companies not have a personnel department? Is the specific character of the company such that it is appropriate not to have one? Do the company's culture and history play a part in this decision? Is the decision perhaps influenced by financial considerations?

(2) How do these companies organize their personnel function? What tasks are taken care of? Who performs these activities and specifically how are these individuals involved?

(3) What are the advantages, disadvantages, and/or bottlenecks of operating without a personnel department?

(4) Are external agencies brought in? What is expected of them?

(5) What special industrial relations are developed in companies without a personnel department?

(6) Can we identify a number of variables that explain the presence or (partial) absence of a personnel management department?

These questions will be examined below with reference to the following Dutch and British case studies (see Appendix 1 at the end of this chapter for more details about the companies):

(1) *J.G. Nelis Building Contractors.* This is a family-owned Dutch building company with various business-units, including earth works, road building, hydraulic works, and equipment leasing. Nelis employs a full-time permanent workforce of some 390 people. Depending on the needs of building projects in progress, this workforce is expanded with temporary staff via subcontractors.

(2) *BSO/Origin.* The Bureau for Systems Development has 80 branches in 14 different countries. The head office is in Utrecht, the Netherlands. BSO employs 4000 people. Our case study focuses on the situation in the Netherlands.

(3) *ABC Technology.* This is a software company which has branches throughout the Netherlands. The total workforce of ABC Technology stands at around 2000.

(4) *Damen Shipyards Gorinchem.* This division of Damen Shipyards employs 450 people. In total, the Damen Shipyards Company employs about 2000 people in various countries.

(5) *Skillbase.* A UK-based consultancy company, Skillbase renders professional services in the field of strategic planning, organizational change, efficiency, human resources, and information technology. It is an IBM spin-off.

In addition to these five case studies, we (Hulleman and Paauwe, 1992; Paauwe, 1991) performed a secondary analysis on seven case studies which were part of a larger study of the environmental and organizational characteristics influencing the formation of human resource management. These case studies were longitudinal, extending over five to seven years, so that we have the additional feature of a dynamic processual perspective. Furthermore, these firms differ in size (number of employees) and represent different branches (dairy, furniture, services, insurance).

Motives for not having a personnel function

Each of the companies prefers to operate without specialist staff and, hence, without a personnel or human resource department. Specifically, they want to keep overhead costs low and to create a flexible organization. A personnel department is considered unnecessarily bureaucratic.

At Skillbase the Managing Director, a former marketing director in IBM-UK, opposes staff departments. He has unfavorable memories of the misery such departments can engender and is a proponent of clarity and simplicity; to him personnel management is emphatically a line management task.

At J.G. Nelis the absence of a personnel department reflects the background of the company's history. Employer–employee relations used to be very weak. As long as the pay was good and on time the workers were satisfied. Recruitment took place only for a specified building project and the governance structure with regard to personnel activities was kept as simple as possible.

The situation at BSO/Origin reflects its organization structure, which operates on the principle of 'cells'; no branch has more than 100 employees. The branch manager is responsible for the local personnel policy and the employees themselves are expected to look after their own personnel concerns.

At ABC the situation is the outcome of a historical process. The company was formed through a number of takeovers, after which the various subsidiaries continued to operate autonomously. Until recently no one felt that there was a need to harmonize the personnel policies of the subsidiaries or to develop a coherent uniform personnel policy for the entire organization.

Damen Shipyards keeps a tight rein on overhead costs and managers are appointed to the task of integral management (see also Matrix section A). Line managers are responsible for policy in their division/unit, including personnel management policies. The fact that this approach precludes a uniform personnel management for all the Damen Shipyards employees is not considered a disadvantage.

Contours of the personnel function

Line management has an important function in each of the five companies and is expected to look after personnel tasks/activities for the personnel in its unit. There is a notable trend to make the organization as decentralized as possible; the divisions or business-units are given great freedom to formulate their policies. At BSO/Origin unit management is implemented very consistently. It is noteworthy, for instance, that the annual labor relations settlement with BSO managers covers not only commercial targets, but also the formulation and implementation of a training program so that there is the correct 'mix' of employees for specialists and function levels and the identification of a number of outstanding performers. In some cases the administrative and accounting department assumes a few tasks, but the emphasis is clearly on having the line management take care of personnel tasks. As Reinier Rijke, one of the BSO/Origin directors, states:

> Our staff is so important that line managers must carry out the various personnel management activities themselves. That's our strength. They know their people personally, the family feeling is all part of the system. On an average, every manager – irrespective of the hierarchical level – spends 30% of his time on personnel issues, 30% on

commercial affairs/business and 30% on technology. The remaining 10% is reserved for troubles that cannot be foreseen.

(PW, special on outsourcing, 1994: March, (18), 25)

On the whole few tasks are contracted out. Generally, the implemented package is limited to the bare necessities: primary personnel planning, restricted evaluation and appraisal procedures, recruitment and selection, and training and development.

Advantages, disadvantages and drawbacks

The management of the organizations studied highlight, in their interviews, the following advantages of not having a personnel department:

(1) *Low overhead costs.* Having no personnel department implies saving on overhead expenses.
(2) *Flexibility.* Every manager is more or less able to alter existing systems and procedures in order to meet changing circumstances, a type of experiential HRM approach (see Chapter 1). For example, higher wages can be offered in the case of labor shortage in certain personnel categories.
(3) *The managers are responsible.* They cannot pass the buck, even if they would like to do so, simply because there is no personnel department. Whether they like it or not, they just have to do the job.
(4) *Tailor made packages.* Personnel activities carried out by the line management are made to fit specific groups. For example, managers can design and implement their own appraisal systems in order to meet the specific needs and characteristics of their own workforce/staff. At Damen Shipyards this led to a situation involving four different systems of appraisal.

However, there are several disadvantages of not having a personnel department:

(1) *Lack of synergy* – there is no opportunity to learn from other specialists.
(2) *Inefficient* – reinvention of the wheel: that is, every unit invents its own personnel systems.
(3) *Unstructured, not policy backed* – hence there is a feeling of operating too much in an ad hoc manner and not taking into account long-term developments with regard to the quality and quantity of future staffing needs.
(4) *No uniformity* – in labor conditions and remuneration, which impedes the exchange of personnel among units.
(5) Line management is often *pressed for time,* to the detriment of personnel tasks and personnel activities that have to be carried

out, including dealing with work-related personal problems of employees.

(6) *Arbitrariness* – due to the lack of procedures and systems in some of our cases and the absence of an institution (like the HRM department) to safeguard the preservation of certain values; favoritism can easily occur in hiring, promoting, and paying employees.

Contracting out of personnel activities

As indicated previously, using external agencies is relatively unimportant. Occasionally a bureau for recruitment and selection or an external consultant is hired in a temporary, advisory capacity. None of the companies do so on a large scale or on a permanent basis, nor do they expect to do so in the future. If external agencies are used, it is because the company lacks expertise. For example, at BSO/Origin a self-developed management development system has been analysed and assessed by an outside consultancy agency, and this company also makes use of a psychological testing agency.

The absence of a personnel department, then, is not occasioned by extensive external handling of personnel matters. Compared to the other firms, ABC technology makes more use of outsourcing, especially with regard to recruitment, selection, training, development, and outplacement.

Industrial relations at company level

The rate of unionization in these companies is low to very low. The workers at J.G. Nelis and Damen Shipyards are somewhat more organized (an average 20%) than those at BSO and ABC Technology (less than 5%). This is partly due to the type of enterprise and the educational level of the employees. The workers at J.G. Nelis and Damen Shipyards are in contact with the unions, though not intensively. In both cases the contacts are related to wage bargaining at the branch of industry level. At Skillbase Limited no one is a member of the unions. In general, in these five companies neither the collective bargaining agreement nor trade unions figure prominently in the shaping of the personnel function.

In the Netherlands so-called works councils have been established in order to provide for legal and formal forms of industrial democracy. The first law on work councils dates back to 1950. Nowadays works councils are mandatory in firms with 100 or more employees, and they exist but with more limited tasks and rights in firms having 35 to 99 employees. Such councils are elected from and by the firm's employees and meet with management at least six times a year. Apart from providing information on a number of issues, management needs the endorsement of the works council to introduce, amend or withdraw measures related to a number of HRM topics such as hours of work and holiday arrangements, pay or job evaluation schemes, health, welfare, and safety regulations, and policies on appointments, promotion, dismissal, training, and employee appraisal. In some instances the works council (if present) plays a prominent role in the shaping of the personnel function. For example, some time ago the J.G. Nelis works council, stimulated by ideas launched at labor congresses, took the initiative to tackle things differently. The council has emphasized that the place of personnel management in an organization is an important one. This initiated a debate about the desirability of a specialist personnel department that, until then, had not been established. BSO did not have a works council for many years, but one was introduced eventually, since in this way possible conflicts could be dealt with as stipulated by recent legislation. At BSO, management laments the consequent loss of informality. ABC has no works council. Although the employees were free to establish one, they felt no need to do so because of their high level of training and individualism. In cases of disagreement employees personally take up the issue with their superiors. The works council at Damen Shipyards functions – just like the one at J.G. Nelis – as a signaling mechanism. The council frequently identifies bottlenecks in the way the personnel function is carried out which are subsequently discussed in management meetings. At both J.G. Nelis and Damen Shipyards, then, part of the management team's agenda – adjustments in personnel management – is set by the works council.

Variables affecting the presence or absence of a personnel management department

With reference to the Aston studies (Pugh, *et al.*, 1968; Pugh and Hickson, 1976) several variables like size, technical system, specialization, (de)centralization and formalization are highly decisive in shaping organizational structure. More specifically, the presence or absence of specialized staff departments often depends, next to the degree of formalization, very much on *size*. Buitendam (1979) concludes that, in the Netherlands, almost all industrial companies employing more than 350 workers have one or more personnel officers. For the United States, Walker (1988) arrives at a ratio of one personnel officer per 100 employees, although the actual ratios vary greatly from firm to firm.

Still, there are exceptions to the rule and our case study evidence shows that they can be explained in terms of variables other than those generally applied in Aston-like studies. Our case studies and literature study point to the following relevant variables:

(1) *Workforce characteristics*:
   (a) the workforce profile
   (b) ratio of wages to overall costs
(2) *Organizational characteristics*:
   (a) organization structure
   (b) nature of the enterprise/technical system
   (c) organizational culture
   (d) history and developmental phase of the firm, and the role of the founder
(3) *Environmental characteristics*:
   (a) trade union influence
   (b) labor market situation
(4) *The role of the works council*
(5) *Management philosophy and strategy, and the available room for maneuvering*

Below we will comment briefly on these factors and describe our findings regarding their practical relevance.

Workforce characteristics

In the area of workforce characteristics, we can think of features of the workforce profile such as size, degree of homogeneity/heterogeneity, types of labor contracts, level of training, age profile, employee turnover, and wages/total costs ratio.

In our case studies *education and training level* were important factors. As employees gain more skills, they become more emancipated and demand more from training policy. They are more individualistic and have higher expectations regarding career opportunities and career counseling in the company. Because of employee training the relationships between employer and employees have changed in those companies studied where employees had a high education level. Kleingartner and Anderson (1987) also found this to be true of high-tech firms and called the phenomenon the rise of the 'gold-collar workers.'

Because highly trained employees place greater demands on training policy and career counseling, management is confronted with the question as to who should take care of these matters. Should a personnel officer do this? Is it perhaps advisable to have the manager of the division or unit do it, since he has detailed knowledge of the work activities and can also function as personal mentor?

If employees are highly skilled, line management will also more readily be able to turn to the tasks of integral management. In our field study, too, it appeared that companies opt for not creating a personnel department and prefer integral management in order to give managers the responsibility for personnel affairs in their division. We found these 'individualist' employees especially in the two software companies (BSO/Origin and ABC Technology). Their employees are highly skilled and are very demanding in matters of training and counseling within the company. In addition, they consider themselves sufficiently independent to look after their own interests. In this context it is not surprising that the degree of unionization in these companies is exceptionally low (less than 5%). Personnel management in these companies can appropriately be termed bottom-up personnel management, because the employees themselves have a prominent voice in the substance of personnel policies.

With regard to the wages/total costs ratio Walker (1988) indicates that, when personnel costs are a significant part of the total costs, personnel activities are contracted out less frequently and the activities are carried out by personnel managers. One would expect, therefore, that a personnel manager will be hired as soon as personnel costs become a major part of total costs. But this did not occur in our case studies. At BSO, for example, personnel costs are a major part of the total costs and yet the explicit decision has been not to appoint a personnel manager. Personnel activities in this company are considered too important to be left to specialist staff. They are, instead, the responsibility of the line managers themselves.

Organizational characteristics

As noted above, major variables of the organization structure are *specialization, (de)centralization* and *formalization.* In particular, the degree of (de)centralization is a structural characteristic which influences the choice for or against a personnel department. Each of our companies without a personnel management department has opted for a decentralized structure and thorough decentralization of competencies and authorizations. The structure is characterized by separate units, each of which is expected to be run at a profit. Almost all responsibilities regarding personnel are delegated as well. The most notable example of this is BSO/Origin, which features almost completely self-contained unit-management with integral management tasks for the managers. Formation of staff departments including personnel is avoided as much as possible. In the other companies, the structure is decentralized in a similar way, though not to the degree found at BSO.

The nature of the company's core activities

Additionally, the nature of the company's core activities and technical systems play a role in the choice for or against a personnel department. For example, Buitendam and Postma (1980) conclude that process-industry companies will more probably have a personnel specialist than companies with batch or single production. Their explanation of this outcome is that, in a process industry such as chemicals, personnel is a more critical factor: the production flow is more vulnerable, and the risks of a breakdown are greater. In such cases a stable workforce, maintenance of skills, and good working and labour conditions are very important. Moreover, the personnel profile is rather heterogeneous: process-industry companies usually have a number of specializations. This situation implies special personnel problems that require the attention of personnel specialists.

Company culture

Further, the research literature mentions *company culture* as a determining factor in the choice for or against a personnel department. In the case studies organizational culture is on the whole informal and internal communication is direct, or at least this is the kind of culture that management encourages. This means that many responsibilities are delegated to the employees. There is a general dislike of strict regulations and procedures concerning personnel; these are considered too bureaucratic. In this type of open culture it is fitting that line managers themselves design and implement appraisal procedures and that they communicate negative messages like dismissals.

At Damen Shipyards, for example, the organizational culture is strongly task- and performance-oriented. The atmosphere and the communication are open and informal, though with a markedly businesslike slant and evident hierarchic lines. The charismatic style of leadership and the vision of the current owner, Kommer Damen (the founder's son), is highly influential in this area and accounts for the aversion to staff departments, overhead expenses and red tape (see also below). At Skillbase the business philosophy can simply be summarized by phrases like 'working hard,' 'making money,' and 'keeping things, including administrative systems and regulations, as simple as possible.' Similarly, our BSO case at the beginning of this chapter spotlights the influence of organizational culture on the way the organization is structured.

The phase of development

Whether a company has or does not have a personnel department also depends on the phase in the company's development. In the pioneering phase management often assumes the additional task of personnel affairs. Once the company reaches the stage of differentiation, a personnel department is likely to be established. The case studies, however, indicate that sometimes a company has reached the stage of specialization or integration and yet has no personnel section.

The firm's founders

In the case of BSO/Origin and Damen Shipyards we noted the dominant position of the firms' founders. Their charisma and vision had a marked impact on the company's culture and consequently on their way of structuring the organization. At Skillbase the emphasis upon simplicity and an aversion to extended manuals can be attributed to the role of the present managing director. He wants to avoid the negative effects of bureaucracy, including a loss of flexibility and an increase in overhead expenses. Gomez-Mejia and Welbourne (1990) in their review of human resource strategies in high technology firms, found that most original founders of high-tech firms have technical backgrounds which make them hostile towards bureaucracy:

> Many of these individuals have been disillusioned by expansive bureaucracy. Much of this bureaucracy stemmed from administrative functions, including the human resource department... When these technical managers initiate their own company, their negative impression of personnel procedures often leads them to curtail the influence exercised by the department. They often do not trust the personnel function to develop systems that will provide equity and harmony essential to maintain the 'happy family' atmosphere that is desired by entrepreneurs. Therefore the founder takes an aggressive and leading role in guiding the human resource function, especially with regard to developing compensation systems.
>
> (Gomez-Mejia and Welbourne, 1990:259)

Environmental characteristics

In this respect we refer to the legal/political systems, the influence of trade unions, and labor market conditions.

Legal systems with regard to the hiring and firing of employees differ considerably between countries. One can imagine that an extended and all encompassing legal system of labor laws in combination with a practice of severe claims either by individuals and/or institutions, if not abiding to these laws, will give rise to specialized departments in order to diminish the possibility of that kind of claims.

When a company is in regular contact with *trade unions* and there is a collective bargaining agreement, there is a high probability that the company has a personnel specialist to carry out the personnel tasks. This depends, however, on the number of trade union members and whether the collective bargaining agreement is company-wide.

In the case studies the rate of unionization is low to very low. In the two software companies (BSO/Origin and ABC) and at Skillbase the trade unions hardly play a role at all. At J.G. Nelis (construction) and Damen Shipyards the rate of unionization is somewhat higher and the trade unions do play a modest role. Contacts with the union are infrequent, however, in part because the collective bargaining agreement was settled at the industrial branch level.

Finally, we must consider the *labor market situation*. When labor is in demand, more time will have to be allotted to hiring than when labor is plentiful. The company will give greater priority to keeping its employees since it will be harder to replace them. This phenomenon is very clear at J.G. Nelis. Some years ago, there was an adequate supply on the labor market; currently, however, skilled labor is much in demand. For this reason J.G. Nelis representatives visit technical schools in the region in order to attract skilled workers. These activities are time consuming, which is why J.G. Nelis is now considering the establishment of a professional personnel department which might take over this function in the future.

Role and position of the works council

The presence of a works council is another factor which helps to determine whether or not the personnel function will be performed by a separate personnel department. If a works council exists, it may be critical of personnel policy, as a result of which improvements may be introduced. This kind of signaling function of works councils is clear at J.G. Nelis. Once the works council was established, there was a growing awareness of the place of personnel policy in overall policy. Works council members attended conferences, noted that things can be done differently, and initiated proposals regarding personnel policy, for example claiming the necessity for a fair appraisal system. At Damen Shipyards the works council has the same effect. In response to questions or suggestions by the works council, the agenda of management meetings regularly contains items concerning personnel activities.

Management philosophy, company strategy and 'room to maneuver'

In addition to the organizational and environmental characteristics discussed above, the management philosophy and the resultant strategic approaches with regard to the structuring of the organization are key factors in the choice for or against a personnel department.

In particular, the management perspective or attitude on staff departments seems to play a role in this choice. In the case studies we noted that management was reluctant to introduce staff departments, since these would raise overhead costs and probably increase bureau-cratic regulations and procedures. BSO director Wintzen, for instance, has outspoken ideas about this and strongly supports a radical form of unit management. Damen Shipyards' CEO also strongly advocates the integral responsibility of line management in combination with an aversion towards specialist staff departments that do not contribute in a direct and visible way to the value generating process.

The perspective of the dominant coalition (often the owner/director in these particular companies studied) can only be translated into practice if there is sufficient room to do so. In the cases of BSO and Damen Shipyards it seems clear that there are no countervailing powers to the vision of top management. In the case of J.G. Nelis there seems to be a shift of power whereby the works council is gaining greater influence. As we see it, management philosophy, company strategy, and available room for maneuvering may well be important reasons for deviating from the 'normal' pattern related to company size and phase of development.

Summary and conclusions

In this chapter we have outlined a number of trends that have an effect upon the personnel function and possible ways of structuring it. We have sketched the historical roots of the personnel function, ending up with the current situation which is characterized by increasing complexity and the growing importance of human resources. This importance is underscored by the shift from personnel management to strategic HRM and by the intensified involvement of regular line management in personnel activities. In terms of the distinction between internalizing and externalizing trends, we presented a broad spectrum of possible ways to structure the personnel function. Sometimes these require minimal interventions; sometimes they are major. We even discussed the most extreme situation of all: personnel management without personnel managers. Through this analysis we were able to gain insight into the factors which have an impact on how the personnel function is structured and shaped.

By way of summary we represent these factors in a conceptual framework shown in Figure 6.8. The arrows underscore the interaction which may occur between the variables over time. A choice made by the management will not only have a bearing on the shaping of the personnel function, but may also alter the initial situation. To clarify the model, we present a synopsis of the assumed relationships. Of course, the combination and the strength of the different variables will determine the outcome in every specific situation.

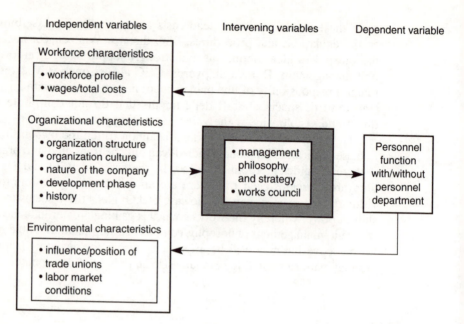

Figure 6.8   Conceptual framework.

Characteristics of the workforce

When the workforce consists of relatively young employees who work full time and employee turnover is low, personnel affairs will require less time and will be more likely an additional task for the line management than if the workforce profile is heterogeneous, many work part time and turnover is high. If the employees are highly skilled, line managers will more probably be charged with integral management, including personnel activities.

Organization structure

Companies with a markedly decentralized organization structure, where line management has an integral management function, are more likely not to form a separate personnel department.

Organization culture

In organizations with an open and informal culture, personnel activities will sooner be part of the task of line managers than in companies whose culture is formal and closed.

Role of the trade unions

Companies with collective agreements and a high rate of unionization will sooner decide to appoint a personnel manager than companies in which no contacts with the trade unions are maintained.

Labor market conditions

If labor is in high demand and, consequently, much time must be invested in recruitment and selection, a company will probably appoint a personnel specialist more readily than if labor supply far exceeds demand.

Role and position of works council

The time at which a works council is formed in a company has an evident signaling function. Such a council expects high standards of personnel policy, and a personnel department will more readily be created.

Management philosophy and company strategy

If top management has an outspoken perspective on the structure of the organization and supports rigorous decentralization based on the idea of employee responsibility and integral management, a personnel department is less likely to be formed than when management does not propagate this point of view.

Framework for decision making

The above model offers insight into a number of variables which have an impact on the structuring of the personnel function. These factors will be filled in as the specific situation calls for and so play a role in the consideration of alternatives and the choices made by the dominant coalition, which usually is the management team. To highlight this process of decision making, we developed a decision tree which pictures the various steps in the process (see Figure 6.9).

A first step is to decide whether a given activity should or should not be carried out. Is it, for example, in this situation appropriate to engage in training, career counseling, and so on? A positive decision leads to a second step: Who should be responsible for the personnel policy and implementation of this task, regular line management or the HRM or personnel department? Our case studies provided a number of weighting criteria, including the opportunity costs for line management on the

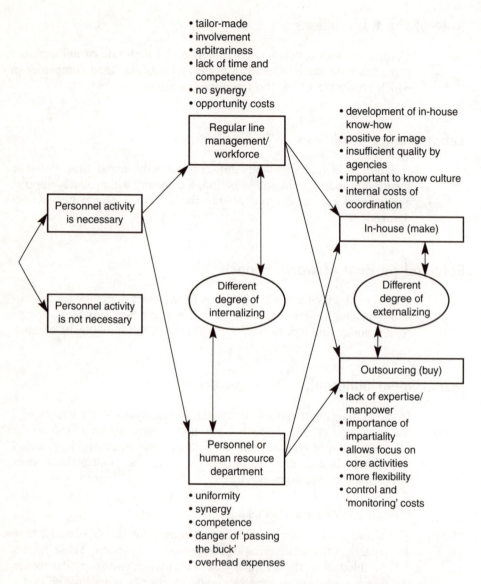

Figure 6.9 Decision tree for weighing staff–line and make/buy alternatives.

one hand and overhead expenses for the personnel department on the other. There is, of course, a 'gray' area of gradations of internalizing as presented in the section on the matrix.

Once the choice is made between regular line management or the specialist HRM department, we arrive at a third step: 'make' or 'buy'? Once again there are criteria that have a bearing on this decision. The conceptual framework of transaction-cost economics can facilitate the weighting here. For example in-house execution of the activities implies internal costs (coordination), while outsourcing will lead to costs associated with monitoring, prevention of misuse, and so on. The choice between in-house and contracting out is often not simple but comprises a large spectrum of possibilities and gradations of externalizing. The scheme we discussed makes clear that, next to determining factors, there is ample room for decision making on the part of the dominant coalition.

Evaluation

It will be clear from the discussion above that a personnel department is no longer established automatically once a certain scale or size is reached. The need for more accurate weighting of criteria in the 'make' or 'buy' decision and the optimal deployment of available resources lead to a large number of alternatives in the process of decision making as to how to carry out the personnel function.

Both our own case studies and the survey by Adams show an increased variety in ways the personnel function is performed. This variety makes it almost impossible to speak of *the* personnel function. The tendency towards outsourcing and towards the application of market forces has brought about a growing demand for specialists in a wide range of different areas. This specialization could imply an increased degree of professionalism and hopefully quality in the rendering of the different specialist services. Based on this reasoning we could expect that by applying market forces and thus increased competition the potential for contributing towards the process of generating added value will increase. At the moment it is still too early to draw that kind of conclusion, since systematic research into the effectiveness of the personnel function under different governance structures is lacking. Moreover, we must also take into account the loss of effectiveness and efficiency of the various personnel activities due to the impossibility of managing, controlling, and monitoring all these fragmented specialist services in a consistent way.

In relation to the effectiveness of the personnel function we must of course pose ourselves the question: *Effectiveness for whom and of what?* A question which reminds us of the fact that the different alternatives for performing the personnel function are of course not only influenced by environmental and organizational characteristics and weighting criteria, but also by power relationships and prevailing norms and values. Recent HRM literature frequently advocates the role of the human resource manager as being that of a business person or business manager. In this regard Shipton and McAuley (1994) present the following role prescriptions for strategic HRM managers:

- seeing themselves as business managers
- identifying closely with management
- viewing people as resources
- describing their roles in ways that other managers can understand
- seeing the rest of the organization, and particularly managers of the senior echelons, as customers
- being able to identify the core values of the organization and being centrally involved in gaining organization-wide acceptance of them.

These role prescriptions in fact imply that the personnel manager acquires a power base by conforming to the dominant culture and principles of the line management. Legge (1978) refers to the 'conformist innovator' who accepts the dominant utilitarian values and bureaucratic relationships within the organization and tries to demonstrate the value added (contribution to the bottom line) of his activities within this framework. This is an attitude and approach which holds a number of evident risks, such as the eventual inability to differentiate HRM from the regular line manager in terms of contribution or expertise, so that the option of personnel management without personnel managers is on the horizon.

In this respect we refer to an interesting conclusion by Purcell (cited in Legge, 1993:21) (in interpreting the Warwick Company Level Survey Data), that personnel considerations appear to have greater prominence in strategic decision making where no corporate personnel department exists, but where a main board director, whose primary responsibility is in personnel/industrial relations, sits on a personnel policy committee whose membership includes non-personnel senior managers, including the chief executive – a situation we also encountered in our case studies mentioned above.

An alternative way of acquiring power – or rather influence – is the 'deviant innovator' approach, whereby the personnel specialist identifies with a set of norms that are distinct from, but not necessarily in conflict with, the norms of organizational success (Legge, 1978:79–85); for example, given the core tasks listed earlier in the matrix section, the personnel manager may retain an important role, especially related to corporate culture and change. In this connection Shipton and McAuley (1994:9) refer to the need for an

> organizational fool, who without danger to himself can take non-consensual stances. . .personnel people are perhaps uniquely fitted for this role because they frequently have the key responsibility for exploring, with members of the organization in which they work, the issues surrounding the management of change and the factors that make it work.

In the end it all boils down to the fact that HRM specialists cannot focus only on criteria such as efficiency, effectiveness, and flexibility. Other appropriate criteria are those of fairness (in the exchange relation between the individual and the organization) and legitimacy (the relation between society and organization). A staff specialist in the area of personnel and organization would be the right person to counter or correct an extreme economic rationality, so that the long-term interests of the various organizational members are kept in mind and the outcomes of organizational effectiveness will benefit the various stakeholders of the firm.

In this respect Kamoche (1994) underlines the inherent paradoxes of strategic HRM as a concept encompassing both the issues of 'strategy' and 'human.' On the one hand, strategic HRM is characterized by the dominant organizational imperative for performance and productivity, which according to Kamoche draws from an industry-based view of the firm and is informed by a rationalistic view of human action. On the other hand HRM is concerned with meeting the complex and often ambiguous needs and expectations of employees, the humanizing of work and a concern with 'equitable' or 'fair' practices, labeled by Hendry and Pettigrew as developmental-humanism.

Amidst these apparently opposing claims, which are subject to the so-called unitarist strategic HRM approach (think of concepts like 'fit', matching business need to human resource practices, and so on.) in order to reconcile latent or manifest differences between strategic demands and human resource needs, we need to describe the performers of the personnel function in their quest for status. Competing with other functional areas like marketing and finance the performers of the personnel function are in search of mechanisms to legitimate their proposals (see Figure 6.10). This was a quest in which until recently the organizational imperative reflected the dominant criteria. But such criteria do not do full justice to the intrinsic complexities of the concept of strategic HRM, which does not simply consist of integrating the human resource dimension into the business strategic planning process (Kamoche, 1994:40). A better way of reconciling both strategic and humane aspects is to use the resource base theory of the firm (see, among others, Paauwe, 1994; Kamoche, 1994:40–1; see also Chapters 1 and 10) as a starting point, because it takes into account the competencies and capabilities of the human resources instead of focusing on dominant business like criteria such as those dictated by the industry-based demands of the specific product/market combination. Kamoche makes a strong plea for this view because in this way it will be possible to take into account the specific nature and complexities of human resources:

> this paradigm emphasises that the skills of employees are conceived of as a vital resource, which the firm is able to build upon rather than simply to exploit rationally and ideologically. Therefore the full potential of HRM can be realized and can be a key determinant in a firm's performance, without the *a priori* imposition of the organizational imperative.
>
> (Kamoche, 1994:41)

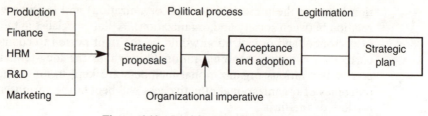

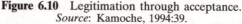

Figure 6.10 Legitimation through acceptance.
Source: Kamoche, 1994:39.

For HRM professionals, working either internally or externally, this paradigm implies a focus on using multi-dimensional/multifaceted approaches in their development and rendering of specialist personnel services. A simple one-sided approach, exclusively based on the strategic demands of the marketplace, is out of the question. Without such an expanded vision the power of the HRM specialists (embedded in or without a specialist personnel department) will decline and possibly die.

References

Adams, K. (1991). Externalisation vs specialisation: what is happening to personnel? *Human Resource Management Journal*, 1, (4), 43.

Aken, J.E. van, Douma, S.W., and Moenaert, R.K. (1993). gastredactie [invited editors], Themanummer Intern Ondernemerschap, *M&O Tijdschrift voor Organisatiekunde en Sociaal Beleid*, 47e jrg., nov./dec. 1993.

Armstrong, M. (1988). The personnel profession in the age of management accountancy, *Personnel Review*, 17, (1), 25–31.

Armstrong, M. (1992). *Human Resource Management: Strategy and Action*. London: Kogan Page.

Atkinson, J. (1984). Manpower strategies for flexible organisations, *Personnel Management*, 16, (8), August, 28–31.

Bakker, J., Paauwe, J., m.m.v. Immerzeel, J. (1989). *Sociaal ondernemingsbeleid: beïnvloeding en vormgeving, Kluwer Bedrijfswetenschappen*, Deventer: Kluwer Bedrijfswetenschappen.

Bartlett, C.A. and Ghoshal, S. (1989). Managing Across Borders, *The Transnational Solution*. Boston, MA: Harvard Business School Press.

Beer, M., Spector, B., Lawrence, P.R., Mills, D.Q., and Walton, R.E. (1984). *Managing Human Assets*. New York: The Free Press.

BSO/Origin, Company report 1992.

Buitendam, A. (1979). *Personeelsafdelingen in de industrie*. Meppel: Konstapel.

Buitendam, A. and Postma, F. (1980), *Personeelsafdelingen in industriële organi-saties*. Deventer: COB-SER, Kluwer.

Carroll, S.J. (1991). The new HRM roles, responsibilities, and structures. In Schuler, R.S. (ed.) *Managing Human Resources in the Information Age*. Washington, D.C.: Bureau of National Affairs, 204–26.

Cascio, W.F. (1992). *Managing Human Resources*, 3rd edn, New York, McGraw-Hill.

Dichter, S.F. (1991). The organization of the '90s, *The McKinsey Quarterly*, 1, pp. 145–55.

Gomez-Mejia, L.R. and Welbourne, T.M. The role of compensation in the human resource management strategies of high technology firms, In: Glinov, M.A., von and Mohrman, S.A. (1990). *Managing complexity in high technology organizations*. New York: Oxford University Press, 255–77.

Guest, D.E. (1987). Human resource management and industrial relations, *Journal of Management Studies*, 24, (5), 503–21.

Guest, D.E. (1989). Personnel and HRM: can you tell the difference? *Personnel Management*, January, 48–51.

Guest, D.E. (1990). Human resource management and the American dream, *Journal of Management Sudies*, 27, 377–97.

Hall, R. (1992). The strategic analysis of intangible resources, *Strategic Management Journal*, 13, 135–44.

Hammer, M. (1990). Reengineering work: don't automate, obliterate, *Harvard Business Review*, July/August, 104–12.

Harrington, H.J. (1991). *Business Process Improvement, the Breakthrough Strategy for Total Quality, Productivity and Competitiveness*. New York: McGraw-Hill.

Hendry, C. and Pettigrew, A.M. (1990). Human resource management: an agenda for the 1990s, *International Journal of Human Resource Management*, 1, 17–43.

Hulleman, A.E., and Paauwe, J. (1992). Personeelsmanagement zonder personeelsmanagers, *M&O, Tijdschrift voor Organisatiekunde en Sociaal Beleid*, mei/juni, 294–316.

Kamoche, K. (1994). A critique and a proposed reformulation of strategic human resource management, *Human Resource Management Journal*, 4, (4), 29–43.

Keuning, D., Opheij, W., and Maas, T.H. (1993). *Verplatting van organisaties*. Assen: Van Gorcum/Stichting Management Studies.

Kleingartner, A. and Anderson, C.S. (1987). *Human Resource Management in High Technology Firms*. Institute of Industrial Relations, UCLA, Lexington Books.

Kluytmans, F. and Paauwe, J. (1991). HRM denkbeelden: de balans opgemaakt, *M&O, Tijdschrift voor Organisatiekunde en Sociaal Beleid*, juni, 279–303.

Legge, K. (1993), The role of personnel specialists: centrality or marginalization. In: Clark, J. (ed.). *Personnel Management, Human Resource Management and Technical Change*. London: Sage, 20–42.

Legge, K. (1978). *Power, Innovation and Problem-solving in Personnel Management*. London: McGraw-Hill.

Manz, C.C. and Sims, H.P., Jr (1993). *Business Without Bosses*. New York: John Wiley.

Mastenbroek, W.F.G. (1993). Organiseren in een historisch perspectief, *M&O, Tijdschrift voor Organisatiekunde en Sociaal Beleid*, mei/juni, 161–71.

Paauwe, J. (1991). Limitations to freedom: is there a choice for Human Resource Management, *British Journal of Management*, 2, 103–19.

Paauwe, J. (1994), *Organiseren, een grensoverschrijdende passie*, Alphen aan den Rijn: Samsom Bedrijfsinformatie, 1994.

Prahalad, C.K. and Hamel, G. (1990). The core competence of the corporation, *Harvard Business Review*, May–June, 79–91.

Pugh, D.S. and Hickson, D.J. (1976). *Organizational Structure in its Context, the Aston Program I*. Saxon House: Aldershot.

Pugh, D.S., Hickson, D.J., Hinings, C.R., and Turner, C. (1968). Dimensions of organization structure, *Administrative Science Quarterly*, 13, 65–105.

Purcell, J. (1985). Is anybody listening to the corporate personnel department? *Personnel Management*, September, 28–31.

PW, Vakblad voor personeelsmanagement (1994), 18, 12 March, Special on Outsourcing. Amsterdam: VNU Business Publications.

Quinn, J.B. (1992a). *Intelligent Enterprise, a Knowledge and Service Based Paradigm for Industry*. New York: The Free Press.

Quinn, J.B. (1992b). The intelligent enterprise: a new paradigm, *Academy of Management Executive*, 6, (4), 48–63.

Schuler, R.S. (1990). Repositioning the human resource function: transformation or demise? *Academy of Management Executive*, 4, (3), 49–59.

Shipton, J. and McAuley, J. (1994). Issues of power and marginality in personnel, *Human Resource Management Journal*, 4, (1), 1–13.

Sisson, K. and Scullion, H. (1985). Putting the corporate personnel department in its place, *Personnel Management*, December, 36–9.

Storey, J. (ed.) (1989). *New Perspectives on Human Resource Management*. London: Routledge.

Torrington, D. (1988). How does human resources management change the personnel function?, *Personnel Review*, 17, (6), 3–9.

Torrington, D. (1989). Human resource management and the personnel function. In Storey, J. (ed.) (1989). *New Perspectives on Human Resource Management*, London: Routledge, 56–66.

Torrington, D. and Mackay, L. (1986). Will consultants take over the personnel function? *Personnel Management*, February, 34–6.

Tyson, S. (1987). The management of the personnel function, *Journal of Management Studies*, 24, (5), 523–32.

Tyson, S. and Fell, A. (1986). *Evaluating the Personnel Function*. London: Hutchinson.

Uijlen, Y. and Paauwe, J. (1994). Internal Research Memorandum on personnel management and unit management, HRS-RU, Rotterdam: Erasmus University. 12 p.

Vries, J.C. de and Paauwe, J. (1994). Internal Research Memorandum on personnel management and outsourcing, HRS-RU, Rotterdam: Erasmus University. 15 p.

Walker, J.W. (1988). How large should the HR staff be? *Personnel*, October, 36–42.

Williamson, O. (1985). *Markets and Hierarchies*, New York: Macmillan.

Wintzen, E.J. (1991). Mens, werk en motivatie, *Economisch Statistische Berichten*, 23 October, 1067–9.

Wintzen, E.J. (1993). Original synergy, *Holland Herald*, 49–51.

Wissema, H.G. (1992). *Unit Management, Entrepreneurship and Coordination in Decentralised Firms*. London: Financial Times/Pitman Publishing.

Appendix 1 Overview of companies

J.G. Nelis Building Contractors

This company operates in western Holland. It is a typical family-owned mid-sized building company with various business-units, including earth works, road building, hydraulic works, and equipment leasing. J.G. Nelis' business philosophy is based on the principles of providing reliability and a customer-oriented approach to building and construction problems. Nelis employs a full-time permanent workforce of some 390 people. Depending on the needs of building projects in progress, this workforce is expanded with temporary staff via subcontractors.

BSO/Origin (Bureau for Systems Development)

This firm, highlighted in our introduction to this chapter, develops software systems. It has 80 branches in 14 different countries. The head office is in Utrecht, the Netherlands. BSO employs 4000 people. Our case study focuses on the situation in the Netherlands.

ABC Technology

This is a software company as well. The firm has branches throughout the Netherlands. The total workforce of ABC Technology stands at around 2000. The case study was conducted at ABC Industrial Automation. The company has opted for an organizational structure which gives the subsidiaries a great deal of autonomy in order to operate flexibly in turbulent and fast-developing markets

Damen Shipyards Gorinchem

This division of Damen Shipyards employs 450 people. In total, the Damen Shipyards Company employs about 2000 people in various countries. Other than shipyards, Damen is able to deliver vessels on short notice because the company has components and kits in stock. These standardized elements can be variously combined so that a large number of types of vessel can be supplied according to the specific customer requirements. The organization in Gorinchem operates with a matrix structure; the two main pillars of this structure are sales and product groups. The products are grouped so as to facilitate sales: offshore and transport, tugs and workboats, fishing vessels, highspeed and naval craft, and dredging equipment. These product groups are set up as profit centers and are free to decide whether to use company facilities (like Parts and Central Engineering) or to turn to some form of external acquisition. In this way marketing conditions are introduced within Damen Shipyards itself.

Skillbase

A UK-based consultancy company, Skillbase renders professional services in the field of strategic planning, organizational change, efficiency, human resources, and information technology. It is an IBM spin-off. Seeking to reduce overhead expenses in 1990, IBM wanted to let go a large number of highly qualified personnel via early retirement schemes. On the other hand, IBM did not want to lose their extended and still valuable expertise. With the aid of two former IBM executives Skillbase was created. Its major objectives are:

(1) the marketing of the skills and experience of former IBM employees, mainly managers and senior professionals, who were entitled to an early retirement scheme;
(2) to have in reserve an organization with a sufficient number of well-qualified and competent staff in order to give IBM the possibility of outsourcing a number of non-core activities or activities for which IBM is temporarily understaffed.

Skillbase employs a small number of core staff employees (about 50) and about 800 employees (so-called A-registrars) who are entitled to perform activities for their previous employer during a period of 90 days after termination. In addition, about 3000 people (so-called B-registrars) are enlisted, of whom about 500 are regularly assigned to projects. With regard to the B-registrars, Skillbase can be considered as a temporary staff agency for highly skilled/trained staff.

7

Management without supervision: how self-managing teams create competitive advantage

In 1987, John Neill led the employees of British auto-parts producer, Uniparts, in a buyout of the company (Economist Publications, 1992a, 1992b). Located in aging buildings in the university town of Oxford, Neill could have discontinued manufacturing and decided to limit Uniparts to marketing and distributing parts from other manufacturers. Located on almost 30 acres of prime real estate, the factory was filled with grimy workshops and dated machine tools. Uniparts built gas tanks and catalytic converters for automobiles. Worker productivity and product quality were both low. Selling off the land seemed like a good way to pay back the US$85 million it cost to buy the business.

But Neill had faith in the factory and the people, yet only if Uniparts adopted 'lean' manufacturing. Uniparts had supplied Rover, an English automaker who had, in turn, teamed with Japan's Honda. Neill turned to Honda (Japan) for help. Honda recommended that Uniparts study the manufacturing methods of Yachiyo Kogyo, Honda's Japanese fuel tank supplier. Uniparts sent a team of workers to Japan, where they learned from the Japanese that attention to quality and defect reduction, not to speed and quantity, mattered most. Japanese workers showed Uniparts how to take responsibility too, even organizing maintenance, repair, and training operations.

Upon their return to England, these fresh converts earned the contempt of their fellow workers. Worker control and participation threatened middle managers; they became hostile. Neill gave the Japanese-trained workers a chance to experiment in a corner of the factory. 'They became the missionaries,' says Neill. The missionaries proved themselves and their methods to their skeptics. Uniparts soon adopted their techniques on a plant-wide basis.

Uniparts eliminated piecework. They placed all workers on a salary. The work process itself changed, shifting from work divided by functions to 'cells,' with small, flexible teams of workers with a variety of tasks. From seven layers of management, Uniparts reduced to three. It added new machines and revived older machines. Fifty-year-old machine presses that had been changed over once a week were now changed over three times a day, allowing production to be more flexible. Inventory turned over 27 times a year, not three or four times. Uniparts reduced the needed manufacturing space by more than half, from 640,000 square feet to 300,000. They reduced the space needed for storage by two thirds, a reduction of almost 50,000 square feet. Mostly through early retirements, Uniparts reduced the workforce from 1000 to 330 employees, while production increased. Uniparts also introduced a type of quality circle – 'contribution circles' – to help cut costs.

By 1991, in the midst of one of the worst automobile recessions ever, Uniparts profits increased nearly 20% for the year, on sales of close to US$1 billion. And, in a country known for fierce union loyalty, trade union recognition ended. All 4000 employees became salaried, just like management. And for a firm once languishing and putting out poor quality parts, Uniparts now supplies parts for Honda and Toyota in England.

Twenty years ago, the notion of employees working without a boss would have been ridiculed. Today, self-managing teams are often used as an effective substitute for the traditional, supervised group. Most important, teams have become a critical ingredient for creating quality and a competitive advantage.

In Emilia-Romagna (Italy), widespread cooperation among management and labor allows small business to manage under very adverse conditions, including unstable government, high interest rates, and even higher taxes. Innovation results from geographic proximity, technical know-how, and economic flexibility – all characteristics of effective teams (Kline, 1994). Recent developments in organization theory recognize the new paradigm of worker–management cooperation embodied in teams. Agency theory addresses the conflict that stems from differences in goals between principal and agent (Eisenhardt, 1989; Pickering, 1993); self-managed teams offer an opportunity for greater alignment between the goals of principals and agents. There is evidence that the inherent conflict between senior management/owners and workers can be resolved through methods such as self-directed work teams (Osterman, 1994). The contract model of employment relations bridges economic and sociological theory of labor (Kalleberg and Reve, 1993); self-managed teams offer an extension of the sociotechnical model of work. The internal labor market of the firm recognizes the vested interest firms have in retaining employees who have received specific training; self-managed teams offer a method for training and retaining highly skilled, cross-functional employees (Soeters and Schwan, 1990; Martin, 1993). The dysfunctional effects of close supervision can be counteracted by effective self-managed teams, reducing the distrust that results from efforts to produce greater work effort through closer monitoring of employees (Frey, 1993).

The K-5 team had been in place for two months when Jorge was first considered to possibly help with some of the technical work on the system. First, he had to be interviewed by two of his prospective fellow workers, Gina and Karl. Being interviewed by peers was a new experience for him. In the past, the personnel manager and the group supervisor had been the only interviewers he encountered before being hired. Gina wanted to know what Jorge knew about the software being installed on the K-5 system. He had worked with the software on his last two assignments; he knew this software very well and answered Gina's questions in a way that seemed to please her.

'Some of the applicants management sent to us didn't know that much about what we do,' she said. 'It's nice to be able to find that out before a person's hired.'

Then Karl asked about Jorge's work habits, his experiences and preferences. This put Jorge off a bit. He looked around for any sign of the group supervisor. Not seeing one, he asked, 'When do I meet the supervisor?'

'We don't have one,' Gina answered quickly, 'and, to be candid, we don't really need one. You may have to get used to that. Is that a problem?'

'Well, who makes final decisions around here?' Jorge asked.

'Like what?' Gina probed.

'For instance, what about working late, buying new equipment, keeping us on schedule,' Jorge listed.

'The team does,' Karl said.

'So who's that?' Jorge asked, getting more frustrated.

'It depends,' Karl replied, 'but 99% of the time it's just us.'

Jorge was silent. This was not something he had experienced previously. He had to think about these new ideas.

A self-managing team is a group of employees who share common goals and who exercise a considerable amount of autonomy and judgment about how to achieve these goals. Most important, a team is a group of employees that works without 'traditional' supervision, if there is any evidence of outside supervision at all. Teams do require leadership, but this comes from within, or from newly designated roles such as 'facilitator', or 'coordinator'. The main theme that we will explore in this chapter is that teams are a means to manage without supervision.

Self-managing teams are growing in numbers and effectiveness for the global corporation. In 1980, one study estimated that about 150 manufacturing plants in the United States used some sort of self-managing team approach. In 1989, it was reported that about 20% of General Electric's 120,000 US employees worked under a team concept. By 1990, it was estimated that about 7% of the manufacturing firms in the United States used a team approach; an estimated number of plants of 'somewhere between 300 and 500.' In 1992, it was estimated that 40% to 50% of all workers would be employed in self-managing teams by the end of the century (Hoerr, 1989; Lawler, 1990, 1990b; Lublin, 1992).

Teams have long been associated with Japanese and Swedish business firms. Use of teams has been more closely associated with the national origin of the firm's managers than the factory's locale. That is, Japanese-run plants in the United Kingdom are likely to employ traditional Japanese features like teams. In 1991, a comprehensive, global study of automobile assembly found that Japanese-managed automobile assembly plants in Japan and the United States used teams for 69.3% and 71.3% of the workforce respectively, while US-managed plants in the United States and European plants used teams for only 17.3% and 0.6% of their workers, respectively (Womack, *et al.*, 1991). A further study of 531 firms – most of them large – reported that work teams were found to be 'very effective' by 64% of the firms that used this method. Over half of the firms had tried work teams. Related team activities reported as being very effective included: involving employees in task forces, small-group meetings, and team-building activities (Fuchsberg, 1993).

However, a study of international applications of quality management found that Japanese firms are not as extensively involved with quality-related teams as many had argued (Ernst and Young, 1991). Sixty-four per cent of Japanese firms had 25% or fewer of their employees involved in teams, and little change in those numbers was likely. Over 80% of German firms involved less than a quarter of their employees in teams. One third of US firms expected to involve over three quarters of their employees in teams in the near future. The rapid growth of self-managing teams is expected to continue to increase.

How self-managing teams developed

Self-managing teams typically involve

> a relatively whole task; members who each possess a variety of skills relevant to the group task; workers' discretion over such decisions as methods of work, task schedules, and assignment of members to different tasks; and compensation and feedback about performance for the group as a whole.
>
> (Manz and Sims, 1987)

Today, the recognition that work groups have the potential for significant self-management has produced an increasing emphasis on team effectiveness and other group-based performance measures.

The development and performance of employees working in groups has been an ongoing managerial concern. Two historical antecedents to the idea of self-managing teams are (1) sociotechnical systems, and (2) quality circles. Attention to the combination of social and technical aspects of work in groups led to the concept of *sociotechnical systems* and the development of autonomous work groups.

Sociotechnical systems

European and, especially, Swedish theorists directed a focus towards the need to structure work in a meaningful way, to satisfy both the technical needs of an industrial society and the social needs of an educated workforce. Historically, group researchers have identified essential *social* and *technical* demands that encourage the development of autonomous work groups. The sociotechnical approach to group and task design has been applied to coal-mining teams and to a variety of industrial settings, including General Foods, General Motors, Cummins Engine, Xerox, Polaroid, IBM, and Procter & Gamble (Hoerr, 1987; Trist and Bamforth, 1951). One study, for example, reported that, following a sociotechnical analysis, a life insurance firm instituted skill-based pay and self-managing teams assigned to manage various geographic regions (Myers, 1985).

As a predecessor to the team concept, a model based on sociotechnical systems was recommended (Cherns, 1977), where

- group members are involved in the design of the group;
- management specifies only minimal conditions, with an emphasis on goals rather than procedures;
- problems inherent to the group task are solved by the group rather than an external authority, for example quality control;
- cross-training, multiple skills of group members, and pay-for-knowledge based systems are used to enhance and reinforce flexibility;
- similar tasks are bundled;
- access to information and feedback for control is available to the group;
- group-based performance leads to group-based rewards;
- the group design provides a high quality of work life for its members, including feelings of self-control and purpose; and
- these changes in work processes require training and rehearsal.

Japanese and European manufacturers provided examples of innovative work group designs. These practices often resulted from the recognition of the inherent inability of traditional group structures and task design to incorporate both assembly-line economies and worker skills, expectations, and demands. ALMEX, a Swedish ticket-machine manufacturer, uses the following principles with its production work groups (Gardell, 1983):

- the group makes decisions in its area of expertise;
- groups exercise collective group responsibility;
- the group leader is elected by the group as the team's contact with management;
- the group decides on the allocation of work;
- there is cooperation with sales and technical personnel outside the group;
- the group is responsible for training, job rotation, and production methods;
- the group coordinates production flow and notes disruptions; and
- failure to achieve internal consensus does not preclude members from seeking outside resolution.

Self-managing teams usually select an internal, full-time member to be the leader/facilitator for the group. The teams themselves are then responsible for many activities and decisions often deemed to be managerial work: budgeting, record keeping, quality and inventory control, training, goal setting, and assessing team performance. For teams, the degree of autonomy ranges from control over group operations and procedures to setting quantitative and qualitative goals (Gulowsen, 1992).

Quality circles

A study of Japanese automotive parts plant reported on 'The well-known "Quality Circle" concept, involving small teams of 5–15 employees. A positive team spirit, along with intense loyalty and high motivation, are further enhanced by effective management communication. Visual communications in the plant – posters, signs, graphs – were extremely numerous' (Deming, 1986). Within the last 20 years, US manufacturing firms used quality circles to respond to worker concerns and demands over the quality of work life, to improve product quality and, above all, to mimic the visible aspect of Japanese success. Sadly, the use of quality circles alone is incomplete, and eventually frustrating and counterproductive without a comprehensive commitment to quality-based management. Problems come with 'taking refuge in formation of QC-Circles for ... employee involvement, employee participation, and quality of work life' (Deming, 1986:85).

At Ford, a 50% decline in sales from 1978 to 1982 prompted a crisis-management response that led to greater employee involvement, such as employee teams doing their own equipment repair and traveling to other plants to study better methods of doing business. 'Our goal was to maximize the contribution of our hourly people,' said Peter Pestillo, Ford's vice president in charge of labor relations. By 1992, Ford had a 33% advantage over GM in assembly labor hours per car, producing a cost advantage of nearly US$800 compared to GM vehicles (Templin, 1992).

Another study of the use of quality circles in Japan and the US noted that in the US circles are used as a formal staff structure; in Japan, circles are informal worker groups (Juran, 1992) (see Table 7.1). US workers are often ill-prepared for the statistical analysis associated with quality circle decision making; Japanese employees typically possess higher mathematical skills. In the United States, the manager appoints facilitators; in Japan, the manager is seen as an advisor or consultant. In the United States, the manager initiates the theme for the circle; in Japan, worker initiative suggests and develops the theme. In the United States, circles meet only during working hours; in Japan they also meet during lunch or after work. In the United States, there are often individual rewards for individual suggestions; in Japan they make team rewards. A further study found that almost 40% of Japanese firms involved over three quarters of their employees in regular meetings about quality, while only 16% of US firms and but 5% of German firms had so many employees meet to review quality (Ernst and Young, 1986). Apparently the Japanese have a stronger informal culture of collaboration, one that crosses hierarchical levels, lunch hours, and worker–manager differences.

One study reports on experiences with quality circles in Japan in 1966. The failure of quality circles in US corporate settings is explained as follows: US management asked quality circles (QCs) to solve problems that were management's own doing, and management did not make a top-down commitment to solving quality problems (Paton, 1992). More recently, QCs have been contrasted with quality improvement teams (teams). The primary result of a quality circle is improved human relations, with a secondary result of improved quality. For teams, improved quality is the primary result, followed by improved participation. While quality circles are from a single department, voluntary, and likely to stay in place for some time, quality improvement teams are drawn from multiple departments; members are assigned to the team and it disbands after the project is done. While QCs continue to grow in use in Japan, the rapid growth in the number of QCs in the United States began in the mid-1970s and peaked in the early 1980s (Juran, 1992).

Table 7.1 Quality circles: United States versus Japan

Element	*United States*	*Japan*
Structure	Formal	Informal
Training in statistics	Poor	Very good
Manager	Facilitator	Advisor/consultant
Source of initiative	Manager	Workers
Meeting time	Work hours only	During and outside of work
Rewards	Individual	Team

Quality circles, often identified as a Japanese managerial practice, are a rudimentary form of self-management. Self-managing teams differ from quality circles in significant ways, including membership, the type and frequency of problems handled, implementation authority, and the relationship of the group to the parent organization (Sims and Dean, 1985) (see Table 7.2). *Membership* in quality circles is limited; they are subsets of a work group, whereas all work group employees are members of a self-managing team; there is no distinction between members and non-members from the work group. As to the *type and frequency of problems handled*, quality circles tend to address relatively few problems usually defined as 'special,' or 'important,' and often on an infrequent basis. Conversely, teams address problems as they arise, even on a continuous basis, and therefore problems are handled more frequently and informally. Problems are identified by the team, not management, and tend to be 'smaller' in nature. For quality circles, *implementation* is often turned over to management, perhaps with ceremonial presentation of the solution. Teams are responsible for implementation of their own solutions, and typically do not require management permission. In terms of their *relationship to the organization*, teams are the basic building blocks of the organization, while quality circles are an overlay feature, supplemental to the basic organizational structure.

Quality circles can evolve into self-managing teams, although this route is rare (Ruffner and Ettkin, 1987). Instead, when management is interested in moving decision making to lower levels of the organization, it typically chooses between quality circles and teams. Quality circles are a much less radical and less risky approach than teams: they are putting a toe in the water; teams mean diving in head-first.

Four recommended stages or 'landmarks' in the development of teams may be identified. First, following the traditional division of labor practices, teams allow members to apply their skills and knowledge to problems compatible with their initial level of expertise, without

Table 7.2 A comparison of quality circles and self-managed teams

Element	Quality circles	Self-managing teams
Membership	Limited subset	All workers are members
Problems addressed	Few, infrequent	All, continuous
Who implements solution	Management	Team
For the organization	Overlay feature	Basic building block
Where	Mature plants	Greenfield sites
Start-up speed and time	Moderate	Long, difficult
Leadership	Initial leader, frequently a supervisor, appointed or elected by management	Elected internal leader; external leader appointed by management
Motivational impact	Moderate to strong	Strong

involving all members in every problem. Second, teams replace the formally designated manager with internally (s)elected leaders. Third, teams schedule weekly meetings and hold additional meetings as needed. Fourth, teams relax the criteria for the implementation of team solutions – that is, they move the responsibility for implementation within the team (Sims and Dean, 1985).

What self-managing teams do

Teams typically are responsible for many decisions – planning work, pacing work speed, managing quality control – that are traditionally made further up the organizational hierarchy. Self-managing work teams are both the result of and the cause of reduced hierarchical levels in organizations. When teams are introduced, it is not unusual for layers of management to be reduced or eliminated, and for decisions to be decentralized to the lowest level.

The following case illustrates the question of just which functions can be undertaken by a self-managing team.

> Marcel is the chief engineer for a large luxury hotel scheduled to open in three months. As chief engineer, Marcel is responsible for the physical plant – electrical, plumbing, construction, maintenance, energy control – of the hotel, and for the workers who do the work.
>
> The physical maintenance operation will be staffed by over 100 workers; they provide round-the-clock service to the hotel and co-ordinate their work closely with the other engineering functions. In delivering quality service to the hotel guests, the maintenance staff represents an often overlooked yet important part of the image of the hotel, as well as the first staff person an irate guest is likely to see if there is a maintenance problem with the guest's room – a dripping sink, a balky air conditioner, or a broken fixture.
>
> Marcel will meet over a period of several days with his area heads, including each of the engineering functions, to develop operational plans and responsibilities. Since close cooperation will be needed across functions and since his managers are seasoned, this meeting was designed so as to hammer out basic service goals and procedures. In an earlier meeting, the management group had decided to organize workers into teams. For the current meeting, Marcel and his area heads need to decide who will have the authority and responsibility for important decisions, once the start-up period has been completed and the system is stable.
>
> Marcel and his managers have written a preliminary list of roles and responsibilities that must be performed for the engineering department to work effectively. The list is not exhaustive, but it is a good start. As the team develops, Marcel expects that the list will expand.

The issue at hand is which of these roles and responsibilities the work team itself should assume. There are some managers who want to 'run a tight ship,' to keep a close rein on the workers and retain management's power to decide. Some are more open to worker participation, what they sometimes call 'Japanese management.'

Marcel's group must decide which roles and responsibilities should be made by management and which by the team. He presented the team members the preliminary list of work decisions and asked them to individually indicate which decisions should be made either by the team or by management. For each decision, team members were asked to mark one of two columns, to identify where responsibility for the decision should typically be placed (see Table 7.3).

This case represents a greenfield approach to designing and implementing self-managing teams. For ongoing operations, the move to teams is likely to involve a change in established practice, often based on dissatisfaction with current practices. The following, composite case represents a typical scenario in this evolution:

Threatened by declining demand, caused in no small part by products that were not price-competitive and often of shoddy quality, the bike manufacturer felt she had no choice but to make a change. She was willing to look at the production process from a fresh perspective.

Table 7.3 Work decisions to be made by the team or by management

	Team	Management
1. Assign individuals to work activities	___	___
2. Set relief and break schedules	___	___
3. Perform housekeeping in engineering area	___	___
4. Select work team leader	___	___
5. Dismiss work team leader	___	___
6. Make minor equipment design changes	___	___
7. Make major equipment design changes	___	___
8. Discipline late/tardy work team members	___	___
9. Train new work team members	___	___
10. Keep timekeeping records	___	___
11. Maintain spare parts inventory	___	___
12. Make quality inspections	___	___
13. Keep quality service records	___	___
14. Prepare labor budgets	___	___
15. Prepare material budgets	___	___
16. Keep daily logs of work-in-progress	___	___
17. Make changes in work practices	___	___
18. Select new work team members	___	___
19. Dismiss work team members	___	___
20. Evaluate team members	___	___
21. Determine pay rates for team members	___	___
22. Conduct monthly safety meetings	___	___
23. Conduct weekly team meetings	___	___
24. Reject work performed if it does not meet quality standards	___	___
25. Review monthly team performance	___	___

Meeting extensively with the workforce, managers found plenty of criticism and some seeds of enthusiasm. Above all, the workers felt that management placed too many obstacles in their way: poor design of the production process, inefficient shop floor management, slow delivery of parts, and an arrogant quality control group.

Management accepted the idea of significant physical rearrangement of the shop floor, in some cases dispatching lengthy assembly lines. A new 'just-in-time' parts delivery system was implemented, first-level supervisors were reassigned to new responsibilities, and the quality control function was turned over to the newly formed work teams.

A marked change evolved among the workers. Workers took more responsibility not only for the quality of their finished work, but also for their workplace. Scrap rates, housekeeping 'demerits,' and rejected bicycle assemblies all declined. Workers opted for a pay-for-skill compensation plan. Adding skills to do multiple jobs led to an increase in base pay, but only after having those skills certified by experienced workers. A proposed plan to remodel the employee rest area was rejected after employees reviewed the cost estimates and their projected impact on plant profitability. A gain-sharing plan was recommended by an 'employee study group.' When a new machine tool was needed, rather than purchasing new equipment, two workers located, inspected, recommended, and received approval to purchase an older piece of equipment from a plant 600 miles away but at a savings of £17,000 for the first year.

How self-managing teams perform

Hard evidence that scientifically evaluates the effectiveness of self-managing teams is scant; relatively little has been published that meets traditional scientific research standards. The typical assessment is qualitative. For example, in the United States, one study asserted that one of the team systems they examined was reputed to produce productivity savings of 30–40% when compared with traditionally organized plants (Manz and Sims, 1987). A second study claimed teams can increase productivity by 30% or more, and can also substantially raise productivity (Hoerr, 1989).

A large glass manufacturer eliminated one management level at their corporate computer center. They substituted a team adviser for three shift supervisors, producing US$150k annual savings and increasing the quality of service. They reported increases in autonomy and responsibility among workers, who experienced more meaningful and productive work (Weiss, 1989). A similar argument has been made for achieving manufacturing excellence, through continuous improvement and team management, the latter entailing worker commitment, self-management, and open communication (Puckett, 1989). In a US insurance firm, change to automation led to a shift from a functional organizational design to self-managing teams, requiring redesigned contingencies to support organizational goals, not simply work unit goals. A twenty-four month follow-up found improved work structure, flows, and outcomes (Frederiksen, *et al.*, 1984).

A UK study reports on how course teams at Saltash and Mid-Cornwall Colleges (UK) assessed customer satisfaction with aspects of their education, including settling into the course, the quality of learning, and the relevance of the course. Initial work by the course teams led to their expressed desire for clearer communication with management. Working with the College Governors, quality teams developed policies as well as improvement issues: communication, management, accommodation, and course evaluation and review (Ellis, 1993).

Those close to the self-management movement informally report substantial productivity savings that typically range from 30% to 70% when compared with traditional systems. Rigorous, scientific evaluation is elusive and difficult. The difficulty of evaluating the team concept is aptly expressed in the following passage:

> The results are often positive. It is hard to predict whether the outcomes will be greater output, better quality, less absenteeism, reduced turnover, fewer accidents, greater job satisfaction, or what, but the introduction of autonomous work groups is often associated with improvements. It is difficult to understand why a particular outcome such as increased productivity occurs in one study and not in another, and why on some occasions nothing improves. Furthermore, what actually causes the changes when they do occur is not known. The approach calls for making so many changes at once that it is almost impossible to judge the value of the individual variables. Increased pay, self-selection of work situation, multi-skilling with its resultant job enrichment, and decreased contact with authority almost invariably occur in autonomous work groups.
>
> (Miner, 1982)

A revealing study of the bottom line effect of team analysis contrasted the success of various changes involving human resources, work structure, and technology – for example, training, reward systems, and work teams. Very strong effects, especially in terms of financial outcomes, were observed with team applications (Macy, *et al.*, 1991). This study is one of the first rigorous scientific efforts that shows the clear financial effect of the team approach in dozens of organizations.

A vast body of experience lies unreported in the scientific literature. Those close to the self-management movement informally report substantial productivity gains and cost savings that typically range from 30% to 70% when compared with traditional systems. Self-managing teams have the potential to exert substantial effects on the bottom line.

Perhaps the notion was captured best by Charles Eberle, a former vice president at Procter & Gamble, who speaks with the advantage of years of practical experience:

> At P&G there are well over two decades of comparisons of results – side by side – between enlightened work systems and those I call traditional. It is absolutely clear that the new work systems work better – a lot better – for example, with 30 to 50 percent lower manufacturing costs. Not only are the tangible, measurable, bottom-line indicators such as cost, quality, customer service and reliability better, but also the harder-to-measure attributes such as quickness, decisiveness, toughness, and just plain resourcefulness of these organizations.
>
> (Fisher, 1991)

Resistance to self-managing teams

Why do companies and employees resist the change to more self-managing teams? There are several philosophical and practical barriers to the ready acceptance of the team concept.

Cultural differences

Cultural differences may give rise to limits of US management thinking, 'A stress on interactions among individuals obviously fits a culture identified as the most individualistic in the world, but it will not be so well understood by four-fifths of the world population for whom the group prevails over the individual' (Hofstede, 1993:92). In contrast to their European and Japanese counterparts, US workers often reflect a tradition of individuality and personal freedom that can, at times, run counter to the collective nature of teamwork. For both managerial and non-managerial employees, an emphasis on team values can threaten not only their traditional views of work, but also their approach to life. Team work that is seen as a threat to individual freedom will be resisted as a matter of culture and values. Many managers have been trained to actively manage in a forceful, autocratic, even threatening way; they may not readily accept the concept of teams. The change to a team approach results in a variety of disincentives to the traditional, hard-charging manager.

Distrust

With a history of management-induced fads and combative industrial relations, some companies do not have the credibility with first-line employees, especially unionized employees, needed to earn the trust to implement teams. If management sees team development as an expense rather than an investment, and employees see teams as another attempt to co-opt employees to management's views, an attempted shift to team values and work will be likely to fail. It is unsurprising that many examples of successful team efforts have come from threatened companies or industries, where workers and management were forced to confront and discard traditional distrust in favor of teams. In one General Motors' assembly plant, traditionally independent quality control functions were turned over to production teams, only to have the decision reversed when quality problems persisted. In a second example, at a paper mill, teams were created after a lengthy collective bargaining process, only to result in the union representatives being voted out of power within a year of signing the agreement.

More teams means fewer managers

Middle management is the primary redundancy when the team approach succeeds. Expensive managers are viewed as overhead, a negative value-added activity. Direct labor – those team workers who add value with quality work, who ensure the continuous improvement, who manage and correct their own behavior – is a relatively small part of the total cost of the process, thus creating high added value. In some cases, the direct labor cost of a product may be less than 5% of the sale price, while indirect labor (management overhead) may comprise 35% of the cost of the product.

A shift to teams and flatter organizations reduces opportunities for advancement in the traditional organizational hierarchy, if only because there is no longer much of a hierarchy. Economic factors, not just the movement to teams, have threatened the career prospects and aspirations of many managers.

Legal threats

Hardened opponents of quality teams have challenged the use of teams by firms in the US courts (Miscimarra, 1992; Nulty, 1993). The international Association of Machinists (IAM) and the United Auto Workers (UAW) have severely criticized worker involvement in teams, arguing that teams undermine the traditional role played by labor unions. Teams, they claim, threaten the very existence of the union, posing a long-term threat to worker job security and other union benefits. When teams resolve grievances, discipline workers and award pay raises, traditional labor union power and roles are threatened. With the declining union representation of the US labor force in the past 50 years, from nearly half of all non-agricultural workers belonging to unions, to about one-sixth of workers in unions, this protest is unlikely to disappear quietly.

In 1992, the US National Labor Relations Board described company-sponsored 'action teams' at Electromation, a small company making electronic parts, as 'sham unions,' agreeing with criticisms from the Teamsters union, which had tried to organize a union at

Electromation's plant. The ruling came a bit late, as Electromation had earlier disbanded the groups. Proponents of quality circles and other management-endorsed teams viewed the ruling as a threat to 30,000 employee empowerment programs found at about 80% of the largest 1000 US companies (Salwen, 1990).

Lack of empathy and understanding

The management of self-managing teams requires the ability to listen, to change views, to empathize, and to change basic behavior patterns. Without an adequate investment in the training and development of new, social work skills, team development will be retarded or thwarted. In the GM case mentioned above, returning the quality control responsibility to the production team reduced quality; training was necessary.

Leading self-managing teams

A team may not have a supervisor, but teams always have some sort of leader. Many self-managing teams elect their own leaders from within their group. Other teams are supported by external leaders typically called facilitators, coordinators, or coaches. Most of all, leaders of self-managing teams do not behave like a traditional boss.

Leading others to be self-leaders sounds paradoxical; many managers are very uncomfortable with surrendering management prerogatives to first-line employees. Yet managers and firms tend to be successful if they recognize the combined impact of changes in products and tasks, in information technology, and in consumer, worker, and managerial demographics, interests, and expectations. A number of steps can be traced during the shift to self-managing teams (Manz, *et al.*, 1990).

To bring about successful team development, the leader must first establish the capacity of the work group to take on these new responsibilities. The manager cannot just cut the group loose. Certain environmental and technological conditions are more likely to be conducive to team development. For example, a greenfield site can be more amenable to teams than an existing plant. Also, a rigid, sequential technology is likely to reduce the potential autonomy of the group.

Next, the manager must take an active role in managing this transition. The leader can encourage:

- *Self-reinforcement*, where team members find ways to identify and administer meaningful, performance-contingent work outcomes for themselves.
- *Self-criticism*, where team members learn to diagnose inappropriate behaviors and engage in appropriate self-reprimands.

- *Self-set goals* for the group, where team members identify and artic-ulate key areas for progress.
- *Self-observation/evaluation*, where team members control their own consequences only after assessing their own behaviors.
- *High self-expectations* or self-efficacy, by developing a culture of constructive risk-taking and success.
- Opportunities for *rehearsal* prior to meeting final work demands, where team members can practice and further develop requisite team skills with less risk to success and self-esteem.
- The *re-design of work* so that the employee draws from the natural rewards that stem from the work itself.
- *Pride* of workmanship, *confidence* and *positive patterns* of thinking.

Overall, the manager of a group in transition to becoming a self-managing team must become a coach rather than a supervisor, and encourage interdependence within the group while discouraging team dependence on the manager. The management focus of the team must become internal. However, the manager must work to assure that the organization actively supports team behaviors, for example, providing needed information, authority, and rewards. The organization must provide the culture for team success, as indicated in the following vignette:

> The training session for new engineering managers was in its third day when Beatrice first noticed her discomfort with what she was hearing. Her education had included two summer internships with manufacturing firms, where the work was routine, dirty, and some-times argumentative. She had often observed bosses exercise their authority on the shop floor through the use of a loud voice, threats, and harsh reprimands. When push came to shove, shoving the hardest seemed to be the preferred practice and the most often recommended management technique. Managers were expected to push and shove. That was their job, they claimed, and not always happily.
>
> But at her new place of employment, a small, new firm producing environmental equipment for recycling hazardous acids, the tenor of the plant was different. And now, the training was unlike anything she had ever received or expected. Managers were taught to be helpful, not forceful. Some of her colleagues labeled it 'unmanaging.'
>
> Beatrice had her own doubts. Her university courses had empha-sized the formal power and expertise expected of a highly trained, effective leader, but the workers here seemed more capable than some of the leaders with her previous employers. The workers sure knew their own jobs better than she did. She compared her experience to a book she had read about a dedicated team of people who designed a new computer under a very tight deadline by tapping their own knowledge and looking within themselves for leadership.
>
> While working under those conditions seemed ideal to her, man-aging under these conditions seemed problematic. Beatrice had trouble with several of the role-playing exercises in which she participated. She

felt less uncomfortable after watching some of the more experienced managers demonstrate how to be helpful without being physically forceful. By the end of two weeks, she had observed other managers, tried out some of what she learned on the floor, read more of the company training materials, reviewed the course CD-ROM training segments twice, and slipped more comfortably into the role playing.

The organization must also provide training for the external leader, to enable her to become the facilitator of a team. Such skills are, in fact, not intuitive. Managers may find team development processes to run counter to well-learned models of active, external supervision.

To lead and effectively employ self-managing teams, management must:

- respect and trust workers to understand, articulate and pursue organizational goals;
- empower workers to solve problems and make decisions;
- cultivate pride in team work – a sense of accomplishment, recognition and realization of potential;
- view leadership as the process of creating an environment for self-management; and
- share the financial results of team and organizational success. Most of all, experience shows that self-managing teams can be a means to manage without supervision.

Now that we have developed a thorough knowledge about teams, we will conclude the chapter with an extensive case study illustrating the major features of team processes and operations.

Case study   IDS: illuminating the concepts[†]

In 1988, after extensive self-analysis, executives of IDS Financial Services in Minneapolis decided to undertake a transition to self-managing teams in their mutual funds operations division. Formerly, the organization and work design of the division could be described as highly differentiated and hierarchical. The change entailed a conversion from traditional supervisors to team facilitator – that is, managing without supervision.

IDS offers a wide range of financial services and products, including personal financial planning, insurance and annuities, mutual funds, certificates, limited partnerships, consumer banking, lending, and brokerage

† This case is abridged from Chapter 4 of Manz and Sims (1993). Barry Bateman was a co-author of the chapter. A more detailed account of teams at IDS is available in the original chapter.

services. The Mutual Funds Operations can be viewed as a service organization that processes information and financial transactions. A typical transaction is the investment of a certain amount of money in an IDS mutual fund for a client, or a withdrawal or redemption from an account. The transactions are carried out by 'core workers,' who undertake the 'back room' operations for the division. Accuracy and absence of errors are critical for maintaining both efficiency and customer goodwill.

Prior to the change in 1988, the employees were organized into specialized roles and departments, and overseen by supervisors who worked in a traditional vertical hierarchy.

Several temporary organizational structures were formed to implement the change to self-managing teams. The effort was launched by a Steering Committee, which consisted of the vice president and his staff of managers, the vice president of information systems, the vice president of human resources, and a consulting team consisting of an internal and an external consultant. The Steering Committee was charged with initiating the change, getting the people in place to actually implement the change, and establishing the overall guidelines for the change.

After considerable discussion, the Steering Committee empowered a design team, a group of 11 employees selected from 57 volunteers. This team consisted of eight core workers, two supervisors, and one assistant supervisor, and was supported by the same consulting team that supported the Steering Committee. Each team member was relieved of his/her regular job, and assigned to the design team full time.

The design team's work consisted of three major steps: developing a plan, conducting the technical (task) analysis, and doing the social interaction analysis. Over a period of eight and a half months, the team conducted their analysis and prepared the new organizational design. Despite difficulties along the way, the design team finally proposed a design that consisted of the following elements:

- teams would be organized according to geographical or regional lines;
- each team would have about 25 to 40 members;
- each team member would be trained to perform multiple skills and tasks;
- each team would be multifunctional – it would include all the different functions and processes within the team;
- each team would be empowered to make the decisions needed to process the work in a timely and accurate fashion;
- supervisors would be eliminated, and replaced by two 'facilitators' for each team;
- information systems would be developed that would provide each team with the information it needs to operate effectively as a small business.

After substantial discussion, the plan was approved by both management and the workforce, and a transition plan was implemented. The transition consisted, first, of a pilot team of about 25 employees who were assigned to a geographical area, and who were empowered to begin operations as an experimental team for several months. Then, the entire organization was converted to teams over a weekend – this change was called the 'big bang.'

Both the pilot team and the subsequent big bang included the conversion of supervisors to facilitators. Not surprisingly, this transition did not always proceed without some difficulties. Indeed, the facilitators found the team environment to be substantially different. Noted one:

> In the traditional system it was clear that I had the final word, and right now it is not clear. That's different. Another thing that's different is that we have changed the tasks. It's one thing to be self-managing in your old room and doing the same function, but now we've put together 20 other types of jobs that we didn't know anything about, so instead of having one set of goals and objectives, we've got a variety of them.
>
> It's frustrating because you felt like you should be knowing it, but you don't, and yet we know that it's unrealistic for us to think at this point that we can know everything. We make it a learning experience, and it takes a lot of time to do that.

Another facilitator noted:

> The thing I've been struggling with is that there's nothing to call my own. Eventually, if they're truly self-managing, it's going to be the team that gets most of the recognition. Now, I get more satisfaction out of helping someone to do something on their own rather than telling them to do it.
>
> In the traditional structure of supervision, you'd have goals and objectives: it was laid out. I always felt I knew what part of the path I was traveling on. Here as a team facilitator, so far I haven't felt that clarified yet, so I don't quite know where we're going.
>
> The reorganization of the task and the structure of the task are one dimension, and the management style or the division of authority is a different dimension.

Despite these problems, overall, the system seemed to work itself out:

> Weekly, we just feel more and more comfortable with it. The pilot team is working. They're getting work done. Things are going fine. I'm delighted. I think that it's going to make jobs a lot more interesting for people. There will be a lot more buy-in to decisions if it's a group decision than if it's mine.

Overall, the results of the transition to teams were quite positive. Team members developed a more personal relationship with their primary customer, the financial planner in the field. Accuracy and quality went up.

Perhaps one of the most interesting indicators of the benefits of moving to the team system was the improvement in flexibility that came when the system encountered a traumatic surge. For example, in 1987, during the mini-crash of the stock market, an extremely large swell in customer telephone calls – mainly requests for redemptions – was thrust upon the division without advance warning. Call volume to the organization quadrupled within a single day, placing a tremendous load on the system. The result was chaos. The average speed-of-answer – that is, how long it takes to begin to service a call – was seven and a half minutes. The system was gridlocked.

Subsequent to the transition to teams, a similar mini-crash occurred in 1989. With no new technology and the same number of employees, the teams handled a larger volume than the 1987 crash, and the average speed of answer was only 13 seconds.

This comparison deserves a second look:

- 1987 (before teams): 7.5 minutes
- 1989 (after teams): 13 seconds

Detailed analysis showed that the improvement in response came from the actions that the teams themselves took to deal with the crisis. As one manager said, 'This team concept really works!' Today, the team system at IDS is alive and well. Their experience is one of the early examples that teams are not only appropriate for manufacturing environments, but will work with knowledge or information workers as well. Most of all, this system is a classic example of how teams can be an instrument of managing without supervision.

References

Cherns, A.E. (1977). Can behavioral science help design organizations? *Organizational Dynamics*, 5, 55–63.

Deming, W.E. (1986). *Out of the Crisis*. Cambridge, MA; MIT Press.

Economist Publications (1992a). Unipartners, *The Economist*, 11 April, 67.

Economist Publications (1992b). Back to the future. *The Economist*, 17 October, 9.

Eisenhardt, K.M. (1989). Agency theory: an assessment and review, *Academy of Management Review*, 14, (1), 57–74.

Ellis, B. (1993). Total quality management in an education and training context. In Shaw, Malcolm and Roper, Eric (eds) *Aspects of Educational and Training Technology, Vol. XXVI*. London: Kogan Page.

Ernst and Young (1991). *International Quality Study: The Definitive Study of the Best International Quality Management Practices*. Cleveland, OH: Ernst & Young.

Fisher, K. (1991). Are you serious about self-management? Paper presented at the International Conference on Self-Managed Work Teams. Dallas, Texas.

Frederiksen, L.W., Riley, A.W., and Myers, J.B. (1984). Matching technology and organizational structure: a case in white collar productivity improvement. *Journal of Organizational Behavior Management*, 6, (3–4), 59–80

Frey, B. (1993). Does monitoring increase work effort? The rivalry with trust and loyalty, *Economic Inquiry*, 31, (4), 663–70.

Fuchsberg, G. (1993). Why shakeups work for some, not for others, *Wall Street Journal*, 1 October, B1, B4.

Gardell, B. (1983). Worker participation and autonomy: A multi-level approach to democracy at the work place. In Crouch, C. and Heller, F.A. (eds) *International Yearbook of Organizational Democracy, Vol. I: Organizational Democracy and Political Processes*. Chichester: John Wiley, pp. 364–5.

Gulowsen, J. (1972). A measure of work group autonomy. In Davis, L.E. and Taylor J.C. (eds) *Design of Jobs*. Baltimore, MD: Penguin, pp. 376–8.

Hoerr, J. (1987). Getting man and machine to live happily ever after, *Business Week*, 20 April, 61.

Hoerr, J. (1989). The payoff from teamwork, *Business Week*, 10 July, 56–62.

Hofstede, G. (1993). Cultural constraints in management theories, *Academy of Management Executive*, 7, (1), 81–94.

Juran, J.M. (1992). *Juran on quality by design: The new steps for Planning Quality into Goods and Services*. New York: The Free Press.

Kalleberg, A. and Reve, T. (1993). Contracts and commitment: economic and sociological perspectives on employment relations, *Human Relations*, 46, (9), 1103–32.

Kline, M. (1994). Tiny business enclave in Italy stares down adversity, *Wall Street Journal*, 18 August, B2.

Lawler, E.E. III (1990a). Speech as Self-Management Conference, North Texas University, Denton, Texas, September.

Lawler, E.E. III (1990b). The new plant revolution revisited, *Organizational Dynamics*, Autumn, 5–14.

Lublin, J.S. (1992). Trying to increase worker productivity, more employers alter management style, *Wall Street Journal*, 13 February, B1.

Macy, B.M., Bliese, P.D., and Norton, J.J. (1991). Organizational change and work innovation: a meta-analysis of 131 North American field experiments – 1961–1990. Working Paper. Texas Tech University.

Manz, C.C., Keating, D.E., and Donnellon, A. (1990). Preparing for an organizational change to employee self-management: the managerial transition, *Organizational Dynamics*, Autumn, 15–26.

Manz, C.C. and Sims, H.P., Jr. (1987). Leading workers to lead themselves: the external leadership of self-managing teams, *Administrative Science Quarterly*, 32, 106–28.

Manz, C.C., and Sims, H.P. (1993). *Business without Bosses: How Self-managing Teams are Producing High Performing Companies*. New York: John Wiley.

Martin, R. (1993). The new behaviorism: a critique of economics and organization, *Human Relations*, 46, (9), 1085–101.

Miner, J.B. (1982). *Theories of Organizational Structure and Process*. Hinsdale, IL: Dryden.

Miscimarra, P.A. (1992). Employee involvement and the law: Outstanding issues. Chicago, 6 April. (Incomplete manuscript.)

Myers, J.B. (1985). Making organizations adaptive to change: Eliminating bureaucracy at Shenandoah Life, *National Productivity Review*, 4, (2), 131–8.

Nulty, P. (1993). Look what the unions want now, *Fortune*, 8 February, 81.

Osterman, P. (1994). Supervision, discretion, and work organization, *American Economic Review*, 84, (2), 380–5.

Paton S.M. (1992). Joseph M. Juran: quality legend, *Quality Digest*, 26, (4), 50–51.

Pickering, A. (1993). The mangle of practice: agency and emergence in the sociology of science, *American Journal of Sociology*, 99, (3), 559–89.

Puckett, J.H. (1989). Manufacturing excellence: A vision of the future, *Manufacturing Systems*, 7, (4), 50–51.

Ruffner, E.R. and Ettkin, L.P. (1987). When a circle is not a circle, *Advanced Management Journal*, 52, (2), 9–15.

Salwen, K.G. (1990). NLRB says labor-management teams at firm violated company-union rule, *Wall Street Journal*, 12 December, A12.

Sims, H.P. Jr. and Dean, J.W. Jr. (1985). Beyond quality circles: self-managing teams, *Personnel*, 62, (1), January, 25–32.

Soeters, J.L. and Schwan, R. (1990). Towards an empirical assessment of internal labor market configurations. *International Journal of Human Resource Management*, 1, (3), 271–287.

Templin, N. (1992). Team spirit: a decisive response to crisis brought Ford enhanced productivity, *Wall Street Journal*, 15 December, A1, A13.

Trist, E.L. and Bamforth, K.W. (1951). Some social and psychological consequences of the longwall method of coal-getting, *Human Relations*, February, 3–38.

Weiss, M. (1989). Human factors: team spirit. *CIO*, 2, (10), 60–62.

Womack, J.P., Jones, D.T., and Roos, D. (1991). *The Machine that Changed the World*. New York: Harper.

8

Managing without quality boundaries

Other chapters in this book have examined the ways in which organizations can be managed without traditional components, including supervisors and full-time employees. In this chapter we look at total quality management (TQ) implementation and its impact on traditional quality boundaries. These boundaries can exist between organization members at different levels in the hierarchy and in different functional areas, and between organization members and their external customers. Proponents of total quality see these quality boundaries as hindrances which keep organization members from focusing on their most important overall goal – the continuous improvement of quality. If the quality goal is met, the organization, its members and its customers benefit. Eliminating traditional boundaries helps to direct the total quality-managed organization toward accomplishment of its goals.

The chapter begins with a brief overview of the elements of a total quality program and the challenges involved in implementing and sustaining it. We then outline some economic and competitive reasons for moving toward a TQ orientation despite the challenges in implementing and sustaining such an effort, and present a short case study of one organization's decision to implement TQ. Next we discuss the elimination of quality boundaries in more detail, providing examples of organizations which have found ways to eliminate these boundaries while obtaining a competitive advantage. We then link TQ ideas to the theories of the firm (agency theory, transaction costs economics, and resource base theory) that have been discussed in previous chapters. A case study of TQ implementation in a European organization is presented to discuss the elimination of boundaries in a real-world setting.

The need for total quality

Total quality management (TQM or TQ) is the popular name for a way of looking at work processes and organizational goals that have been revolutionizing organizations since the 1950s. The four most visible proponents of this outlook are Deming, Juran, Crosby, and Taguchi, although many others have written on the topic and served as TQ consultants. The quality movement began in post-war Japan and focuses on using measurable data in tandem with an understanding of statistical variance to systematically eliminate problems in the process of delivering a product or service to the customer. Although the authors' approaches to the challenge of continuous quality improvement differ, their writings share some common themes:

(1) *Customer focus.*   TQ organizations must focus on customers and on satisfying their needs. They must also be capable of reacting quickly to changing customer needs.
(2) *Continuous improvement.* TQ organizations use a scientific approach to problem solving coupled with ongoing step-by-step improvements to all work processes.
(3) *Management by fact.*   TQ organizations are data driven and all decisions are determined from verifiable data collected over long periods.
(4) *Process management.*   TQ organizations focus on the process rather than on the target. This encourages employees to think for themselves and reduces the natural tendency to lay the blame for defects elsewhere.
(5) *Total participation.*   TQ enables an organization to develop horizontal, cross-functional and vertical teams that greatly assist in involving everybody in the organization in improvement programs.
(6) *Visible effective leadership.*   TQ efforts require active commitment at all levels of management (Tuttle, 1991).

Differing interpretations of the main tenets of the TQ movement, coupled with customization of TQ efforts by individual organizations, has led to some confusion about TQ which its original advocates did not intend. In this chapter, we will use the definition put forward by Shiba, Graham, and Walden (Shiba, *et al.*, 1993). They define TQ as an evolving system, developed through analyzing successful practices in industry, for continuously improving products and services to increase customer satisfaction in a rapidly changing world. The chief scientist and Corporate Vice President of Xerox, John Seely Brown (who is responsible for such innovations as Ethernet, bitmapped displays, and object-oriented programming), argues that the most powerful ideas in the leadership-through-quality movement are:

(1) Learning from and listening to the customer.
(2) The ability to listen to the workforce to drive constant improvement.
(3) Rewarding 'out of the box,' or creative, thinking about radical innovation while simultaneously pursuing incremental innovation and listening to customers.

If an organization can do all three of these, then it has implemented TQ. Brown observed: 'It took me a long time as a researcher to appreciate the power of the quality movement because it has been oversold and bureaucratized. But there are a few simple, wonderful principles that can help show how to capitalize on the accelerating pace of change' (Nee, 1993:24–34 (25)).

Although the quality movement started in Japan in the 1950s, it only gained widespread popularity in Europe and the United States in the 1980s. Increased global competition and the increasing pace of technological advances led executives to reconsider quality as a competitive advantage, not just as a component of a product or service. One Total Quality writer, Genichi Taguchi, defined the necessity of thinking about quality in terms of loss to society. He proposed that if a product fails, then someone somewhere has suffered a financial loss of some kind. Hence, he concluded that poor quality results in a loss to society as a whole.

According to Taguchi, a manufacturer who knowingly allows a defective product to be shipped from his or her factory is worse than a thief. If a thief steals an item worth US$20, then he/she has taken only US$20 from the victim. However, a manufacturer could have repaired the defective product within the factory for, say, US$10. If the defective product were shipped, then someone would have to spend in excess of US$10 to have the defective product either repaired or replaced. So in order to save US$10, the manufacturer is inflicting a greater loss on society and, in Taguchi's view, this 'crime' is worse than stealing. Taguchi believes that everyone is someone else's customer. In his view, manufacturers should concern themselves with the lifetime of the product and not just the limited period specified on the warranty (Taguchi, 1989).

Deming's (1986) 14 points for management are:

(1) Create constancy of purpose toward improving product and service.
(2) Adopt the new philosophy, that change is needed.
(3) Cease dependence on inspection to achieve quality.
(4) End the practice of awarding business on the basis of price tag.
(5) Improve product and service constantly and forever. This will constantly decrease costs.
(6) Institute training on the job.
(7) Institute leadership with the goal of helping people and machines to do a better job.
(8) Drive out fear so that all may work effectively.
(9) Break down barriers between departments.

(10) Eliminate slogans, exhortations, and targets for the workforce which ask for zero defects and increased productivity.
(11) Eliminate work standards or quotas and substitute leadership.
(12) Remove barriers that rob the hourly worker of his [or her] right to pride of workmanship.
(13) Institute a vigorous program of education and self-improvement.
(14) Put everyone to work on the transformation.

An unmagnetized piece of iron is an analogy for many traditional organizations. Each department has north and south poles, but the poles are not necessarily aligned with the strategic goals of the business. Similarly, within many organizations barriers between departments, lack of trust among employees, and lack of leadership from senior management and direction from customers may result in the constituent elements of the organization not aligning properly. Market share and profitability decline as a result. Where TQ is successfully implemented, all of the forces within an organization pull in the same direction. Everyone participates in a continuous improvement program through which internal and external customer needs are satisfied.

Implementing and sustaining total quality

Even after altering the climate and goals of the organization to make them more consistent with TQ methods and ideology, it is difficult to sustain the TQ initiative. There are several conditions for implementing and sustaining TQ. These conditions may not have been met by all TQ organizations, but they are part of the success stories of many.

The first condition for sustaining TQ is *organizational learning*, which is a process whereby organizational members in one or more companies share their insights to avoid reinvention of methods already in existence (re-inventing the wheel), in order to improve more quickly and to create a quality culture which will influence society as a whole. Among TQ organizations, enthusiastic borrowing is replacing the 'NIH' (not invented here) syndrome (Garvin, 1993). Milliken Corporation, a Baldrige award winner, has called this process the SIS system ('Steal ideas shamelessly'). Ray Stata of Analog Devices, Inc. feels quite strongly that organizational learning was a crucial factor in his company's progress toward better quality. He writes, 'In fact, I would argue that the rate at which individuals and organizations learn may become the only sustainable competitive advantage, especially in knowledge-intensive industries' (Kofmann, *et al.*, 1994:64). At Analog Devices, a producer of integrated circuits and systems that convert between analog and digital data, organizational learning took the form of practitioner–academic partnerships and more traditional learning methods such as books, seminars and professional trainers, but other organizations have used many other methods.

A second condition for successful TQ is another form of organizational learning. It is *benchmarking*, which refers to comparing a firm's activity to a comparable activity being completed at another firm. Through benchmarking and societal learning the barriers between organizations are broken down. One organization may look to another as a benchmark in a certain area, as many look to L.L. Bean to set the example for distribution. Benchmarking is used by similar and dissimilar firms (Bounds, *et al.*, 1993).

The third crucial condition which must be met in order for TQ to be successful is the *active support of the change* at all levels of management. Further, all levels of the organization must be actively involved in implementing and sustaining it. Thus traditional barriers and boundaries between managers and non-managers, between managers and lower-level managers, and between line and staff positions, must be weakened or eliminated. Deming includes the concept of breaking down barriers in several of his 14 points (above). The amount of information exchanged increases dramatically when boundaries are eliminated, and all parts of the organization benefit from the insights and experience of every organization member.

Another critical dimension of TQ is *shared understanding* of the organization's goals and objectives. This requires more than just the ability to parrot a slogan. Shared understanding is constructed, not transmitted. Trust and understanding are developed through informal processes rather than by means of formal structures. Breaking down boundaries between departments and creating an environment that seeks the causes of problems rather than looking for blame is not an easy exercise. Organizations must learn to do things differently, but in order to do this we must first look at everything from a different perspective – the perspective of a potential customer. This is the fundamental difference between the traditional market approach and the emphasis on the customer in the philosophy of TQ.

To see the organization and its products as the customer sees them requires a fundamental shift in how people in organizations think and behave; that is, a paradigm shift. As Nee said, 'To get people to understand a [paradigm] shift you can't just do it intellectually. You don't talk somebody into changing his/her religion!' (Nee, 1993:25). Traditionally we perceived the manufacturer's liability as ending after some specified period of time had elapsed post-purchase. However, the customer evaluates a product's quality for the entire period in which he or she owns the item, not just during the warranty period. Taguchi's definition of TQ earlier in this chapter is a good example of how organizations must fundamentally alter their views on warranty and liability in order to fully adopt the TQ mind-set.

Olian and Rynes (1991) have identified three critical factors in achieving the shift in organizational thinking which is necessary in order to implement TQ: organization process, metrics or measurement, and stakeholder support. The categories include the following:

(1) *Organizational process:*
    (a) communication and vision
    (b) team building
    (c) reward and recognition
    (d) recruitment and selection
    (e) training
(2) *Metrics or measurement:*
    (a) customer reactions
    (b) operation measures
    (c) financial measures
    (d) employee contributions
(3) *Stakeholder support for TQ commitment from:*
    (a) top management
    (b) middle management
    (c) professional staff
    (d) line staff

Central to the successful implementation of TQ is the establishment of quality goals. These goals may seem at first unattainable. For example, Motorola reduced defects from over 6000 to less than 40 per million in five years, but set an even more challenging goal of cutting defects by a further 90% every two years throughout the 1990s (Economist Publications, 1992a). This practice of setting impossible goals seems to run contrary to the accepted belief that people will not accept goals they perceive as unachievable (Locke and Latham, 1990). Many TQ programs address challenging goals in a non-traditional way – by setting targets for the entire organization, rather than for individuals. In a TQ organization, each employee is trained to redefine his or her function in the organization. Each employee becomes both a supplier and a customer; a link in the quality chain. This attitudinal adjustment is similar to aligning the magnetic poles within a piece of steel or iron, and the effect can be dramatic. Some dramatic data on the impact of TQ training come from Motorola. Based on two systematic studies of its training efforts, Motorola estimates that it earns US$30 for every US$1 invested in TQ training (Blackburn and Rosen, 1993).

A piece of iron does not remain permanently magnetized; a sudden fall or sharp blow can distort the magnetic alignment. Similarly, TQ organizations are susceptible to forces impelling them to revert to former non-TQ styles of management. Short-term economic pressures on the organization can make a reversion to 'seat of the pants' management look attractive if and when the TQ effort becomes stalled and the initial enthusiasm has faded.

Case study **Analog Devices, Inc.**

TQ initiatives not only represent a fundamental change in organizational culture for individual participants, they may represent a threat to the structure of the organization itself. At Ray Stata's company, Analog Devices, Inc., his well-thought-out TQ efforts seemed to be working to change the culture – quality measures, including rate of defects and on-time delivery rate, were extremely positive. However, the organization's financial performance did not improve, and in fact financial pressures were beginning to build. Stata's experience is not unique; others have experienced this paradox (Kofmann, *et al.*, 1994). Stata's partnership with several leading academic experts on TQ led to some conclusions about the nature of TQ change and how to best sustain it.

The research team at Analog developed a detailed historical picture of the TQ effort there. They then constructed a simulation to test their hypotheses about the situation and its development. They found that the success of the TQ effort led to lower prices and excess capacity. This in turn contributed to lowered earnings and lowered market value for the products. This poor financial result undermined the TQ continuous improvement effort. Not enough effort went to capitalizing on the benefits that TQ had brought to the organization; instead, the financial results took top priority and eventually layoffs occurred. This was bad for morale, especially among employees who had worked hard for TQ.

The research team found that management support for TQ dropped off after the initial implementation. Line managers were expected to take time from their normal duties to work with TQ teams, and they lacked time, experience and training. Analog also lost ground because, even though Analog was practicing organizational learning, its competitors were too. Furthermore, parts of the organizational structure, such as the accounting function, did not keep up with the new realities of life with TQ, and even the traditional method of setting prices had to be reevaluated.

Analog was able to survive with its TQ effort intact because management recommitted to the quality effort for the long haul, acknowledging the complexity of the change. Adoption of a long-term focus rather than panic over short-term financial distress resulting from excess capacity helped the organization to learn how to plan better to capitalize on the benefits which would continue to result from TQ in many areas throughout the organization. As the researchers noted, 'A focus on early results may lead to excess capacity, financial stress, downsizing, low morale, and the collapse of commitment to the program. Improvement programs can fail not in spite, but precisely because of their early success' (Kofmann, *et al.*, 1994:30).

The tendency to lose enthusiasm for change efforts is a natural one. The changeover to TQ can threaten organizational members' entrenched positions and leave them not knowing their place in the organization. It has been suggested that for TQ to be implemented successfully and sustained over the long term, it should be implemented neither radically (leaving members unsure of their future) nor incrementally (which allows for loss of enthusiasm and the perception that TQ does not have full management support). In the 'middle ground' change can be implemented most effectively (Reger, *et al.*, 1994).

TQ and economic realities

Despite difficulties in implementing and sustaining the change effort, there are several cogent reasons for using TQ. The increased pace of global competition, fueled in large part by the success of the Japanese economy in recent years, has caused many to examine the management techniques that contributed to Japan's success. The Japanese had developed sophisticated quality improvement programs and had been refining them throughout the 1980s. They had invested heavily in TQ while protecting their home market from imports. If US and European companies were to compete, they would have to meet or exceed Japanese quality standards. To get there, however, they needed to appreciate a fundamental principle of TQ – that the organization focuses not on reducing costs but on producing high-quality products, delivered reliably, with lower costs and flexible production processes (Bounds, *et al.*, 1994).

Western management consultancy in the post-Second World War era traditionally emphasized the relationship between cumulative production and unit costs, using a new model of the production/price relationship. Market analysts had identified that in general, each time production rates doubled, unit costs fell by 25–30% of their previous levels. As a company produced more units, there were corresponding increases in experience, knowledge, and technical ability which would enable the company to produce future products more efficiently; this in turn resulted in greater market share, the production of additional units, and so on.

This model had a profound effect upon the pricing strategies of manufacturing companies. According to this model, the market leader (in terms of the cumulative number of units produced) could dictate price to the market. The market leader could, in theory, strategically determine the market price and thereby dictate the profit margins of its competitors.

In contrast, Japanese manufacturers believe that price is controlled by the market and that, without a formal cost reduction program, most companies will fail to reduce overheads. Shiba and colleagues (1993) outline the widespread Japanese strategy of keeping costs 10% lower than competitors' prices. Furthermore, Japanese engineers and managers cooperate in cross-functional teams specifically to reduce costs. The senior managers work with suppliers of materials and parts and they audit and invest in suppliers' businesses to obtain cost reductions. Jones (1993) reports that the Nissan Plant in Sunderland UK is as productive as any in Japan. However, only 30% of its European sub-suppliers would match their Japanese counterparts for efficiency, quality, and cost. This shift in emphasis from controlling prices to controlling costs and its associated emphasis on value over price caught many market leaders unawares.

The combination of considerable erosion of market share and shift in the emphasis on value and cost reduction over price has compelled many companies to look closely at TQ for survival. However, as noted by Bernardo DeSousa of Ciba-Geigy Ltd, most European companies have introduced TQ because of pressure from customers, a crisis, or a potential crisis (Niven, 1993:27). In contrast, more and more US companies are implementing TQ to obtain a competitive advantage (Lawler, et al., 1992).

But does TQ always work? There is some international data on this issue. For example, Fuchsberg (1993) reports from a study of 531 companies that 68% have used some form of TQ and 61% have conducted team building activities, while 61% have established small group meetings with employees. Total quality management *has* saved money when implemented successfully. Globe Metallurgical, a Baldrige Award Winner in 1988, cut costs by 17 million (15% of sales revenue) between 1986 and 1990 (Roth, 1991). The Conference Board reports that companies implementing TQ experience savings in process costs, and gains in other measures including profits and return on investments. In its survey of 20 studies of TQ the Board concluded that 'TQ efforts are often, but not always, considered by executives to have a beneficial effect on their firm's performance' (The Conference Board, 1993:5). It also observed that the extent to which companies use the standard TQ techniques (such as Statistical Process Control) is related to the success of their programs. When a company fails to follow TQ practices and adopt its philosophy completely, problems can develop.

While an article in *The Economist* focuses on the 'cracks in quality', it does highlight two important issues. First, Florida Power and Light, a US utility company famous for its quality programs and the first non-Japanese winner of the Deming prize, similarly has had serious misgivings about its quality programs, as has British Telecom. Yet when interviewed by *The Economist*, both companies indicated that their quality programs had *failed to retain a customer focus* over time – one of the cornerstones of TQ. They have now refocused their priorities, and 'customers now count for everything' (Economist Publications, 1992b).

A second issue highlighted by the article is that Western companies possess only a *limited amount of cumulative experience* with TQ. The average length of time Honda, Nissan, and Mitsubishi have been involved in TQ is 30 years. For Motorola, Texas Instruments, Hewlett Packard, and Xerox, their average experience with TQ is less than 10 years (Economist Publications, 1992b). Finally, The Conference Board report found 'no substantial evidence that TQ is having a negative impact on company performance' (The Conference Board, 1993:6).

In sum, TQ is a management philosophy and a system for focusing effort on customers' needs and continuous improvement of every aspect of the business. It is a transformation in how we do business. External forces, including outside consultants, may act as a catalyst but alone cannot ensure the survival of a TQ program. The impetus must come from inside the organization. To provide the conditions necessary to initiate a TQ program requires considerable effort and commitment; to maintain the momentum is equally difficult. TQ is a necessary but not sufficient condition for the survival of many, but not all, companies. Still, as Seely Brown indicated, the basic principles of customer focus and continuous improvement within a learning organization are very powerful concepts and, if implemented correctly, will make significant contributions to any organization at any time, now or in the future (Nee, 1993).

Removing quality boundaries

In his ground-breaking book *Out of the Crisis* (1986), W.E. Deming addressed the topic of organizational barriers. Point number 12 of his 14 points is to 'Remove barriers that rob people of pride of workmanship' (above). By this, he meant that our idea of employees as lazy, reluctant, and careless was grossly unfair. J.M. Juran cited a figure of 85% as the proportion of quality errors which can be directly attributed to the system, not the employee. Deming later amended this figure to 94%. The remaining 6% of errors are due to 'special causes,' which include worker error and other sources of non-systematic problems, such as weather conditions (Deming, 1986:315). He believed, and most TQ adherents believe, that people are already doing their best on the job. They may experience barriers to accomplishing their highest level of performance, but most of these barriers are placed in their way by the organization, deliberately or inadvertently. In a recent US television commercial for Saturn automobiles (a TQ organization), a worker explains how he shut down the production line one day in order to fix a problem. This action was unheard of in the traditional automobile plant of the past. In the commercial, the worker explains that people *want* to put out a good product – they just need the chance to do so. By eliminating the boundary between the worker and the production process, Saturn has effectively removed a barrier to pride of workmanship.

In the next section, we will discuss three types of quality boundaries which are commonly found in organizations; boundaries between levels, between departments, and between the organization and the customer. We will look at how removing these boundaries, or making them more permeable, is a crucial component of TQ efforts, and can benefit any organization.

Eliminating boundaries between organizational levels

In the TQ organization, management's job is to train and encourage employees, and to work with them to fix system problems, in order to help employees to reach their full potential – to achieve pride of workmanship. Organizational boundaries which prevent communication from flowing between levels in the organization may prevent the good ideas and insights of line workers from reaching the top, or may prevent valuable information held by top management from reaching those who can use it in delivering the product or service.

Deming included 'drive out fear' as one of his 14 points (above). He explains that workers can only do their best when they feel secure about their position in the organization. They must feel free to express opinions and make suggestions, to 'rock the boat' by challenging the conventional wisdom (Deming, 1993). Sometimes existing policies need to be questioned in order for knowledge breakthroughs to occur.

One of the ways a TQ implementation can break down boundaries between levels is in the training process. Having employees from various levels attend training together accomplishes two purposes. First, it demonstrates a strong commitment from top management to spread the ideas of TQ throughout the organization. Second, it places all learners, regardless of level, on an equal playing field on which they are all students. In this atmosphere, it may be easier to talk about problems in the organization in new ways.

Quality circles have often been used as a way to eliminate boundaries between levels. In a quality circle, employees from different levels work on eliminating the 94% of defects which result from the system. Although the popularity of quality circles has waned in recent years, the basic idea behind them is sound – get a group of people together to focus on a problem or situation and let them pool their knowledge so as to arrive at the best solution.

Although TQ programs do not necessarily involve eliminating levels of management, some organizations discover that the employee empowerment which results from a total quality effort may make some lower and middle-level managerial functions unnecessary. For example, when line workers learn to do their own record keeping and problem solving, the foreman/woman's job duties may change drastically from performance evaluator and disciplinarian to facilitator. In some organizations the role of these managers is further reduced because unit members work in self-managed groups, only consulting management when serious problems arise or when approval is needed for making a major change (see Chapter 7).

When Spectrum Control, Inc. implemented its quality program, a process engineer at one of its divisions decided to write to a vice president for advice about a problem he had been experiencing for many years. There was a serious quality problem with the solder used to make a company product. The engineer wrote to a company vice president to ask for help, but got none. Undaunted, he sent copies of his next letter to several top executives, including the president. When top management realized that their spoken commitment to quality did not match their actions (and this gap was reflected in ongoing quality problems) they decided to become more involved in quality training, reviewing the programs, attending sessions, and making changes where needed. The process engineer understood the value of breaking the boundaries between organizational levels. His refusal to give up on quality in the face of indifference forced his organization to rethink its commitment to quality and the valuable resource it had in its employees (Bartol and Martin, 1994).

Eliminating boundaries between departments

Point 9 of Deming's 14 points is 'Break down barriers between staff areas' (above). Effective implementation of TQ is virtually impossible without extensive communication between functional areas, because the focus of strategies for eliminating defects is the process of delivering the product to the consumer in its entirety. If Production, for example, cannot realistically meet a deadline which has been promised by Marketing, the customer will not be satisfied because the deadline will not be met. If, however, Marketing and Production talk about what constitutes a reasonable deadline, and Marketing agrees to check with Production before finalizing contracts, the customer is much more likely to be pleased with the outcome.

Quality circles and other quality teams are often cross-functional as well as being composed of employees at various levels. A special type of team recommended by Juran is the quality-improvement team. The goals of these teams are to reduce instances of poor quality and/or to improve quality (Juran, 1989). The Hallmark Card company developed product teams for each holiday and for special occasions such as birthdays. The teams, which are composed of members from the creating, manufacturing, and marketing departments, work closely together so that they can minimize cycle time. The cross-functional teams have sped up the process of getting cards to the customer and have saved money for Hallmark (Stewart, 1992).

Training programs which include members of various departments, functions and work units serve to spread enthusiasm about TQ throughout the organization. They serve a further purpose of spreading useful ideas, insights, and even respect from one area to another. Because trainees generally start on the same level with regard to the skills needed to work in a TQ environment (statistical process control – a set of data-based process management tools – for instance), camaraderie is maximized and intimidation is minimized. Because organization members will need to continue learning forever if they want to be part of the learning organization, the experience of training should be as positive as possible.

Eliminating customer–organization boundaries

TQ programs are known for their 'customer focus', and slogans relating to the customer always being right are only outnumbered by slogans relating to the importance of quality. Slogans aside, the serious TQ organization is deeply committed to providing the highest quality product to the customer that is possible on that particular day. Quality has been defined as 'fitness for use' by Juran (1989) and as the avoidance of loss by Taguchi (1994); though there are many others, almost all of the definitions currently in use have the *customer's impression of quality* as their means of defining success or failure.

Consider the very popular definition of quality as 'the extent to which a product or service meets and/or exceeds a customer's expectations' (Reeves and Bednar, 1994). In the past the customer's expectations might have been deemed less important than cost considerations. However, what has brought us to TQ is the consideration that this strategy may not work in today's competitive environment. In order for the average organization to survive, it must have customers, because satisfied customers come back themselves to do further business with the organization and recommend the product to others. Customers consider many aspects of products when deciding if they like their purchases, but low price and attractiveness mean nothing if products are not usable.

TQ organizations need to have ways to find out what their customers want. Marketers, of course, have been conducting focus groups and having consumers complete surveys for many years. However, the exponential increase of customer surveys in service organizations such as fast food restaurants (and even the telephone company!) is a sign of growing recognition of the importance of each customer to the survival of the business. Juran (1989) gives detailed instructions for managers as to what questions they should ask their customers to determine both their known needs and their underlying needs and desires (such as the desire for status). He makes three major points about the information-gathering process: (1) it must be an integral part of the quality planning process; (2) it must be thorough; and (3) it must be acted upon. The more systematically information is gathered from customers, the more permeable the artificial boundary between the organization and its customer becomes.

At Mutual Benefit Life, turnaround time for insurance applications was a problem for customers. The application process, which had formerly involved up to 30 steps, was streamlined by creating a special position, the 'case manager.' This employee is responsible for seeing an application through the entire process. In this case, both interdepartmental boundaries and customer organization boundaries had to be crossed in order to determine what customers needed (fast turnaround) and then to devise a way to satisfy that need (create a boundary-spanning position) (Bounds, *et al.*, 1994).

Case study   Implementation of TQ breaks down barriers

ABC is a US multinational manufacturing facility located in the west of Ireland. Its distance from the European mainland and the absence of an adequate transport infrastructure were perceived as impediments to further expansion of the facility. The corporation was seriously considering relocating the facility either elsewhere in Ireland or on mainland Europe.

The workforce was aware of both the escalation of operating costs and the dissatisfaction of the corporate head office with the overall performance of the facility. The combination of fear and inadequate information led to deep worker mistrust of management. It was often necessary to refer industrial relations disputes to an independent third party for mediation. Serious industrial relations problems emerged, particularly in respect to such issues. The point was reached where communications between management and the workforce was almost exclusively conducted through union representatives. In these circumstances, and given that in this area few other sources of employment were available to the workforce, workers became very protective of their specific jobs and tasks within the facility.

Due to the nature of the health care industry in which ABC operated, quality assurance was of the utmost importance. However, quality was perceived as the sole function of the Quality Assurance Department. If defective product was shipped inadvertently, Production accepted no responsibility for the defect. 'That is what we employ these quality assurance people for anyway!' was the commonly heard phrase among production workers. Likewise, Quality Assurance accepted no responsibility for either timely deliveries or productivity. It was seen as Production's responsibility to produce a sufficient amount of good product to meet customer demand.

Just as there was no communication between Quality Assurance and Production, there was no interaction between Production and the external customer. While Quality Assurance saw its role as being clearly defined by external customer requirements, Production did not view the Quality Assurance department as its customer, and once the Quality department approved a consignment, that was the end of Production's responsibility. Quality costs were very high, scrap and rework were the norm – and quality had been inspected into the product, rather than being an integral part of the product from the start. The philosophy of prevention rather than detection of defects, and the concept of getting everything right the first time, were alien to the prevailing culture within the company.

A situation arose in which an important customer needed product urgently. The Government had decided to treat victims of an international catastrophe. The chief executive asked Quality Assurance to ship from stock. Their reaction was: 'We will ship but you must sign and accept responsibility.' This evidence that the product's quality was no one's responsibility led to a reevaluation of priorities. At this point the chief executive officer and a small number of key executives decided to implement a TQ program. External consultants delivered a five day executive development program to the CEO and those that directly reported to him. Training materials were purchased from the consultants and modified by the training manager to meet the specific needs of the organization. Participants were encouraged to try out different options; formal training was structured on a 'need to know' basis; and the general philosophy was 'apply, learn and re-apply.' Clearly the emphasis was on application and involvement as opposed to formal training.

The training program was cascaded through the organization, and the CEO and the top management led by example. The CEO relocated his office in the center of the factory floor. Quality-related issues were promoted to the top of the agenda for the weekly management meeting. Everyone, including the CEO, began to wear the same or similar color overalls or coats to visibly demonstrate 'constancy of purpose' (Deming's point number 1, above).

A problem occurred in the process of adopting the training program to ABC Company. The maintenance department had been organized along traditional lines (workers performing a limited number of tasks), while the TQ training program assumed that multi-skilling was in place; that is, workers were to perform a variety of tasks. Hence the sequence of activities within the purchased program had to be altered. All references to operators assuming full responsibility for quality were deleted from the early texts, and only after a series of experiments were completed were these references gradually reintroduced.

The quality control and quality assurance functions were separated into different units. Quality inspectors were redeployed within the company. They were gradually relieved of their responsibility for final inspection and integrated into the operation of the production lines. The title 'quality control inspector' was replaced by 'quality technologist.' Quality technologists were encouraged to take responsibility for overall output of the production line, particularly for the number of units produced. Similarly, production workers operating within quality improvement teams were encouraged to assume responsibility for making items 'right the first time.' Every aspect of the business was carefully examined and better solutions were eagerly sought.

Overall, the changes were very successful. The outcomes of this quality initiative included the following:

(1) 1992/1993 production figures exceeded 1986 figures but at lower cost per unit (US$1.15 per unit in 1986 and US$1.10 per unit in 1993).
(2) The number of categories of employees was reduced from 12 in 1986 to three in 1993.
(3) No official or unofficial industrial relations issue occurred in 1992/1993.
(4) This is now the most productive site in the corporation and a decision has just been announced to build a third manufacturing facility there.

Skeptics may argue that the benefits detailed in the previous paragraph resulted from technological investment or changes in the workforce and would have happened even if the TQ program was not introduced. However, consider the following:

(1) No major technological investment occurred at the facility between 1986 and 1992.
(2) There was no influx of new workers: in fact, 15% of the workforce took redundancy or early retirement packages between 1986 and 1992.

The major lessons learned at ABC were these:

- Exposing everyone in the organization to customers' requirements and customer complaints (breaking down the barriers between the organization and its customers) resulted in everyone within the company becoming acutely aware of the need for quality.
- The TQM program released the repressed energy and tacit knowledge of the workforce, and when this energy was harnessed, considerable benefits accrued (breaking down barriers between levels).

- Everyone in the organization become conscious of his/her role as someone else's customer (breaking down barriers between departments) (McCarron, 1994).

Total quality and other theories of the firm

Unlike most other theories of management, the theory underlying total quality management is rooted in a set of values. A primary value of TQ is that work should be an enjoyable activity for all employees. They have the respect of their co-workers (at all levels) and the freedom to make their own decisions about how the work will be done. TQ proponents believe that if the organizational structure promotes respect, continuous learning and continuous improvement, the relationships between people will be cooperative and productive, resulting in positive organizational outcomes including survival. TQ does not threaten the existing hierarchy of the organization; rather, it changes the responsibilities and rights of managers and employees. More fundamentally, TQ organizations focus on delivering the best possible product or service to the customer.

Economics-based theories of the firm, including agency theory, transaction costs economics and the resource base theory of the firm, have a different perspective on the relationships between people in organizations. The fundamental disagreement between these theories and TQ is their focus on the monetary value of people rather than their value as human beings. In the next section, we will discuss each of these economics-based theories and its link to TQM.

Agency theory (see Chapter 3) looks at the relationship between the organization's agents (its managers) and principals (employees) primarily as an adversarial relationship. Principals are assumed to be acting in their own self-interest. Because agents cannot fully know employees and thus cannot completely control their behavior, employing people involves risk. This risk can be minimized through control mechanisms which appeal to the principals' self-interest. Operationalizations of this theory in organizations take the form of contractual relationships between management and employees (Masterton, *et al.*, 1994). Examples include fixed job descriptions, lengthy policies and procedures manuals for employees, and detailed disciplinary policies. On the contrary, TQ organizations tend to have open-ended job descriptions and comparatively few rules and policies (and these may be set by teams of employees from various organizational levels). Practices resulting from agency theory tend to be static, while TQM practices tend to be more dynamic.

The transaction costs view (see Chapter 3) again focuses on the costs of doing business rather than the benefits. Transaction costs are the losses incurred when we exchange goods and services with others within our own organization or with outside parties. Losses occur when working with humans because we are not completely rational when making choices, and because humans act opportunistically. The environment also contributes to transaction costs, because we are faced with so many exchanges, and the choices available in the marketplace are so varied and complex. To avoid costs we tend to seek more stable relationships, like organizations, in which we can keep closer track of those with whom we do business. Like agency theory, the transaction costs approach recommends controls to minimize costs; within organizations these could include job descriptions, procedure manuals, and especially employment contracts (Scott, 1987). Outside organizations, controls could generally include contracts and the formation of long-term relationships.

As noted above, TQ diverges sharply from theories such as agency theory and the transaction costs view which see humans as opportunistic. However, TQ does resemble transaction costs theory in that TQ organizations tend to foster long-term relationships with suppliers, vendors, and customers. In TQM organizations, the reason for fostering long-term relationships is so that information may flow freely between the parties, benefiting both, and so that the parties can benefit from each others' continuous improvement initiatives. Again, TQ tends to focus on the *benefits* of interactions between people and between organizations, while agency theory and transaction cost theory tend to focus on possible *losses* from these interactions.

The resource base theory of the firm looks at the individual resources that organizations possess (see Chapter 1). These resources tend not to move fluidly across organizations, so they constitute relatively long-lasting advantages, but their value can change over time. Resources fall into three main categories – physical capital (access to raw materials, work processes, location, and plant and equipment), human capital (the organization's members, including their knowledge, skills, and abilities), and organizational capital (the organizational structure and relationships between members). Some of these resources are unique to one organization, but many are common to some or all organizations. It is the job of managers to manage and build these resources in order to sustain competitive advantage relative to other organizations.

Competition against other organizations for market share is at best a subordinate goal for TQ organizations. At worst, it is seen as a destructive force. Writers on TQ differ in their view of competition between employees within the organization, but generally agree that the aim of producing a good product is more important than competing with organizations for business. As Deming states:

> If economists understood the theory of a system, and the role of cooperation in optimization, they would no longer teach and preach salvation through adversarial competition. They would, instead, lead us into optimization of a system, in which everybody would come out ahead.
>
> (Deming, 1993:75)

As discussed above, TQ organizations have flexible and changing boundaries between people and departments and between the organization and its customers, suppliers, and vendors. The resource base view sees organizational resources as something to hold onto, rather than something to share for the mutual benefit of all parties. However, the idea that resources change in value over time is consistent with TQM ideology. The idea that managers are responsible for ensuring that the value of resources continues to grow might give rise to such initiatives as employee training programs and customer surveys, which are commonly found in TQ organizations. It is in the aim of these initiatives that the difference between the resource base view and the TQM view is clearly identified. TQ organizations see a better product or service as the ultimate goal of organizational strategy, while resource base organizations see competitive advantage as their ultimate goal.

The future of total quality

As reported by The Conference Board, TQ 'appears to represent a long-term effort on the part of many . . . companies to make significant changes in the way they operate' (The Conference Board, 1993:5). Further, more and more companies are getting involved in TQ efforts (Lawler, *et al.*, 1992). Although as noted above, there are many variations of TQ methods and disagreements over philosophy, TQ's impact on the way people think about their jobs and their organizations is significant and ongoing. Problems with TQ seem to result from attempting to change the organization too fast, or not fast enough (Reger, *et al.*, 1994), or when TQ is looked at as a cure-all for severe organizational problems.

In a TQ organization, there are no boundaries to quality. Barriers which previously existed between organization members, between functions and departments, and between the organization and its external customers only serve to hinder the constant flow of information which is necessary to understanding and improving quality. They must be removed. These boundaries were, after all, created – they do not exist naturally. They were originally created for a variety of reasons, and persisted for political reasons (or through inertia), becoming an intrinsic, unquestioned part of almost all organizations. Adopting TQ methods and ideas forces organizations to look at these artificial boundaries and barriers with a critical eye, asking whether or not they contribute to meeting the organization's goals.

Point number 1 of Deming's 14 points is 'Create constancy of purpose for improvement of product and service.' If the organization's purpose is constant, members will find quality barriers and boundaries frustrating, and will act to remove them, as did the process engineer in the case of Spectrum, Inc. above. In the past 20 years, we have learned to our detriment that placing limits on quality is at best a waste of time and at worst a contributor to organizational decline. Managing without quality boundaries is not only desirable but necessary, for to do otherwise is to create conditions that can lead to organizational failure.

The research on TQ in organizations still lags far behind its practice. Part of the problem in identifying areas for research into TQ is the breadth of its focus – writings on TQ address such divergent topics as strategic management, human behavior, and competitive advantage. However, some recent research has been undertaken to identify the theoretical underpinnings of TQ writers such as Juran and Deming, and to link this underlying theory to what we know from past research in the fields of organizational psychology/behavior, human resources management, and strategy. The next step will be to conduct empirical research in field settings, in order to, first, identify what aspects of TQ are more or less successful in various types of organizations and why, and eventually to identify the components of a successful TQ program.

References

Bartol, K.M. and Martin, D.C. (1994). *Management*, 2nd. edn. New York: McGraw-Hill.

Blackburn, R. and Rosen, B. (1993). Total quality and human resources management: lessons learned from Baldrige Award-Winning Companies, *Academy of Management Executive*, 7, (3), 49–66.

Bounds, G., Yorks, L., Adams, M., and Ranney, G. (1993). *Beyond Total Quality Management: Toward The Emerging Paradigm*. New York: McGraw-Hill.

The Conference Board (1993). Does quality work? A review of relevant studies. Report 1043, The Conference Board, New York.

Crosby, P. (1979). Quality is free: the art of making quality certain. New York: McGraw-Hill.

Deming, W.E. (1986). *Out of the Crisis*. Cambridge, Massachusetts: MIT Center for Advanced Engineering Study.

Deming, W.E. (1993). *The New Economics for Industry, Government, Education.* Cambridge, MA: MIT Center for Advanced Engineering Study.

Economist Publications (1992a). Future perfect, *The Economist*, 4 January, 61.

Economist Publications (1992b). The cracks in quality, *The Economist*, 18 April, 67–8.

Fuchsberg, G. (1993). Baldrige awards may be losing their luster. *Wall Street Journal*, 19 April.

Garvin, D.A. (1993). Building a learning organization. *Harvard Business Review*, 71, 78–91.

Jones, A.K.V. (1993). Nissan's quality requirements for its European suppliers. First Newcastle International Conference on Quality and its Applications, University of Newcastle, 1–3 September.

Juran, J.M. (1989). *Juran on Leadership for Quality: An Executive Handbook.* New York: The Free Press.

Kofmann, F., Repenning, N., and Sterman, J. (1994). Unanticipated side effects of successful quality programs: exploring a paradox of organizational improvement, Working paper, Sloan School of Management, MIT.

Lawler, E.E. III, Mohrman, S.A., and Ledford Jr., G.E. (1992). *Employee involvement and TQM: Practices and results in Fortune 1000 Companies.* San Francisco, CA: Jossey-Bass.

Locke, E.A., and Latham, G.P. (1990). *A Theory of Goal Setting and Task Performance.* Englewood Cliffs: Prentice-Hall.

Masterson, S.S., Olian, J.D., and Schnell, E.R. (1994). Belief versus practice in management theory: contrasting models and levels of total quality management and agency theory. Working paper, University of Maryland.

McCarron, P. (1994). Sustaining TQM in a unionised environment. Working paper, University of Limerick.

Nee, M. (1993). John Seely Brown, *Upside*, December, 24–34.

Niven, D. (1993). When times get tough, what happens to TQM? *Harvard Business Review*, 71, May–June, 20–34.

Olian, J.D. and Rynes, S.L. (1991). Making total quality work: aligning organizational processes, performance measures, and stakeholders, *Human Resource Management*, 30, (3), 303–33.

Reeves, C.A. and Bednar, D.A. (eds) (1994). Defining quality: alternatives and implications, *Academy of Management Review*, 19, (3), 419–45.

Reger, R.K., Gustafson, L.T., DeMarie, S.M., and Mullane, J.V. (1994). Reframing the organization: why implementing total quality is easer said than done, *Academy of Management Review*, 19,(3), 565–84.

Roth, E.F. (1991). Winds of change, *World*, 25, (2), 10–18.

Scott, W.R. (1987). *Organizations: Rational, Natural and Open Systems.* Englewood Cliffs, NJ: Prentice-Hall.

Shiba, S., Graham, A., and Walden, D. (1993). *A New American TQ.* Portland, OR: Productivity Press.

Stewart, T.A. (1992). Are you flat, lean, and ready for a bold new look? Try high-performance teams, redesigned work, and unbridled information, *Fortune*, 18 May, 96.

Taguchi, G. (1989). *Introduction to Quality Engineering.* Dearborn, MI: Asian Production Organization.

Taguchi, G. (1994). Cited in Reeves, C.A., and Bednar, D.A. (eds) (1994).

Defining quality: alternatives and implications, *Academy of Management Review*, 19, (3), 419–45.

Tuttle, T.C. (1991). Implementing total quality, *The Maryland Workplace*, 12, (1), 4–5.

9

Managing without a complete, full-time workforce[†]

Throughout the industrialized world there has been a dramatic increase in non-traditional work arrangements in the past 20 years, such as the use of part-time and temporary employees, subcontracting, home-based work, and flexitime or flexible working hours. To manage a company without a complete full-time workforce is becoming increasingly common. News from the business press supports that belief, and so do data on the number of workers who are not full-time employees. Of course, employing part-time and temporary workers is not new. But the way in which these people are being used, and the magnitude of their use is new.

Contrary to popular belief, this increase is, in fact, occurring not only in the United States but also in Europe, although it is generally recognized that Europe has been less successful than the United States in creating jobs because of its rigid labor markets and high cost of labor. Still, this dramatic increase of new work arrangements in Europe and the United States – and even in Japan, but in a different way, as we will see – suggests that the nature of work and employment relationships have been radically altered in the industrial world, regardless of the nation in which the work is accomplished. Thus it is not surprising that managers are interested in many of the related topics treated in this book, including managing without supervisors, quality inspectors, and traditional organizational structures, all of which are directly related to the manner in which different types of workers are utilized.

Throughout this book we have emphasized several theories that help to explain the move toward managing without traditional methods, particularly the resource base theory of the firm and transaction cost economics. These two theories are particularly helpful in explaining why

† Martin Gannon would like to acknowledge the financial support provided by the General Research Board and the Center of International Business, Education, and Research, University of Maryland at College Park, in the writing of this chapter.

the move away from a traditional, full-time workforce has accelerated in recent years. While economists have identified the four elements of a productive economy as land, labor, capital, and entrepreneurship, they have generally treated labor as a given until very recently. Gary Becker's classic work, *Human Capital* (1960), caused a major reconsideration of this perspective, as he and others have shown that the optimal and planned mix of these four elements when considered in combination rather than individually significantly determines effective output for organizations and the entire economy. More specifically, Becker showed that labor is not a given but, rather, can be treated as capital so that if a company invests in its workers it can obtain a stream of returns over time, thus separating human capital from raw labor.

Similarly, Oliver Williamson's (1985) analysis of the importance of transaction costs (the costs simply of doing business) demonstrates that they are critical to an organization's success, and a large proportion of such costs involve employees and managers. In some firms labor costs range between 75% and 90% of total costs. It is little wonder, then, that there has been a tidal wave of change when managers consider the pivotal role of labor, how to manage it effectively, and how to reduce labor costs.

In this chapter we first explore this issue of managing without a complete, full-time workforce by presenting two short case examples which bring into perspective the staffing and scheduling challenges facing managers. Next, we highlight the core and ring strategy of employment, which is a method for continually readjusting the number of different types of employees needed to produce the final good or service; we also address the changes in the employment relationship that have occurred in the areas of part-time employment, temporary employment, and other forms of contingent employment such as short-term employment contracts and subcontracting. In the third section of the chapter we present the case for the core and ring strategy in detail or the justification for managing without a complete, full-time workforce. The next section focuses on the problems that occur in managing without a full-time, complete workforce. In the final section we offer some suggestions and guidelines that managers can use to effectively manage different types of workers and work arrangements.

Issues and challenges facing managers

Several forces are driving the trend toward managing without a complete full-time workforce, and we expect it to continue. There are many positive aspects of managing partly with full-time regular employees and partly with part-time, temporary, or short-term contract workers. But there are problems and unresolved issues, too. To illustrate, we begin with two short case studies of managing without a complete full-time workforce, which show some of the potential gains and also some of the downside problems.

Case study   **Second thoughts about cost effectiveness**

The company is a large US multinational corporation. It manufactures electronic control instruments and systems at a major site in the West for industries as diverse as oil refining and food processing. The 800 employees at this site include scientists, customer service representatives, and production workers. Production operations are carried out in roughly 40 work units that are managed according to a team approach.

The company adopted a strategy of operating without a complete full-time workforce nearly a decade ago. Of the workforce of 800 people, more than 200 are temporaries provided by temporary help and staffing firms. The company wants the staffing temporaries to work at one job in one work team for nine months to one year. The staffing temporaries tend to be younger than the regular core employees, and all of them are in the entry-level job grade, as are over half of the regular core employees.

Three key factors shape this company's practice of managing without a complete full-time workforce. First, the company went through several rounds of severe layoffs around the time of the recession of 1981–2. This bad experience resulted in a wish to protect the employment of core employees in the future by providing a buffer against fluctuations in the company's demand for labor over the business cycle.

Second, because the company produces large systems for customers to order rather than standardized products, its need for workers varied irregularly with ups and downs in customer orders and delivery dates from week to week and month to month within a year. Adding and subtracting temporary workers could help the company cope with peaks in demand and prevent paying for idle labor during slack periods.

Third, many managers believed that temporary workers would be cheaper than regular core employees. The wage rate paid to temporaries was about a dollar an hour less than the wage rate paid to regular employees doing the same job, and of course the company paid no fringe benefits to the temporaries. The temporary help and staffing firm's fee was less than the benefits for regular employees, so the total payment made for temporaries was less than the total compensation of regular employees by about US$1.50 an hour.

However, the belief that staffing temporaries are cheaper than regular employees is now being called into question, for two reasons. First, managers realize that in a high-technology business like theirs, a substantial amount of training is required. Initial training for all new workers consists of formal classroom training in technical skills for three to five days, and then on-the-job training at the job site with an experienced employee for six to eight weeks. Continuing classroom training is conducted periodically during the year on topics ranging from manufacturing processes to teamwork skills. All of the training is paid for by the company in the form of direct costs such as trainers' salaries and training facilities, and in the form of the opportunity costs of wages paid to trainees and supervisors when neither is producing output.

Because staffing temporaries are not permitted by the client company's policy to stay at the company longer than one year to avoid the appearance of an employment relationship, there is not much time for the company's training investment to be recovered. In fact the average length of service is less than seven months. There is a continual inflow of new temporaries who require new doses of training. Only a few of the trained temporaries are hired into the core. Maybe the company's expenditure on training is not an investment after all, but just another employment cost that wipes out the low-wage advantage of temporaries.

The second reason to doubt whether the staffing temporaries are cheaper than core employees arises from the company's recently adopted goal to achieve world-class manufacturing standards. This means reducing the unit cost of production and increasing customer service to match the best results obtained by any company worldwide. Some managers wonder if temporary employees make it hard to achieve this goal.

Aside from questions about their training cost, there is a broader question of their effectiveness. This has nothing to do with their individual productivity, which is not measured but thought to be okay. Instead, it is a question of whether work teams can really function effectively if temporary workers are continually coming and going.

Case study   **Differences in managing contingent labor in the United States and Germany**

The company is a major US multinational corporation in the consumer products business. It has customers in just about every country of the world and facilities in every continent. The business is seasonal. Customers' demand for the company's products surges in the holiday-rich fourth quarter and slacks off in the first and second quarters. The company's demand for labor varies accordingly.

The company has similar production and distribution facilities in the United States and Germany, as well as in other countries. In both the US and German facilities, thousands of orders come in from the field every day. The orders are assembled, packaged, and shipped within two days. Neither facility produces for inventory nor ships from inventory. Both facilities require substantial numerical flexibility in their workforces. They achieve it in different ways.

In the US facility, contingent workers are on-call, in-house temporary employees who are on the company payroll. They are used when needed, with a one-day notice, and they are used heavily. The operation has far less than a complete full-time workforce. In the peak fourth quarter, the on-call workers account for nearly a third of the workforce and even in the slack fourth quarter, their numbers do not fall below a quarter. Business volume in the peak fourth quarter is a modest 1.2 times above the slack first quarter.

The on-call, in-house temporaries at the US plant are hardly temporary; their average length of service is about three and a half years. About three-quarters of them eventually are hired into the core workforce. As on-call workers, they are paid the same wage as core employees but not all benefits.

In the German facility, contingent workers are short-term contract workers who are on the company payroll. They work for three to six months, but there are not so many of them. In the peak fourth quarter they account for less than one-seventh of the workforce, and in slack periods only a few of them remain. This quite small use of contingent workers contrasts with quite large swings in the German plant's business volume – twice as much in the peak fourth quarter as in the slack first quarter.

Although the German contingent workers' short-term contracts are sometimes renewed, these workers spend less than a year at the company on the average, and less than half of them ever join the core workforce. They are paid equal wages and equal benefits as core employees.

The German plant has more need for numerical flexibility but uses fewer contingent workers than the US plant, and the German plant uses contingent workers differently. Why? The answer is partly differences between US and German labor laws, partly differences in labor markets, and partly differences in management preferences driven by differences in national culture.

The German facility gets some numerical flexibility from its core workforce via the traditional use of overtime, which carries a wage premium of only 25%. The US facility, facing a 50% wage premium, does not use overtime. It adds a second shift instead if more output is needed. It does not get flexibility from its regular core workforce.

The US managers use contingent labor not only as a buffer for core employees and to gain numerical flexibility, but also as a screening device and entry port into the company. Contingent workers can be screened during three years of experience before they become regular employees; no one joins the core workforce at the US plant without first being an on-call worker. The long service of the US 'temporary' workers would be illegal in Germany where short-term contracts cannot be renewed past one and a half years of service. The German facility also faces a tight labor market so that people who do not want contingent employment probably can find other jobs. The US facility faces a slack labor market, so workers will wait three years for a job in the core.

Questions and potential answers for companies

The decade of the 1980s introduced qualitative changes in the business environment. Beginning, in the early 1980s, with the worst business recession that many countries had endured since the 1930s, companies faced challenges to their way of doing business that have not gone away but instead have become more pressing in the 1990s. The business environmental changes that companies face might be characterized on the demand side as product market turbulence and global competition, and on the supply side as workforce diversity.

The sources of turbulent product markets and global competition are many – deregulation of product markets, privatization in foreign industries, the success of Japanese companies and new Asian competitors, economic integration in Europe, the freeing up of East European industry, and the prospect of freer trade in North America are just some examples. Taken together, turbulent product markets and global competition mean that product life cycles are short, new products appear frequently, technology advances rapidly, production processes are improved continuously, management practices change regularly, and competitive strategies are redesigned often. To succeed in this business environment, companies must be able to change rapidly, and they must continuously reduce costs.

How can companies make their organizations adaptable to rapid change? How can they manage their human resources to reduce costs? The concrete issues that companies face are those of how to increase individual labor productivity and work unit performance, how to minimize wage and benefit payments, how to tailor labor input to labor requirements, how to adjust job tasks and employee skills to changes in production processes, and how to make labor cost respond to the financial circumstances of the company.

Companies also face issues on the supply side. The labor force is increasingly diverse. This means that workers are increasingly different from each other and different from those in past. They are no longer mainly middle-aged white males. Workers are increasingly young or old, female, Black or Hispanic or Asian, immigrants, single parents, and openly gay. Different demographic and personal traits translate into different aspirations and expectations from the workplace, and different management practices from employers.

One potential type of solution toward which many companies are moving is *flexibility* – flexibility in the way the company employs, deploys, and compensates labor. Managers want to be able to increase and decrease labor input as labor demand fluctuates and the labor input needs to become more variable and less fixed as output volume fluctuates. Managers want to be able to move people to jobs that need to be done and away from jobs that are unnecessary. They want to be able to pay people more when the company is succeeding and less when it is not.

All of these problems that managers need to solve can be described as types of flexibility needs. Organizational flexibility refers to structural interventions to achieve flexibility in the ways that people think and act, as exemplified by decentralizing and delayering. Numerical flexibility refers to staffing options such as temporary and part-time employment that enable the company to rapidly change the number of workers or the hours they work. Temporal flexibility means scheduling options such as flexitime that give employees a range of choice about when and where they work. Functional flexibility refers to the ability of workers to use a range of skills to do a range of tasks, as acquired through cross-training and lateral mobility. Labor cost flexibility means that total payments made to labor vary with the company's earnings picture as achieved by incentive pay or profit-related pay.

Types of workers and employment relationships

From the Second World War until the 1980s most firms in the industrialized world offered stable, full-time employment to their workers. However, alternative arrangements began to increase during the 1980s and their growth continues to be strong. In this section we describe the core and ring strategy or model of new work arrangements, whereby a small group of workers and managers constitutes the core that management wants to keep as regular, full-time organizational members; most of the other people completing the company's work constitute the rings around the core, that is, the firm has varying levels of commitment to them and can let them go contingent upon its needs. We then focus specifically on part-time employment, temporary employment, and other forms of contingent relationships.

As indicated in Figure 9.1, the firm invests heavily in the training of a core group of mostly full-time managers and employees, many of whom are cross-trained in a variety of functions and activities so as to maximize *functional* flexibility in using them. (For a widely cited discussion of the core and ring strategy, see Atkinson, 1984.) Some part-time employees are also in the core and receive wages and fringe benefits comparable to full-time employees but pro-rated to their hours of work; sometimes they also obtain some non-pro-rated fringe benefits such as complete health coverage. The core can include two workers sharing a regular full-time job and people who voluntarily accept a temporary reduction in full-time employment during an economic downturn. The firm maximizes both functional and *numerical* flexibility by such arrangements.

Outside of the core, there are rings of casual, part-time employees and short-term contract employees; staffing temporaries; and outsourcing and subcontracting. As employment moves away from the core to the periphery, functional flexibility declines and numerical flexibility increases.

In addition, there are specialized work arrangements such as flexitime, that is, everyone works during a peak work period such as 10 am until 3 pm, but an employee's starting hour determines his or her finishing hour: workers starting at 8 am finish at 3 pm, and so on. Flexitime has grown dramatically in the United States. It was virtually

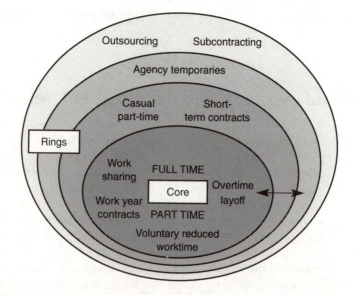

Figure 9.1 The core and ring strategy and different types of flexibility (numerical, temporal, functional, and labor cost).

non-existent in 1970, but one recent study of 1034 US firms indicated that 60% of them offer it, even though only about a quarter of their workforces takes advantage of it (Fierman, 1994).

Similarly, many individuals now perform their corporate jobs at home: in the United States, there are now 7.6 million Americans who work at least part of the time at home, and this figure represents an increase of 15% from 1992 to 1993 (Shellenbarger, 1993a). Such forms of specialized arrangements that are available to regular full-time employees and some part-time employees strengthen the overall flexibility of the firm and constitute effective motivational tools for keeping outstanding employees.

Part-Time Employment

In this section, we describe the levels and patterns of usage of part-time and temporary workers, and we trace their trends over time. The number of part-time employees in the United States was 22.6 million in 1992, accounting for 19.2 percent of all employment.[†] Among these part-time employees, about 20–25% are involuntary part-timers – they work part-time because of slack work on their regular full-time job or because they cannot find a full-time job. The rest of the part-time employees regularly work part-time and voluntarily choose that labor force status.

Time trends

While the absolute numbers of part-time employees has increased quite steadily over the years, so of course has the entire workforce. As a result, voluntary part-time employment has not increased as a share of the labor force in the past 25 years; it has stayed around 13–14%. However, the use of involuntary part-time employment has been increasing gradually from less than 3% 25 years ago to 5–6% recently (see Figure 9.2).

This time trend masks the cyclical nature of the use of involuntary part-time employment. During recessions, such as in 1975, 1982, and 1991, companies need less labor and correspondingly increase their use of part-time employment. During periods of solid economic growth, such as the period from 1984–9, demand for labor increases and less part-time employment is involuntary.

---

† These data and those to follow for the United States are tabulated from unpublished data from the US Bureau of Labor Statistics. Among the US government publications that report statistics on part-time employment are *Employment and Earnings* and *Monthly Labor Review*.

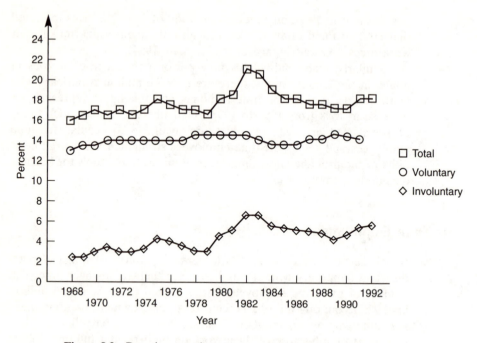

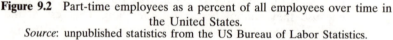

Figure 9.2   Part-time employees as a percent of all employees over time in
the United States.
Source: unpublished statistics from the US Bureau of Labor Statistics.

Occupations

The jobs that part-time employees are typically hired to do are different
from the jobs that full-time employees do in some respects. Compared to
full-timers, voluntary part-timers have a less even occupational distribution.
They are less likely to be managers at the top end, and less likely to be
craft or repair workers, or factory or transport operators at the bottom end.
Instead, voluntary part-timers are more likely to be sales people, administrative or clerical employees, and especially service workers. However, there
is little difference in the proportionate number of voluntary part-timers and
full-timers who are professionals or technical employees (see Figure 9.3).

Involuntary part-time employees are in turn somewhat different
from regular part-timers insofar as they are more concentrated at the
bottom end of the occupational distribution. Involuntary part-timers
are less likely than regular part-timers to be professionals or administrators, and more likely to be equipment operators (Figure 9.4).

Gender and age

Whereas men make up 58% of all full-time employment, women are
in the majority among part-time employees, constituting 69% of voluntary part-timers and 51% of involuntary part-timers. Women part-time

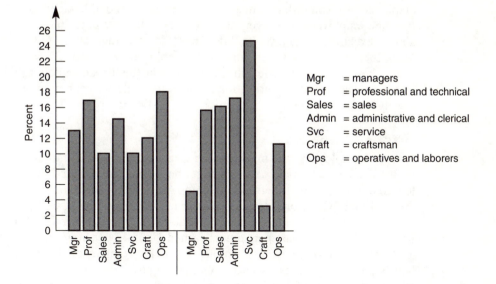

Figure 9.3   Occupations of full-time and voluntary part-time employees in the United States, 1992.

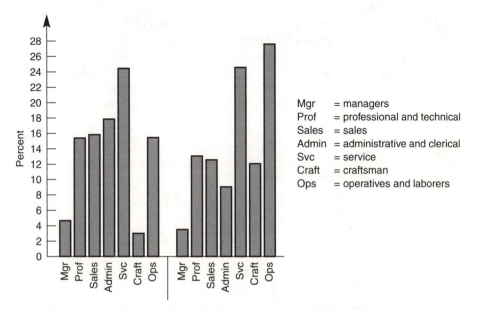

Figure 9.4   Occupation of voluntary and involuntary part-time employees in the United States, 1992.

employees are somewhat younger and older and less middle-aged than full-time employees. However, men who are voluntary part-timers are almost exclusively very young (age 16–24) or old (age 60 or older). Only 26% of voluntary part-time male employees were age 25–59 in 1992 whereas 84% of male full-timers were in this broad middle-age category. The age distribution for involuntary male part-timers more closely resembles the age distribution for full-timers.

Wages

Part-time employees earn much smaller wages than full-time employees on the average, and male part-timers get both absolutely and relatively less than female part-timers. When comparing hourly-paid employees in 1991, men who worked part-time earned just over US$5 per hour, which was just over half as much per hour as that earned by men who worked full-time; female part-timers earned US$5.42 per hour, or 73% as much as full-time women employees. (The comparison between hourly-paid employees, which excludes many people, does not adequately account for differences in the jobs that part-time and full-time employees do, and thus cannot be used to judge company pay practices.) However, the pay gap between full-time and part-time women has been widening (it was 83% 20 years ago) (see Figure 9.5).

Usage in other countries

The United States occupies the middle ground in its extent of use of part-time employment compared to other industrialized countries. Although exact statistical comparisons are quite difficult because of national differences in definitions and data collection, it appears that the highest-usage countries are the Netherlands, where one-third of all employment was part-time in 1990, and the Scandinavian countries, where the level was from 23 to 26%.[†] In contrast, some southern European countries have very low levels of part-time employment, as

Table 9.1 Change in the percent of part-time employment in different countries

Country	1979	1990
United States	16.4	16.9
Netherlands	16.6	33.2
United Kingdom	16.4	21.8
Japan	15.4	17.6
Germany	11.4	13.2
Spain	N/A	4.8

† The source for these and the following data for other countries is the International Labor Organization, *Part-Time Work* (1993), Report V(1) of the International Labour Conference 80th Session, 1992, Geneva, International Labour Office.

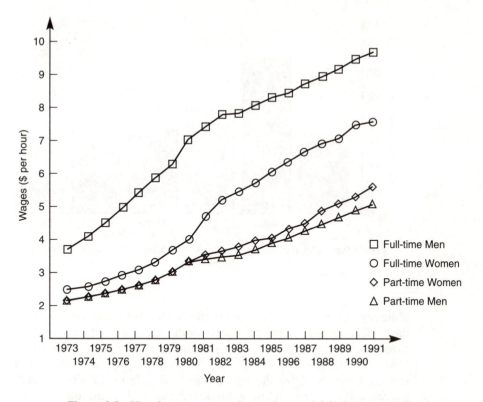

Figure 9.5   Hourly wage rates of part-time and full-time men and women.
(Median rates for hourly paid workers.)
Source: unpublished statistics from the US Bureau of Labor Statistics.

exemplified by Spain with less than 5%. Germany uses somewhat fewer part-timers than the United States, while Japan's use is about the same as the United States (see Figure 9.6). In both Europe overall and in Japan, part-time employment increased considerably faster than full-time employment during the 1980s, whereas in the United States there was scarcely any change in the ratio of part-time employment to full-time employment in this time period (see Table 9.1).

Temporary workers

In the area of temporary workers, the United States experienced unprecedented growth during the 1980s; Manpower, Inc. recently replaced General Motors as the largest issuer of W2 tax forms[†],

---

† W2 tax forms are given to all salaried employees, and deductions from the total salary include various types of taxes, employee pension contributions, employee health care costs, and so on. These forms are sent automatically to the Internal Revenue Service.

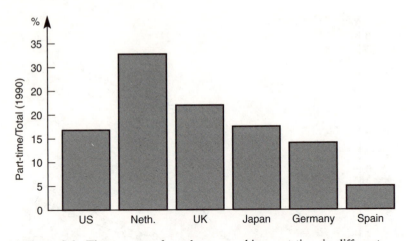

Figure 9.6   The percent of employees working part-time in different
countries.

although many of its temporary workers are employed for only a few days. The largest share of this growth has occurred among those workers who are sent out on assignment by temporary help staffing firms. In 1970, there were only 184,400 temporary workers supplied by staffing firms; by 1990 the figure was 1.165 million. In terms of 1992 payroll dollars, 47% of these employees worked in the office/clerical sector, and 27.5% in the industrial sector. However, there were significant numbers in the technical (10%), professional (5%), and medical sectors (9%), and some specialized US staffing firms now provide scientists, engineers, and even temporary CEOs.[†]

Reasons for use

A large-scale study by Katherine Abraham (1988), the US Commissioner of Labor Statistics, indicates that firms report various reasons for the use of temporary workers provided by staffing firms, short-term hires, and on-call workers, such as special projects, seasonal needs, and identifying good candidates for regular jobs (see Table 9.2). Also, the same survey indicated that many more firms increased rather than decreased their use of staffing temporaries, short-term hires, contracting, and subcontracting between 1980 and 1985, thus suggesting that firms tend to use multiple approaches to solving their staffing problems.

[†]   These data were derived in studies of staffing temporaries completed by the National Association of Temporary and Staffing Services, Alexandria, Virginia. Figures identical or almost identical to these have been published by the US Department of Labor. The data on staffing temporaries in Europe are derived from a study of over 180 sectors of the European Union's industry, *Panorama of EC Industry: 1991–1992*. This report and related ones can be obtained from the Confederation Internationale des Entreprises de Travail temporaire (CIETT), London.

Table 9.2   Percent of respondents reporting various reasons for the use of staffing temporaries, short-term hires, and on-call workers[†]

	Staffing temporaries	Short-term hires	On-call workers	Any of the preceding
Special projects	70	56	51	77
Seasonal needs	24	53	39	52
Provide buffer for regular staff against downturns in demand	14	8	20	22
Any of the above	79	84	73	90
Fill vacancy until a regular employee is hired	61	15	34	60
Fill in for absent regular employee	74	42	68	80
Either of the above	88	48	72	89
Identify good candidate for regular jobs	16	14	9	23
Special expertise possessed by flexible staffer	12	13	34	29
Prefer not to hire regular employee for some ongoing jobs	15	10	13	20
Other	2	10	9	11
Sample size	338	282	158	412
Total number	339	282	161	413

† Abraham (1988).

Usage in Europe

In the EU (previously the EC), employment of staffing temporaries is about 1% of total employment, which is about equal to the percentage in the United States, but 2% in France and the Netherlands. Generally speaking, temporary employment increases during economic upturns both in the United States and Europe as firms seek to meet higher production goals; during downturns, firms tend to eliminate the use of temporaries before considering the reduction of regular part-time and full-time employment. These patterns have been consistent both in the United States and Europe since temporary help firms came into existence in 1947, and they support the argument that firms had been using a core and ring strategy for decades before the concept became well known during the 1980s, even if they did not consciously recognize this fact and used it rather unsystematically.

Also, although European labor laws are in a state of flux because many of the European governments want to decrease labor market rigidities, Germany has more restrictions on the use of temporaries than most European countries, and Spain, Greece, and Ireland legally prohibit their use. A summary of the legal restrictions in Europe is presented in Table 9.3.

Table 9.3 Legal restrictions in the use of staffing temporaries in European countries

Country	Belgium	Denmark	Germany	France	Ireland	Luxemburg	Netherlands	Portugal	UK
Forbidden to use	YES	NO	NO	YES	NO	NO	NO	YES	NO
Restricted to sector(s) of the economy	YES	NO	YES	YES	NO	NO	YES	NO	NO
Restricted by collective bargaining agreements	YES	NO	NO	NO	YES	NO	YES	N/A	NO
Govt/industry program to make temporary workers into permanent ones	NO	NO	YES	NO	NO	NO	NO	NO	NO
Duration (employment in months)	6	–	6	18	12	–	6	6	–
Contract renewable with agency	YES	NO	YES	N/A	YES	YES	YES	YES	YES
Temporary worker employed by only one staffing firm	YES	NO	NO	YES	NO	NO	YES	YES	NO
Written contract with the temporary employee	YES	N/A	YES	YES	N/A	N/A	NO	YES	YES
Insecurity bonus	NO	NO	NO	YES	NO	NO	NO	NO	NO
Equal treatment: temporary and regular workers	YES	YES	NO	YES	NO	NO	YES	YES	NO

Outsourcing and downsizing

Outsourcing and subcontracting constitute another work arrangement that has grown dramatically in recent years. Precise figures are not available in this area, but between 1980 and 1987 the number of self-employed workers in the United States increased from 8.5 to 9.6 million (13%) and the number of business service workers rose from 3.3 to 5.1 million (55%). Many of these workers are engaged in outsourcing and contract work. By comparison, the civilian labor force only increased by 12% during this period.

There is an ongoing debate about the advantages and disadvantages of downsizing the workforce, a concept which is consistent with the core and ring strategy. Companies such as Kodak and IBM have had successive labor cuts as they have faced unprecedented turmoil and competition, and even white-collar workers and managers are no longer relatively secure in their jobs, even during periods of prosperity. There are, however, alternatives to downsizing, and these include retraining workers during economic downturns, a moratorium on hiring, voluntary leaves and reductions in working hours, pay reduction, work sharing, early retirement programs, lean staffing, and the use of contingent workers. Japanese automotive firms in the United States have retrained workers during economic downturns, as has the US firm, Harmon International Industries; the Communications Workers of America and AT&T have started a pilot program under which employees who would have been discharged during an economic downturn work as in-house temporaries for nine months, after which they are guaranteed full-time, regular employment; and many companies now hire staffing temporaries under a 'temp to permanent' arrangement if the individual's performance is satisfactory. Such approaches seem necessary if firms want to maintain a loyal workforce, and a recent large survey suggests that continual downsizing has already significantly weakened employee loyalty to companies (Shellenbarger, 1993b).

Further, although we have focused mainly on the United States and Europe, some attention should be devoted to the distinctive labor system that Japan has been using since the Second World War, as it constitutes a core and ring approach. A rather small percentage of workers and managers is guaranteed lifetime employment after graduating from college until age 55 or 60; in 1980 this percentage was approximately 35 but it has since declined to about 28. Only the larger and more prosperous companies have been able to offer this form of employment, and the percentage is declining at least in part because they can no longer afford the costs associated with the guarantee. Still, large Japanese companies have followed the core and ring strategy since the Second World War and will probably continue to do so, but in a much reduced fashion.

The case for continuous workforce readjustment

A company using the core and ring strategy implicitly accepts continuous workforce readjustment as a way of life. It is our contention that companies must accept continuous readjustment, as turbulent product markets, rapid changes in technology, and global competition force them to accept flexible workforce arrangements. A company must be able to shift quickly the products and services that it makes and sells, the methods used in production, and the location of production. The cost of production must be continuously reduced even as quality must be increased. Even Michael Porter's famous distinction between a differentiation strategy, whereby a premium can be asked for a distinctive product or service, and a low-cost-leader strategy, has been expanded to incorporate a 'speed' strategy, whereby a company beats its competitors in the introduction of new products and services (Dess and Miller, 1993).

In 1967 James Thompson became famous when he argued that the major problem facing modern firms is not profitability per se but managing external environmental uncertainty so that long-term profitability can be achieved. According to Thompson, firms should 'buffer' and protect their technical and productive core, and researchers following his line of reasoning have shown that the core and ring strategy is designed to achieve this outcome. Thus Alison Davis-Blake and Brian Uzzi, using large databases available through the US Department of Labor, have found support for the following hypotheses (Davis-Blake and Uzzi, 1993):

(1) Jobs requiring high levels of firm-specific knowledge are less likely to be filled by temporary workers than jobs requiring low levels of firm-specific training.
(2) Firms will increase their use of temporary workers during periods of economic prosperity.
(3) The larger the establishment, the more likely it is to use independent contractors to handle specialized and intermittent work that can be performed better and at less cost by the contractors; smaller firms do not have as much financial flexibility as the larger firms, and thus cannot afford to contract out as much.
(4) Smaller and less prosperous firms will tend to meet increased demand by hiring more temporary workers.

Such research confirms that companies are either systematically or unsystematically readjusting their workforces continuously so that the core is treated differently from the rings surrounding it. It also suggests that companies can take specific actions to manage effectively this continuous process of readjustment.

To achieve workforce flexibility, the numbers and types of employees and the skills they possess must be quickly adjustable. Companies can achieve numerical flexibility by adjusting the total amount of labor time as demand rises and falls, either by changing the number of people at work or by changing the number of hours put in by the people at work. Temporal flexibility can be achieved by distributing labor time over the day, week, month, or year in a variable manner. Thus some workers can be employed as regular, full-time employees only for some months of the year, and other workers can be treated as contingent or peripheral.

To supplement numerical and temporal flexibility, companies can emphasize functional flexibility by equipping workers with multiple skills through functional cross-training and designing jobs to embrace multiple tasks. Intracompany transfers of workers from jobs with slack to jobs with peak loads may reduce the amount of change needed in the number of workers or the hours they work.

To achieve labor cost reductions, companies can systematically contain expenditures on wages and benefits, and they should realize that many firms do not blindly follow industry norms in this regard (Davis-Blake and Uzzi, 1993). Labor productivity must increase, and there must be a close fit between the workload and the workforce so that labor is paid when it is needed but not otherwise. Aside from wages and benefits, companies can try to reduce other employment and human resource management costs by refining their hiring and performance evaluation practices. In addition, labor costs can be made to vary with the economic success of the firm so that when earnings fall, so does labor expenditure, thus maximizing labor cost flexibility.

Previously we have highlighted some of the reasons why companies use staffing temporaries, short-term hires, and on-call workers (see Table 9.2). It is now possible to connect such reasons with the types of flexibility that companies need: functional, temporal, numerical, and financial or labor cost. First, temporary workers permit the company to achieve numerical flexibility because they can be brought into the workplace at a moment's notice. If no work is available, they do not come to work. Such workers also meet the company's need for functional flexibility because different temporaries with different skills can be brought into the workplace on short notice.

Part-time employees (casual or hourly, but not regular or salaried part-time workers) also give the company numerical flexibility in the same way that temporaries do, and in addition, they may work a variable number of hours each day, for example, seven hours one day and three hours the next. Casual part-timers also provide a company with such temporal flexibility.

Both temporary and part-time workers provide labor cost flexibility insofar as their use enables the company to fit the workforce closely to the workload. No idle labor time is paid for. Additional labor cost savings may be achieved from temporary workers if the one payment made to the staffing company for their services that includes their wages and staffing fee is less than the wages and benefits received by regular core employees. Also, labor cost savings can be achieved from part-time employment if they are paid the same wage rate as full-time employees but receive fewer benefits than them or none at all. Existing US labor law permits both unequal pay and unequal benefits for part-timers. Practices vary in the EU countries, but in general part-time employees are better protected than in the United States. Nevertheless, there is a growing movement to reduce labor costs through such approaches.

Further, temporary employees enable managers to save labor costs because in some ways managing them is easier than managing regular employees. Hiring, firing, appraising, and counseling temporaries does not require the paperwork or care needed for regular employees. Not only does this save money in the short run, but it also makes the manager's job easier to perform. It remains to be seen if this route to ease and cheapness is in the firm's long-run interests; the two cases at the beginning of this chapter indicate that the issue is very complex and must be decided situationally.

Problem areas

Several issues arise in the management of people who are not regular full-time employees. One set of issues affects the bottom line directly – the performance and cost effectiveness of part-time and temporary workers. Another issue in a state of flux is the potential for legal difficulties stemming from the sometimes questionable employment status of contingent workers. A third issue is the equity with which contingent workers are treated compared to regular core employees.

Performance

When human resource managers or operating managers are asked about the performance of their contingent workers, they typically reply that it is 'about the same' or 'maybe not quite as good' as the performance of regular core employees. If contingent workers are not employees on the payroll, it is unlikely that the company really knows what their performance is simply because it is not measured or assessed.

In general, there are reasons to doubt that casual part-timers or staffing temporaries will be as high-performing as regular core employees doing similar jobs, although such a prediction depends on the type of job and the nature of the labor market.

Individual productivity depends on skill and effort. Skill in turn depends on formal education, practical training, and experience. Even if contingent workers have education equal to that of core employees, they are unlikely to have as much training or experience if they do not have an ongoing attachment to an employer. At the least, they will not have as much experience on their current job assignment. Of course, for some jobs experience may not count for much, or job skills can be learned very quickly if the jobs are very simple to do.

On the other hand, sometimes contingent workers, especially short-term contract workers or some staffing temporaries, are hired specifically because they have specialized skills that can be brought to bear immediately on a particular task. In this case, we are not comparing contingent workers to core employees because they are not doing similar jobs.

Effort also affects individual productivity, and effort depends to some extent on motivation or commitment and rewards. It is hard to imagine that contingent workers, who by definition have little or no attachment to their current workplace, can have high commitment to it. And if contingent workers are paid either smaller wages or receive fewer benefits than core employees, the reward system does not encourage superior effort from them. However, particularly in the United States, many temporary employees are hired under a 'temp to perm' arrangement. Frequently such temporary employees, after proving themselves on the job, are offered permanent positions. Also, some temporary employees have increased their salaries three or four times in a year because of skill upgrading.

However, for some types of routine machine-paced or highly structured jobs, we might question the extent to which effort and hence commitment really matter. If pay is piece-rate, and holding the job requires a minimum output level, then perhaps neither skill nor effort are central factors, and satisfactory productivity is achieved by virtue of turnover until the right contingent worker is found.

In fact, some types of jobs may be performed better by contingent workers. Jobs that are repetitive or stressful are better performed in short stretches, such as part-days or part-weeks. For these jobs, part-time and temporary workers may do better than full-time long-service employees.

Performance in many work settings is not only a matter of individual productivity but also a matter of teamwork. Good teamwork requires a mutual understanding that is developed with work mates through time. If contingent workers come and go quite rapidly, they cannot contribute to the development of high performance through teamwork. What matters to managers ultimately is the performance of their work unit as a whole, more so than the productivity of given individuals.

Finally, the performance of contingent workers might be different from core employees if the supply of people who are available for part-time and temporary work is systematically different. If part-time and temporary work appeals to qualified people who cannot work full-time continuously, such as students, retirees, or some parents of young children, then contingent work taps into a new source of labor supply and broadens the labor pool. In this case, contingent workers might outperform core employees. On the other hand, if labor markets are tight, and contingent jobs are perceived to be 'bad' jobs that regular employees do not have to take, then contingent workers are among the least skilled and experienced and accordingly will turn in poorer performance than core employees.

Cost effectiveness

Cost effectiveness is what company managers really want to achieve with contingent labor. Cost effectiveness refers to how much value of output workers produce compared to how much it costs to employ them. It depends on productivity and on wages and benefits, which together make up unit labor cost, given by expenditure on wages and benefits divided by output. It is possible for high-wage labor to be cost effective if it is also high-productivity labor; if contingent labor is low-wage labor, it can be cost effective as long as productivity is not also low.

This point is illustrated by one of the authors' case study work with two companies that use contingent workers in data entry operations. In these two companies, the wages and benefits paid to contingent workers is 12–14% lower than for core employees, while the measured productivity is 7–9% lower. This means that the unit labor cost of contingent labor is 5–6% lower (Nollen, 1993).

Costs of employment go beyond wages and benefits, and include costs such as recruiting, training, and human resource management services such as employee assistance programs. These costs are often overlooked because they are regarded as 'overhead,' and it is hard to quantify them. But these costs may be critical to the cost effectiveness of contingent labor because they are fixed with respect to the amount of time a worker puts in, and because some of them are incurred by the company up-front.

If training is regarded as an investment in human capital, then the company that pays for the training expects to recover its investment over time. It does so if the trained workers produce value of output that exceeds the wages and benefits they are paid. The key element is that training investment is recovered only if the trained worker stays on the job or in the company long enough to pay it back. But contingent workers by definition are not long service workers; temporary and casual part-time workers expect to move on after a while, and the company uses them precisely because they are expected to be let go after a while. If they leave before the company's training investment is paid back, then the training investment is instead just another cost of employment, as if the contingent worker's wage rate were higher or an extra benefit were paid.

Most jobs require some training, even entry level or routine jobs that often are done by contingent workers. The training may be formal classroom training or it may be informal on-the-job training conducted by the supervisor. In the former case, a trainer's salary is being paid and space is being used. In the latter case, a supervisor is being paid but not for producing output. In both cases, the contingent worker-trainee's wages are being paid although little output is being produced at first.

From the case study research of cost effectiveness conducted by the authors in three companies, training costs were not recovered in two cases. For example, from 12 to 20 months was required to recover training costs, but the average time on the job of the contingent workers was only 8–14 months. Thus the unrecovered training costs are added to the costs of employing contingent workers, and this caused their otherwise lower unit labor costs to become instead higher costs.

Legal issues

Company managers need to address potential legal issues in the use of temporary workers. Legal issues can arise out of the potentially ambiguous employment status of some contingent workers. The question is whether or not, if not when, an employment relationship is established between staffing temporaries or short-term contract workers and the company at which they work. In the case of temporaries provided by temporary help and staffing firms, the courts have established a principle of co-employment, that is, while the temporaries are legally employees of these firms, both these firms and the client firms have specific responsibilities toward them.

This question is important because contingent workers who are not on the payroll of the company where they work are not fully covered by protective labor legislation because they are not legally permanent or regular employees of that company. Therefore these contingent workers have little if any recourse if they are adversely affected by problems such as discrimination by race, gender, age, or other prohibited categories, or sexual harassment, or wrongful discharge. However, if the contingent worker can establish that he or she had an employment relationship, then a lawsuit against wrongful discharge or other violation can be brought. If temporary workers acquire these rights, then some of the manager's freedom not to manage them is lost, and companies are then responsible for some of the costs of regular employment.

A second type of legal issue arises from the use of independent contractors rather than staffing temporaries. These contingent workers have no income taxes withheld (so it is easier for them to cheat on tax payments), nor are payments made by an employer for unemployment insurance or workmens' compensation. This is not a problem if the independent contractors are really independent, but some may actually have an employment relationship with the company where they work (sometimes these people are laid-off employees who return to do the same job they were doing), and in this case all of these taxes should be paid by the company.

The danger in the case of short-term contractors and staffing temporaries who are not really independent and who really are functioning as employees is that the company may be able to escape legal obligations as well as moral duties.

While it is not clear when or what constitutes an employment relationship for workers who are not officially employees, some companies restrict the length of time that a temporary or contract worker can spend continuously at the company (often the limitation is less than one year). Another factor is the extent to which the company guides and directs the work of the contingent worker. Some companies have a staffing firm representative permanently located on-site to function as a quasi-supervisor for the agency's temporaries located there in order to minimize the co-employment relationship.

These legal issues do not occur in the same way in some European countries because the use of contingent workers is more strictly regulated. For example, short-term contract workers in Germany cannot by law exceed 18 months of service at one company. As indicated previously, some European countries such as Germany are in the process of loosening their labor laws so as to facilitate the use of non-traditional employees. In 1980, for example, Germany with a population of 64 million had only 75,000 agency temporaries while the United States, with a population of 227 million, had 416,000. In Germany, such workers could receive sick pay even if they never showed up for an assignment due to illness. Today the German situation is changing, and approximately 1% of the German labor force is now in the temporary category. We can expect to see similar changes in other European countries as labor constraints on the operations of markets are removed.

Equity

The growing use of casual part-time and temporary workers has been accompanied by growing concern about the equity with which these people are treated compared to their regular full-time employee counterparts. Is the segmentation of the labor market being increased? Is the dual labor market being reinforced in which the primary sector of core employees is increasingly better off and the secondary sector of contingent workers becomes increasingly worse off, at least in relative terms?

The equity concerns arise first because of the widespread belief that contingent workers are paid smaller wages than regular employees, or even if wages are equal, that the benefits they receive are less if not zero. (Of course, aggregate statistical comparisons are not satisfactory to prove this point; comparisons between people doing similar jobs are required.) A second equity concern arises from the lack of social protections afforded to contingent workers by labor law in the United States, as mentioned above in connection with legal issues. The third equity concern stems from the likelihood that contingent workers are unable to take advantage of as much opportunity to develop their human capital as core employees are – most notably continuing training and career development.

If compensation, social protections, and human capital development are inferior for contingent workers, then companies that use them need to reexamine their management of them, and to look into just how much inequity is being promulgated. To do that, two tests can be applied.

First, how many people want contingent work? Is the supply of people with little or no attachment to an employer (at least at the current time in their work life) in balance with companies' demand for them? How many people prefer the freedom to come and go that temporaries have? How many people prefer to avoid the implicit obligation to undertake the retraining and relocation that often accompanies membership in the core? If the supply is roughly equal to the demand, then we might infer that the labor market is working successfully and the terms and conditions of work for contingent labor are satisfactory compared to core employment.

Second, what resources and choices do contingent workers have? Do they have less human capital from education, training, and experience than core employees? Are they disproportionately representative of disadvantaged groups in the labor market? If the answers to these questions are yes, then the people who do contingent work have inferior choices about their work life compared to core employees. If they do not have viable alternatives to contingent work, then even labor supply–demand balance does not ensure equity for contingent workers.

Guidelines and suggestions

In this section we offer some guidelines and suggestions so that companies can take advantage of managing without a full-time complete workforce while alleviating some of the potential problems of this type of workforce management. Specifically, we profile different ways of optimally using temporary and part-time employment, and contracting and subcontracting arrangements.

As our previous discussion suggests, it is important for a company to systematically use a core and ring strategy and avoid random and unsystematic approaches. Clearly smaller and less profitable companies need to use a different approach than large companies, and it is for this reason that they tend to use more temporaries and fewer contracting arrangements. Also, both small and large companies need to use several work arrangements simultaneously to take advantage of the different types of flexibility. In this regard, companies must pinpoint the type or types of flexibility – numerical, functional, temporal, and cost – that they seek to maximize through the use of each non-traditional work arrangement, for otherwise they cannot know or measure whether they are achieving their objectives.

However, managing without a complete full-time workforce can succeed in some cases but should be limited in its use in other cases. Using contingent workers successfully requires that they achieve good individual productivity, incur reasonably low recruiting and training costs, and remain with the company for a reasonable length of time. Because long length of service is inherently contradictory to the concept of contingent employment, its use is inherently limited.

Further, as our case examples demonstrate, contingent labor probably cannot be used as a usual large-scale staffing practice in work units in which work is accomplished mainly in groups rather than by individuals. As Lorenzi, Sims, and Manz show in Chapter 7, such group-oriented approaches are becoming increasingly popular, and they neutralize many of the advantages associated with using contingent labor.

Also, it should be stressed that achieving workforce flexibility and reducing labor cost can be achieved through better use of the core workforce. In fact, companies are moving in this direction as they downsize or rightsize, as members of the core, whether managers or employees, are required to take on additional tasks and responsibilities (functional flexibility).

There are some best management practices that companies can follow if they hope to stimulate good performance among their contingent workers and avoid such dysfunctional consequences as excessive absenteeism and rapid employee turnover. These include:

(1) Linking pay both to performance and time on the job.
(2) Paying benefits that have special value in meeting the needs of contingent workers, and these include partial tuition reimbursement for young student workers, flexitime, job sharing, and day care centers.
(3) Offering contingent workers access to core employment through such devices as 'temp to perm' arrangements, which is already

occurring for 40% of temporary employees hired by staffing firms in the United States.

(4) Training supervisors to be attuned to the special needs of contingent workers.

(5) Hiring workers on short-term contracts as the needs of the work setting permit to provide both workers and the company with a small amount of certainty in their relationships.

(6) Minimizing training costs for new contingent workers by demanding that they possess minimum abilities and skills, or using them only in jobs that have small initial training needs. (Note: staffing and temporary help firms such as Manpower now provide specialized training of their temporaries, and offer vacation benefits that are directly related to length of service.)

Finally, it is possible to obtain flexibility among core employees, even if the workforce is not a complete, full-time workforce and experiences staffing shortages. Some ways to achieve company goals of flexibility and cost reduction aside from the use of temporary or casual part-time employees are:

(1) Including part-time employees in the regular core workforce, but making their hours of work variable within pre-set limits.

(2) Using work sharing for full-time employees who agree as a group to voluntarily cut their hours of work and pay during slack times.

(3) Introducing a voluntary reduced work time option for individual full-time employees who, with supervisory approval, temporarily cut back their hours of work.

(4) Writing annual work hours contracts for employees who agree to distribute a pre-set number of hours of work across the year according to company demand for labor.

As this discussion implies, there is a large number of options that companies can pursue to obtain different types of flexibility within the core and ring. While space precludes describing all of them, these guidelines and suggestions constitute a starting point for a company to systematically and proactively plan a core and ring strategy rather than being reactive to problems as they arise and pursuing random and unsystematic approaches that frequently fail to maximize different types of flexibility. Although there is no perfect organization, the core and ring strategy is perfectly compatible with such concepts as the virtual corporation, the horizontal corporation, the network corporation, and even self-managing teams, all of which are described fully in other chapters of this book. Both the resource base theory of the firm and transaction cost economics strongly suggest that managers should emphasize a systematic core and ring strategy to avoid problems, maximize flexibility, and manage external environmental uncertainty so that long-term profitability becomes a reality.

References

Abraham, K. (1988). Flexible staffing arrangements and employers' short-term adjustment strategies. In Hart, R.A. (ed.) *Unemployment and Labor Utilization*. Boston, MA: Urwin Hyman.

Atkinson, J. (1984). Manpower strategies for flexible organizations, *Personnel Management*, August, 28–34.

Becker, G. (1960). *Human Capital*. Chicago, IL: University of Chicago Press.

Davis-Blake, A. and Uzzi, B. (1993). Determinants of employment externalization: a study of temporary workers and independent contractors, *Administrative Science Quarterly*, 38, 195–223.

Dess, G. and Miller, A. (1993). *Strategic Management*. New York: McGraw-Hill.

Fierman, J. (1994). Are companies less family-friendly? Fortune, 21 March, 64–7.

Nollen, S. (1993). Exploding the myth: is contingent labor cost effective? Paper presented at the conference on Reinventing the Workplace: new perspectives on flexibility in tomorrow's competitive company, New York, 16 June.

Shellenbarger, S. (1993a). Some thrive, but many wilt working at home, *The Wall Street Journal*, 14 December, 1993, B1 and B6.

Shellenbarger, S. (1993b). Work-force study finds loyalty is weak, divisions of race and gender deep, *Wall Street Journal*, 3 September, B1 and B8.

Thompson, J.D. (1967). *Organizations in Action*. New York: McGraw-Hill.

Williamson, O. (1985). *The Economic Institutions of Capitalism*. New York: The Free Press.

10

Competitive advantage through strategic innovations in human resource management

In this chapter we summarize the evidence presented in this book on the contribution of strategic innovations in human resource management (HRM) to the achievement of competitive advantage. This summary highlights the fact that strategic innovations in HRM have a powerful role to play in liberating the organizational culture so that it becomes both entrepreneurial and motivating. To accomplish this goal, however, is by no means as straightforward a task as is commonly envisioned, and the practicing manager faced with the task of implementing such innovations needs to recognize that there are both threats as well as opportunities involved.

The sequence in which we address the major strands and themes of this book is as follows:

(1) new perspectives on theory
(2) new perspectives on organizational practices and management
(3) lessons learned
(4) human resource systems of the future and their impact on key stakeholders (the top management team, line managers, the human resource department, employees, and stockholders).

New perspectives on theory

In Chapter 1 we developed a new integrative perspective on creating sustainable competitive advantage through an emphasis on developing human resource capabilities, which extends the traditional twofold distinction between overall cost leadership and differentiation to encompass a fivefold categorization of world-class capabilities: the ability to produce products and services 'right the first time,' speedily, on time, cheaply, and flexibly. Using the resource base theory of the firm, we demonstrated that sustainable competitive advantage is intimately tied to the input, throughout, and output of human resource processes in the firm. These behavioral control systems, of course, must be linked to the overall competitive strategy of the firm and need to combine both algorithmic and experiential features (Gomez-Mejia, 1992).

However, it is our contention that creating a sustained competitive advantage is, in many ways, an illusory quest, as companies have found it possible and frequently relatively easy to emulate one another's products and services through reverse engineering, to reduce drastically the length of the product lifecycles for many goods and services, and to replicate the rivalrous moves of competitors in areas such as advertising and price cuts. Also, because of such factors as computerization, increases in advertising expenditures, and the speed of information flows, it is difficult to hide information from competitors in order to build barriers to entry and maintain a sustainable competitive advantage (Smith, *et al.*, 1992). Under such conditions the one resource that is most strategic is the one that is most difficult to copy due to the socially complex nature of its formation – human resources.

Further, there are specific criteria that are used in the resource base theory of the firm to indicate whether a resource provides a source of sustainable competitive advantage, and theoretically human resources meet *all* of these criteria, not just one or a few of them. Human resources are valuable, rare, hard to imitate, and non-substitutable.

Also, the formation of these five world-class competitive capabilities identified above needs to be understood in terms of the interaction of human resource processes and organizational processes which encourage the creation of knowledge capital. These organizational processes include total quality, concurrent engineering, just-in-time production, and computer integrated manufacturing.

Of course, the bottom line is profits, and we have highlighted the payoff to investing in human resources to create these world-class capabilities, namely the ability to create, secure, and defend market share. We have also broadened the conception of firm resources to include the top management team, which is in and of itself a strategic human resource. The composition and the behavior of the top management team is itself influenced by the human resource policies and practices of the firm: selection of team members for compatibility, individual and group rewards, and a concurrent focus on both individual and group efforts.

In addition, the top management team seeks to generate rents or profits, but there are several different types, and these include Ricardian, Schumpeterian/entrepreneurial, and quasi-rents or profits. Thus the top management team must be clear as to the specific types of profits it is seeking to attain.

As this discussion implies, the top management team or dominant coalition has several different functions, including the crafting of strategy, creating a distinctive organizational culture, and developing a coherent human resource strategy and employment philosophy. Thus the top management team is more than a group of strategy makers: it is a major subsystem unto itself that is critical for the overall functioning of the organization. Many companies seem to recognize this fact. For example, they use the Myers-Briggs personal preference inventory – the most widely used personality measure currently available, based on Carl Jung's theory of four dimensions of personal preferences – to profile the personalities of top-management team members so that each member understands the personality proclivities of other team members, and their respective strengths and weaknesses (Moore, 1987). Frequently the top managers receive their scores profiling their personalities on these four dimensions – for example, being a person who makes either 'thinking' decisions involving objective criteria or 'feeling' decisions involving subjective criteria – and then they go through a series of exercises so that they can become sensitive to the strengths and weaknesses of the personalities of other members of the top management team.

In seeking to maximize organizational performance, the top management team often reconfigures the resource base of the firm, including the organizational structures, routines, and processes. Usually this reconfiguration triggers a chain reaction in the human resource systems of the firm to support these changes. Innovations in HRM are thus set in motion. However, downstream to the top management team, the value-enhancing impact of organizational innovations may have unanticipated – even dysfunctional – consequences. This outcome occurs because of the fact that the successful implementation of these innovations is dependent on the extent to which the human resource subsystems are synchronized and integrated with each other, and these include the traditional subsystems such as selection, socialization, performance evaluation, rewards, and training and development; and the contemporary extensions of them noted directly below.

The categorization of HRM innovations which are identified include introducing radically new organizational structures and forms, de-emphasizing formal planning systems, altering the traditional ownership structure of the firm, implementing a unitarist ideology between management and employees, empowering line managers to handle traditional and historically specialized HRM activities, utilizing quality circles and self-managing teams, internalizing the quality ethos so that there are no quality boundaries, and creating new types of employment relationships involving a permeable core and ring strategy.

This categorization and detailed subsequent analysis provides new insights into theoretical issues, such as the classic shareholder-employer-employee agency problem. Organizational structures, viewed from the perspective of transaction cost economics, are designed to minimize transaction costs for shareholders. In complex and uncertain external environments, long-term commitments to employees tend to increase transaction costs, for example, retirement benefits must be met.

Transaction costs in and of themselves help to explain why many contemporary organizations are behaving as they do. Thus these organizations seek to form network partnerships of a lateral or a horizontal nature with other companies, and are even experimenting with virtual forms of structure so that long-term commitments can be avoided. The transaction costs associated with such forms are much lower than those found in the traditional vertically integrated organization, even though the integrated organization has the decided advantage of building effective barriers to entry. The drive to eliminate transaction costs implies an increasingly unpredictable future for employees – a challenge for unions to respond to in the next decade.

Moreover, agency theory, which is closely related to transaction cost economics, provides even more detailed insights into the motivational reactions of organizational members. The institutional reality is that innovations designed to reduce the incentives to shirk in labor contracts are not always operable as illustrated by our analysis of buyouts. Theoretically buyouts and particularly employee buyouts can be expected to confer significant motivational advantages because of the fact that employees as owners have new reasons to be productive and committed to the organization. However, in reality the agency problem persists (despite the fact that overall agency costs seem to be reduced) and endures because, in many employee buyouts, managers continue to be the dominant shareholders and continue to act as managers, reinforcing the traditional dependent role of employees in the employer–employee relationship. Also, information asymmetries in buyouts often results in employees buying only a small proportion of the total company shares available.

Further, transaction cost economics argues that contractual relations among and within firms are the result of efficiency-seeking behavior in a world of limited information and incomplete enforcement possibilities (Oster, 1990). Viewed from the perceptual lens of the manager who prefers to exercise unchallenged autonomy and control in the workplace, trade unions epitomize frictions in labor contracts and potentially expose managers and shareholders to ex post holdups.

However, our analysis of the Catch-22 phenomenon in union avoidance is both consistent with, and seemingly contradictory to, the above propositions. It is true that managers in large non-union companies do seek to avoid exposure to holdups in wage bargaining by avoiding unions, but paradoxically they find themselves in a situation in which they must provide the same or equal conditions to those practiced in comparable high-wage unionized environments.

From a collective action perspective, non-union employees in such large companies represent 'free riders' (Flood, 1993). That is, once large non-union employees are benefiting from the spillover effect of union-derived wages, there is little incentive for employees to form a union provided that management has created a carefully constructed and equitable internal labor market. However, organizational culture and context specific factors such as the social legitimacy enjoyed by unions in any particular country also impinge upon the union avoidance decision. The British Workplace Industrial Relations survey data, for example, indicate that non-unionism in the private sector leaves many non-union employees at a relative disadvantage to their unionized counterparts (see Chapter 5).

In addition, the efficacy of the contingency or situational framework was challenged in our analysis of the factors determining the presence or absence of specialized personnel departments within organizations because of the neglect of one important variable, namely managerial ideology. According to the Aston researchers (Pugh, *et al.*, 1969), as company size increases, there is a tendency to add specialized functions such as the personnel department. Some managers in our study indicated that, no matter how large their organizations became, they regarded specialized personnel departments as expensive and dispensable overhead. This aversion toward specialized staff, coupled with the twin objectives of reducing overhead costs and maintaining a flexible organization, explains in large part the motivation to empower line managers to carry out traditional personnel activities. In the extreme, both the HRM department and personnel managers would vanish, and their routine functions such as payroll would become the responsibility of such departments as accounting.

Once again, transaction cost economics helps us understand these research results. This field of economics posits that organizations develop hierarchy as an alternative to contracting in freely competitive markets when there are demonstrable efficiencies to be gained and where potential 'moral hazard' problems exist. Moral hazard problems develop when one party in a contract or transaction hides information from another party and behaves opportunistically in the search for profits. Having the specialized personnel department inside the organization is analogous to the 'make-hierarchy' decision while outsourcing the personnel department and activities is similar to the 'buy-contractors' decision of transaction cost economics. Specialized functional departments are sometimes viewed as moral hazards because there is an in-built incentive on their part to hide information in order to gain power and exalt their status in the corporate hierarchy.

From a line management perspective, personnel departments are sometimes viewed as 'trash cans' or a collection of incidental, peripheral and unrelated activities. Therefore line managers often believe that they can achieve significant economies by purchasing specialized personnel activities in the open market. However, this approach can bring its own special problems as insider knowledge, frequently a key factor in sensitive personnel issues, is lost when core personnel functions such as appraisal are contracted out.

Conceptually one can also conceive of certain personnel management specialists as possessing 'asset specificity' – in the language of transaction cost economics – because of their distinctive knowledge, which is difficult to replicate. Such specialists are perhaps less likely to see their activities outsourced provided they can successfully demonstrate the non-substitutability of their expertise to top management. Paradoxically, there are incentives for personnel managers to encourage strong unions to increase awareness among line managers of the 'special' knowledge of collective bargaining which seasoned industrial relations practitioners have.

Top managers of large organizations who both desire decreases in overhead costs and simultaneously believe in the supremacy of the line managers empower them to perform specialized personnel activities while outsourcing some of the more routine activities, such as payroll and employee training and development. Transaction cost economics would argue that this outsourcing pattern reflects the desire on the part of owners or shareholders to reduce transaction costs and the 'moral hazard' problem.

An alternative open-market approach is to create an internal market for personnel services within the organization. This can be achieved through a zero-based budgeting approach in which the personnel department receives no budget at the commencement of the fiscal year. Instead, line managers purchase the services of the personnel department, which motivates the HRM managers to be more efficient and tends to reduce transaction costs.

Still, our research highlights that high transaction costs persist under this new governance arrangement involving outsourcing. This is due to the lack of coordination between managers of various departments within the organization in the creation of defensible and equitable human resource practices in the areas of selection, recruitment, appraisal, rewards, and development.

Transaction cost economics also helps us understand the popularity of lean production methods, the objective of which is to cut costs dramatically and in whatever way possible. Lean production is a set of management practices designed to reduce transaction costs. Three of the non-traditional methods discussed in this book really reflect lean production and combine both motivational and financial advantages. These methods are: using self-managing teams, empowering employees to be responsible for quality through self-monitoring activities, and emphasizing a permeable core and ring hiring strategy. When self-managing teams are utilized, the workers are responsible for their tasks, and they allocate resources and duties to accomplish them. When employees are empowered to be responsible for the quality of the products or services they produce, barriers between individual organizational members, departments, and the customers tend to be minimized, thus decreasing transaction costs. Frequently, management can reduce transaction costs by outsourcing a particular function such as payroll, subcontracting for a specific activity, and hiring part-time and temporary workers and managers. For example, although hiring a temporary CEO for a one- or two-year period would have been considered extreme 10 years ago, today doing so is quite common, especially when radical changes such as downsizing are necessary, and the rationale for this change is that transaction costs are reduced.

Organizations, as we have seen, are continually faced with greater dynamism and complexity in their external environments in today's world. Developments such as intensified competition, shortened product lifecycles, accelerated technology, the emergence of information distribution networks such as the much vaunted 'infobahn,' and the growing pluriformity of consumer preferences are but some of the factors we have identified in this book. From the point of view of internal organization there are three general kinds of response intended to enhance adaptability to rapidly altering conditions.

A first type of reaction is interventions designed to reduce the number of levels in the hierarchy and its concomitant 'command and control bureaucracy.' Rearrangement of the organizational structure along these lines seeks to put output and customers back to center stage. Examples of interventions of this kind which we have examined have included de-layering, network forms of organization, and the creation of entrepreneurial internal market systems.

Structural adjustments which shift the focus to output and the customer are useful but, as we have seen, do not suffice to bridge the gap between strategy formulation and execution. Successful strategy implementation implies that front-line personnel need to be called upon and equipped to assume greater autonomy and responsibility. This leads to a second series of reactions to increasing dynamism and complexity: interventions which involve increasing the competencies and responsibilities of employees at every level of the organization. Examples documented in this book have included empowerment, policy deployment task forces, self-managing teams, and the creation of the so-called 'learning organization'.

These two types of reactions have one crucial factor in common, namely that, within strategic policy frameworks, each of them enhances the self-regulating capacity of those immediately involved, while on the other hand they simultaneously intensify mutual dependence. Mastenbroek (1993) describes this as maintaining the balance of tension between autonomy and interdependence. The third type of reaction, for which the first and second are in fact prerequisites, consists of interventions centering on business processes (Hammer, 1990; Harrington, 1991):

business process re-engineering, time-based competition, strategic quality management initiatives, and business process improvement.

Unlike sections and functions, which are organized vertically, these processes cut across the organization horizontally. Interventions on behalf of business processes therefore mean that the familiar image of the organization as a layered cake of functions, sections, and hierarchic levels will disappear. In its place we get an organization based on a new design that accords a central place to processes of management and business and that leads to output and added value.

Due to growing dynamism, more top-down control and command just does not work. To cope with increasing complexity we need to introduce enhancement of the capacity of self-regulation via strategic policy frameworks, in combination with more subtle and better-internalized forms of coordination. In short, the commitment and energy of employees at all levels are becoming utterly critical. Thus we have shown that some companies want to minimize or eliminate HRM departments so that line managers and workers at all organizational levels are directly involved in personnel and people activities as demonstrated by the discussion of top management teams.

Moreover, there is still another important reason for the growing significance of strategic human resource management, as recent publications in the field of strategic management reflect. To ensure a maintainable competitive edge the emphasis is less on existing products, services, and markets, and more on core competencies (Prahalad and Hamel, 1990) and capabilities (Bartlett and Ghosal, 1989) which guarantee continuity in the flow of new products and services for the future.

The competencies and capabilities of particular relevance in this regard relate to issues such as the firm's capacities in the following broad areas: knowledge and its transmission, technology, speed, adaptability, the capacity to combine distinct technologies and production techniques, communication, and the ability to transcend the boundaries of sections and functions in establishing a cooperative and coordinating structure within the firm. All of these capacities represent assets and/or resources to the firm. Quinn (1992:62) describes these capabilities in terms of 'knowledge-based service activities,' which constitute the core of an 'intelligent' business:

> Physical positions like a raw material source, a plant facility, or a product line rarely constitute a maintainable competitive edge today. This is especially true of manufactured products. They can be too easily bypassed, back-engineered, cloned, or slightly surpassed in performance. A truly maintainable competitive edge usually derives from developing depth in skill sets, experience factors, innovative capacities, know-how, market understanding, data bases, or information distribution systems – all service activities – that others cannot duplicate or exceed.

Recently survey research among top managers (Hall, 1992) has established that intangible resources such as product or company reputation, employee know-how and skills, company culture, and networks contribute most to the success of the companies studied. If these sources are lost, replacement or restoration takes far longer than would the construction of, say, a new hangar. That is to say, these resources are not only hard to replace but they are also not easily imitated, which is advantageous for maintaining a sustainable competitive advantage.

Towards a human resource base theory of the firm

These principles undergird the resource base theory of the firm. It is therefore appropriate to use that theory as a starting point to develop a conceptual framework for structuring human resource management. A key objective of this structuring is that it should contribute to the realization of maintainable competitive advantage.

As Mahoney and Pandian (1992) point out, the resource base theory of the firm integrates a number of theoretical traditions, namely strategic management, organizational economics, and industrial organization. Importantly, the theory helps to explain how to achieve a maintainable competitive edge which does not depend on characteristics of the industrial sector but which is related to the heterogeneous and unique character of the firm's own internal resources. The resource base view of the firm holds that to maintain a competitive edge, these resources must fulfill at least four conditions/characteristics: they must be valuable, scarce, imperfectly imitable, and imperfectly substitutable. These characteristics are introduced in the conceptual model below which refines the resource base theory of the firm as the 'human resource base theory of the firm' (see Figure 10.1) (Paauwe, 1994:32).

We will now discuss the various components of the conceptual model.

Reconciling tensions between the logic of the market *and* social norms, values and expectations: the P–M–T (Product–Market–Technology) and S–C–L (Social–Cultural–Legal) dimensions

Two dimensions in the environment dominate the crafting of HRM. On the one hand, HRM is to a large degree determined by demands arising from relevant product/market combinations and the appropriate technology (P–M–T dimension). These demands are usually expressed in terms of criteria such as efficiency, effectiveness, flexibility, quality, and innovativeness. The P–M–T dimension represents the tough

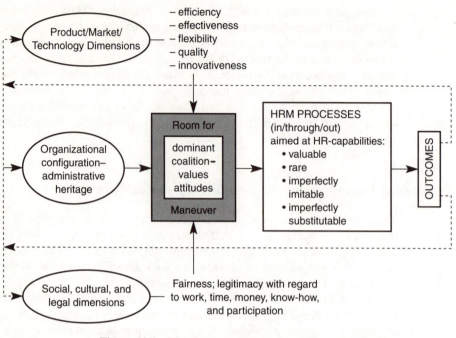

Figure 10.1   The human resource base theory of the firm.
Source: Paauwe, 1994.

economic reality of national and international industrial competition. On the other hand, it is important to remember that the *so-called* 'free market' is embedded in a socio-political and cultural context (S–C–L dimension). Prevailing values and norms and their institutionalization channel the outcomes of the market process in ways that simultaneously do justice to the dictates of fairness and legitimacy. In Europe, for example, trade unions possess a much higher status than in the United States with its free market ethos.

Fairness

Watson (1977) refers especially to a 'fair' arrangement in the agreed exchange between the individual as employee and the organization as employer. Elements in this exchange are not only time, money, and labor, but information, know-how, and voice or the ability to express dissatisfaction fully as well.

Legitimacy

This has to do with the same elements, but collectively, whereby the parties involved are interest groups (employees, unions, government) rather than individuals. It is not, of course, the case that between them these two dimensions are the exclusive and complete determinants of the HRM structure and its concomitant activities (which would imply a deterministic perspective on contingency); nevertheless their impact is of great significance.

Administrative heritage

In addition to the above two dimensions, historically growth configurations of firms also have their bearing on the structuring of HRM. These configurations may be looked upon as the outcome of past choices of strategy in interaction with the way structuring issues were originally posed and the organization culture this has engendered. Mintzberg (1979) offers examples of such configurations (as ideal types). Specifically for international operating companies Bartlett and Ghoshal (1989) make use of a typology of firms which includes multidomestic, international, global, and transnational forms. These authors reserve the term 'administrative heritage' for the influence of structures, methods, competencies, values, and so on, which originated in the past, and they consider this heritage an important influential factor (for better or worse) in continued organization structuring, including the structuring of HRM.

Dominant coalition

The processes of decision making and choices made by the dominant coalition – the TMT (Top Management Team) – must also take into account key sets of actors within pluralistically led organizations. Examples of important actors are the various executive and governing authority boards, middle and lower level management teams, works councils, and of course the personnel department. These actors all have their own norms and values, shared with others to a greater or lesser degree.

Room to Maneuver

The shaded area in Figure 10.1 represents the available room for the dominant coalition to maneuver in *shaping* HRM. Depending on the situation, this leeway may be expansive or restricted. Examples of relevant circumstances are the market position, the degree of labor union organization, labor–capital ratio, and financial health of the company. In the case of an organization with a market monopoly, for instance, maneuvering room is obviously sizable. But when the manufacturers are many, competition keen, and financial resilience is low there will be little room for structured HRM activities (Paauwe, 1991).

HRM activities and processes

If we subdivide the various personnel activities on the basis of a simple 'flows' model, we can see the distinctive in-, through- and outflow of human resources. For the first phase we can think of activities and processes such as recruitment, selection, and numerical flexibility. The second phase includes activities like assessment, reward, training, management development, and achieving functional flexibility. For the last phase we think of topics such as *age-conscious* personnel management (Nicholson, 1993), cut-back discharge arrangements, and retirement plans.

All of these generic references – if we are to believe the more practice-oriented publications in personnel journals – are becoming widespread. A genuine contribution by HRM to sustainable competitive advantage, however, does not arise unless the 'trade/exchange' between the individual and the organization is structured in such a way that we can speak of *unicity* (the literature on the resource base theory – Mahoney and Pandian, 1992 – of the firm calls this 'heterogeneity') for the company involved, in other words, an arrangement between the individual and the organization that is *firm-specific*. This unicity is valuable, scarce, virtually inimitable, and difficult to replace in the short run.

The resource base approach focuses on the key success factors of individual firm behavior to achieve firm-specific advantages by a portfolio of differential core skills and routines, coherence across skills, and unique proprietary know-how. Consider the following examples from our experience and research:

(1) A container shipment company in which all employees are given the opportunity to traverse all functions (10 functions listed from low to high), both in terms of the required training and the necessary practical experience. In this way the company achieves a unique optimization of functional flexibility, which ensures an important and very likely decisive advantage in the area of flexible and high-quality employee effort. As to the aspect of fairness: employee rewards reflect their qualifications, regardless of the actual function in which the employee is engaged.

(2) An international publishing company, able to monitor with great accuracy, via an extensive system of monthly data codes, the personnel development (size, costs, build-up, qualifications) of each business-unit, which allows the head office to provide continual improvements in efficiency and effectiveness.

(3) A large brewery, where all available methods to direct personnel are reviewed and adjusted for mutual consistency (horizontal integration) and for their contribution to strategic objectives.

Outcomes

HRM activities structured according to the above analyses are, of course, oriented to the realization of certain objectives or outcomes. Beer and colleagues (1984) mention four of these:

(1) *Commitment.* To what extent is HRM policy aimed at strength-

ening the bond employees have with their work and with the organization of which they are a part?

(2) *Competence.* To what extent is HRM policy able to recruit,
retain, and develop personnel with the capabilities, skills, and
knowledge needed by the organization and society now and in the
future?

(3) *Cost-effectiveness.* How effective and efficient are the results of
the HRM policy as implemented in relation to labor costs,
secondary labor conditions, personnel turnover, truancy, strikes,
and so on?

(4) *Congruence.* To what degree does the HRM policy and its activities achieve congruence or harmonization among the distinct
personnel categories, in the relation between organization and
society, between employee and family and the relation with
personal aspirations of individuals?

These outcomes in turn should contribute to the realization of long-
term objectives such as individual well-being, effectiveness of the organization, and social well-being. Such objectives are inspired by a
stakeholder approach to the organization in the sense that, in the
process of choosing objectives, the desires and demands of involved
parties inside and outside the firm are satisfied, as are the demands of
effectiveness and fairness. It can be said, therefore, that both the HRM
objectives and the long-term goals fit into the context of the P–M–T
and S–C–L dimensions. Recent approaches to HRM (Walton, 1985)
recognize this need for appropriate fit and congruence among personal,
industrial and social objectives. Still, many HRM approaches tend to
be oriented one-sidedly to company objectives and so HRM managers
tend to lose sight of the S–C–L dimension, with its criteria of fairness
and legality/legitimacy. It is our contention that unless organizations
recognize and accept the legitimate claims of employees for full organizational citizenship, then the search for human resource base sources
of sustainable competitive advantage will be considerably reduced and
impaired.

Social changes

Employees (and, if applicable, their trade union representatives) are
likely to experience far-reaching social changes that are bound up with
a unique and hence company-specific HRM structure – changes in the
sense that employee commitment to the organization will need to be
strong. Such commitment does not rest merely on a labor contract and
its package of labor conditions, but is based also on organization specific
know-how, capabilities, and competencies; is linked to status and
trust; and implies a far stronger type of commitment. Conversely, for
its competitive advantage the company itself will come to depend
increasingly on the capacities and know-how of its employees.

Vulnerability increases for both the organization and the individual in this situation.

Viewed from this perspective one wonders whether this type of high commitment and high obligation HRM can or will apply to all personnel or just to the happy few. The core–peripheral employee distinction is relevant here. Peripheral personnel categories may well be fated to a permanent secondary labor market segment.

A second possible consequence is that all components in the structure of the exchange between the individual and the organization become incorporated into the set of psychological, knowledge-based and ultimately moral contracts developed between the organization and employee under the rubric of the human resource strategy developed by the dominant parties involved. This would include not only time, labor, and money, but information and voice as well. Thus industrial democracy and participation (co-determination) would become tools of management in the struggle for a sustainable competitive edge. The distinction between formal (say, works council and union-based channels of communication) and informal or management initiated forms of consultation and voice will, under such a scenario, lose its relevance. Trade union objectives such as looking after the interest and emancipation of employees could potentially be taken over by HRM policy, at least for the happy few or the core members. Does this mean that the trade union is relegated to bargaining in the secondary segments of the labor market alone? Or will it rather ensure itself of a maintainable niche in organizations and institutions via enhancement of the competencies and capabilities of employees, for example, by way of novel approaches to the quality of working life, or new efforts toward training and development, or support of various forms of workers' participation/voice? Unless the challenges posed by the latter are responded to, unions will play a less than full role in the emergent industries of the next century within currently industrialized nations.

New perspectives on practice: the Catch-22s of organizational life

The research and analyses reported throughout the book have emphasized that there are few if any panacea-like solutions for organizational problems. The Catch-22 scenario which was developed in Chapter 5 also has relevance for many of the issues addressed in the book – union avoidance, decentralization of the specialist personnel function, core–periphery manpower strategies, self-managing teams, and total quality initiatives.

In Chapter 5 the Catch-22 of union avoidance was highlighted, that is, that large companies who wish to remain union free must grapple with the 'spillover effect' of unions, that is, non-union companies must match the wages, benefits, and conditions negotiated by unions on behalf of their members if they are to resist potential unionization drives in an external environment where unions enjoy a strong social legitimacy.

Union organizers are apt – and perhaps rightly so – to see non-union members in high wage non-union organizations as 'free riders' enjoying the gains of collective action conducted by unionized workers in other sectors of the economy. The 'spillover' effect of unions coupled with the need to create conditions conducive to high performance in organizations – that is, the creation of a robust organization culture which is impervious to unionization drives – leads to the development of high wage and high motivation employment systems in such organizations.

In Chapter 6 the Catch-22 involved in the decentralization of the HRM function was identified. Our analysis demonstrates that the aboli-tion of the HRM department can potentially lead to the phoenix-like resurgence of the HRM department at the level of line managers in managing that is ad hoc and frequently ineffective. Frequently trans-action and coordinating costs within the firm increase. For example, a simple discrimination problem handled improperly may lead to a court case and the loss of millions of dollars.

In Chapter 9 the Catch-22 of avoiding a large core workforce was highlighted. We discovered that this frequently leads to potentially frac-tured organizational cultures, inexperienced workers with less commit-ment to the organization, difficulties in the use of self-managing teams, and even higher costs than alternatives, such as overtime for regular workers. Core–periphery strategies may well imply that such organiza-tions face enormous difficulties in pursuing 'unique' strategies that cannot easily be imitated. Sometimes, of course, transaction costs are reduced. Each situation must be analyzed separately and carefully.

In Chapter 7, the Catch-22 of self-managing teams was discussed, and our analysis illustrates the fact that self-managing teams do work but only under particular conditions. In addition, we identified that it is very important to distinguish between self-managing teams and other participative mechanisms such as quality circles. In Chapter 8 where managing without a traditionally based quality control function was discussed, we discovered that total quality management works effec-tively only when traditional quality boundaries between organizational members, levels, and functions, and the organization and its customers are minimized. However, frequently, organizations widen rather than narrow such boundaries, especially during periods of financial distress when the easiest target for cost-cutting is TQM innovations and initiatives.

Lessons learned

Throughout the book we have identified lessons for the practicing manager. All of those lessons are related to the theoretical frameworks we have used, namely agency theory, transaction cost economics, and the resource base theory of the firm.

(1) Making one change without considering interactions. This point highlights the fact that when a company makes one change, it needs to consider how it will interact with other key organizational factors. For example, Chapter 9 presents a case study of a company that used self-managing teams and temporary hires among its engineering staff. However, the temporary engineers became so numerous that the self-managing teams were not able to function effectively. Hence transaction costs, instead of declining, actually increased.

(2) Another lesson learned in this book is that world-class competitive capabilities consist not only of cost containment and differentiation as traditionally envisioned in many strategic management texts, but also as a simultaneous combination of the five factors of cost, speed, quality, dependability, and reliability. Taken all together these constitute adaptive efficiency.

(3) The top management team was identified as a critical resource. This is sometimes neglected in contemporary management texts with their focus on delayering – inducing corporate anorexia in some cases – and middle and lower level management teams. The same types of issues – involving social integration, leadership style, and the need to balance both group maintenance and task centeredness needs – that affect the effectiveness of self-managing teams also pertain to the top management team. In addition, the top management team has a critical role to play in the strategic crafting of organizational strategy in order to reap entrepreneurial rents or profits.

(4) Another lesson learned is that there are widespread common myths and ignorance in relation to the usage of core-periphery workers. For example, some US writers tend to emphasize that the United States has a more flexible market structure because of the use of temporary and part-time employees when, in fact, many countries in Europe actually surpass the United States in terms of their usage of atypical forms of employment. Additionally, as noted in point 1 above, frequently the use of peripheral workers is ill-advised.

(5) Looking to the United States as a model for the reduction of labor market rigidities is problematic and perhaps fallacious. While the United States has created many more jobs than Europe in recent

years, a large number of them tend to be low-skilled and low-paid. Both US and European managers need to learn from one another rather than blindly copying one another's systems.

(6) Low growth rates in the European Union have prompted a widespread debate that unions are too strong, and that they are seen as propping up an unsustainable welfare system which leads, in turn, to an inimicable environment for the creation of small and medium-sized enterprises. However, the research on the non-union situation highlights the fact that, even when companies avoid trade unions, their cost structures are very often comparable to unionized firms. There is also considerable evidence on differences between union and non-union firms which would seem to suggest that the absolute presence of a union is not a major determinant in productivity differences. Unions do seem, however, to have a major influence in terms of their allocative effects on shareholder wealth, that is, distributing wealth created within enterprises away from shareholders towards employees. However, our discussion of the human resource base theory of the firm suggests that perhaps this is not necessarily a bad situation, particularly when such resources represent the key source of sustainable competitive advantage.

(7) Another lesson learned is just how critical it is that management make clear distinctions when introducing a particular new work practice method. The manner in which, for example, quality circles differ from self-managing teams has important implications in relation to the level of voice which is afforded to employees.

(8) Our discussion on managing without traditional owners highlights the fact that the frequent assumption that privatization in itself provides endless benefits both in terms of privatizing the employment contract and also developing an entrepreneurial organization is not necessarily correct. That is, the agency problem of motivating employees endures even in buyout situations though on balance we conclude that overall agency costs are reduced.

(9) Another lesson is that total quality management fails when it is not embedded in a learning culture or learning organization. Most importantly, we have emphasized the need for a learning organization in which commitment is high but changes, including downsizing, must be accepted continuously. While we have described *only* some of the characteristics of learning organizations, it is clear that they are radically different from the traditional bureaucratic organizations. In addition, we have seen that for organizations to reap the benefits of TQM, a longer-term focus is often required due to the potentially disruptive effects on organizational routines that TQM initiatives may have, leading to a spiralling effect which can bring about financial distress in the medium term.

Human resource systems of the future: impact on key stakeholders

Our book has highlighted several major organizational trends which will affect the crafting of human resource systems in the future. These include the trend toward empowerment of the line manager, the simultaneous devolution of control to employees, the scaling down of large-scale bureaucratic forms, the emerging pre-eminence of core–periphery employment relationships, and the development of performance contracts which incorporate both behavioral and output control aspects.

(1) Devolution to the line manager is a widespread trend as organizations delayer and attempt to reduce coordinating costs. For example, there is a clear trend away from centralized personnel departments towards the empowerment of line managers in terms of motivational responsibilities and the handling of grievance and discipline issues with their direct subordinates. This necessarily leads to a requirement for managers to combine both traditional leadership and modern facilitation skills when managing.

(2) The trend towards the empowerment of employees has led to the creation of self-managing teams, renewed emphasis on statistical process control, and the elimination of traditional quality boundaries. However, in many cases the transfer of power is more superficial than real, ultimately reducing the potential benefits to be gained from such initiatives.

(3) The scaling down of large-scale bureaucratic forms to more flexible and entrepreneurially-based units raises a key issue in relation to stockholder interests, namely eliminating overhead and feather-bedding in employment contracts. When accomplished skillfully, such scaling down can reduce transaction costs associated with prolonged delays in managerial decision making in the bureaucratic organization.

(4) Core–periphery employment relationships including subcontractor arrangements will have a very powerful impact on trade unions and union organizing difficulties. They also affect the human resource department and create potentially two sets of psychological contracts – one for core workers and one for periphery workers. Such contracts will have a Janus-like impact upon the human resource specialists who are likely to be tough in their dealings with periphery workers but simultaneously extremely facilitative with core workers. Unions are beginning to react negatively to the core–peripheral distinction, as their power can easily be eroded. The European Union's Social charter guaranteeing minimum standards of treatment for all workers in EU countries will, when fully

adopted in each of the member states, redress some of these issues in favour of employees and unions.

(5) Performance contracts for top managers are creating some paradoxes, for example, such managers are being asked to elicit high commitment from organizational members while reducing transaction costs through downsizing, lean production, and other methods that increase the responsibilities and burdens of employees.

In summary, this book has relied upon agency theory, transaction cost economics, and the resource base theory of the firm to create a 'human resource base theory of the firm.' We have expanded the distinction between cost leadership and differentiation to highlight the five characteristics of world-class competitive capabilities: producing products or services right the first time, speedily, on time, cheaply, and flexibly. Given this view of the world, it is our contention that the human resources in the firm are much more critical than other resources which can be copied and imitated quickly. While our refined version of the resource base theory of the firm is still exploratory, it does suggest that organizations and markets have changed fundamentally and that, as a result, non-traditional and innovative methods of managing and working are not only desirable but necessary.

References

Bartlett, C. and Ghosal, S. (1989). *Managing Across Borders: Transnational Solutions*. Boston, MA, Harvard Business School Press.

Beer, M., Spector, B., Lawrence, P.R., Mills, D.Q., and Walton, R.E. (1984). *Managing Human Assets*. New York: The Free Press.

Flood, P. (1993). An expectancy value analysis of the willingness to attend union meetings, *Journal of Organizational and Occupational Psychology*, 66, 213–23.

Gomez-Mejia, L.R. (1992). Structure and process of diversification, compensation strategy, and firm performance, *Strategic Management Journal*, 14, 381–97.

Hall, R. (1992). The Strategic Analysis of Intangible Resources, *Strategic Management Journal*, 13, 135–44.

Hammer, M. (1990). Re-engineering work: don't automate, obliterate, *Harvard Business Review*, July–August, 104–12.

Harrington, H.J. (1991). *Business Process Improvement, the Breakthrough Strategy for Total Quality Productivity and Competitiveness*. New York: McGraw-Hill.

Mahoney, J.T. and Pandian, J.R. (1992). The resource base view within the conversation of strategic management, *Strategic Management Journal*, 13, 363–80.

Mastenbroek, W.F.G. (1993). Organiseren in een historich perspectief, *M&O Tijdschrift voor Organisatienkunde en Sociaal Beleid*, 3, 161–71.

Mintzberg, H. (1979). *The Structuring of Organizations*. Englewood Cliffs, NJ: Prentice-Hall.

Moore, T.M. (1987). Personality tests are back, *Fortune*, March 30, 74–82.

Nicholson, N. (1993). Purgatory or place of safety? The managerial plateau and organizational agegrading, *Human Relations*, 46, (2), 1369–89.

Oster, S. (1990). *Modern Competitive Analysis*. London: Oxford University Press.

Paauwe, J. (1991). Limitations to freedom: is there a choice? *Human Resource Management*, 2, 20.

Paauwe, J. (1994). *Organiseren, een grensoverschrijdende passie*. Alphen aan den Rijn: Samsom Bedrijfsinformatie.

Prahalad, C.K., and Hamel, G. (1990). The Core Competence of the Corporation, *Harvard Business Review*, May–June, 79–91.

Pugh, D.S., Hickson, D.J., Hinings, C.R., and Turner, C. (1968). Dimensions of organization structure, *Administrative Science Quarterly*, 13, 66–105.

Quinn, J.B. (1992). *Intelligent Enterprise: A Knowledge and Service Based Paradigm for Industry*. New York: The Free Press.

Smith, K.G., Grimm, C., and Gannon, M. (1992). *The Dynamics of Competitive Strategy*. Thousand Acres, CA: Sage.

Walton, R.E. (1985). Toward a strategy of eliciting employee commitment based on policies of mutuality. In: Walton, R.E. and Lawrence, P.R. (eds) *HRM Trends and Challenges*. Boston, MA: Harvard Business School Press.

Watson, T.J. (1977). *The Personnel Manager: A Study in the Psychology of Work and Employment*. London: Routledge and Kegan Paul.

About the authors

Hans Bruining (PhD, Erasmus University Rotterdam) is Associate Professor in Business and Organization, Rotterdam School of Economics, at the Erasmus University Rotterdam and Director of the Dutch Management Buyout Research Unit which is a member of the British Centre for Management Buyout Research in Nottingham. He undertook the first major study of management buyouts in the Netherlands and has written a number of articles and books in the area of performance improvement after management buyout.

Stephen J. Carroll Jr. (PhD, University of Minnesota) is Professor of Management and Organizational Behavior at the University of Maryland, College Park, Stephen Carroll has authored or co-authored 10 books, four monographs, and over 100 articles, including *Managing Organizational Behavior* (1994) and *Performance Appraisal and Review Systems* (1983). A Fellow of the Academy of Management and the American Psychological Association, he consults widely and has served as a Fulbright Research Professor in Japan.

Patrick C. Flood (PhD, London School of Economics) is Associate Professor of Human Resource Management and Assistant Dean for Research, College of Business, University of Limerick, Ireland. His previous co-authored books include *Personnel Management in Ireland* (1990) and *Change and Continuity in Irish Employee Relations* (1994). In 1993 he was a Fulbright Professor at the University of Maryland, and in 1995 the EU Post Doctoral Fellow, Centre for Organizational Research, London Business School. Professor Flood also co-edits the *Journal of Irish Business and Administrative Research*.

Martin J. Gannon (PhD, Columbia University) is Professor of International Management, University of Maryland at College Park. His nine books include *Understanding Global Cultures: Metaphorical*

Journeys Through 19 Countries (1994), *Dynamics of Competitive Strategies* (1992) and *Management* (1988). He has also served as a Fulbright Research Professor in West Germany and as the John F. Kennedy/Fulbright Professor at Thammasat University in Thailand. Gannon has published 75 articles and papers and has served as a consultant to many private firms and government agencies.

Julie Kromkowski (MAS, The Johns Hopkins University) is PhD Candidate at the University of Maryland, where she is completing her dissertation on the relationship between Deming's theory of feedback as implemented in the TQ organization and individual performance outcomes. Ms Kromkowski was an employee benefits specialist in the private sector for 10 years before resuming her studies.

Peter Lorenzi (PhD, The Pennsylvania State University) is Dean and Professor, College of Business Administration, the University of Central Arkansas. He has written widely on management issues and his latest book, *Management*, was published in 1994. He has also co-authored *The New Leadership Paradigm: Social Learning and Cognition* (1992).

Charles Manz (PhD, The Pennsylvania State University) is an Associate Professor of Management at Arizona State University. He is co-author of *Superleadership* (1989), which was awarded the Styble-Peabody Prize for the best book in Human Resources in 1989 and which has been translated into several languages. He also co-authored *Business Without Bosses* (1993). Professor Manz has held a Marvin Bower Fellowship at the Harvard Business School.

Eamonn Murphy (PhD, National University of Ireland) is Lecturer in Statistics and Business Mathematics in the College of Engineering and Science, and Director of Research, National Centre of Quality Management, University of Limerick, Ireland. He has written widely on quantitative quality techniques, especially experimental design.

Stanley Nollen (PhD, University of Chicago) is Professor of International Business and Director of the Center for International Business, Education, and Research (CIBER) at Georgetown University. His research on part-time and contingent employment has resulted in the publication of numerous management articles and books, including *Permanent Part-Time Employment: the Manager's Perspective* and the forthcoming *The Contingent Workforce*.

Judy D. Olian (PhD, University of Wisconsin, Madison) is Professor of Human Resource Management, Associate Dean for Academic Affairs in the School of Business, and Director of the IBM-TQ Program at the University of Maryland, College Park. She was the recipient of an American Council of Education Fellowship and has served as Special Assistant to the President of the University. She has published in such places as *Research in Personnel/Human Resource Management* and *Organizational Behavior and Human Decision Processes*.

Jaap Paauwe (PhD, Erasmus University Rotterdam) is Professor of Business Organization at the Rotterdam School of Economics, Erasmus University Rotterdam, and Director of the Human Resource Systems Research Unit. He has written and co-authored seven books on human resource management and many articles. He is the editor of *M&O* and research fellow of the Tinbergen Institute. In 1991 he was Academic Visitor at the London School of Economics.

Henry P. Sims, Jr. (PhD, Michigan State University) is Professor of Organizational Behavior in the College of Business and Management, University of Maryland. He is co-author of the award-winning *Superleaderhip* (1989) described above (see under Charles Manz). Author or co-author of four books and numerous articles, Professor Sims consults widely and is involved in several executive training programs.

Kenneth A. Smith (PhD, University of Maryland) is Assistant Professor of Strategic Management at Syracuse University, New York. His recent PhD thesis at the University of Maryland was concerned with the relationship between the composition of the top management team and the competitive performance of US high technology companies. He has published in *Administrative Science Quarterly* in the area of Top Management Teams.

Bill Toner (PhD, London School of Economics) was a member of the lecturing staff of the National College of Industrial Relations, Dublin, from 1974 to 1991, specializing in Industrial Relations and Personnel Management. He currently works as a researcher on social issues.

Theo Van Neerven (MSc., Personnel Sciences, Katholic University, Brabant, Tilburg) is working as a junior researcher at the Tinbergen Institute Rotterdam, the Netherlands. He is a member of the Human Resource Systems Research Unit which is part of the Department of Business and Organization of the Rotterdam School of Economics, Erasmus University. His background is in personnel science. Currently he is writing his PhD thesis on different patterns of investment in human capital and their consequences for the existence and development of internal and external labour markets.

Stefan Wally (PhD, New York University) is Assistant Professor of Strategic Management in the College of Business and Management,

University of Maryland. His research has appeared in the *Academy of Management Journal, Journal of Business Venturing*, and *Global Human Resource Management*, an edited book of readings. His business experience includes work with McKinsey & Co. and the American Management Association.

Author Index

Abowd, J. 156, 181
Abraham, K.G.
  (1988) 292, 293, 306
  (1990) 25, 27
Adams, K. 199, 200, 204, 207, 209, 227, 230
Adams, M. 261, 264, 270, 276
Adler, N.J. 101, 102
Aken, J.E., van 191, 230
Alderfer, C.P. 167, 181
Alderson, S. 68
Allen, T.J. 50, 68
Alter, C. 10, 13, 28
Ancona, D.G. 31, 54, 55, 67
Anderson, C.S. 218, 231
Applegate, L.M. 67
Armstrong, M. 194, 196, 230
Arrow, K. 90, 102
Atkinson, J. 198, 199, 203, 230, 286, 306

Badaracco, J.J 99, 103
Bain, G.S. 152, 181
Bakker, J. 189, 230
Bamforth, K.W. 239, 256
Bannock, G. 113, 137
Bantel, K.A. 31, 32, 42, 44, 53, 67, 70
Barbash, J. 166, 181
Barnard, C.I. 84, 103
Barnett, W. 55, 69
Barney, J.B.
  (1991) 6, 11, 27, 34, 37, 67
  and Tyler, B. (1992) 57, 67
Barry, T. 155, 181
Bartlett, C.A. 193, 230, 314, 317, 325
Bartol, K.M. 268, 276
Bateman, B. 251
Beaumont, P. 148, 163, 181, 183
Becker, B.E. 156, 181
Becker, G. 280, 306
Bednar, D.A. 269, 277

Beer, M. 13, 27, 194, 230, 318, 325
Berger, C.J. 8, 27
Blackburn, R. 262, 276
Blau, P.M. 50, 67
Bliese, P.D. 246, 255
Blyton, P. 151, 164, 181
Boudreau, J.W. 8, 27
Bouma, J.L. 117, 137
Bounds, G. 261, 264, 270, 276
Bourgeois, L.J. 55, 67
Bowen, D.E. 14, 29
Bower, J.L. 35, 58, 67
Bowman, E.H. 38, 67
Bradley, K. 131, 132, 133, 137
Bradley, S.P. 86, 103
Bradsher, K. 27
Brant, R. 23, 24, 27
Brett, J.M. 152, 153, 181
Brown, C. 155, 156, 176, 181
Brown, K.G. 41, 68
Bruce, R. 67
Bruijn, R.P. 118, 120, 137
Bruining, J. 137, 327
  (1989) 112
  Bruijn et al. (1990) 118
  (1992/3) 105, 109, 111, 114, 120
Bryce, M. 69
Buitendam, A. 217, 220, 230
Burns, T. 85, 103
Buzzel, R.B. 160, 181
Byrne, J.A.
  (1993) 84, 97, 103
  and Brant, R. (1993) 23, 24, 27

Caines, P. 87, 103
Caldwell, D. 55, 69
Carroll, S.J. 327
  (1991) 196, 231
  (1993) 89, 101, 103
  Martell, K. and (1993) 101, 104
Cascio, W.F.

and Ramos, R. (1986) 8, 27
(1992) 189, 202, 211, 231
Cash, J.I. 31, 67
Castanias, R.P. 38, 40, 45, 48, 49, 56, 67
Caves, R.E. 34, 41, 67
Chaganti, R. 53, 67
Chandler, A.D. 85, 103
Cherns, A.E. 239, 254
Clark, J. 231
Clark, K. 155, 181
Coase, R.H. 18, 27, 91, 103
Cohen, W.M. 50, 53, 67
Coleman, H.J. Jr. 31, 70
Conner, K.R. 6, 11, 27
Connolly, R.A. 155, 181
Cook, M. 8, 27
Copeland, T.E. 119, 137
Coyne, J. 105, 109, 112, 113, 138
Crosby, P. 258, 276
Cyert, R.M. 42, 67

Dainty, P. 31, 67
D'Aveni, R.A. 42, 48, 67, 68
Davidow, W.H. 27
Davis-Blake, A. 296, 297, 306
Dean, J.W.
 Sims, H.P. and (1985) 242, 243, 256
 Snell, S.A. and (1992) 8, 29
Delbridge, R. 11, 27
DeMarie, S.M. 264, 275, 277
Deming, W.E. 258, 276
 (1986) 240, 254, 259–60, 261, 266, 268, 271
 (1993) 267, 275, 277
Dess, G.G. 43, 67, 296, 306
Dichter, S.F. 191, 231
DiMaggio, P.J. 88, 103
Donnellon, A. 249, 255
Douma, S.W. 230
Dubin, R. 167, 182
Durham, C. 14, 29

Eisenhardt, K.M. 67
 (1988) 55
 (1989) 236, 254
 (1990) 31
Ellis, B. 246, 254
Elsheikh, F. 152, 181
Erez, M. 101, 103
Ernst and Young 238, 241, 254
Ettkin, L.P. 242, 256
Evans, P. 5–6, 15, 18, 29

Fama, E.F. 116, 137
Fayol, H. xiii, 84, 103, 190
Fell, A. 189, 232
Ferlie, E. 88, 104
Fernie, S. 3, 27
Fierman, J. 287, 306
Finkelstein, S. 32, 42, 53, 67, 68
Fiorito, J. 163, 181

Fisher, K. 247, 254
Flatt, S. 32, 44, 53, 69
Flood, P. vii, 327
 (1991) 87, 103
 (1993) 311, 325
Fotos, C.P. 35, 68
Foulkes, Fred K. 165, 166, 181
Fredrickson, J.W.
 (1984) 246, 254
 (1989) 53, 68
Freeman, R.B. 155, 156, 181
Frey, B. 236, 255
Frey, S.C. 100, 103
Fuchsberg, G. 238, 255, 265, 277
Fukutomi, G. 35, 68

Galbraith, J.
 (1973) 86, 103
 (1977) 31, 68, 103
Gale, B.T. 160, 181
Gannon, M. viii, 308, 326, 327–8
Gardell, B. 239, 255
Garvin, D.A. 260, 277
Gast-Rosenberg, I. 8, 29
Geber, B. 14, 28
Ghoshal, S. 193, 230, 314, 317, 325
Gillen, D.J. 101, 103
Glinov, M.A., von 231
Goffman, E. 93, 103
Goldstein, S.G. 133, 137
Gomez-Mejia, L.R. 67
 and Welbourne, T.M. (1990) 221, 231
 (1992) 13, 28, 308, 325
Goodman, P.S. 12, 28
Gourlay, S. 147, 182
Graham, A. 258, 265, 277
Gratton, L.C. 8, 13, 28, 30
Green, F. 181
Grimm, C.M.
 and Smith, K.G. (1991) 53, 68
 Smith, K.G. and (1992) 308, 326
Guest, D. 182, 231
 (1987) 163, 194
 (1989/90) 194
 and Hoque, K. (1994) 12, 28, 161
 and Rosenthal, P. (1992) 182
Gulowsen, J. 240, 255
Gupta, A. 44, 68
Gustafson, L.T. 264, 275, 277

Hage, J. 10, 13, 28
Hall, R. 7, 28, 193, 231, 315, 325
Hambrick, D.C.
 (1987) 32, 43, 45, 47–8, 53, 66, 68
 Finkelstein, S. and (1989/90) 53, 67, 68
 and Fukotimi, G. (1991) 35, 68
 Michel, J.G. and (1992) 52, 69
 (1993) 44, 52, 55
 and Mason, P.A. (1994) 44, 49, 68
Hamel, G. 193, 232, 314, 326

Hammer, M. 191, 231, 313, 325
Hampton, W.J. 20, 28
Hanney, J. 112, 137
Harrington, H.J. 191, 231, 313, 325
Harris, R. 163, 181
Hausman, J.A. 86, 103
Hawes, W.R. 150, 182
Helfat, C.E. 38, 40, 45, 48, 49, 56, 67
Hendry, C. 194, 229, 231
Heneman, H. and R. 8, 28
Herst, A.C.C. 105, 109, 111, 114, 118, 120, 137
Heskett, J. 10, 28
Hickson, D.J. 217, 232, 311, 326
Hinings, C.R. 217, 232, 311, 326
Hirschey, M. 155, 181
Hite, G.L. 119, 137
Hoerr, J. 238, 239, 255
Hofstede, G.H.
  (1984) 174, 182
  (1993) 247, 255
Hoque, K. 12, 28, 161, 181
Huiskamp, M.J. 106, 137
Hulleman, A.E. 212, 213, 231
Hunger, J.D. 34, 70
Hunter, J.E. 8, 29
Huxley, J. 178, 182
Hyman, R. 167, 176, 177, 182

Iaquinto, A. 53, 68
Ichniowski, C.
  (1986) 156, 182
  (1993) 15, 28
Immerzeel, J. 189, 230
Izumi, H. 17, 28

Jackson, S.E. 26, 28, 31, 42, 44, 53, 67
Janis, I.L. 68
Jensen, M.C. 116, 137
Johannesen, J. 133, 137
Jones, A.K.V. 265, 277
Jones, C.S. 113, 137
Jones, D. 11, 17, 29, 30, 238, 256
Jong, A.C., de 112, 118, 120, 123, 125, 128, 129, 137
Juran, J.M. 241, 255, 266, 269, 270, 275, 277

Kahn, R.L. 44, 68
Kakabadse, A. 31, 32, 43, 66, 67, 68, 69
Kalleberg, A. 236, 255
Kamoche, K. 229, 230, 231
Kanter, R.M. 4, 21, 28
Kaplan, R.S. 105, 116, 137
Kaplan, S.N. 114, 138
Karr, A.R. 12, 28
Katz, D. 44, 50, 68
Katz, H.C. 156, 158, 159, 161, 162, 165, 182
Kaufman, R. 17, 28
Kay, J. 38, 68

Keating, D.E. 249, 255
Keck, S.L. 32, 42, 68
Keuning, D. 191, 231
Kieschnick, R.L. 105, 138
Klandermans, P.G. 152, 153, 154, 182
Kleiner, M. 156, 157, 182, 183
Kleingartner, A. 218, 231
Kline, M. 236, 255
Kluytmans, F. 194, 231
Kochan, T.A. 28, 156, 158, 159, 161, 162, 165, 182
Kofmann, F. 260, 263, 277
Kornhauser, A. 167, 182
Kotter, J. 10, 28
Krafcik, J.F. 11, 17, 22, 28
Kravetz, D.J. 101, 103
Kristof, A. 14, 28, 41, 68
Kromkowski, J. 328

Lado, A.A. 28
Latham, G.P. 262, 277
Lawler, E.E. 238, 255, 265, 275, 277
Lawler, J. 153, 182
Lawrence, P.R. 194
  and Lorsch, J. (1967) 85, 86, 103
  Beer et al. (1984) 13, 27, 194, 230, 318, 325
Lazo, M. 84, 104
Ledford, G.E. 265, 275, 277
Legge, K. 197, 228, 231
Lengnick-Hall, C.A. and M.L. 58–9, 68
Levine, D. 16, 28
Levinthal, D.A. 50, 53, 67
Lichtenberg, F.R. 138
Locke, E.A. 262, 277
Lockwood, D. 167, 179, 182
Long, R.J. 133, 138
Lorenzi, P. 328
Lorsch, J. 85, 86, 103
Lowe, R. 11, 28
Lowman, C. 163, 181
Lublin, J.S. 238, 255

Maas, T.H. 231
McAuley, J. 227, 228, 232
McCarron, P. 273, 277
MacDuffie, J.P. 11, 17, 22, 28
McGovern, P. 159, 162, 182
McGregor, D. 4, 29, 190
Mackay, L. 198, 204, 232
McKee, L. 88, 104
McKersie, R.B. 158, 159, 161, 165, 182
McLouglin, I. 147, 183
McMahan, G.C. 7, 8, 9, 30
McWilliams, A. 7, 8, 9, 30
Macy, B.
  (1991) 246, 255
  (1993) 17, 28
Maguire, M. 91, 104
Mahoney, J.T. 38, 69, 315, 318, 325
Malone, M.S. 27

Mangham, I.L.   93, 104
Manz, C.   328
  and Sims, H.P. (1987)   31, 69, 238, 245, 255
  et al. (1990)   249, 255
  and Sims, H.P. (1993)   191, 202, 231, 251, 255
March, J.G.   42, 44, 67, 69
Martell, K.   101, 104
Martin, D.C.   268, 276
Martin, R.   236, 255
Mason, P.A.   42, 44, 49, 68
Mastenbroek, W.F.G.   191, 231, 313, 326
Masterson, S.S.   273, 277
Meckling, W.H.   116, 137
Medoff, J.   155, 156, 176, 181
Metcalf, D.   3, 27
Meyer, J.W.   88, 104
Michel, J.G.   32, 42, 52, 69
Miles, R.
  and Snow, C.C. (1978)   43, 69
  and Snow, C.C. (1992)   98, 99, 104
  et al. (1992)   31, 70
Miller, A.   43, 67, 296, 306
Mills, D.Q.   31, 67, 194, 230, 318, 325
Millward, N.   12, 29, 151, 183
Milner, S.   163, 183
Milward, M.   150, 183
Miner, J.B.   246, 255
Mintzberg, H.
  (1979)   44, 69, 317, 326
  (1987)   31, 69
Miscimarra, P.A.   248, 255
Moenaert, R.K.   230
Mohrman, S.A.   231, 265, 275, 277
Moore, T.M.   309, 326
Mullane, J.V.   264, 275, 277
Murphy, E.   328
Murray, A.I.   32, 42, 69
Myers, A.   32, 68, 69
Myers, J.B.   239, 246, 254, 255

Nadler, D.A.   54, 55, 67
Nee, M.   259, 261, 266, 277
Nejad, A.   131, 132, 133, 137
Nelson, F.D.   163, 181
Neumann, G.   156, 183
Nicholson, N.   318, 326
Nickelsburg, G.   156, 182
Niven, D.   265, 277
Nolan, R.L.   86, 103
Nollen, S.   300, 306, 328
Norton, J.J.   246, 255
Nulty, P.   248, 255

O'Bannon, D.P.   42, 55, 70
Olian, J.D.   328-9
  and Rynes, S.L. (1991)   15, 19, 20, 29, 262, 277
  Smith, K.G. *et al.* (1993)   42, 55, 70
Oliver, N.   7, 11, 14, 29

Olson, C.A.   156, 181
Opheij, W.   231
O'Reilly, C.A.   32, 44, 53, 55, 69
Oster, S.   7, 19, 29, 310, 326
Osterman, P.   236, 256
Overington, M.A.   93, 104
Owers, J.E.   119, 137

Paauwe, J.   vii, 165, 329
  Vries, J.C., de and (1984)   205, 206, 232
  (1989)   106, 138
  Bakker, J. *et al.* (1989)   189, 230
  (1991)   213, 232, 317, 326
  Kluytmans, F. and (1991)   194, 231
  Hulleman, A.E. and (1992)   212, 213, 231
  (1994)   229, 232, 315, 316, 326
  Uijlen, Y. and (1994)   206, 207, 208, 232
Pandian, J.R.   38, 69, 315, 318, 325
Pascarella, P.   35, 69
Paton, S.M.   241, 256
Penrose, E.T.   58, 69
Peteraf, M.A.   38, 41, 69
Peters, T.J.   59, 69
Pettigrew, A.M.
  (1985)   12, 29
  Hendry, C. and (1990)   194, 229, 231
  et al. (1992)   88, 104
Pfeffer, J.
  (1983)   49, 69
  (1992)   86, 93, 104
  (1994)   3, 11, 21, 24, 26, 29
Pickering, A.   236, 256
Pierce, R.   14, 29
Pilarski, A.   156, 182
Poel, J.H.R., van de   117, 138
Porter, M.E.   296
  Caves, R.E. and (1977)   34, 41, 67
  (1980)   34, 69, 160, 183
  (1985)   7, 29, 35, 36, 37, 69
Postma, F.   220, 230
Powell, W.W.   88, 93, 103, 104
Prahalad, C.K.   193, 232, 314, 326
Prennuski, G.   15, 28
Price, R.   152, 181
Puckett, J.H.   246, 256
Pugh, D.S.   217, 232, 311, 326
Pugh, M.F.   148, 183
Purcell, J.   203, 228, 232

Quinn, J.B.
  (1980)   31, 69
  (1992)   193, 232, 314, 326
Quinn Mills, D.   13, 27, 169, 183

Ram, M.   162, 183
Ramamoorthy, N.   101, 103
Ramos, R.   8, 27
Randlesome, C.   68

Rankin, T.   12, 29
Ranney, G.   261, 264, 270, 276
Reed, T.F.   148, 183
Reeves, C.A.   269, 277
Reger, R.K.   264, 275, 277
Repenning, N.   260, 263, 277
Reve, T.   236, 255
Richard, R.   156, 183
Richards, E.   163, 182
Riley, L.W.   246, 254
Robbie, K.   105, 112, 113, 138
Roos, R.   11, 17, 30, 238, 256
Rosen, B.   262, 276
Rosenthal, P.   182
Ross, A.M.   167, 182
Roth, E.F.   265, 277
Rowan, B.   88, 104
Rozell, E.J.   14, 30
Ruback, R.   155, 184
Ruffner, E.R.   242, 256
Rynes, S.L.   15, 19, 20, 29, 262, 277

Salancik, G.R.   86, 104
Salwen, K.G.   249, 256
Sambharya, R.   53, 67
Sapienza, H.J.   48, 69
Schendel, D.   138
Schlosser, M.M.   100, 103
Schmidt, F.L.   8, 29
Schneider, B.   9–10, 14, 29
Schnell, E.R.   277
Schonberger, R.J.   21, 29
Schoonhoven, C.B.   31, 67
Schuler, R.S.
    Jackson, S.E. and (1990)   26, 28
    (1992)   195, 196, 197, 203, 232
Schulman, L.E.   5–6, 15, 18, 29
Schwan, R.   236, 256
Scott, A.   147, 183
Scott, W.R.   104, 274, 277
Scullion, H.   203, 232
Scully, J.A.   42, 55, 70
Shaw, K.   15, 28
Shaw, M.E.   50, 69
Shellenbarger, S.   287, 295, 306
Shiba, S.   258, 265, 277
Shipton, J.   227, 228, 232
Shook, R.L.   20, 29
Siegel, D.   106, 138
Simon, H.A.   42, 44, 69
Sims, H.P.   329
    and Dean, J.W. (1985)   242, 243, 256
    Manz, C. and (1987)   238, 245, 255
    Kristof, A. et al. (1993)   41, 68
    Manz, C. and (1993)   31, 69, 191, 202,
        231, 251, 255
    Smith, K.A. and (1993)   34, 42, 47, 60,
        70
    Smith, K.G. et al. (1993)   55, 70
Singh, H.   105, 114, 138
Sisson, K.   12, 29, 160, 183, 203, 232

Slack, N.   viii, 6, 29
Smart, D.   150, 182
Smart, M.   182
Smith, D.K.   35, 70
Smith, K.A.   329
    Kristof, A. et al. (1993)   41, 68
    and Sims, H.P. (1993)   34, 42, 47, 60,
        70
    Smith, K.G. et al. (1994)   55, 70
Smith, K.G.   viii, 42, 53, 55, 68, 70, 308,
    326
Snell, S.A.   8, 29
Snow, C.
    Miles, R.E. and (1978)   43, 69
    et al. (1992)   31, 70
    Miles, R.E. and (1992)   98, 99, 104
Soeters, J.L.   236, 256
Sonnenfeld, J.   84, 104
Spector, B.   13, 27, 194, 230, 318, 325
Stalk, G.   5–6, 15, 18, 29
Stalker, G.M.   85, 103
Sterman, J.   260, 263, 277
Stevens, M.   150, 182
Stewart, T.A.   269, 277
Stogdill, R.M.   55, 70
Storey, J.
    (1989)   194, 232
    and Sisson, K. (1994)   12, 29, 183

Taguchi, G.   258, 259, 269, 277
Taylor, A.   83, 104
Taylor, F.W.   84, 98, 104, 190
Templin, N.   256
Terpstra, D.E.   14, 30
Thigpen, P.   30
Thomas, S.   156, 183
Thompson, J.D.   296, 306
Thompson, S.   105, 112, 113, 138
Thurrow, L.C.   9, 30
Tighe, C.   178, 182
Toner, B.   156, 163, 164, 168, 169, 170,
    171, 172, 173, 174, 175, 176, 177, 178,
    179, 183, 329
Torrington, D.   198, 199, 204, 232
Trist, E.L.   239, 256
Truss, C.   13, 30
Turnbull, P.   151, 164, 181
Turner, C.   217, 232, 311, 326
Tuttle, T.C.   278
Tyler, B.   57, 67
Tyson, L.D.   16, 28
Tyson, S.   189, 195, 232

Uijlen, Y.   206, 207, 208, 232
Uzzi, B.   296, 297, 306

Van de Vall, N.   153, 183
Van Neerven, T.   329
Vesey, J.T.   16, 30
Visser, J.   152, 183
Vries, J.C., de   205, 206, 232

Walden, D. 258, 265, 277
Walker, J.W. 217, 219, 232
Wally, S. 329
Walters, J.A. 69
Walton, R.E. 13, 27, 194, 230, 318, 319, 325, 326
Waterman, R.J., Jr. 59, 69
Watson, T.J. 316, 326
Weber, M. 84, 104, 156, 182
Weiss, M. 245, 256
Welbourne, T.M. 221, 231
Wernfelt, B. 6, 11, 30
Weston, J.F. 119, 137
Wheelen, T.L. 34, 70
Wiersema, M. 32, 53, 70
Wilkins, A. 37, 70
Wilkinson, B. 8, 29
Williamson, O.E.
 (1975) 91, 104

 (1985) 198, 200, 232, 280, 306
 (1986) 18, 30
Wilson, M.C. 13, 28
Wintzen, E.J. 187, 188, 189, 223, 232
Wissema, H.G. 191, 232
Womack, J.P.
 et al. (1990) 11, 17, 30
 et al. (1991) 238, 256
Wood, R.E. 91, 104
Woodland, S. 3, 27
Woodward, J. 85, 104
Wright, M. 105, 109, 112, 113, 138
Wright, P.M. 7, 8, 9, 30

Yorks, L. 261, 264, 270, 276
Yukl, G.A. 54, 70

Zimmerman, M.B. 155, 156, 183

Subject Index†

ABB (Asea-Brown Boveri) 99, 100
ABC Technology
  absence of personnel department 214,
    216, 217, 219, 221
  implementation of TQ 270–3
  overview 213, 233
absorptive capacity 50
acquisitions 99
adaptive capability 17–18
AES Corporation 37, 48
  boundary management 55–6
  core values 46–7, 50, 56, 60, 61–2
  establishment of team culture 60–1,
    65
  profitability 62–3
  project development teams 40–1, 62–3
  results 65
  strategic planning 39, 59, 63–5
  top management team 32, 50, 51–2,
    53, 54, 60, 61
  overview 33–4
age
  of part-time workers 290
  and TMT composition 49
agencies
  in-house 199, 207
  see also consultancies
agency theory (AT) xiv, xv, 56, 102
  link to TQM 273–4
  and management buyouts 114–17,
    118–20, 121–2, 134–5, 310
  and organizational structuring 90–3
  principal–agent relationship 115–17,
    236, 273
  and unionism 154
AKZO Coatings 207–8
algorithmic HRM systems
  defined 13

alliances, strategic see strategic alliances
ALMEX 239–40
American Airline 38
Analog Devices 260–1, 263–4
Apple Computers 24
Asea-Brown Boveri (ABB) 99, 100
asset specificity 92, 312
Atlas Venture 144–5
auto assembly plants
  study on 11, 17

Bakke, D.W. (AES) 33, 46, 47, 51–2, 60,
    61
banking industry 14, 37
Bell South 9
benchmarking 261
Boekhoven-Bosch 107–9, 129, 139
boundaries, elimination of quality see
    quality boundaries
boundary management 55–6
Britain see United Kingdom
British Airways 14
British Telecom (BT) 265–6
Brown, John Seely 258–9
BSO/Origin (Bureau for Systems
    Development) 198, 223
  case study 187–9
  culture 220, 221
  decentralization of 219
  industrial relations 216, 217
  and internalizing 198, 214
  overview 213, 233
BT (British Telecom) 265–6
business processes see processes
business strategies see strategy
buyer
  relationship with supplier 99, 100
buyouts see management buyouts

† Numbers in bold denote major section/chapter

capabilities, competitive
  achieving through HRM   **12–18**
  characteristics of   viii, 13, 307–8, 314,
    325
  simultaneous combination of to form
    world-class competitive capability
    viii, xvi, 5–6, 13, 73, 185, 322
Caterpillar Tractor   37
CEOs (Chief Executive Officers)   49, 54,
    91, 102, 313
CFNR (Compagnie Française de
    Navigation Rhénane)   140
Citibank   37
collective bargaining   166–7, 173, 176,
    221
commitment, employee   122, 123, 314,
    318, 319–20
competencies, core   193, 314
competition, globalization of   73–4, 80,
    98, 99, 284
competitive advantage   5, **35–7**, 97
  and achievement of simultaneous
    combination of competitive
    capabilities   viii, xvi, 5–6, 13, 73,
    185, 322
  conditions for   37
  emphasis on core competencies for
    193
  HRM as source of   **11–18**
  human resources as critical source of
    7–11, 26, 42, 190, 308, 315
  importance of self-managing teams
    236
  increased focus on by organizations
    73–4
  and profitability   38, 40, 41–2
  and resource base theory   7–11, 34–5,
    37, 56, 274, 308, 315
  and TMT   42, 45–6, 53–4, 55, 56–8, 66
  value creation as basis for   36–7
competitive capabilities *see* capabilities,
    competitive
concurrent engineering   16, 101, 308
consortia   99
consultancies
  external   198, 199, 208–9, 216
  internal   199, 207–8
contingent workers   295, 322
  cost effectiveness of   300–1
  differences in management of in the
    US and Germany   282–4
  disadvantages of   25
  equity concerns   302–3
  guidelines for successful use of   303–5
  legal issues concerning   294, 301–2
  performance of   298–300
  and teamwork   299, 304
  see also part-time workers; temporary
    workers
contract management   206
contracting out *see* outsourcing

contracts, performance   325
core-and-ring strategy
  defined   xvi, 285
  in Japan   295
  and personnel activities   198, 199, 203,
    204–5, 210
  and workforce   280, **285–98**, 304, 305,
    321
Corning Glass   14
cost capability   16–17
Crown van Gelder   143
culture, company
  determining factor for presence/
    absence of personnel department
    220, 221, 224
customers
  focus on by TQ organization   258,
    259, 261, 266, 269–70, 273
Customs and Excise   205–6

Damen Shipyard Gorinchem
  absence of personnel department   214,
    215, 216, 217, 220, 221, 222, 223
  overview   213, 233
De Reus   143
decentralization   16, 101, 194–5, 219
decision-making
  forms of strategic   54
  framework for presence/absence of
    personnel function   225–7
  improvement of quality in management
    buyouts   116–17, 121–2, 124,
    129–31, 133
defensive buyouts   109–10, 111
Denmark
  unions in   152
dependability capability   15–16
deregulation   82
Diamond Star Motors   20
dismissal
  of unsatisfactory workers   169–70
Dordtse Kil Holding   140–1
downsizing   73, 74, 100, 295, 304, 313,
    323
Du Pont   149

Eastern Europe   80
Economist, The
  article on TQ   265–6
Electromation   149, 248–9
Elsevier   107, 139
emergent strategy
  AES components   59–65
  concept of   59
Emilia-Romagna (Italy)   236
employees
  commitment of   123, 314, 318, 319–20
  effect of organizational restructuring
    on   80, 102
  leasing of   210
  in management buyouts   **125–9**, 136

and share ownership 131–4
  see also contingent workers; part-time
      workers; temporary workers;
      unions; workforce
entrepreneurial profits 38, 40, 43, 48, 49,
      55
Europe
  use of contingent workers 293–94, 302
experiential HRM systems 13, 160
external boundary management 55–6
external consultancies 198, 199, 208–9,
      216
externalizing xvi, 18–19, 197–8, 226–7
  case studies 205–6, 207–8, 209
  changes brought about by 187, 200,
      204–11, 312
    contract management 206
    core/peripheral personnel activities
      204–5
    in-house units 199, 207
    external consultancy 198, 199,
      208–9, 216
    internal consultancy 199, 207–8
    leased employees 210
    teleworking 211
  defined 186, 200
  see also outsourcing

firm-specific skills 48, 49, 318
flexibility 122–3, 285
flexitime 285, 286–7
Florida Power and Light 265–6
Ford Motor Co. 99, 100, 240–1
founders, firm's 221
fringe benefits
  in union/non-union companies 168
Fujitsu 89–90, 92, 98, 101

gain-sharing plans 17
General Electric 21, 237
General Motors *see* GM
generic skills 48
Germany
  and teams 238
  unions 154
  use of contingent workers 283, 290,
      291, 302
Globe Metallurgical 265
GM (General Motors) 82–3, 248, 249
  Saturn division 14, 15, 17, 202–3, 267
gratuity schemes 127
grievance procedure
  in union and non-union companies
      171–2
group orientation *see* teamwork
GTI (Groep Technische Installatie) 126,
      127, 130–1, 132, 139–40

Hallmark Cards 269
hierarchy
  as base of power 4
    to business processes 97–8, 191, 192,
      314
    removal of levels of 190–1
    and transaction cost theory 311
Holland *see* Netherlands
home working 287
Honda 15, 20
horizontal organizations
  and management of business processes
      97–8, 191–2, 314
HRM (human resource management)
  alternative forms of 26–7
  changing roles of managers 195–7
  consequences of organizational
      restructuring on 100–2
  dimensions which effect **315–20**
  interaction with other organizational
      processes 7
  source of competitive advantage
      11–18, 26–7, 318
  traditional approaches to 26–7
  types of systems 13
  see also strategic HRM
human resource base theory of firm xvi,
      315–20, 323
human resources
  defined 6–7
  as source of competitive advantage
      6–11, 26, 42, 190, 229, 308, 315
  TMT seen as strategic 32, 42–6, 66,
      308, 322

IBM 169, 173, 209, 234, 295
IDS Financial Services 251–4
IMPROSHARE plans 17
in-house agencies 199, 207
incentive systems 17, 85
  gain-sharing 17
  managerial 56
  merit pay scheme 174
  and unionism 173, 174
  see also reward systems
individualism
  belief of by non-union companies
      173–4
industrial relations
  in management buyouts 129, 131
  see also unions
industry-specific skills 48
information asymmetries
  and principal–agent relationship in
      buyouts xv, 90–1, 92, 116, 121,
      310
information processing 9, 80–1, 85–6, 91
institutional theories
  on organizational structuring 88–9, 97
internal consultancies 199, 207–8
internalizing xvi, 18–19, 198, 200–1, 223,
      227, 312
  changes brought about by 187, 200,
      201–4, 211–17

core/peripheral personnel activities
203
integral management   201–2
personnel management without
personnel managers   211–17
self-managing teams *see* self-
managing teams
defined   186, 198
investors
relationship with managers in buyouts
117, 118, 119
Ireland
unions in   153, 159, 162, 163, 165, 178
isomorphism   88–90

Jaguar Cars   7
Japan
core-and-ring system   102
relationship between US companies
and   101
self-managing teams   235, 238
TQM   258, 264, 265
unions   155, 177
use of part-time employment   290, 291
use of quality circles   240, 241–2
job profiles   129
job security
in union and non-union companies
169, 177
joint ventures   23, 87, 99f

Kingston Technology   23, 26
knowledge   97
focus on by some industries   98–9
seen as asset   50, 193, 314
Kodak, T.A.   295
Komatsu   37

labor *see* workforce
leadership   4
importance of in TQ philosophy   22
in self-managing teams   249–51
lean production   22, 98, 312–13
learning organizations   313, 323
leased employees   210
legal systems   221
and contingent workers   294, 301–2
legitimacy   316–17
through acceptance   229, 230
Levi Strauss   11
Lincoln Electric Company   84
line management *see* internalizing
line manager   324
at AES   61
assignment of integral management to
195, 202
and human resource utilization   4,
193–4
in non-union companies   165
personnel activities carried out by
215, 220, 309, 311–12, 314, 224

role of   185–6, 197
in TQ organizations   21, 22, 26
management
Deming's 14 points of   259–60, 261,
266, 267, 268, 271, 276
traditional theories of   84–5
management buyouts (MBOs)   xv, 91,
105–42, 310, 323
advantages   112, 134
branches of industry for occurrence in
112
case studies
Boekhoven-Bosch   107–9
primary analysis (Appendix 1)
139–42
secondary analysis (Appendix 2)
143–5
contribution of HRM to success of
106–7, **122–34**, 135–6
decision making improvement   116–17,
121–2, 124, 129–31, 133
defensive   109–10, 111
deployment of personnel   124–6
division between shareholders and non-
shareholders   131–4
duration of success   111, 113, 135
motives for   109–10, 111
offensive   109–10, 111
and performance improvements
105–6, 111–14
reasons for   106, 113–18
reduction in agency costs   117,
118–20, 121–2, 134–5
principal–agent relationship   115–17,
121–2
relationship between investors and new
managers   117, 118
reward structure   120–1
and role of TMT   114
managers
and power relationships   93
redundancy of if team approach
succeeds   248
role   35
in virtual companies   25–6
see also line manager; personnel
manager; TMT
managing without
full-time workforce   **279–305**
personnel managers   **185–230**
quality boundaries   **257–76**
supervisors   **235–54**
traditional owners   **105–36**
traditional strategic planning   **31–66**
traditional structures   **73–102**
unions   **147–80**
managing without traditional methods
defined   xiv–xvi
market testing   205–6
Martinus Nijhoff International   128, 141

matrix organizations   99
Mazda   20, 21
Medequip   18
Merck   38, 49
mergers   99
merit pay schemes   174
merit systems
   creation of in management buyouts
      126
Microsoft   38
Midway Airline   35
Milliken   21
monopoly profits   41, 43, 48, 55
Motorola   9, 262
Mutual Benefit Life   270
Myers-Briggs personal preference
      inventory   309

Nagle, Roger   24
Naill, Roger (AES)   51, 60
National Energy   76–9
National Freight Consortium see NFC
National Health Service see NHS
Nelis (J.G.) Building Contractors
   absence of personnel department   214,
      216, 217, 222, 223
   overview   233
Netherlands
   management buyouts in   107–10,
      111–12
   and paternalism   189
   personnel officers in   210, 217
   teleworking   211
   unions   154
   use of part-time employment   290
   works councils   107, 216–17
network organizations   xv, 92–3, 99, 101,
      211, 305, 310
New Universal Motor Manufacturing
      Company (NUMMI)   11, 17
New York Telephone Company   9
NFC (National Freight Consortium)
      132–3, 145
NHS (National Health Service)   87–8, 92
non-traditional methods
   defined   xiv–xvi
non-unionism   323
   Catch-22 of union avoidance   151,
      165–6, 210–11, 310–11, 321
   and company culture   176–7
   and competitive advantage   180
   difficulties associated with   149–51
   elimination of triggers to unionize
      162–3
   employment costs   168
   flexibility   179–80
   grievance procedure   171–2
   HRM policies and   163–5
   improved communications   174–6
   model of strong non-union culture
      164

personnel policies   167, 169
   reasons for emergence of   154–5, 158,
      159, 160–1
   strategies in relation to   161–3
   types of non-union companies   165–6
   unacceptable face of   150
   see also unions
NUMMI (New Universal Motor
      Manufacturing Company)   11, 17

offensive buyouts   109–10, 111
organizational learning
   importance in the sustainment of TQ
      260–1
organizational (re)structuring   xiii,
      73–102, 309
   case studies
      General Motors   82–3
      NHS   87–8
      Powertech   74–9, 81, 93–5, 96
   characteristics of recent changes in
      79–80
   consequences for HRM   100–2
   effect of technology on   80–1, 82
   in the future for world-class competi-
      tion   97–9
   increased complexity of   98, 190–3,
      313–14
   problems with   102
   reasons for   73–4, 80–2, 83–4, 85, 96–7,
      310, 317
   reasons for failure of non-traditional
      98, 99
   theories based on economics for   90–3
   traditional theories of   85–90
outsourcing   63, 185, 227
   of personnel activities   185, 198–9, 204,
      208–9, 210–11, 216, 312, 313
   of workers   23, 25, 295
   see also externalizing

part-time workers   **287–91**
   advantages   297, 298
   cost-effectiveness   300–1
   equity concerns over   302–3
   occupations for   288, 289
   performance   298–300
   usage in other countries   290–1
   voluntary and involuntary   287, 288,
      289
   wages   290, 291
   see also temporary workers
pay-for-performance schemes   84, 91, 164
Pepsi Co. Inc.   21
performance contracts   325
performance management system   16
peripheral workers see contingent
      workers
personality profiles   309
personnel management   3, **185–230**
   advantages for not having   215

alternative ways of performing   197–9
  externalizing *see* externalizing;
    outsourcing
  shift from specialist staff to line
    management *see* internalizing
  case studies for not having   213, 233–4
    BSO   187–9
  challenge of increasing complexity
    190–3
  conceptual framework   224
  developments in   3, 190
  disadvantages for not having   215–16
  effectiveness of   227
  and management buyouts   136
  models of   195–6
  motives for not having   213–14, 311
  origins of   189–90
  process for decision-making as to
    presence/absence of   226–7, 228
  union role in companies without
    216–17, 219, 221–2, 225
  variables effecting presence/absence of
    217–27, 311
    environmental characteristics   221–3,
      225
    management philosophy   222–3,
      225–7
    organizational characteristics
      219–21, 224
    role and position of works councils
      222, 225
    workforce characteristics   218–19,
      224
personnel manager   312
  changing roles and expectations for
    195–7
  role prescriptions   227–9
  see also line manager
Plasthill   143
P–M–T (Product–Market–Technology)
    dimension   315–16, 319
Polaroid   149
Powertech   85
  chronology of organizational changes
    81
  development of   **74–9**
  employee reaction to recent changes
    78–9, 80
  and information systems   86
  internal structural changes   94–5, 96
Preston Trucking   22
principal–agent relationship   236, 273
  see also agency theory
privatization   81–2, 323
processes, business
  from hierarchy to   97–8, 191, 192, 314
Procter & Gamble   247
profit-sharing schemes   126–7
profitability   38, 40, 41–2, 308
Proforms   125, 144
project development teams   40

at AES   40–1, 62–3
PTT Post (Mail)   206

qualities, managerial   45, 47–8
quality
  definition of   269
quality boundaries, elimination of
    266–73, 275–6, 313, 321
  between departments   268–9
  between organizational levels   267–8
  case study (ABC)   270–3
  customer and organization   269–70
quality capability   13–14
quality circles (QCs)   16–17, 239, **240–3**
  compared with self-managing teams
    242, 321, 323
  and elimination of boundaries   267,
    268–9
  US compared to Japan   241
quality improvement teams   241, 268–9
'quality organization' *see* TQM
quasi profits   40, 41, 44, 49, 54–5

Rabofacet   207
recruitment
  in TQ organizations   20, 21
resource base theory (RBT)   **6–11**, 56
  and competitive advantage   7–11,
    34–5, 37, 56, 274, 308, 315
  and competitive disadvantage   37
  and concept of value chain   37
  focus on human resources as critical
    source of competitive advantage
    6–11, 26, 42, 190, 229, 308, 315
  human resource base theory   xvi,
    315–20, 323
  link with TQM   274–5
  and management buyouts   310
  and profitability   38, 40, 41–2
  and unionism   154, 156–7
reward systems   16, 62, 90–1
  gain-sharing plans   17
  in management buyouts   120–1
  pay-for-performance schemes   84, 91,
    164
  performance management system   16
  in TQ organization   20, 21
Ricardian profits   38, 40, 48, 49, 54

Sant, Roger W.   33, 46
Saturn plant (GM)   14, 15, 17, 202–3, 267
S–C–L (Social–Cultural–Legal) dimension
    315–16, 319
security, job
  in union and non-union companies
    169, 177
selection processes   8, 14, 16, 101
  in non-union companies   164–5
  in TQ organizations   20, 21
self-managing teams   191, **235–53**, 312,
    321, 324

advantages xvi, 236
case study (IDS) 251–4
compared with quality circles 242, 321, 323
defined 237
development of 238–43
functions 202–3, 238, 240, 243–5
importance of for creating competitive advantage 236
increase in numbers 237–8
leadership of 249–51
performance 245–7
reasons for resistance to 247–9
in TQ organizations 20
shareholders 91, 309–10
in management buyouts 118, 131–4
short-term contractors 293, 302
SHRM *see* strategic HRM
SHV 139–40
Skillbase 216, 220, 221, 222
overview 213, 233–4
sociotechnical systems 239–40
Sony 24
Southwest Airlines 14
Spectrum Control, Inc. 268, 276
speed capability 14–15
steel industry
study on impact of HRM on cycle time 15
strategic alliances 23, 87, 98, 99, 101, 191
strategic HRM 106, 122
characteristics 185, 194
core activities 203
and creation of competitive advantage 136
emergence of 193–4
lack of generalized movement towards 12
paradoxes 229
reasons for growing significance 190–3, 307–15
role prescriptions for managers of 227–8
traditional approaches to 58–9
values of 129
see also HRM
strategy
defined 38
formulation 31, 43–4, 59
implementation 44, 59
sub-contracting xvi, 295, 324
Suiker Unie 141–2
supervision, managing without *see* self-managing teams
supplier
relationship with buyer 99, 100

task management 54–5
Taylor Jones 75–6
teams 238

advantages 16, 17, 65, 236
case study (IDS) 251–4
and contingent workers 299, 304
effect on HRM systems 101–2
emergence of 80
establishing of 59–61
importance of in TQ organization 20–1
see also quality circles; self-managing teams; TMT
technology
central role in creation of VC 24
effect of change in on unions 159
effect on organizational restructuring 80–1, 82
and expanded opportunities for teleworking 211
relation between structure and 85
as a resource substitution 10–11
teleworking 211
temporary workers **291–4**, 304
case studies 281–4
cost effectiveness of 210, 300–1
differences in management between the US and Germany 282–4
disadvantages 25
equity concerns over 302–3
increase in 279, 292, 296
legal restrictions in using 294, 301–2
performance of 298–300
reasons for use of 292, 293, 296, 297
in unionized organizations 169
usage in Europe 293, 294
see also part-time workers
TMT (top management team) **31–66**, 317
case study (AES) 32, 33–4, 50, 51–2, 53, 54, 59–65
composition of 43–4, **45–56**
age 49
and competitive advantage 42, 45–6, 53–4, 55, 56–8, 66
importance of combination of skills 47, 49
qualities and skills 45–6, 47–50, 53, 56, 57
structure of team 52–3
tenure and succession 52, 53
effectiveness 44–5
Hambrick on 32, 45, 47–8, 49, 52–3
and HRM 58–65, 66
and incentives 56
and personality profiles 309
processes central to function of 54–6
relationship between members of 50, 52, 55
role xv, 32, 35, 43–5, 50, 308–9, 322
size 50
as a strategic human resource 32, 42–6, 66, 308, 322
substitutes for 57–8
and upper echelon theory 42

TOP (Trimfus Onion Products) 141–2
top management team *see* TMT
total quality management *see* TQM
TQM (total quality management) 5, 18,
   19–22, 98, **257–75**, 321
  agency theory link to 273–4
  case studies
    ABC 270–3
    Analog Devices 260–1, 263–4
  as a competitive advantage 19, 259
  conditions for success 260–2, 264
  customer focus 258, 259, 261, 266,
    269–70, 273
  defined 258–9
  Deming's 14 points for management
    259–60
  effectiveness 265–6
  and elimination of quality boundaries
    266–73, 275–6, 313, 321
  and establishment of quality goals
    262
  factors in achieving shift in organiza-
    tional thinking 262, 264
  future 275–6
  HRM in 20–2
  popularity 259
  at Powertech 78, 94
  principles 19–20
  problems with 275, 323
  reasons for using 26–4
  research into 276
  resource base theory link with 274
  themes 258, 259, 264, 266
  and training 20, 21, 267, 269
  transaction costs theory link with 274
  values of 273
trade unions *see* unions
training 14, 16
  for contingent workers 300–1, 305
  greater attention to in buyouts 128
  in non-union companies 164
  in TQ organization 20, 21, 267, 269
transaction costs theory xiv, 324
  basis for internalizing/externalizing
    decision xv, 186, 198, 199, 226–7,
    311–12, 313
  and core-and-ring strategy 305
  defined 274
  and hierarchy 92, 93, 311
  and lean production methods 312–13
  link with TQM 274
  and move away from full-time
    workforce 279–80
  and organizational structuring 91–3,
    96, 310
  and self-managing teams xvi
  and union joining 154, 158
Trimfus Onion Products (TOP) 141–2

unions **147–80**, 221, 323
  agency theory link to 154

avoidance of *see* non-unionism
and collective bargaining 166–7, 173,
    176, 221
  in companies without a personnel
    department 216–17, 219, 221–2,
    225
  core–periphery employment relation-
    ships
    impact on 324–5
  culture 177
  disadvantages 156–8, 168, 169–71, 176,
    178
  effect on competitiveness 154–6, 157
  functions 163–4, 165
  grievance procedure 171–2
  growth of 147, 152–3
  and hiring temporary staff 169
  international changes in density of
    148
  levelling of wages 173–4
  in management buyouts 131, 136
  reasons for joining 152, 153–4
  threatened by team culture 248–9
  see also works councils
Uniparts 235–6
United Kingdom
  contracting out of personnel activities
    198
  HRM study in 11–12
  management buyouts 109, 112, 113
  quality teams 246
United Parcel Service 84
United States 322–3
  deregulation of private firms 82
  flexitime growth 286–7
  and individualism 173–4
  management of contingent labor
    282–4, 287, 288, 289, 290–2, 293,
    299, 302, 303, 305, 322
  number of personnel officers to
    employees 217
  relationship between Japanese
    companies and 101
  and self-managing teams 237–8,
    245–6, 247
  teleworking 211
  unionism 147, 149–50, 153, 154–6,
    159, 161, 165
  use of quality circles 240–1
'upper echelons' theory 42
UT-Delfia (UTD) 144

Vagelos, Roy 49
value chain viii, 36, 37
values, personal
  at AES 46–7, 50, 56, 60, 61–2
  and effect on executive contribution to
    TMT 45–6
Van Marken 189
Van Nelle 144
VC *see* virtual corporation

Venture Capital Companies 112
virtual corporation (VC) 5, **22–6**, 305
  characteristics 18–19, 23–4
  defined 23
  guidelines to establishing 24–5
  HRM in 5, 25–7
  use of contingent workers 25

wages
  and collective bargaining 166–7, 173
  in non-union companies 168
  in management buyouts 127
  for part-time workers 290, 291
  total costs ratio 219
WalMart 20
WFS (Workforce Solution) 209
Wolters Kluwer 141
women
  and part-time working 288, 290, 291
work sharing 305
workers see employees
workforce, managing without complete
    279–305
  case studies 282–4
  core-and-ring strategy 280, 285–7, 296,
    304, 305, 321
  labor cost reductions 297–8

need for flexibility of by companies
    285, 296–8
part-time workers see part-time workers
problems arising from **298–303**, 321
  cost effectiveness 281–2, 300–1
  equity concerns 302–3
  guidelines for alleviation of 303–5
  legal issues 301–2
  performance 298–300
  reduction of in buyouts 124–5
  training costs 300–1
reasons for 279–80, 297–8
temporary workers see temporary
    workers
outsourcing 23, 25, 295
Workforce Solution (WFS) 209
works councils
  in management buyouts 127–8, 130,
    131, 136
  in the Netherlands 107, 216–17
  role of 222, 225
  in United States 149, 150
world-class competitive capability see
    capabilities, competitive
Xerox 21, 35

zero-based budget 206, 312